THE YEARS OF HARVEST

A History of the Tule Lake Basin

Third Edition

By
Stan Turner

Spencer Creek Press
28498 Spencer Creek Road
Eugene, Oregon 97405

The Years of Harvest
A History of the Tule Lake Basin
By Stan Turner

Published by:

Spencer Creek Press
28498 Spencer Creek Road
Eugene, OR 97402
(541) 484-6226

Library of Congress Publication Data:

Turner, Stan
The Years of Harvest: A History of the Tule Lake Basin
Call Number: F863.S6 T87 1987
LC Control Number: 88143974

Third Edition

Copyright © 1987, 2002 by Stan Turner

Printed in the United States by Maverick Publications

ISBN 0-9721170-0-8

Front and rear cover photos by author and Kathleen Turner

Additional copies may be ordered from:

Spencer Creek Press
P.O. Box 25458
Eugene, Oregon 97402
(541) 484-6226

CONTENTS

PREFACE

"Where is Tule Lake?" I have often been asked. "And why have you spent so much time writing about it?"

For me the answers are obvious, but to explain my interest in the Tule Lake Basin in one quick sentence is impossible. I have invested too much personal time, and the basin is far too complex to give a simple description. It has been a crossroad for key developments in Western American history. For as long as ten thousand years, the Tule Lake Basin was inhabited by successive waves of Indian settlers, among the most recent being the Modoc tribe. In the early 1800s, fur trappers and explorers mapped the region and established routes along the shores of Tule Lake. These trails were followed by thousands of white emigrants and gold seekers, who flocked to Oregon and California. In 1872, friction between whites and Indians led to the Modoc Indian War and focused national attention on Tule Lake and the Lava Beds. In the late 1800s, two small irrigation projects in the basin proved the feasibility of irrigated farming. By the turn of the century, one of the West's most unique land reclamation and irrigation programs was begun in the Klamath and Tule Lake basins, and Tule Lake itself was drained. The early 1900s also heralded government-sponsored homesteading in the basin, and through 1949, thousands of acres of rich lake-bottom farmland were given away to veterans of World War One and Two. Tule Lake gained notoriety during the Second World War with the construction of the largest relocation center for Japanese-Americans in the United States. A prisoner of war camp for German soldiers was also built in the basin at the same time. Today, Tule Lake is best known for its agricultural products. Less known by many westerners is the basin's unique beauty and its great variety of recreational facilities, including the Tule Lake National Wildlife Refuge and the Lava Beds National Monument.

*   *   *   *

I first heard about the Tule Lake Basin in the spring of 1973. I had been teaching a course on Asian Americans at South Eugene High School, and one of the units focused on the internment of Japanese-Americans during the Second World War. I had placed a map on the bulletin board, which identified the location of the ten major camps in the United States. Several students noted that one of them, Tule Lake, was only two hundred miles south of Eugene, *near the city of Klamath Falls. By coincidence, I mentioned Tule Lake to Karen Brothers, a neighbor, several days later and discovered that she had been born and raised in the basin. She subsequently drew a map for me with directions on how to reach the site of the former internment camp.*

In August of 1973, my wife, our two boys, and I drove through the Tule Lake Basin on a trip to Central California. We stopped briefly at Newell, the site of what had once been the Tule Lake Relocation Center (later I would learn that the camp became a segregation center for allegedly disloyal Japanese-Americans and resident aliens, and that it did not cease operation until March of 1946). I took a few photographs. We then hurriedly drove on to the Southwest through the Lava Beds National Monument. Here, a major portion of the Modoc Indian War had been fought. After a quick stop at Captain Jack's Stronghold, site of the Modoc headquarters, and at the Lava Beds National Monument Visitors Center, we left the basin.

Though the visit to Tule Lake was brief, it made a lasting impression. One of the things that struck me was that the basin was an ideal destination for historical field trips for high school students. The climate and topography were distinctly different from Eugene, and the drive to the basin took a relatively short four and a half hours. Campsites were readily available. But most importantly, the basin provided a base for studying a great variety of topics, both historical and environmental. Students could have an opportunity to experience on-site history related to the Modoc War and Japanese Internment. They could study the basin's unique geography, and they could observe its rich abundance of wildlife. I was excited about the possibilities for student field trips to Tule Lake.

In October of 1973, thanks to the support of Cliff Moffitt, Glen Trusty, Melva Ellingsen and other officials from the Eugene Public Schools, twenty-seven students from South Eugene High School were given permission to spend three days in the Tule Lake Basin. Several South Eugene faculty members, including Al Fletcher, Jacob Veldhuisen, and Barbara Johnstone, agreed to help me supervise the field trip.

In preparation for our departure, the students pored over topographical maps of the Tule Lake Basin and studied the Modoc Indian War. Several Japanese-Americans, who had been internees at Tule Lake, came to South Eugene High School to talk with the students about their experiences. Finally, on Friday morning, October 12th, we transported the students to Tule Lake in a caravan of vans and cars. For the next three days, the Park Service at the Lava Beds gave us presentations. We interviewed fifteen basin residents on their impressions about the Japanese-American internment camp, and we scrambled through countless lava tubes and climbed to the top of nearby volcanic hills to study basin wildlife and geology. When we returned to Eugene, the students wrote reports on their findings. These were of a quality and depth that would not have been possible had we just covered the topics in class. The experience had left a lasting impression on all of us.

The success of that first field trip to Tule Lake has since led me to offer historical field trips to high school students on an annual basis. Generally, the target sites have alternated between locations in eastern Oregon and the Tule Lake Basin of northeastern California. The program has now been in operation for more than twelve years. In 1981 the real foundation for this book was laid. I received a grant from the Bethel-Eugene- Springfield Teacher (BEST) Center to offer a program for talented and gifted high school students on conducting historical research. Because of my familiarity with the basin, I chose Tule Lake as the focus of the project. For two weeks in July, I worked with eleven students, developing their research skills. As the project took shape, we decided to make the study as comprehensive as possible. Each student was assigned a major area of responsibility. Topics included: early Modoc history, land reclamation and irrigation, homesteading, internment, and contemporary basin lifestyle and economics. Then from August 1 to 9, the eleven students, my family and I camped out at the Tulelake-Butte Valley Fair Grounds. During the week, the students interviewed over thirty people, and they spent countless hours gathering information at the Klamath County Pioneer Museum, the Bureau of Reclamation's offices in Klamath Falls, the Tule Lake National Wildlife Refuge headquarters, and the Tulelake-Butte Valley Fairgrounds' Historical Museum.

When the students returned to Eugene, they spent the next three weeks writing reports on their findings. Several of the monographs became models to help other students learn how to write research papers. Additionally, some members of the project made class presentations during the regular school year concerning their experiences.

The students' research and reports, as well as my own background experience and work, became the nucleus for this book. Since the fall of 1981, much of my spare time has been spent doing additional research. During the summer of 1984, I was fortunate to secure support and guidance to complete the project from Dr. Edwin Bingham, Professor Emeritus from the University of Oregon's History Department. From June through August, I lived in the Tule Lake Basin while finishing my research. Eighty pages of student monographs grew to more than six hundred pages of manuscript.

Work continued on the project after I returned to Eugene. However, progress was slowed by the demands of work at the University of Oregon's College of Education, and it took nearly three more years to complete the writing. The final product is a blend of historical description and first-person narrative. Much of it is based on accounts gleaned from letters, diaries, manuscripts, newspapers, and tape-recorded interviews. Personal experiences of individuals have been used wherever possible to present the richness and diversity of developments in the Tule Lake Basin.

Although I assume total responsibility for the contents of The Years of Harvest, there still remains a strong core of contributions from students of the 1981 historical research project. The following graduates from South Eugene High School deserve both recognition for their work and my deepest appreciation for helping lay the foundation for this book. They include: Sam Adams, Bart Aikens, Daphne Berdahl, David Carmichael, Josh Goldstein, Mark Lewinsohn, Arman Maghbouleh, Becky Medler, Andrew Purkey, Jay Schwarzhoff, and Jim Stow.

*   *   *   *

2002 Update

The luxury of a novelist is that he can plan the entire story from beginning to end. There's relatively little worry about outside events changing the plot. However, when attempting to write a comprehensive history, the ongoing dilemma is when to stop—the present keeps marching along, introducing new events and providing different interpretations of what has gone on in the past. Such is the case with this book. When The Years of Harvest was first published in 1987, the Tule Lake Basin was in a period of relative stability. In the next fifteen years, significant events would *leave their mark. Farmers faced declining crop prices because of foreign and domestic competition. Drought plagued the basin multiple times. But the greatest impact came when three fish, the short-nose and Lost River suckers and the coho salmon were placed under the protection of the Endangered Species Act. The listing of these three fish, and the measures taken by several government agencies to protect them, would plunge the basin into one of its most severe crises. For the first time in the history of the Klamath Reclamation Project, irrigation water was denied to Klamath and Tule Lake Basin farmers. The ensuing struggle over who should receive water would pit basin farmers against environmentalists, wildlife preservations, Indian tribes, Pacific Coast fishing interests, the U.S. Fish and Wildlife Service, National Marine Fisheries Service and even the Bureau of Reclamation. To adequately cover the events from 1987 to 2002 would require a book in itself. However, a two part epilogue has been added to this new edition*

There were two choices in updating this book: undertake a major rewrite of many of its chapters, or add an epilogue offering an overview of the events. The latter choice was taken. The "Epilogue" is divided into two parts. The first discusses the events from 1987 to 2002—with a particular emphasis on the water crisis of 2001. The second part looks at the impact of those events on the town of Tulelake and the basin's residents.

The water crisis is far from over. As future events unfold it is hoped that all parties will keep in mind that there needs to be a balance in whatever decisions are made. Species protection is fundamentally important, but so is the well-being of several thousand people. The Klamath and Tule Lake Basins can either become a showplace for cooperative ventures which support farming and species protection or the poster-child from an ongoing battle over conflicting agendas and a scarce resource—water.

ACKNOWLEDGEMENTS

There were many people who graciously gave of their time to make this book possible. As previously mentioned, the work of eleven South Eugene High School students during the summer of 1981 was invaluable. But there were also many others who also provided assistance.

The following people played pivotal roles during the research phase of the book: Bill Whitaker, who first suggested that I look at a general history of the Tule Lake Basin; Dan Fults, Manager of the Bureau of Reclamation's Klamath Project, and Jim Bryant, Repayment Specialist for the Klamath Project, who together made it possible to make extensive use of the Project's files, maps, and photographs; Bob Fields, Project Leader of the Klamath Basin Wildlife Refuges, who provided valuable information on the history of wildlife preservation in the region; the staff of the Klamath County Museum, who arranged for the use of the museum's photographic files, old newspapers, and book collection; the University of Oregon Library's Oregon Collection and microfilm section, which provided a wealth of information on historical development in the basin; Dorothy Embertson of the Tulelake-Butte Valley Fairgrounds Museum, who patiently pored though the museum's files and collection to find documents, photographs and articles related to homesteading, Japanese internment, and the development of the city of Tulelake; Ralph Morrill, Manager of the Tulelake-Butte Valley Fairgrounds and Cindy Wright, Business Manager, who together opened the facilities for research and provided copies of key historical documents; Jim Sleznick, Head Ranger and Supervisor at the Lava Beds National Monument, Gary Hathaway, Head Ranger-Interpreter, and Woody Gamble, Monument Interpreter and Photographer, who collectively provided access to the Monument's files, photographs, and book collection; Jack Turner and Kathy Method, both formerly of the Bethel-Eugene-Springfield Teachers' (BEST) Center, whose support led to the acquisition of grant money for the first stages of comprehensive research; the administrative staff of the Eugene Public Schools, including Donald Jackson, Principal, and Wayne Hill, Vice Principal of South Eugene High School, whose continued support for student field trips to Tule Lake made the initial research possible; and the following individuals who were willing to share their personal knowledge about the Tule Lake Basin:

Dorothy Ager
Earl Ager
Portia Aikens
Robert Anderson
Clyde Barks
Cindy Bell
Clifford Bell
Betty Lou Byrne
Mrs. Roy Campbell
Gertrude Christy
Paul Christy
Joe Cordonier
Dan Crawford
John Cross, Sr.
Marvin Cross
Betty Darling
Marguerite Dayton
Regina Frey
Marie Gentry
Lavada Hance
Lorna Hanson

David Hatfield
Helen Helfrich
Paulette Hinds
Clyde Huffman
Frank Hunnicut
Marian Hunnicut
Robert Jones
Louis Kalina
Vaclav Kalina
George Katagiri
Frank King
Ginger King
Amy Kolkow
Phillip Krizo
Barbara Krizo
Kenneth Lambie
Winifred Lambie
Chet Main
David Misso
Edward Miyakawa

Ralph Morrill
John Moore
Bertha Myers
Karen P. Nelson
Charles Palmerlee
Clifford Parker
Donald Porterfield
Frankie Porterfield
Paul Rogers
Otto Schaffner
Ethel Scott
Burris Short
Victoria Thaler
Wallace Trujillo
Denise Walker
Ada Wosnum
Hugh Wosnum
Bill Whiteaker
Andy Wilkins
Cindy Wright

A special thank-you is extended to David Misso who, over the years, has kindly allowed students, my friends, and my family to stay at his home in the Tule Lake Basin. David's hospitality, his humor, and his candor have been invaluable in seeing this project through to its completion.

I must express my affectionate appreciation to my wife, Kathleen Podley Turner; my mother-in-law, Jesslyn Gates Podley; my parents, Stanton A. and Edith B. Turner; former English teacher Eleanor McLendon; and social studies teacher Deb Monnier; all of whom spent many hours proofreading rough draft copies of the manuscript.

Finally, to my children, James and Michael, I must both thank them for their help, and reassure them that they really do have a father! Certainly they must have wondered at times who that stranger was who came back to the house after spending eight weeks at Tule Lake, or who became engrossed with the word processor night after night!

In my attempt to thank individuals who made significant contributions, I have no doubt left several key people out. To those *who are not mentioned, my apologies and my sincere thanks for your support.*

> *Stan Turner*
> *Eugene, Oregon*
> *June, 1987*

2002 Update

This updated version of The Years of Harvest *is in large measure thanks to the support and encouragement of a relative newcomer to the city of Tulelake, Jessie Larson. A tireless and enthusiastic eighty-year-old, she contacted me multiple times in the winter of 2001-02, asking if copies of the original book were available. Learning that it was long out of print, we then discussed the possibility of not only a reissue but updating the book as well— leading to this revised edition. I can't thank her enough for the time she spent finding information, sending me documents, and arranging for a meeting that I had with a number of basin residents—including some of the original homesteaders—at the Tulelake-Butte Valley Fairgrounds. I also want to thank Cindy Wright, Manager of the Tulelake-Butte Valley Fairgrounds, for the interviews she helped arrange, the documents shared and for the photographs she helped me find. She is also to be commended for her Herculean effort to plan and direct the construction of a new fairgrounds museum that will showcase the history of the basin's development. When completed in the summer of 2002, it will rival any museum of comparable size in terms of layout, content and information.*

A number of individuals named in the original Acknowledgements assisted in the update of this book. They included 1940s homesteaders Paul Christy, Ralph Morrill, David Hatfield, and Barbara and Phil Krizo. Joe Cordonier and David Misso also provided additional help. Collectively, they were joined by a number of new contributors, including:

Luis Aceves	*Venancio Hernandez*	*Sharron Molder*
Kathy Ackley	*Nancy Huffman*	*Phil Norton*
Mike Byrne	*Frances Johnson*	*Suzanne Russel*

Earl Danosky	*Denny Kalina*	*Fred Simon*
Bob Galeoto	*Steve Kandra*	*John Staunton*
Fe Galeoto	*Renee Kohler*	*Joe Victorine*
Bill Ganger	*Jessie Larson*	*Roy Walldin*
Tony Giacomelli	*Joan Loustalet*	*Woodhouse Family*

I also wish to thank my daughter-in-law, Katherine Turner, who patiently proofread every chapter. Her work was invaluable. Finally, my deepest appreciation to my wife, Kathleen, who again and again, read and re-read the manuscript and offered her gentle but wise suggestions for improvement.

Stan Turner
Eugene, Oregon
June, 2002

The Tule Lake Basin looking west toward "The Peninsula."
*(Photo by Mary Hyde. Courtesy Tulelake-Butte Valley Fair,
Museum of Local History)*

CHAPTER 1

AN INTRODUCTION TO THE TULE LAKE BASIN
Its Geography and Geology

Nestled comfortably in a large oval bowl ringed with brown, juniper dotted hills lies the Tule Lake Basin. Its northern fringe spreads across the border from California into Oregon, and a narrow band of black-topped highway connects the basin with the city of Klamath Falls, twenty-three miles to the northwest.

At four thousand feet in elevation, the broad, flat former lake bed floor gracefully sweeps southward in all directions to blend into distant hills and volcanic tableland. Intermingled along its edges is ample evidence of a shoreline that one hundred years ago defined the basin's most prominent feature, a large expansive lake. At that time, a profusion of tule reeds marked the many shallow parts of the lake, giving the body of water its name. Drained and opened to farming in the early to mid-twentieth century, it now hosts some of the most productive and profitable farmland in the United States.

Subdued hues of brown, gray, and red color the remarkably rich soil. In the spring and summer, the basin is covered by a patchwork of green and amber fields of wheat, potato vines, onion stalks, and horseradish. All are testimony to the hard work of three generations of Tule Lake homesteaders.

In the winter, icy winds chill the countryside and bring a dusting of snow whose whiteness offsets the drab brown color that permeates the entire region. Thermometers may plunge to thirty degrees below zero Fahrenheit. Springtime is unpredictable. A single week may bring a howling blizzard, relentless rain and sunshine with cloudless, deep blue skies. Summers are usually mild with temperatures rarely exceeding one hundred degrees. The fall brings crispness to the air and a bright yellowing to leaves of the few shade trees that cluster next to neat farmhouses.

The basin's climate challenges the farmer. Frosts can occur every month of the year, limiting the variety of crops that can be grown. Annual rainfall averages nine to twelve inches, making irrigation a necessary part of farming. The wind is nearly constant and at times is strong enough to blow away topsoil and newly planted seed.

The features of the Tule Lake Basin are well defined. It is thirteen miles wide, east to west, by fifteen miles long. Lost River enters from the north through a relatively broad, flat opening between the Klamath Hills and Stukel Mountain. On the west side, the basin is bordered by the narrow, steep slopes of Sheepy Ridge. On the eastern side, it abuts the gentle rolling Clear Lake Hills. Two thirds of the way down the basin, three volcanic formations protrude from the lake bed floor. The most prominent is The Peninsula. This relatively broad brown cinder cone, topped on its southeastern edge with lava ramparts, can be seen for miles. Further to the south, the last of the flat fertile land runs into a chaotic landscape of twisted and broken volcanic rock known as the Lava Beds.

Tule Lake's Geologic Origins

The Tule Lake Basin and its adjacent neighbors, the Upper and Lower Klamath Basins, are part of three major geologic regions of North America known as the Basin and Range, the Pacific Rim of Fire, and the Lakes Region. Characterized by rippled, relatively narrow mountain ranges and wide dead-end valleys, sprinkled with black lava and red cinder rock, these regions are products of millions of years of westward-drift by the North American continent—a phenomenon that continues today.

It its infancy, fifty to one hundred million years ago, the entire region was relatively flat and could be scarcely identified from the surrounding countryside. Contact between the westward drifting North American Continent and a huge undersea formation known as the Pacific Plate generated tremendous internal pressure on the earth's surface. Occasionally some of this enormous energy was released as molten basalt rock that welled up from great cracks and spread out over much of the earth's surface. When it hardened, it formed a crust from ten to several hundred feet thick. As the westward movement of the continent continued, this solid but fragile surface yielded to the unrelenting internal pressure and began to fracture. Large chunks of material were tilted upward, often at crazy angles. To the west, abrupt fractures and ribbons of downward-flowing lava formed what became known as Sheepy Ridge. This narrow, spiny formation soon separated the Lower Klamath and Tule Lake basins into two distinct regions. On the east side, the softer and broader features of the Clear Lake Hills were more gently thrust upward. Scattered about were flat chunks of basalt that remained in horizontal positions, perched table-like on the upthrusted earth.

Not all of the pent-up energy generated by contact between the North American Continent and the Pacific Plate was spent uplifting the continent's western margin. Part of it caused North America to recoil from the Pacific Plate. In the process, the entire Basin and Range region stretched apart. In uniform fashion, row after row of linear fractures appeared, creating a series of elongated mountain ranges and basins, each generally running north to south.

In the Tule Lake Basin, the recoil phase widened the separation between Sheepy Ridge and the Clear Lake Hills. Between them, a deep valley appeared whose floor was of thick basalt. Over time, this valley began to fill with sediments. Volcanic ash, cinders, pumice, pulverized lava, and rotting organic matter were deposited, principally by the action of wind and water erosion. Eventually, the valley became a shallow basin. Water flowing from the north formed a lake, and wave action smoothed out each new contribution of waste rock and decayed material. So deep were these deposits that the present-day city of Tulelake had to sink a well nearly 3,000 feet into the former lake-bed before bedrock and potable water were found.

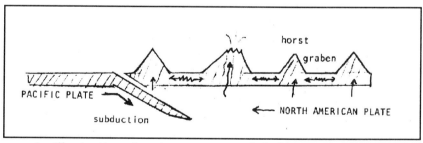

An illustration showing continental drift and subduction.
(Sketch by author)

The Impact of Volcanic Activity

While internal pressure was forcing the region up and the recoil effect was creating a proliferation of mountains and valleys, a third force was also at play—that of volcanism. As the North American continent moved westward and rode over the Pacific plate, the friction of the two surfaces grinding together turned the rock underneath into a superheated plastic mass. The internal pressure was enormous and the molten material worked its way to the surface through a series of fractures on the western side of the Basin and Range region. It spewed from giant fissures and built great conical mountains, jagged and broken peaks, symmetrical cinder cones, and deep depressions known as "caldera." Much of this activity created the great Cascade Mountain Range, which passes just to the west of the Tule Lake Basin, but volcanic activity also affected the basin itself.

Sometime between ten and fifteen million years ago, a series of volcanic eruptions began to alter the basin's character and create many of its contemporary features. Much of the volcanism was concentrated to the south in what is known today as the Lava Beds. But the basin itself was also the scene of several important volcanic phases. One to 1.8 million years ago, brown and gray 4508 feet Cayuse Mountain, a rather rounded and squat cinder cone, appeared in the southwestern corner of the basin. At about the same time and several miles to the north, "The Peninsula" poked its volcanic nose from the ground. It first spewed cinders and then, in its dying phase, capped itself on its southeastern side with lava. The semi-molten rock was pushed upward by the prevailing westerly winds and then solidified, forming ramparts that looked very much like the walled fortifications of a castle.

As volcanic activity in the basin continued, other formations joined The Peninsula. Brown and black Prisoners' Rock and a gray cinder and sand covered mound (labeled today on maps as the Sand Spit) appeared just to the south. Due east, a rather oddly shaped butte known as Horse Mountain also took form. It began as a volcano, its rim neatly defined by a ring of lava. But after its eruptive stage ended, its center bowl was filled with pumice, ash, and bits of coarse red lava dumped there by other erupting volcanoes. The piled debris was then smoothed and rounded by the wind, softening Horse Mountain's features.

Twenty miles southeast of the Tule Lake Basin is one of the largest volcanic formations in the region. Known as the Medicine Lakes Highlands, its most recent building period extends to at least 100,000 years ago. Located adjacent to the Lava Beds, this area is the product of a large subterranean fissure which channeled massive amounts of volcanic material toward the surface. The outpourings of lava spread in all directions and created huge concentric rings, each building on top of the next. The product was a "shield volcano," whose gradually rising slopes towered 4000 feet above the basin.

Though the Medicine Lakes Highlands' eruptive cycle is currently dormant, volcanic activity in the entire region is far from over. It is safe to predict that there will be future volcanic episodes. Each will add refinement to the features of the Tule Lake Basin and the surrounding hills.

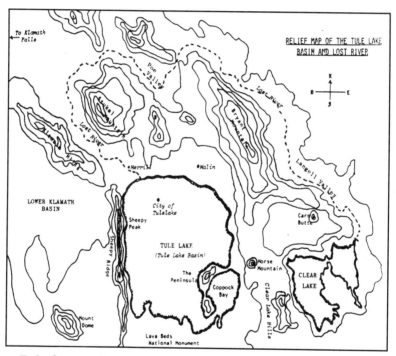

Relief map of the Tule Lake Basin and route of Lost River.
(Sketch by author)

The Changing Climate

Not only did the shape of land in the Tule Lake Basin undergo change; so did its climate. Two to three million years ago, the basin was considerably more tropical. The land was lush with vegetation. Wild pigs inhabited the area, as did mammoths, sloths, small horses, and camels. At several sites, remnants of these animals have been found. A construction crew working on an irrigation ditch near Merrill, Oregon uncovered ancient bones that "... were found to be the fossil remains of an enormous camel about twice the size of the present day Arabian camel." [1] Work on the Lost River Slough uncovered fossilized bones of a mammoth. In time, as the shape of the land changed, so did the climate and the wildlife. The American camel and mammoth disappeared. Today these animals have been replaced by antelope, big horn sheep, mule deer, marmots, jack rabbits, and millions of migratory birds.

The Mystery of Tule Lake's Water

Changes in the geography of the Tule Lake Basin contributed to the unusual way that water flows into the basin. The primary feeder is Lost River, whose headwaters are at Clear Lake. This body of water lies six miles due east of Tule Lake and is about 400 feet higher in elevation. Because the Clear Lake Hills and Bryant Mountain separate the two lakes, Lost River begins its journey by flowing northward into Oregon's Langell Valley. At one time, the river nearly became lost here (hence its name) as it fanned out to form an expansive marsh. At the northwest end of Langell Valley, Lost River snakes southwest past the foot of Bryant Mountain and enters Poe Valley. Here, the flow turns to the north and then arches west through a narrow gap that divides Stukel Mountain from the hills immediately to the east of the city of Klamath Falls. Finally, Lost River heads south through a valley flanked by Stukel Mountain on the east and the Klamath Hills on the west and enters the Tule Lake Basin. By journey's end, its circuitous route covers more than seventy miles.

Though the source of Tule Lake's water is unique, the lake itself offers the curious investigator several tantalizing mysteries. Ample evidence shows that in the years prior to reclamation Tule Lake greatly fluctuated in size. Written records from as early as the 1820s describe a northern shoreline running approximately three miles southeast of the present town of Merrill, Oregon. By the 1890s, a series of wet winters filled the lake to such a point that its shoreline was less than a mile from Merrill. However, these written records represent an extremely short period of time in geologic history. An examination of the cliffs along the eastern side of Sheepy Ridge and the abrupt western side of Prisoners' Rock provide a much longer record of changes in the level of Tule Lake. The highest water marks or wave cuts show that at one time the lake was as much as 32 feet higher than its meander line in the 1850s. [2]

Herein lies a mystery. It is obvious that the lake increased in volume during years of high precipitation, but Tule Lake was a dead-end as its southern outlet was blocked several million years ago by massive lava flows. Where then did the water go? Did it merely evaporate into the atmosphere, like the water did in many of the Basin and Range valleys? Or was there a subterranean fissure that siphoned water away?

Although evaporation did help lower the level of Tule Lake, it does not seem to have been the primary cause for the fluctuating water levels. Lakes that are subject to a great deal of evaporation build up large deposits of alkali. This was true of Lower Klamath Lake, immediately to the west of the Tule Lake Basin. It was also true of many lakes to the northeast, including Oregon's huge Lake Abert. Very little of the soil in the Tule Lake Basin had a high alkali content, so evaporation does not seem to have been the major cause for the loss of the lake's water. What then?

There is strong evidence to suggest that at least part of Tule Lake's fluctuating water level was due to the existence of subterranean outlets from the lake at its southern end. Geologic record indicates that at one time water from Tule Lake flowed south into the Pit River drainage system. Then, a series of volcanic eruptions in the Lava Beds and Medicine Lake Highlands spread lava over much of the region south of the lake, effectively blocking the further exit of water. After the volcanic activity stopped, it left behind a great network of cracks, fissures and lava tubes. The subterranean drainage theory suggests that water from the southern end of Tule Lake moved through a myriad of cracks and fissures in the lava and reappeared some sixty miles to the south as large springs near Pitville, California. These springs fed into the Pit River. Between 1906 and 1920, when the U.S. Reclamation Service was draining the lake, the volume of water flowing out of the Pit Springs was reported to have been substantially reduced.

Most engineering reports completed for the U.S. Reclamation Service concede that some underground seepage did take place at the southern end of Tule Lake. However, the size and rapidity of that drainage is subject to some degree of debate.

Rachael Applegate Good, author of the *History of Klamath County, Oregon*, published in 1941, mentioned the possibility of a subterranean channel in Tule Lake. Her book reported that it was located in an area known as Coppock Bay, at the southeast end of the basin. Supposedly, the water was drawn so quickly into the drainage hole that it created a large whirlpool. Good stated, "There is an Indian legend that about [1846] ... or somewhat later, a canoe on the surface of Tule Lake was seen to spin rapidly and sink as though drawn by some subterranean outlet." [3]

When a geologic study of Tule Lake was done by the Reclamation Service, no evidence was found of a large whirlpool. However, those who supported the whirlpool theory suggested that it had disappeared prior to recorded time because it had become clogged with debris and its main channel had been cut off by a series of earthquakes. Skeptics doubted these claims. Among them were two engineers, C.E. Hayden, who was director of the Klamath Reclamation Project in the 1930s, and John C. Cleghorn, who was part of a 1910 U.S. Reclamation Service engineering party.

C.E. Hayden believed that only a small volume of water seeped out of Tule Lake. His view was that the greatest variation in water levels was caused by evaporation coupled with cycles of wet and dry years. Water purity was maintained, and alkali build up minimized because of the large volume of water entering the lake.[4]

Cleghorn suggested that long term changes in the water levels of both Tule Lake and Lower Klamath Lake might have been caused by the shifting of an earthquake fault at Keno, south of the present city of Klamath Falls. If the fault movement partially blocked the outflow of the Klamath River, it would have backed up the river, causing water to flow into both lakes.[5]

Cleghorn also challenged the whirlpool drainage theory. He acknowledged that Indian legend suggested that a large whirlpool once existed but he claimed "... this could have been caused by wind-driven currents."[6] He went on to report that between 1910 and 1912, the U.S. Reclamation Service (later the Bureau of Reclamation) sought to expedite the drainage of Tule Lake by attempting to locate the main site of seepage. The Bureau focused their search in Coppock Bay, near the site of the reported whirlpool. Their activities included blasting holes into the lava rock at the edge of the lake, in an area several miles south of Prisoners' Rock, Cleghorn reported:

> ... I made a trip across [Tule Lake] in a launch with
> Project Engineers Patch and Mosier about 1910 or
> 1912. A few men were working on a crack about three
> feet wide [but] the prospect [of large scale drainage]
> did not seem promising to me.[7]

The holes dug by the Reclamation Service did eventually
provide some drainage for the lake, but it never reached the
volume that would have caused a large whirlpool. Yet even after
the reclamation project ended at Tule Lake, the legend of a great
whirlpool in Coppock Bay persisted. In fact, it was enhanced
when a lava tube was discovered in the lakebed at the southern
end of the bay. Local residents named it the "Glory Hole" and
claimed that it was the source of a great whirlpool. Through this
hole, they said, water cascaded underground, working its way
south to feed the springs near Pitville, sixty miles away.

Whether or not the Glory Hole of Coppock Bay actually was the
site of major drainage in Tule Lake is difficult to prove. Yet the
theory remains intriguing. Earthquakes and debris may well have
filled an underground labyrinth of lava tubes that once channeled
water south. It is known that some water still seeps into the Glory
Hole. It is currently used to drain surplus water from surrounding irrigation canals. The rate of flow is not spectacular, but
the water does disappear—somewhere.

The Tule Lake Basin Today

The Tule Lake Basin has undergone many changes in its
geography and climate. It has also been host to a great variety of
human inhabitants. The earliest visitors were Native Americans
who passed through thousands of years ago as part of a long
migration that began in the northern regions of Asia. Some Native
American groups took up residence in the region and their
descendants remained for hundreds—perhaps thousands—of
years.

Beginning in the mid-1800s, the lives of Native American
residents were abruptly changed. Streams of explorers, military
scouts, and settlers, whose ancestors were from Europe, traveled
through the basin. Some settled at the north end of Tule Lake.
Local tribes resisted this invasion, but they were not able to
dissuade these invaders. Instead, the basin's earliest inhabitants
were forcibly removed and the land opened to white settlement.

Change accelerated in the basin. Irrigation projects fostered a boom in agriculture, the offer of free land for homesteading drew new waves of settlers, and the need for commercial centers led to the founding of several towns. Today, there are four viable communities in the Tule Lake Basin. On the Oregon side of the border are Merrill, founded in the 1890s, and Malin, settled in 1909. The two communities on the California side are considerably younger. The City of Tulelake was opened for settlement in 1931. (The reader will probably notice the variation in spelling of Tule Lake between the body of water and the town. The combined word "Tulelake" came about to differentiate the city from the remnants of the drained lake). The last community settled in the basin was Newell. Located just to the east of The Peninsula, this townsite was originally part of a large internment camp built to house Japanese Americans and Japanese resident aliens during World War II. The camp closed in 1946 and in 1951 Newell was given townsite status.

One of the Tule Lake Basin's fundamental problems is its obscurity. Residents of western Oregon and Washington frequently drive through the center of the basin as they head south on Highway 139 to Reno and Carson City. Anxious to get to the twenty-four hour frenzy of Nevada's casino life, most drivers hurriedly press on, oblivious to the basin's diverse topography and distinctive beauty.

The basin is a lost stepchild. Sharing much in common with southern Oregon, but located just across the state line in remote corners of California's Siskiyou and Modoc counties, she occasionally suffers from an identity crisis. News, radio and television programs, major purchases of equipment and supplies, and entertainment all focus on Klamath Falls and the State of Oregon. But laws and administrative decisions affecting the basin come out of Sacramento and the county seats in Alturas and Yreka. The fate of Tule Lake is like so many communities located near borders between states. In the absence of natural divisions—particularly rivers—surveyors and mapmakers found it easiest to draw a straight line, ignoring the unity that comes with common geography.

A Purpose and a Goal

The chapters that follow are an attempt to unify the fragmented history of the Tule Lake Basin. They explore why this land of rugged contours and relatively harsh climate created a unique bond with the people who lived there. If this region's history becomes less obscure as a result of the information shared in this book, then an important goal has been achieved. Starting with an account of the region's earliest Native American settlers and ending with a description of its contemporary inhabitants, you are invited to share in the Tule Lake Basin's "years of harvest."

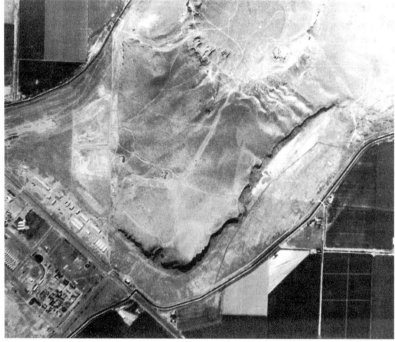

An aerial view of the eastern side of The Peninsula clearly shows its volcanic origins. *(Photo courtesy Bureau of Reclamation)*

A ground level view of the cinder and rampart formation known as "The Peninsula" located near the southern end of the Tule Lake Basin. *(Photo by author)*

Rounded and dome-shaped Horse Mountain rising from the basalt table land to the southeast of the Tule Lake Basin. *(Photo by author)*.

CHAPTER 2

THE FIRST INHABITANTS

In the late 1800s it was fashionable within the fledgling science of archaeology to suggest that Native Americans inhabited the Americas only a relatively short 5,000 years ago. This conclusion was based upon the limited work that had been done on early sites of habitation and upon studies done by ethnographers. This conclusion might have also been reached because of the unfortunate view expressed by many early archaeologists and anthropologists that non-whites were an inferior or less civilized branch of Homo sapiens.

Today, scientists are divided between those who believe people first arrived in the Americas 15,000 years ago, and others who maintain that the arrival date goes back at least 35,000 to 40,000 years BCE ("before common era"). There is some evidence to support both theories. In 1961, on Santa Rosa Island, off the coast of California, a group of archaeologists carefully excavated a hunting site that yielded both projectile points (arrowheads and spearheads) and the burned bones of pygmy mammoths that had been apparently cooked over an open fire. Using the Carbon 14 dating technique, which measures minute amounts of radio-activity left in once living material, it was ascertained that this site had been occupied at least 27,000 years ago.[1] In Lewisville, Texas, a site containing cooking hearths, waste flake from projectile points, and split and charred animal bones were dated to be 38,000 BCE.[2] Finally, along the Columbia River at The Dalles (pronounced "dalz"), an excavated site revealed reworked stone tools dated to be from 25,000 to 30,000 years old.[3]

The discoveries at Santa Rosa, Lewisville, and The Dalles have been viewed with caution by some anthropologists. They do not reject the great antiquity theory but instead point out that the frequency of these discoveries is presently very low, greatly increasing the possibility of error. Until more conclusive proof can be produced, via additional site discoveries, the conservatives feel more comfortable saying that humans clearly arrived in the Americas somewhere between 9,000 and 15,000 years ago. This is based upon the fact that a significant number of sites in the Basin and Range region have been dated to this time period.

What is known, with a much greater degree of accuracy, is that the early pioneers of the Americas came from the Asian continent. Most of them were members of nomadic tribes following herds of caribou, the main staple in their diet. Twice in recent geologic times there have been opportunities for travel between Asia and the Americas. In the period from 35,000 to 40,000 years ago and again from 15,000 to 20,000 years BCE, a general cooling trend caused an enormous amount of water to be transformed into glacier ice. During both of these periods, the ocean levels were substantially reduced. The result was the exposure of an expansive land bridge in the area of the Aleutian Islands that connected the two continents together. With the proximity of the Japanese Current, the newly exposed land may well have had a relatively mild climate during all but the winter months, far from the image frequently given of great expanses of ice and snow replete with the sting of frigid air.[4] It seems likely that human migration across the land bridge came about as the caribou herds expanded their grazing range eastward. Gradually, small bands of people moved onto the North American continent and established modest settlements in ice-free areas south of the Arctic Circle. In time, the more adventurous began to follow a corridor devoid of glaciers that led them into the Basin and Range country far to the south. From there, dispersal over the rest of North and South America took place.

What evidence do we have of the land bridge theory and the migration patterns? First, an increasing number of sites of antiquity have been discovered in the far northern region of the Americas. On the Arctic Coast at a site called Trail Creek, a 13,000-year-old camp was discovered in 1949. In the Yukon Territory, a site excavation in the 1960s unearthed a caribou bone scraper that was estimated to have been used about 25,000 years ago.[5] In addition, many sites in the Great Basin have been dated to be as old as 13,000 to 15,000 BCE, indicating that this was one of the oldest regions for permanent settlement in the Americas.

What brought people to the Great Basin at such an early time in human history? Clearly it was because of its hospitable environment. Weather cycles were changing, and the glaciers of the Pleistocene epoch, which had covered expansive regions of the North American continent, were in retreat. Land east of the Cascade Range in Northern California and eastern Oregon was particularly attractive to these early settlers. Here, a profusion of lava caves provided shelter, obsidian flows yielded precious material for making projectile points for arrows and spears, and large lakes attracted not only human settlers but great herds of game animals and water fowl.

Four phenomena generally dictated the length of continuous habitation in the high plateau region east of the Cascades: climate, availability of food, unusual geologic events, and displacement by intruders. For example, it is known that there were a number of significant shifts in weather patterns from 12,000 years ago to the present that altered living habits. From 12,000 to 7,000 years ago there was a general warming trend, but enough rainfall was present to support large lakes and grasslands. This period attracted a fair number of inhabitants to the Lakes country. From 7,000 to 5,000 years ago there was a very hot, dry period. Mountain glaciers practically disappeared and major lakes on the east side of the Cascades dried up. Many people were forced to move out as the traditional sources of food, particularly big game, began to disappear. Then another wet cycle occurred which lasted from 4,000 to 2,000 years ago. Lakes refilled, large game animals and migratory birds returned, and new waves of people occupied long abandoned caves and campsites. Finally, in the period from 2,000 years ago to the present, the climate turned drier; dry enough to cause the disappearance of a number of lakes, but not to the severity of the 7,000 to 5,000 year period. Some people were displaced, but others were able to maintain settlements that were still function-ing when the first Europeans arrived on the scene in the 1500s to 1800s.[6]

Within the proximity of the Klamath and Tule Lake basins, there have been a number of archaeological digs that have provided important information on the length of human presence in North America. Less than one hundred miles northeast is an unusual volcanic formation in the high desert plateau of Oregon known as Fort Rock. Until 2,000 years ago, a huge lake surrounded its steep walls, and lapped at a basalt and lava outcropping on a peninsula to the west. There was a cave in this outcropping, modest when compared with others in the Great Basin, but conveniently located and connected to the main shore by a narrow neck of land. The inhabitants who lived there were occasionally forced to leave when the level of the lake rose to cover the peninsula, but for thousands of years it provided a stable place of residence. Birds and large game were plentiful and the tule reeds and sagebrush on the surrounding land provided material for clothing. Then sometime around 7,000 years ago, the last inhabitants of the cave were forced out. Storms were no longer able to escape the clutches of the Cascade Mountains, and the lake began to evaporate. Eventually it completely disappeared, and so too did the inhabitants of the Fort Rock region.

In 1938, Dr. Luther Cressman of the University of Oregon was alerted to the possibility that a cave on the property of rancher Reubon Long might contain artifacts of interest to an anthropologist. When Cressman arrived and began to excavate the site, he soon encountered a layer of volcanic ash covering the cave's floor. As he began to carefully remove the ash he came upon one of the most important and unusual artifacts to be found in the Great Basin. Gingerly, he lifted from the floor of the cave a number of sandals made from the fiber of sagebrush. They were later dated to be at least 9,000 years old. Cressman also discovered many other important artifacts, including crescent shaped scrapers, projectile points, and a variety of charred bones and organic material which provided clues to the lifestyle and diet of the cave's former inhabitants. But the sandals remained the most singular of the discoveries. How could they have possibly survived for such a long period of time? As Cressman probed the question, the answer became obvious. Essentially three factors helped preserve the sandals: the arid desert environment of the plateau, the cave itself, which provided shelter from adverse elements, and the layer of lava ash. But where did the ash come from?

About 6,800 years ago, Mount Mazama, located approximately sixty miles southwest of Fort Rock, violently exploded. So great was the blast that 4,000 feet of the 12,000 feet volcano was blown away. Ash was carried great distances, raining down on practically all regions of the Pacific Northwest, and even going into the Canadian provinces of British Columbia, Alberta, and Saskatchewan.[7] It was this explosive episode that provided the protective blanket of ash for the Fort Rock sandals. As for Mount Mazama, when the eruptive period ended, rain and snow melt gradually filled an enormous depression in the center, forming one of Oregon's most beautiful natural sites, Crater Lake.

In subsequent years, the Reub Long Cave was further excavated and a extensive operation was carried out by Cressman and Stephen Bedwell in the early 1970s. Their discoveries were invaluable. The artifacts they found indicated that human habitation in the Lakes Country extended back perhaps as long as 14,000 years ago. Furthermore, an analysis by Cressman and Bedwell of the stone tools found in the cave was later used as a model for studying other Lakes Country sites suspected of being of great antiquity. Such sites included those found at Clear Lake and along Lost River, both in close proximity to the Tule Lake Basin.

Although no sites in the Klamath and Tule Lake Basin region have been specifically dated as old as the one near Fort Rock, several excavations have established occupation dates as early as 7,000 years ago.[8] However, a number of stone tools have been found in the area from the Lower Klamath Basin to Clear Lake which may indicate a much older period of human habitation. These include crescent-shaped scrapers, similar to artifacts found at Fort Rock, and finely made projectile points, very much like those of the Llano Culture of the Southwest. These discoveries have led one amateur archaeologist, Carrol B. Howe, who has done an extensive analysis of artifacts in the Klamath Basin region, to suggest that it may be the oldest continuously lived in region in western North America.[9]

Howe's suggestion does not imply that this habitation was not without interruptions. Probably, the dry cycle of 7,000 to 5,000 years ago caused dislocation. In addition, it is highly suspected that around 4,000 years ago an eruption in the Medicine Lake Highlands forced settlers to flee clouds of ash that rained down upon the area.[10] A similar event probably occurred 2,000 years later, and more recent volcanic events in the Lava Beds area probably also displaced people. However, based on the number of artifacts and sites discovered in the region, it seems clear that it was a popular place for human settlement; one that saw the presence of human beings for an enormously long period of time.

In the past one hundred and fifty years, the record of human habitation in the Tule Lake and Klamath basins has become progressively better, thanks to the availability of written records. The diaries of early white explorers give us some clue as to the nature of the people living there, but in the 1850s ethnologists began to gather formalized data on tribal groups of First Americans. This was fortunate primarily because of the rapid rate at which tribal culture was being altered and destroyed because of white intervention. Even the ethnologists themselves were not always objective, describing their subjects as hostile, sullen, crafty, and cruel.

What is known through written record is that, by the 1800s, tribal groups living in the vicinity of the Tule Lake and Klamath Basins included the Pit River Indians, Shastas, Klamaths, and Modocs. But in attempting to discover exactly when the ancestors of some of these people arrived in the basin, ethnologists and archaeologists alike were stymied. The reason for this is best summarized by Albert Samuel Gatschet, who in 1890 wrote in frustration, "The Klamath people possess no historic traditions going further back in time than a century, for the simple reason that there was a strict law prohibiting the mention of the person or acts of a deceased individual by using his name.[11] This was also true for the Modocs, so generally all information about these two tribes had to come from observing and recording present traditions and technology. Excavation of abandoned sites also was used as an aid in attempting to learn about their past history. When Dr. Luther Cressman conducted studies on Klamath tribal artifacts and villages, he came to believe that the people had been present in the area for a considerable period of time. In a monograph presented to the American Philosophical Society in 1956, he pointed out that:

> The examination of the economy of the Klamaths shows an adaptation to the particular ecological conditions of the area that bespeaks a long period of occupation. While there was no overall Klamath community, only a series of villages among which there were often raids ... each group had a recognized home area to which it always returned at the close of the seasonal movements in search of the particular resource available at special seasons and places.[12]

Aside from establishing dates of arrival for the Klamath and Modoc people, an equally nettlesome problem has been the attempt to determine whether or not the Klamaths and Modocs are related to each other. The experts offer mixed opinions. Albert Gatschet states in his 1890 study that "The two bodies of Indians ... are people of the same stock and lineage through race, language, institutions, customs, and habitat."[13] Historian and ethnologist Theodore Stern concurs. In his book *The Klamath Tribe, A People and Their Reservation* he writes, "Despite their differences, the two peoples retain[ed] a substantial common base: they spoke dialects of the same language and felt their political separation to have been a recent event."[14] One historian, Keith Murray, goes as far as establishing a year of separation for the two groups. In his book *The Modocs and Their War* he claims "Ethnologists find that villages which are distinctly Modoc began about 1780."[15]

Not all scholars of Klamath and Modoc history and culture agree that the two are related to each other. Verne F. Ray in his book *Primitive Pragmatists, The Modoc Indians of Northern California* states, "The Modocs shared fewer culturally diagnostic traits in common with the Klamath than they did with the Achomawi."[16] According to Ray, the Modocs were pragmatic, borrowing what they felt useful from other tribes living around them. They felt themselves ethnically and culturally unique and in Ray's opinion, were more closely related to California Indians than they were to the Klamaths. As proof, he cites that both their religious beliefs and styles of warfare were different from the Klamaths.[17]

The debate over whether or not the Klamaths and Modocs are part of the same group is healthy for the purpose of more thorough cultural analysis of both tribes. What can be said with certainty, though, is that by 1800 the Klamaths and Modocs were living in distinct regions. The Klamaths resided in the area of the Sprague and Williamson rivers and Upper Klamath Lake. The Modocs' region included the Lower Klamath Basin, Tule Lake, Lost River, and Clear Lake. Occasionally the two groups had contact with each other in a cooperative manner, principally through trade, but there was antipathy in their relationship. This would have great significance by the 1860s.

As the principal inhabitants of the Tule Lake Basin, the Modocs had a total population of less than 1,000. Their villages ranged in size from twenty to forty persons, and they identified themselves with regional names. Those who lived in villages east of Lost River Gap (today Olene, Oregon) on Lost River called themselves Kokiwas or "people of the far out country." People who lived south of Lost River Gap along both the river and the shores of Tule Lake were known as Paskanwas, meaning "river people." Finally, Modocs who resided west of Tule Lake and Sheepy Ridge in the Lower Klamath Basin called themselves Gumbatwas that translates as "people of the west." When a person was born in a village within one of the three regions, he or she retained part of that regional identification, but there were no restrictions limiting personal movement from one region to another.[18]

During the cold, harsh winters, the Modocs lived in one of twenty semi-permanent settlements. The greatest number was located along Lost River, and at least seven were on the shores of Tule Lake.[19] Their primary form of shelter was the wickiup, which was constructed by digging a saucer-shaped depression, ranging in depth from six inches to four feet. A domed network of willow poles was erected over it, and the poles were covered with woven mats made of tule reeds. Over this structure, a layer of earth was added to provide insulation against inclement weather. Each wickiup had a hole at the top for ventilation and light, and its entrance was generally situated facing towards the east.

In the spring of each year, the Modocs would dismantle their wickiups and move to traditional fishing sites, primarily along Lost River. Here they caught red suckers, one of the staples of the Modoc diet, and a variety of other fish including mullet, minnows, steelhead and freshwater clams. Much of their catch was dried and ground into a meal for later use. Other food gathering was divided by sex. The men hunted game animals including deer, antelope, mountain sheep, rabbit, marmot, and ground squirrel. Their favorite hunting sites extended from the southwestern half of Goose Lake to Clear Lake, Lost River, and Tule Lake. The Lava Beds area south of Tule Lake was frequently hunted for larger game. Women were responsible for gathering the seed of the wocus, a type of pond lily, and the roots of the camas plant, a main staple in their diet. These tuberous roots were dried and then ground into a powder for winter use.

The social structure of the Modoc tribe extended beyond a simple division of labor between men and women. There were complex provisions made for leadership, religious practices, family structure, warfare, and recreation. Modoc leadership was divided into three major powers, which included religious, political and military. Each leader was selected by meeting certain qualifications. The religious leader, known as the shaman or medicine man, attained his power through dreams, religious pilgrimages (especially to Crater Lake, which possessed mystical qualities), and the successful practice of medicine. He had to be a creative storyteller, able to relate to other tribal members vivid details of dreams involved with the contact between the spirit world of humans and animals. Though a shaman was considered a person of great power who could cure ills, he was also considered dangerous. Among other things, the shaman could remove a political leader (or chief) from power. Consequently, although it was considered bad luck to kill a shaman, most fell victim to intrigue and few died of natural causes.[20]

The political leader, called La-gi, held the most powerful and most permanent position. Though he yielded his authority to a war chief during times of conflict, the La-gi was the spokesman for the tribe. Selection of a political leader was based on wealth and the number of children he produced. However, the major factor was an individual's oratorical ability. If one was a particularly good speaker, it was possible to become the spokesman for the village and perhaps even the entire tribe.[21]

A military leader was selected on the basis of his fighting prowess and tactical skills. He also had to win the respect of the tribe through the strength of his personality. During times of conflict, he took over tribal leadership from the La-gi. During peacetime, he assumed a secondary role. Though the military leader was important, the tribe did not engage in continual warfare. In fact, before the 1850s, skirmishes were generally limited to fights with the Pit River and Shasta tribes. When a war party was organized it usually consisted of between ten and one hundred men. Women often accompanied the war party, but they did not engage in combat. In a skirmish, it was not unusual for the Modocs to take captives, and prisoners were frequently sold as slaves to the Klamaths and other northern tribes.[22]

The religion of the Modocs focused on a belief that the world was a flat disk whose center was located on the east side of Tule Lake. Because of its circular, dome-shape appearance, Horse Mountain, called Coyumnok by the Modocs, may have been the focus of their religious attention. Within their religious cosmology, they believed that the stars, sun and moon had always existed. Though their mythology mentioned no specific time for the earth's creation, they did possess legends on its origin. According to Modoc theology, the creator, Kumookumts, who had both male and female body parts, created the earth-disk by weaving land around Earth's center. When Kumookumts was done, he then created all the Indian tribes using two methods. Either seed was scattered about the land and from the seed humans grew, or he plucked hair from his armpits and from these sprang the people of the earth. It is not clear whether the Modocs had a preference between these two legends of their own creation.[23]

Many natural occurrences were warnings to the Modocs. Signs of impending death included a coyote's bark, the night call of a loon, or an owl's hoot. If someone killed a snake, then the death of the killer would follow. If they saw a frog die, it would bring a dry spring. Eclipses were caused by a hungry bear that ate the sun or moon. In order to restore the orb he had swallowed, a helpful frog would urinate on the bear until he threw it back up.[24]

To the bane of historians, any mention of a person who had died was forbidden by Modoc custom. When death occurred, the body was cremated. If possible, the funeral pyre was erected at the same site where the parents or grandparents had been cremated. Disposing of the body was always done during daylight hours, and all personal possessions of the deceased were destroyed. From that time on, all memories of the person were to be erased, and to even dream about the deceased was considered bad luck.[25]

Modoc marriages took place within a few months after puberty. The marriage itself was arranged by the respective parents of the bride and groom. In order to maintain the population of the tribe, couples were expected to have many children. Infant mortality was high though, and the average size of a Modoc family, including parents, was five. Within a marriage and within Modoc society in general, the quality of a man was judged by his speaking ability, wit, bravery, and his hunting skills. A woman was expected to be hard working. "It was said that a girl who was efficient at root digging was always beautiful."[26]

Within Modoc society, men held superior positions to women, and wives had to follow the dictates of their husbands. During the 1850s the power that the Modoc men held over their women came to play an important part in the tribe's relationship with white gold miners. In Yreka and other mining settlements, the Modoc men would prostitute their wives in return for trade goods. Cruel as this practice may seem, they had engaged in this practice with neighboring Modoc bands long before the arrival of the white miners.[27]

The Modocs were expert weavers, and they used the abundant tule reeds of Clear Lake, Lost River and Tule Lake to fashion both clothing and baskets. Clothing styles were usually designed to fit individual taste. For the most part, men wore a simple loin cloth during the summer months, and the women a wrap-around skirt. Clothing was made both out of woven reeds and animal skins. Generally, the men wore the skins from groundhogs, and women preferred coyote.[28]

For recreation, the Modocs enjoyed gambling and playing games. A rudimentary game of dice, using pieces that contained designs or spots, was one popular form of gambling. However, the Modocs wagered over almost all forms of competition, and a skillful gambler earned high status within the tribe. Games included ball-kicking, which was similar in many ways to soccer; distance running, usually from five to six miles; and the rolling of hoops made from braided tule reeds. Another popular sport was the use of bow and arrow to shoot at bundles of tules that were thrown into the air.[29]

The Modocs made extensive use of water transportation, particularly before the introduction of the horse that first became available in the first quarter of the nineteenth century. A number of different craft were used to ply the waters of the lakes and rivers in the Klamath and Tule Lake basins. One was the raft, which was made from bundles of tule reeds that were tied at each end and then lashed together or from pine, willow and juniper logs. Another was the two-man dugout canoe. These were made by burning the top of a log lengthwise and then carving out the center. Watercraft were most frequently used on Tule Lake. The wide, clear expanses of water provided an abundance of fish, waterfowl, tule reeds and wocus. Attesting to the intensity of activity on Tule Lake, many stone fishing weights and boat anchors were found by basin farmers after the lake was drained.[30]

Beyond their cultural practices and technology, the Modocs were considered to be fiercely independent and ready to protect their land. The only tribe they had the least bit of reservation about fighting were the Shastas to the west. Unfortunately, much has been made of this independent trait; particularly by historians who describe in detail alleged Modoc attacks on settlers coming into the Tule Lake Basin. There is little doubt that the Modoc were participants in some of the raids, but equally responsible were the Pit River and other tribes desperately attempting to hold on to their land in the face of white intrusion.

In the first quarter of the nineteenth century, the Modocs met the first Anglo-European explorers; so too did the Klamaths and other tribes of the Lakes country. Those encounters were the beginning of a lengthy and tragic period in the history of the Tule Lake Basin.

The lava fields at the southwest end of the Tule Lake Basin.
(Photo by author)

CHAPTER 3

EXPLORERS AND TRAILBLAZERS

On September 19, 1826, trapper and explorer Peter Skene Ogden, in the employ of the Hudson's Bay Company, left "The Dalles" outpost on the Columbia River. His mission was to explore uncharted regions to the south and to ascertain their potential for beaver and other animals whose skins could be used in the thriving fur trade. Ogden's expedition first took him through eastern Oregon. In a zigzag pattern, he followed the Deschutes River south and then the Crooked River east to Harney and Malheur lakes. Ogden and his men then moved westward along the Williamson River; by early December they were along the eastern shore of Upper Klamath Lake.[1]

The weather was usual for that time of year, a mixture of snow, rain, and annoying fog. Frequently, their pace was slowed while the expedition searched for food, which was acquired both through hunting and trade with local tribes. Evidently one main staple was dog, for it was often mentioned by Ogden in his journal. One such acquisition was noted for Tuesday, December 6, 1826. (Actually it was the 5th, somewhere on the trip Ogden had gotten off by one day). "We succeeded in trading at a cheap rate [for] 40 Dogs and some small Fish not more than two inches in length and far from being good."[2]

At this point in Ogden's trip, his actual location becomes a bit murky. According to K.G. Davies, who edited the Hudson's Bay Record Society's publication of *Peter Skene Ogden's Snake Country Journal, 1826-27*, the trapper and his men spent several weeks in the vicinity of Upper Klamath Lake. They then headed due south, skirting along Lower Klamath Lake, and set up camp on Willow Creek at the southwestern end of the basin.[3] However, the late Devere Helfrich, Klamath Basin historian and former editor of the Klamath County Historical Society's *Klamath Echoes*, disagreed. He believed that Ogden traveled as far south as the outflow of Upper Klamath Lake and then headed southeast toward the Lost River Valley and Tule Lake.[4] When one consults Ogden's journal, one finds his cryptic descriptions of the region's topography make it difficult to pinpoint his actual location. Based on the evidence presented, Helfrich was apparently correct. For example, after moving south from Upper Klamath Lake, Ogden made the following notation on Friday, December 15th:

> Our Horses look'd wretched this morning after the stormy night it would not require six nights more of such weather to reduce the number of our Horses, but our Guide promises as we shall not long be troubled with Snow at present we have 12 Inches. Our course South East.[5]

This direction would have taken the expedition to the Lost River Slough, and not to the Lower Klamath Basin. Other segments of Ogden's journal are not as helpful in confirming his location. Too frequently he used generic terms to describe the countryside. He had a penchant for depicting streams and rivers as being "well lin'd with Willows" and the land as being filled with "Swamp and Lakes." However, interspersed within his daily entries he did include specific references to unusual geographic formations. Based on extrapolations of this information and on the findings of Devere Helfrich, the following narration of Ogden's trip through the Tule Lake Basin has a reasonable degree of accuracy.

For four days, the expedition slowly worked its way down the Lost River Valley, searching for signs of beaver. On December 20th (19th), while looking for a ford across Lost River, Ogden's party had its first contact with members of the Modoc tribe. Ogden recorded the subsequent events:

> We dried our Lodges and at 10 A.M. we started and advanced six miles over a plain where we reached the river a fine looking stream well lin'd with Willows and had some difficulty in discovering a fording place but on our Guides calling out to some Indians who were on the opposite side they came and pointed out a suitable spot had the water been two inches deeper without the assistance of rafts we could not have cross'd, we succeeded however without wetting any thing ...[6]

This is a significant entry. It is the first known written record of contact between Anglo-Europeans and the inhabitants of the Tule Lake and Lower Klamath basins. It is also the first written description of what is now known as the Stone or Natural Bridge. For much of its journey through the Lost River Valley, the banks of Lost River are steep, making it extremely difficult to cross.

However, at Stone Bridge, which is about two miles southeast of
the present city of Merrill, Oregon, Lost River crosses a smooth
outcropping of rock. The depth of the river has varied here,
according to the level of Tule Lake, from about six inches to over
fifteen feet. Normally, this ford was navigable and at the time that
Ogden crossed on Stone Bridge, the depth of Lost River must
have been about three feet deep.

Modoc assistance in finding Stone Bridge was not the only
encounter that Ogden's expedition had with the tribe. On
January 2, 1827, Ogden and his men camped out at a recently
abandoned Modoc village. It was probably located at the
southeastern end of Tule Lake at a spot now known as Scorpion
Point. As was normal for that time of year, the weather was cold,
especially at night. Ogden wrote:

> This morning Mr. McKay and all the Hunters started
> in quest of Deer ... at midnight I overtook the Camp at
> the Indian Village seen on the 28th [27th of December]
> ... The Natives since we passed here have abandoned
> their Village but we could not discover what course
> they have taken—altho mild in the day the nights are
> cold and from total want of wood is probably the cause
> of their departure. We took the liberty of demolishing
> their Huts for fire wood at least the men I have warn'd
> them if the Natives should complain of this burgalary
> (sic) rather than it should be a cause of quarrel that
> they should pay for the theft so far all shall be fair on
> our side—I should certainly regret that our side
> should cause a quarrel with these Indians, for so far
> their conduct towards us has been certainly more
> correct and orderly and worthy of imitation by all ...[7]

Unfortunately we have no written record concerning the
reaction of the Modocs to their destroyed village. Certainly their
feelings would have been much less magnanimous than those of
Ogden! He and his men compounded their darkening reputation
the next day. On January 3rd, several members of the expedition
moved to another camp, again in the proximity of Scorpion Point.
Ogden recorded:

> Here a number of Indians collected round our Camp
> complaining of starvation but we could afford them no
> relief in regard to food for the last four days we have
> been without ... consequently many curses are

bestowed on this Country and justly so for certainly it is poverty itself it cannot even support its own inhabitants still less a few solitary strangers amongst the number first rate marksmen and hunters. [8]

Again, speculation must step in, but clearly the denial of food by these white strangers must have left an indelible mark on the minds of the starving Modocs. It was an omen of things to come.

Ogden's expedition remained in the general area of the Tule Lake and Lower Klamath basins until May, 1827. They then traveled south to pick up the Pit River, where they changed direction and headed east and north to Goose Lake. Finally, they backtracked through Oregon to the Columbia River. Ogden reported to the Hudson's Bay Company on the experiences of his expedition soon after, and the first edition of his journal was made available for public use. Sadly, it became a blueprint for the future invasion of Modoc and Klamath territory by white explorers and settlers.

It was nineteen years later when the second intrusion of whites into the Tule Lake Basin took place. On May 1, 1846, Captain John C. Fremont arrived at the shore of Tule Lake. He was on a survey and scouting mission for the United States government, mapping a region still relatively uncharted and unknown to those not living in the basin.

Technically, Fremont was trespassing on Mexican land, something he had done several times in the past. His actions were simply the nature of the times. The United States had already declared that "Manifest Destiny" was its cause celebre, and all land from the Atlantic to the Pacific oceans was destined to be under American control. There was also a touch of Anglophobia in Fremont's action. Because of the active Hudson's Bay post at Fort Vancouver on the Columbia River, there was fear that Great Britain might take control of the far west if the U.S. didn't, so the Captain was under orders to gather all the intelligence information he could. This would be Fremont's last expedition, War with Mexico would break out only a month and a half after he entered the Tule Lake and Klamath basins, and he would be called south to serve in a new role.

When Fremont entered the Tule Lake Basin, he sketched its topography and lake onto his maps, assigning various geographic features their first Anglicized names. In his diary, he recorded: "On the first of May I encamped on the southeastern end of a lake, which afterward I named lake Rhett in friendly remembrance of Mr. Barnwell Rhett, of South Carolina ..."[9] Five days later, Fremont and his men camped near Stone Bridge and named the water flowing by there McCrady River, using the name of a boyhood friend.[10] Though Rhett Lake would appear on some early survey maps of the Tule Lake Basin, Fremont's names were only temporary. Geographers and mapmakers tended to prefer the names "Lost River" and "Tule Lake."

Fremont's survey party continued their expedition by going up the Lost River Valley and then turning west to cross Link River between Lake Ewauna and Upper Klamath (today the site of Klamath Falls, Oregon). Heading north again, he and his men circled Upper Klamath Lake and in the process engaged in two battles, in all likelihood with people of the Klamath tribe.

In the meantime, Senator Thomas Hart Benton from Missouri sent Marine Corps Lieutenant Archibald Gillespie to find Fremont. Benton, whose daughter was Fremont's wife, wanted to persuade his son-in-law to lead a war of liberation in California should war with Mexico break out. In his search for Fremont, Gillespie posed as an emissary of the United States government. His travels first took him to Monterey, the Mexican capital of California. When he discovered that Fremont was scouting an area somewhere near the Oregon-California border, he hired Peter Lassen, a blacksmith by trade, to guide him north.[11]

In May, Gillespie and Lassen entered the Klamath Basin and soon located Fremont. On the day of their arrival, Fremont's small camp was attacked by Klamaths who were by now wary of these well-armed intruders. Three of Fremont's Delaware Indian scouts lost their lives. The casualties would have been higher had it not been for the alertness of Kit Carson, who had been helping guide the expedition. Sensing trouble, Carson had warned his companions in time for them to take defensive action.[12]

There is some confusion as to where the attack on Fremont's expedition actually took place. Denny Creek on Upper Klamath Lake is one location frequently cited. Fremont's party had engaged the Klamath Indians in several skirmishes around Upper Klamath Lake, and the proximity of the expedition to Klamath tribal territory would have made the Denny Creek campsite a likely spot.[13] However, two months later, when pioneer scout Lindsay Applegate was passing though the basin, he and other members of his party discovered an unusual campsite along Lower Klamath Lake. Applegate wrote of this event:

> We could see columns of smoke in every direction, for our presence was already known to the Modocs, and the signal fire telegraph was in active operation. Moving southward along the shore we came to a little stream coming in from the southward, and there found pieces of newspapers and other unmistakable evidences of civilized people having camped there a short time before. We found a place where the turf had been cut away, also the willows near the bank of the creek, and horses had been repeatedly driven over the place. As there were many places where animals could get water without this trouble, some of the party were of the opinion that some persons had been buried there and that horses had been driven over the place to obliterate all marks and thus prevent the Indians from disturbing the dead. The immense excitement of the Indians on our arrival there strengthened this opinion. Colonel Fremont, only a few days before, had reached this point on his way northward when he was overtaken by Lieutenant Gillespie of the United States army with important dispatches and returned to Lower California.[14]

There are several explanations for this event. Fremont may have been mistaken on the location of the skirmish, or more likely another unrecorded party of whites came under fire. By this time in history, the expeditions of Peter Skene Ogden and John C. Fremont were not the only ones to enter the basin. Mountain men, trappers, and travelers had passed through, but if they recorded the events, the information was either lost or never published.

Wherever the attack took place, Fremont and his men quickly recovered, and they left immediately for the Sacramento Valley. In an area near Sutter Buttes (north of Sacramento), Fremont and his expedition camped out. While there, the Captain was approached by a contingent of Americans to lead an attack against the Mexican government at Sonoma. He refused.

Nevertheless, the American insurgents made their move and on June 14, 1846, Mexican official Mariano Guadalupe Vallejo officially surrendered the town. As soon as Fremont received word of the capture of Sonoma and the surrender of Vallejo, he and his men assumed command of the ragtag American forces. His opportunistic move would earn him the reputation, though inaccurate, of being one of the principal liberators of Northern California.[15]

There was only a brief two-month respite between Fremont's contact with the people of the Klamath and Tule Lake Basins and the arrival of another expedition of whites. The new group, known as the Applegate-Scott expedition, was not there to map the region for military and scientific purposes. Instead they were looking for a shorter and more direct route for white settlers coming from the east to the Oregon Territory. The origin of the Applegate-Scott expedition began in 1843 when Jesse, Lindsay, and Charles Applegate left the state of Missouri with the intent of settling in Oregon. It was an arduous journey for the Applegates, and one marred by tragedy.

After traveling west across Nebraska and Wyoming on the Oregon Trail, their party stopped briefly at Fort Hall in southeastern Idaho. They then traveled in a northwest direction to Fort Walla Walla. There, they built log rafts to float down the Walla Walla and Columbia rivers toward their Willamette Valley destination. For 150 miles, the raft trip was uneventful, and then disaster struck. The memoirs of Lindsay Applegate vividly described the event:

> We did well 'till we reached The Dalles, a series of falls and cataracts. Just above the Cascade mountains one of our boats, containing six persons, was caught in one of those terrible whirlpools and upset. My son, ten years old, my brother Jesse's son, Edward, same age, and a man by the name of McClellan, who was a member of my family, were lost. The other three who escaped were left to struggle the best they could until we made the land with the other boats. It was a painful scene beyond description. We dare not go to their assistance without exposing the occupants of the other boats to certain destruction.[16]

This fatal episode had a profound impact on the Applegate family. When they finally reached their new home on Salt Creek, near the present town of Dalles, Oregon, the Applegates reflected on their grief. Lindsay Applegate wrote, "That long and dreary winter, with its pelting rains and howling winds, brought sadness to us. We resolved if we remained in the country to find a better way for others who might wish to emigrate."[17]

Grief was not the only motivation for the Applegates to contemplate a new route to Oregon. Like so many Americans, they had been infected with Manifest Destiny. By the 1840s, people were clamoring for not only Mexican territory, but also British held land from the Columbia River north to the 54th parallel (which would have included the present state of Washington and the Canadian provinces of British Columbia and Alberta). One popular theory of the time was that by encouraging large-scale settlement in Oregon, a staging ground could then be established for expansion to the north ... or to the south. In addition, any designs that the British might have on Oregon territory would be discouraged.

The first person to organize an expedition to look for an alternate route to Oregon was Levi Scott, a resident of Polk County, Oregon. Scott believed that a trail leading into the territory from the south and east was feasible. In May of 1846, he left with a group of men and headed down the Willamette Valley and into the Calapooya range. But the expedition ended quickly. Scott's men became weak-hearted. They feared they would be attacked by Indians resentful of their intrusion, and they returned to their homes in the central Willamette Valley only several days after their departure.[18]

Hearing of Scott's ill-fated search for a southern route to Oregon, Jesse and Lindsay Applegate offered their assistance in organizing a new expedition. Under their leadership, fifteen men were recruited, including mountain man Moses Harris, who had previously run a set of traps in the Klamath Basin.[19] The Applegates prepared for the trip by reading excerpts from Peter Skene Ogden's journal and pouring over newly published maps which covered an area from southern Wyoming to California and the Oregon Territory. Based on the information they gathered, they joined Levi Scott in the firm belief that a southern route into Oregon was possible.

On June 21, 1846, with men and provisions secured, the Applegate-Scott party left the Polk County settlement of Dallas. Their route took them south paralleling a course very close to that of the present Interstate 5 highway system from Eugene to Ashland. On June 30th, they turned southeast and began to cross the Cascade Mountains. Three days later they were in the Klamath Basin and on July 4th camped along the shores of Lower Klamath Lake. It was here that Lindsay Applegate later reported that they had found evidence of "civilized people having camped a short time before," and he speculated that this was the site of the attack on John C. Fremont's scouting party.[20]

The fifteen-man expedition spent the day of July 5th working their way along the twisting shoreline of Lower Klamath Lake, heading toward its southern end. The events that took place next were immensely important to the future of the Tule Lake Basin and are best described by Lindsay Applegate:

> We camped on the lake shore and the next morning, July 6th [1846], we ascended a high rocky ridge to the eastward for the purpose of making observations. Near the base of the ridge, on the east, was a large lake, perhaps twenty miles in length. Beyond it, to the eastward, we could see a timbered butte, apparently thirty miles distant, at the base of which there appeared to be a low pass through the mountain range which seemed to encircle the lake basin. It appearing practicable to reach this pass by passing around the south end of the lake, we decided to adopt that route and began the descent of the ridge.[21]

The expedition had been standing on Sheepy Ridge or Gillem's Bluff when they made their observations. The mountains they were looking at in the distance were the Clear Lake Hills. Lindsay Applegate continued his narration:

> We soon found ourselves in the midst of an extremely rugged country. Short lava ridges ran in every conceivable direction, while between them were caves and crevices into which it seemed our animals were in danger of falling headlong. The further we advanced the worse became the route, so that at length we decided to retrace our steps to the smooth country.[22]

The expedition had a difficult time returning to navigable ground and in the process became separated from one of its members, David Goff. Evidently Goff had discovered a band of mountain sheep and gone in pursuit, unaware that his comrades had left. While chasing the sheep about, he came upon a band of Modocs who had been carefully watching his moves. Curious at first, the Modocs suddenly turned and ran to their canoes, perhaps fearful that the rest of Goff's party was close behind. Meanwhile, the main party was riding along the west side of Tule Lake. They spied a considerable number of canoes crossing the lake near the Peninsula. Soon after, David Goff appeared on his horse, riding along the lake's western shore. He rejoined the party, regaling in telling the story of his adventure.

At noon the men stopped for lunch at a large meadow at the north end of the lake. Several hours later, they resumed their journey and Lindsay Applegate chronicled another important event.

> We repacked and started on our way towards the timbered butte, but had not proceeded more than a mile before we came suddenly upon quite a large stream [Lost River] coming into the lake. We found this steam ... very deep, with almost perpendicular banks, so that we were compelled to turn northward, up the river. Before we proceeded very far we discovered an Indian crouching under the bank, and surrounding him, made him come out. By signs, we indicated to him that we wanted to cross the river. By marking on his legs and pointing up the river, he gave us to understand that there was a place above where we could easily move across. Motioning him to advance, he led the way up the river about a mile and pointed out a place where an immense rock crossed the river. The sheet of water running over the rock was about 15 inches deep.[23]

This description of Stone Bridge marked the third time that a written record had been made by whites about the natural ford across Lost River. Prior entries had been for mapping and survey purposes; the Applegate record went much further. Stone Bridge now became designated as an important segment of a new route to Oregon, a route that would not just bring small bands of trappers and explorers but entire wagon trains of settlers. The tenuous relationship between whites and native inhabitants of the basin would soon explode into violent confrontation because of this discovery.

After crossing Stone Bridge, the Applegate-Scott party continued east. They blazed a trail that passed to the north of Clear Lake and crossed the outlet that formed the headwaters of Lost River. They then traveled east past Blue Mountain and around the south end of Goose Lake. Next the party moved through Fandango Pass in the Warner Mountains and began to head southeast as they entered Nevada. The journey took them through the Black Rock Desert and southeastward to the Humboldt River. Here they stopped and five members of the Applegate-Scott party were selected to continue on to Fort Hall, in southeastern Idaho. Their plan was to intercept wagons trains coming west as part of the 1846 migration and convince them to take the newly blazed southern route.

On the morning of July 25th, Moses Harris, John Owens, Henry Boygus, David Goff, and Jesse Applegate left for Fort Hall. Prior to their departure, they had made an agreement with the main party to rendezvous at a spot called Thousand Spring Valley (also known as Hot Springs Valley). After leaving the main party, they followed the Humboldt River in a northeasterly direction. On the journey, one of the five men, Henry Boygus, went on a scouting mission in search of friends he thought might be in the area. Boygus disappeared and it was assumed by the remaining four men he had been killed by Indians.[24]

The advance party reached Fort Hall the last week of July. Their first act was to announce the discovery of a new, shorter route to Oregon. Since Jesse Applegate had been one of the main leaders of the expedition, the route became known as the Applegate (or Southern Emigrant) Trail. It was also Applegate who became the party's central spokesman, and he attempted to persuade pioneers he met at Fort Hall, including several former acquaintances, to try the new route. Though more than 450 wagons and 2000 people had already passed by the fort, Applegate was able to convince some 450 to 500 people, traveling in about 90 to 100 wagons, to take the southern trail.[25]

Near the end of the first week in August 1846, the first wagon train to try the southern route to Oregon left Fort Hall. On August 11th, the vanguard of this train met the main party of the Applegate-Scott expedition at Thousand Spring Valley. Problems developed almost immediately. In his enthusiasm to convince people to take the new route, Applegate had neglected to clarify to members of the wagon train that they would have to help clear the trail. In fairness to Applegate, it should be also mentioned that the expedition members, who had been left in the Humboldt sink to work on the trail while waiting for the first wagon train to arrive, had not been able to get as much done as planned.

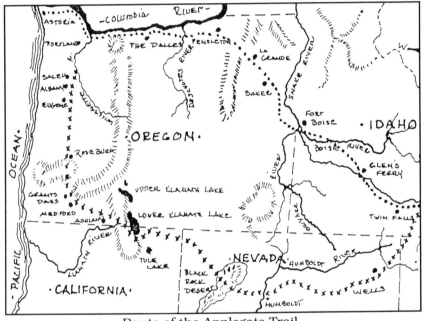

Route of the Applegate Trail.
(From Dr. Frances Haines, The Applegate Trail: Southern Emigrant Route, University of Oregon)

The wagon train's progress was extremely slow. The trip along the Humboldt River and then northwest through the Black Rock Desert saw the pioneers working endlessly clearing bush and removing boulders from their path. It wasn't until late September that they reached Tule Lake and the Klamath Basin. By October the wagon train had crossed the mountains to the west in an area where the Siskiyous and Cascades met. They descended into the Rogue River Valley and headed north. Their route became torturous as they crossed Canyon Creek and soon after encountered the first of Oregon's infamous rain.

The rain slowed the wagon train to a crawl; it took the settlers a week to go twenty-eight miles from Canyon Creek to a ford across the Umpqua River. Oregon pioneer Tabitha Brown later described how terrible this stretch of the journey had been for her. She wrote: "I rode through in three days at the risk of my life on horseback, having lost my wagon and all that I had but the horse that I was on."[26] Brown also remembered that the canyon was littered with "dead cattle, broken wagons, beds, clothing and everything but provisions."[27]

Meanwhile, the Applegate-Scott party had departed the main wagon train. Lindsay Applegate recalled that:

> Road working, hunting, and guard duty had taxed our strength greatly, and on our arrival in the Umpqua valley, knowing that the greatest difficulties in the way of immigrants had been removed, we decided to proceed at once to our home in the Willamette [Valley]. There we arrived on the 3rd day of October, 1846, having been absent three months and 13 days.[28]

The Applegates' departure may have been a grave mistake. By the first week in November, the pioneers were desperate for food and supplies because their progress had been so slow. Several men were sent ahead into the Willamette Valley to find provisions. Later, they returned and met the wagon train, as it was moving into the southern end of the Willamette Valley. Finally, on December 25, 1846 the first major group of white settlers to use the Applegate Trail reached their destination in the area around Polk County. But they were only the vanguard of a larger wagon train that was still on the trail.

The main section of the 1846 wagon train using the Applegate Trail ran into even more difficulty than the lead group. Continual delays, scarce food, Indian attacks, and disease took their toll. In addition, the pioneers ignored Jesse Applegate's warning that they had to move on as rapidly as possible to avoid Oregon's harsh winter weather. Coming from the east and mid-west, it was difficult for them to imagine how miserable the continual dampness of a winter in western Oregon could be. Unfortunately, they soon found out. The rains began as soon as they entered the Rogue River Valley. Their progress was slowed even more when they reached Canyon Creek. The incessant downpour turned everything to mud. Those at the end of the wagon train became so desperate for food that they ate raw the flesh of animals that had died along the trail.[29]

When word reached members of the main wagon train that the Applegates had gone home, there was a great deal of dissension. The pioneers claimed that they had been abandoned. One member of the train, Jesse Quinn Thornton, who later became a Supreme Court Justice of the State of Oregon, called Jesse Applegate a "voracious and commissionless captain" who had given misleading information.[30] Tabitha Brown referred to Jesse as that "rascally fellow" who decoyed three or four wagon trains to follow his miserable trail.[31] But in truth, the Applegates were deeply concerned about the fate of the main wagon train. Jesse Applegate noted that:

> As soon as we could possibly make the arrangements, we sent a party with oxen and horses to meet the immigrants and aid them in reaching the Willamette Settlements. For this assistance we made no demand, nor did we take them for the use of the road as was alleged by parties inimical to our enterprise. [32]

Though Jesse and Lindsay Applegate were severely criticized for leading that first group of pioneers on the Southern Emigrant Trail, they were in the long run vindicated in their effort to open a new route to Oregon. The next year a stream of immigrants came across Applegate's route with only one wagon lost. In reference to the 1847 wagon train, Jesse Applegate noted that "these immigrants ... redeemed the character of the road." [33]

The Applegates could look with pride at their accomplishments. However their actions and those of other white explorers and settlers permanently altered the lifestyle of the area's first occupants. The native tribes, whose ancestors had occupied the land for thousands of years, would not yield easily to the newcomers. Soon the Klamath and Tule Lake basins would be sites of violent confrontation.

The "Stone Bridge" ford before Lost River was dammed.
(Photo courtesy Klamath County Museum)

Anderson-Rose Dam, built in 1921, spans Lost River at the site of
the "Stone Bridge". *(Photo by author)*

Upper Klamath Lake and Mt. McLaughlin.
(Photo by author)

CHAPTER 4

EARLY RESISTANCE TO WHITE SETTLERS

The Applegate Trail ushered in a new chapter in the relations between the tribes of the Klamath and Tule Lake basins and Anglo-Europeans. The cumulative effect of the Ogden and Fremont expeditions and the influx of new settlers and travelers upset a delicate balance that had been centuries in the making. In the past, there had been warfare between the Klamaths, Modocs, Shastas, Pit Rivers and Snakes but evidence suggests that it had never threatened an entire culture. Instead, it involved skirmishes that were usually focused on territorial rights, or on retaliatory raids rooted in continuing feuds. The philosophy imported by whites was entirely different. They considered the "First Americans" to be impediments to civilization, best dealt with by removing them from land that could be "better used" for farming and industry and confining them to reservations. Many tribes resisted such encroachment, but in spite of outstanding skills in warfare, superior firepower and greater numbers overcame them. The Modocs and Pit Rivers were resolute in their efforts to hold onto their land.

The Applegate Trail was the catalyst that led to open conflict in the Tule Lake and Klamath basins. Beginning with the first train of 1846, long lines of wagons, horses, cattle, and hundreds of settlers snaked across sacred Modoc land and traveled by their villages. Dust rose high in the air. The jingle of harnesses, the creaking of wheels, and shouts of encouragement to horses and oxen disrupted the placid setting. Game not shot by the emigrants was frightened away by the clamor. It was too much for the Modocs to cope with, and their first attack on a wagon train was recorded in that year. It was not a spectacular raid. Barking dogs warned the emigrants of the impending assault, and a strong show of force caused the Modocs to back away.[1]

Though the impact of the attempted raid was inconclusive, the site selected by the Modocs was ideal. As the Applegate Trail moved west out of the Clear Lake Hills, it passed just to the north of Horse Mountain (called Raspberry Mountain by the emigrants) and descended through several gullies before it paralleled Tule Lake. It was hilly terrain, with an abundance of table rock that provided excellent cover. The trip from Clear Lake to Tule Lake often took wagon trains more than a day, and the settlers were anxious to reach a spot where their stock could slake their thirst and water barrels could be refilled. Concentrating on reaching Tule Lake, their alertness to possible attack was diminished. So frequently did attacks take place here that it earned the name Bloody Point.

Meanwhile, Modoc resistance to white intrusion solidified in 1847 when a smallpox epidemic swept the tribe. There was little doubt that it had been introduced by infected whites.[2] Not only did the epidemic decimate Modoc villages but it took the lives of many of the traditional leaders. Consequently, leadership fragmented among the younger Modocs. Lacking the discipline of their elders, they broke into smaller bands and began to vent their frustration by indiscriminately attacking wagon trains passing through their land.[3] This was only one of a series of events that led to an escalation of violence.

In 1848, gold was discovered in the hills east of Sacramento and the Applegate Trail took on new significance. Some of the earliest gold seekers were not from the east, but rather from the Pacific Northwest. In the summer of 1848, two major wagon trains—one from Oregon and the other from Washington Territory—headed south down the Applegate Trail. Their journeys took them through the Willamette Valley, past the Umpqua and Rogue rivers and southeast into the Klamath Basin. As the trail approached the Clear Lake Hills, the wagons branched off to the right, following the eastern shore of Tule Lake. Further south, they moved through Big Valley, passed near Mount Lassen, and picked up Deer Creek, which they followed into the Sacramento Valley.[4]

Gold seekers from the east also utilized segments of the Applegate Trail. Branching off from the Oregon Trail at Fort Hall, they came as far west as Goose Lake and then turned south to follow the Pit River on a route blazed by Peter Lassen. It too led into the Sacramento Valley. From 1849 to 1851, it is estimated that between 10,000 and 15,000 people used the Applegate and Lassen trails on their way to the California gold fields.[5]

In 1849, the first violent deaths on the trail between Goose Lake and Tule Lake were reported. A party of miners was attacked, allegedly by Modocs, and twenty-five were killed.[6] In September of 1850, a badly wounded man staggered into Jacksonville, Oregon and announced that he was the only survivor out of 80 who had been attacked at Bloody Point. In this case, the survivor's story was substantiated when Colonel John Ross led an armed party to the site and discovered "stripped and mutilated bodies of men, women, and children (lying) amidst the charred ruins of prairie schooners."[7] There was no proof that the Modocs were responsible for this atrocity but, because of their past resistance, it was assumed by whites that they were the guilty party.

The hysteria this attack and others generated left an indelible mark on emigrants, government officials, and even historians. In September of 1854, Joel Palmer, Superintendent of Indian Affairs for Oregon described the Modocs and Pit Rivers as being "tribes (who) have always evinced a deadly hostility to the whites, and the Modocs boasted of having within the last four years murdered thirty-six ..."[8] In 1905, historian F.A. Shaver claimed in *An Illustrated History of Central Oregon* that:

> Innocent and unoffending immigrants, accompanied by their families, passing through the Modoc country along the old southern road [Applegate Trail], were attacked and butchered indiscriminately by these painted savages; their property confiscated or destroyed; their bodies inhumanly mutilated, and left unburied, a prey to wolves. In some cases the victims of these Modocs were caused to suffer excruciating tortures before relieved by death. In some cases girls were kept among them as captives for months; to suffer more than torture, with death only to crown their miserable existence. More than three hundred immigrants are known to have been slain in this manner by Modoc Indians.[9]

There is no doubt that groups of Modocs participated in attacks on white immigrants, but the hysterics of such descriptions were unfair and distorted. In his book, *The Modocs and Their War* Keith Murray points out that:

> It is impossible to state accurately how much damage was done to the trains. Since the Modocs did more damage than any of the other northern California Indians, legend later ascribed many killings to them that never took place. Claims of damage were often based on the wildest of rumors. Killings to the number

of 350 were laid at the door of the Modocs, but this number included people killed well outside of Modoc territory - along the coast, in the Umpqua and Rogue River valleys, at the head of the Deschutes, and even on the Columbia.[10]

In 1851, gold was discovered in Yreka, California and the next year in Jacksonville, Oregon. These two strikes caused a new wave of fortune hunters, merchants, and settlers to surge along the Applegate Trail. Once again, the Modocs and other tribes mobilized and used guerrilla tactics to harass the latest intruders. In August of 1851, the Modocs captured a string of packhorses and mules. The owner, Augustus Meamber, hurried on to the fledgling mining town of Yreka and convinced twenty of its inhabitants to return with him to Tule Lake in an effort to retrieve his property.

One of the members of the group was Ben Wright, who had already earned a sordid reputation as an Indian fighter. Wright was from Indiana and had come out to Oregon in 1847. In that year, Reverend Marcus Whitman and his wife, Narcissa, were killed by members of the Cayuse tribe. The Cayuse believed that the Whitmans were responsible for severely disrupting their lives. Part of the Oregon Trail passed by the Whitman Mission at Walla Walla, and endless lines of wagons crossed Cayuse land. Their food supply dwindled as game was frightened away, and an outbreak of smallpox decimated their ranks. Finally the Cayuse rose up in rebellion and unleashed their vengeance on those living at the Whitman Mission. It was a tragic event.

When an army was organized to avenge the death of the Whitmans, Ben Wright willingly joined. His participation in the Cayuse War helped him develop a taste for fighting Indians, and he brought this penchant with him when he arrived in Yreka in 1851. He immediately set about making his accomplishments known. He bragged of the scalps he had taken, and the noses and fingers he had cut from the bodies of Indians. In his blood quest, he soon earned the reputation of being "the acknowledged champion Indian fighter in Northern California."[11] Consequently, when he heard of Meamber's need for a party of men to retrieve his lost animals, he eagerly joined.

Several days later, the Yreka party reached the Lost River Valley and soon located Meamber's missing stock in a Modoc village. The miners set up camp several miles away. Early the next morning, fifteen members of the party crept up to the village and launched an attack. Women and children were taken hostage and several Modoc men were killed. Most of Meamber's horses and mules were recovered and the miners returned to Yreka in triumph. Ben Wright was among the most boastful of their accomplishments.[12]

In 1852, raids on wagon trains using the Applegate Trail resumed and Ben Wright and the miners of Yreka rallied once again. Wright led a band of fifteen men to The Peninsula, at the southeastern end of Tule Lake. There they set up a long-term camp and began patrolling the area around Bloody Point. During this time, Wright met with Modoc leaders in several villages, demanding that they return property allegedly stolen from the emigrants. He also questioned them about the possible location of hostages taken during raids on wagon trains.

During the months that Wright and his men were camped at The Peninsula, the emigrant trail from Clear Lake to the Klamath Basin was free from Indian raids. In the monotonous days that slipped by, Wright began to mull over several plans that might be employed to set an example for any Indian contemplating future attacks against whites. Out of these considerations came a durable legend and a tragic plan of action. It began when Wright sent several of his men back to Yreka for supplies. Allegedly, his shopping list included a packet of strychnine powder, to be purchased from a local doctor. When the supplies reached the camp at The Peninsula, Wright invited the Modocs to a feast. Legend suggests that he planned to poison them. However, only a few Modocs accepted the invitation and later Wright denied the story. He implied that using poison was against his "code of ethics." Instead, he devised a more direct and bloody method for dealing with the Modocs.[13]

In November of 1852, Wright moved his camp to Lost River. As yet no skirmishes had taken place, and his men were anxious to find some dramatic way to deal with the Modocs so that they could return to Yreka in triumph. At the time of the move to Lost River, rumors began circulating that the Modocs were planning a surprise attack. Ben Wright seized the opportunity and devised a bold, diabolical plan. He selected a village along Lost River and secretly had his men take positions around its perimeter. Then Wright walked into the camp alone and asked to see the village leader. He claimed that he was there to once again demand the return of all stolen property and seek information concerning white hostages. When the Modocs indicated that they had no such property to return, Wright opened fire with a concealed pistol, killing the village's second-in-command. At this signal, Wright's men also began firing their guns at the helpless Modocs. When the smoke cleared, forty-one people of the village were dead and only five had escaped the carnage.[14] Wright and his men immediately began to mutilate the bodies of the Modocs. Then replete with scalps and other body parts, the men returned to Yreka, where they were met with wild jubilation. From the perspective of the residents of the gold rush town, the Modocs had been taught a lesson and the attacks at Bloody Point had been avenged.

As for Ben Wright, he continued to make a reputation for himself as an Indian fighter, but he was not discriminating in his vengeful attacks. Many innocent Indians were killed along with a few who were actually guilty of killing whites. In February of 1856, Wright's violence finally caught up with him. An Indian woman, whom he had abused by stripping her naked and whipping her through the streets of Port Orford, lured him to a campsite at the mouth of the Rogue River. There, several of her friends ambushed him. It was reported that the woman helped mutilate his body and that she ate a portion of his heart. The end was perhaps fitting for Wright, for he died in the same indignity that he had inflicted on so many of his victims.[15]

The massacre of forty-one Modocs in 1852 had an effect on the number of raids along the California section of the Applegate Trail. For about five years, relatively few attacks took place. Then in 1857, the fighting resumed. Eight emigrants were killed in the vicinity of Goose Lake. In 1859 a small group of settlers was caught in a fusillade at Bloody Point.

It was a tenuous and confusing time in the relationship between whites and Indians. On one side, white immigrants and settlers were beseeching the United States government for military protection and for the opening of more western land for settlement. On the other, the Modocs were desperately trying to hold onto their land and their culture; but the Modocs witnessed many forces working against them. Young men of their villages were lured to communities like Yreka, where they could mingle with a society far different than their own. Repeated visits brought about changes in their dress styles and habits. Modocs who remained on their traditional lands watched anxiously as a seemingly endless stream of wagons moved by their villages, knowing that sometime in the near future some of those people would take up residence along Lost River and in the Tule Lake Basin. Above all, for all Modocs the Ben Wright massacre was burned deeply into their spirit. It was a sign of the power and vengeful nature of their enemy. In this uneasy time, it must have crossed the minds of most Modocs that their way of life was in peril.

The Lava Beds and Schonchin Butte. *(Photo by author)*

Lower Klamath Lake and Mt. Dome.
(Photo by author)

CHAPTER 5

A PRELUDE TO CONFLICT

At the dawn of the 1860s, the Modocs and other local tribes continued to harass travelers using the California segment of the Applegate Trail. In 1861, there were attacks at Goose Lake and Bloody Point. Herds of cattle and horses accompanying the wagon trains became a choice target, and over 900 head were stolen that year.[1] 1861 also marked the appointment of Lindsay Applegate as Indian Agent for the Lakes Region. Rather than using his new position to establish friendly relations with the tribes he was charged with monitoring, he took it upon himself to organize a militia of forty-three men to patrol the emigrant trail that bore his family name.[2] Their presence was effective. They rescued one wagon train under attack at Bloody Point; for the remainder of the year, other emigrants who passed through the area were unmolested.

In spite of Modoc involvement in the wagon train raids of 1861, the strength of their militancy was beginning to wane. One of the principal leaders, Old Chief Schonchin, actively sought to end hostilities, though he angrily told men such as Lindsay Applegate that it was the stupidity of whites that had caused warfare in the first place. They had trespassed on Modoc land, they had blamed the Modocs for raids carried out by the Pit Rivers and Snakes, and they had wantonly killed Modoc men, women, and children. But Schonchin was a realist; he knew that it was futile to continue armed resistance. In reviewing sixteen years of conflict he stated, "I think if we kill all white men, no more come. We kill and kill but, all time, more come and more come like grass in spring. I throw down my gun. I say 'I will fight no more. My heart is sick. I am old man'."[3]

Old Schonchin's action brought about a pronounced change. By 1862, it had become so quiet at Lost River and Tule Lake that "Oregon Superintendent of Indian Affairs, William H. Rector evaluated the Modocs as more of a nuisance than a real problem."[4] It should be pointed out, however, that this newly placid nature might have also come about because of a steady decline in the use of the Applegate Trail as new roads west had been opened by the 1860s and reduced traffic through the basin.[5]

The new tranquility in the basin was not shared by the nation as a whole. The Civil War was already into its second year, its terrible carnage reaching out to touch the lives of nearly every American family. Though the war was concentrated in the Southeast, there was concern on the part of the United States Government that Southern sympathizers might try to initiate hostilities in sections of the Great Plains and far west. Several measures were taken to prevent this. In 1862, Congress authorized that federal money be spent to underwrite the construction of a transcontinental railroad. The immediate objective was to link the country together, east to west, in order to provide a more efficient means for deploying troops, equipment, and Union supporters. In the same year, Congress passed the Homestead Act. This legislation was initially designed to attract pro-Union settlers to sparsely populated regions in the mid- and far west by offering them free land. Later, it became one of the country's most successful experiments in land distribution, providing for immigrants and American citizens alike an opportunity to farmland that they might not have otherwise been able to afford. Finally, as part of the wartime budget, Congress authorized funds for military protection in each of the northern and western states. Money was to be spent on the formation of state militias and on the construction of garrisons and armories. It was under the auspices of this act that a permanent military presence was introduced to the Lakes country.

In March of 1863, Major C.S. Drew arrived in the Klamath Basin. Under orders issued by the War Department, he was to survey the region for a suitable site on which to construct a fort. Soldiers stationed there were to carry out two primary responsibilities: one, to prevent any uprisings by Southern sympathizers, and two, to protect emigrants and local settlers from Indian attack. Drew's arrival had been preceded by heavy lobbying on the part of the State of Oregon, the Applegate family, and the residents of Yreka and Jacksonville. Their motivations had been only loosely connected to the sizable number of Southerners living in the area. Many of them had come west to escape the war, not to start a new one. Instead, the lobbyists saw an opportunity to end the Indian attacks on emigrant wagon trains and local settlers through military intervention.

Major Drew traveled extensively in southeastern Oregon and the Klamath Basin looking for sites that offered a combination of strategic location, forage for stock, and wood for both construction and fuel. When he finally sent his recommendation to the Army's Department of the Pacific in San Francisco, he shocked nearly everyone who had originally promoted the garrison. Instead of selecting a site near the Applegate Trail or in the proximity of white inhabitants, Drew opted for a spot fifty miles to the north in Wood River Valley, located halfway between Upper Klamath Lake and Crater Lake.

Drew's decision was immediately attacked and he was personally accused of both stupidity and corruption. However, the Major defended his choice by pointing out that Wood River Valley met all of his criteria. There were broad meadows where stock could be pastured, at least six streams were available for drinking water, and there was an abundance of trees that could be used for lumber and firewood.[6] In addition, he claimed that a major road, passing through the site of the fort, was soon to be constructed from Jacksonville to the Klamath Basin. Soldiers would be needed to help construct and protect the road, and, once completed, it would provide a means of deploying troops over a broad area of southern Oregon.

Because of the clamor over Major Drew's decision, in November of 1863 the Department of the Pacific sent Captain James Van Voast to conduct an investigation. After surveying the site and inspecting the buildings already under construction, Captain Van Voast reported:

> There can be no question of the fitness of the place selected for the new fort if only the considerations are the health of the troops and the concern for their support. It also appears equally clear that as a strategic position taken for the purpose of holding in subjection the Indians that are considered hostile, it offers many advantages. Indeed, with the limited means at Colonel Drew's disposal, for the construction of the new fort in that section of the country, it is hardly possible that one could have been located which would have afforded greater advantage and secured like protection to emigrants and to citizens ... [7]

What Drew and Van Voast neglected to note was that the fort was so remote that it could offer little immediate aid in the event of an emergency. On closer inspection, the site was not the ideal place of habitation it had been touted to be. Supplies were slow in arriving, and the winter snows often remained for much longer periods than anticipated. But in spite of its drawbacks, the garrison was in operation by the end of 1863 and commissioned under the name "Fort Klamath."

Meanwhile, the town of Yreka, located about fifty miles to the west of the Klamath Basin, was undergoing significant change. The crude shanties and flimsy tents that had been hastily erected by miners more concerned about "striking it rich" than living in comfort were being replaced with permanent buildings of wood, brick, and stone. The town had become a community center for the smattering of settlers, miners, trappers and traders who inhabited the surrounding Siskiyou Mountains. It was a source of supplies, a place to hear the latest news, and it afforded a venue for social events and recreation for those who were living solitary lives in the hills.

Equally important, Yreka had become a magnetic attraction for local Indians, especially the Modocs. The younger, more adventurous braves began to frequent the town, adopting some of the clothing styles of the residents, and learning to speak rudimentary phrases in English. But much of what was offered in Yreka, particularly material goods, was beyond the means of most Modocs. As a resource-poor tribe, they had little to offer in trade save one item: their women. The Modoc men soon learned that in a mine town such as Yreka, which was principally inhabited by lonely men, female companionship was in high demand and short supply. It was a Modoc custom to allow friends and visitors sexual privileges with their women. In a sadly perverse way, this tradition was transformed into an item of barter with the inhabitants of Yreka. Some of the younger Modoc girls, barely beyond puberty, were sold to the local miners as "companions," while Modoc wives were recruited as prostitutes.[8]

For many residents of Yreka, the presence of the young Modoc males and their wives provided comic relief. Jokes were frequently made about their strange dress habits that mixed white and Indian styles together. They were viewed as indolent and often given anglicized names that either described their physical features or that made them appear foolish. But not all inhabitants of Yreka held the Modocs in contempt. Some seemed to genuinely demonstrate compassion for these pragmatic and fiercely independent people. Two such residents were Judge A.M. Rosborough and Elijah Steele.

Steele and Rosborough were an interesting pair. Steele had come to Yreka after practicing law in New York and Wisconsin. He had been drawn to California because of the gold rush, but had done poorly in the diggings around Yreka. Next, he had a brief stint in the butchering business, but it also went sour and so he returned to practicing law. Steele soon acquired a partner, A.M. Rosborough, who had previously been an Indian agent for the Northern California region. The presence of Indians in Yreka captured the attention of the two men and, before long, they had befriended a young Modoc that Steele took to calling Captain Jack. Why Steele chose this name is unclear, but certainly one reason was because in the Modoc he was called Kientpoos. Translated it meant "man-with-heartburn," an unflattering title reputedly bestowed upon him because of a sensitive and nervous temperament.[9]

Steele had earned himself a reputation for firm but fair dealings with local Indians and he was appointed Indian Agent for Northern California in 1863, whereupon, he immediately he went to work to bring peace and stability to the region. He convinced the Shastas, Modocs, and Klamaths to stop warring against each other, and he concluded a peace treaty with the Humboldt and Mendocino tribes in which they agreed to stop attacking whites.[10] But Steele's most important accomplishment came in early 1864, when he met with representatives of the Klamath, Modoc, Shasta, Hamburg, and Scott Valley tribes. Steele persuaded them to sign an agreement in which they pledged to live in peace among themselves and with whites, blacks, and Chinese living in the territory. The Indians also agreed to enter towns unarmed, to refrain from alcohol, and to stop selling their women into slavery. Individuals who did not live up to the treaty were to be turned over to the soldiers at Fort Klamath. Captain Jack was present at these proceedings and he was instrumental in getting Modoc approval. The tribes signed the treaty on Valentine's Day, February 14, 1864.[11]

In the process of negotiating the Yreka Treaty, Elijah Steele promised the Modocs that he would do all that was within his power to secure protected land for them along Lost River. But when he presented the treaty and his proposition for a Modoc reservation to the Superintendent of Indian Affairs in California and to the Commissioner of the Indian Bureau in Washington, D.C., he was rebuffed and the proceedings declared invalid. The Bureau felt that the treaty gave the Indians too much freedom. In the meantime, Steele's position as Indian Agent was abolished through political action. Apparently his work in Northern California had created jealousy among some California politicians and a new agent, Austin Wiley, replaced him.[12] On April 1, 1864, J.W. Perit Huntington was appointed Indian Superintendent of Oregon. Following the action taken by the Indian agency in California, he too declared Steele's Yreka agreement invalid and then announced that a new round of negotiations with local Indians would begin in the near future.

Six months later, on October 9, 1864, Huntington met with representatives from the Klamath, Modoc, Paiute, and Snake tribes at Council Grove, located one mile north of Fort Klamath. His intent was to create an Indian reservation in the area around the northern end of Upper Klamath Lake and Fort Klamath. The meeting at Council Grove was similar to most negotiation sessions with Indians at the time. A sizable contingent of soldiers was present to "maintain order." Promises were made that every tribe would be fairly compensated for the land they relinquished to the federal government (though most of the Indians present did not understand that the relinquishment was permanent). They were assured that they would be well taken care of on the reservation and that they would receive a steady supply of food and blankets. They were also guaranteed that they would live unmolested.

In many ways, the Council Grove Treaty was unfortunate. Though it established a sizable plot of land north of Upper Klamath Lake for the four main tribes, the reservation encompassed most of the Klamath Tribe's traditional hunting grounds. Naturally, they considered themselves to be in a position of "superior" ownership over other tribes who would join them there. For the Modocs, the treaty was a disaster. Not only did they have to move more than fifty miles north from their former village sites, but now they were confined on the same land with their traditional enemies, the Klamaths.

When Superintendent Huntington negotiated the Council Grove Treaty, he made an important tactical mistake. He and his agents focused their attention on Old Schonchin and gave only brief recognition to younger Modoc leaders such as Captain Jack. This was unwise because Jack had played an important role in the Yreka Treaty negotiations with Elijah Steele. Furthermore, Jack's family had some of the deepest ties to the land along Lost River, particularly at Stone Bridge. Consequently, when the Modocs moved to the Klamath Reservation, Captain Jack and his band made little effort to adjust to their new surroundings.

Unhappy with life on the Klamath Reservation, Captain Jack and his followers returned to Lost River in 1865. Near Stone Bridge and the northern end of Tule Lake, they re-established their village and resumed many of their traditional ways. They fished the lake, hunted in the Lava Beds, and the Modoc men— particularly Captain Jack—began to visit Yreka once again.

With the return of the Modocs to Lost River, old fears were rekindled among settlers in the Klamath Basin. Trepidation over potential conflict with the Modocs was not their only concern. The Council Grove Treaty had technically ended any claims the Modocs had to land along Lost River and Tule Lake. This meant that the area was now available for white settlement. Consequently, mounting pressure was put on the Klamath Agency to return the Modocs to the reservation. In 1866, Lindsay Applegate met with Captain Jack and attempted to persuade the young Modoc leader to return to the Klamath Reservation. Jack flatly refused. The next year, Indian Superintendent Huntington tried to entice Jack to return to the reservation with promises of food and supplies. Again, Jack refused.

In 1868, Ulysses Grant was elected President. Under his administration, the Bureau of Indian Affairs announced a new approach to working with Indian tribes known as the Quaker Policy. The name came from the religious affiliation of the program's leading advocates. According to Columbus Delano, who later became Secretary of the Interior, it was to do the following: first, "it proposed to place the Indians upon reservations as rapidly as possible, where they [could] be provided for in such manner as the dictates of humanity and Christian civilization require." Translated into laymen's English, this essentially meant confining them to one location where they could be controlled. Second, for "Indians who persistently refused to go upon a reservation, and determined to continue their nomadic habits, accompanied with depredations and outrages upon ... frontier settlements" it gave the President the power "to treat such band or tribe with all needed severity ..." Third, the program was "to see that all supplies ... [of] food or clothing ... are procured at fair and reasonable prices, so that the Indians meriting these supplies may receive the same without having the funds of the Government squandered in their purchase." Fourth, "it is the purpose of the government to procure competent, upright, faithful, normal, and religious agents to care for the Indians ... [and] to aid their intellectual, moral, and religious culture, and thus to assist in the great work of humanity and benevolence which the peace policy means." And finally, fifth, "to establish schools, and though this instrumentality of the Christian organizations, acting in harmony with the Government ... to build churches and organize Sabbath schools, whereby these savages may be taught a better way of life than they have heretofore pursued, and be made to understand the comforts ad benefits of Christian civilization and thus be prepared ultimately to become citizens of this great nation."[13]

It was under the Quaker Policy that Alfred Meacham was appointed Indian Superintendent of Oregon in 1869. The new Superintendent was a devout member of the Methodist Church and a staunch Republican. He had previously worked as a toll road operator in the Blue Mountains of Oregon.[14] A compassionate man, Meacham honestly wanted to establish a system of fair treatment for Indians living on the Klamath Reservation. One of his first tasks was to attempt to persuade Captain Jack and his Lost River band of Modocs to return to the Klamath Reservation. In December of 1869, he decided to meet personally with Jack and his people. Among those he asked to accompany him were Frank and Toby Riddle.

The Riddles were an interesting couple that soon would play an important role in the events unfolding in the Klamath Basin. Frank Riddle had been a gold miner in the Yreka area and had purchased Toby from the Modocs when she was twelve years old. Though she was technically Riddle's slave, she was treated with a great degree of kindness. In 1869, when Meacham became Indian Superintendent, he ordered an end to Indian slavery. Riddle had a choice. He could release Toby and allow her to return to her village, or he could marry her. He chose the second option. Toby was pleased with her husband's choice and felt indebted to Meacham for the edict that led to her marriage.

The Riddles had maintained close contact with the Modocs along Lost River. They were capable of interpreting the Modoc language and had a reputation for fair-mindedness in working with both whites and Indians. Meacham called upon these talents when he asked them to participate in his December 1869 meeting with Captain Jack.

When the negotiations party left Fort Klamath, it included Meacham, the Riddles, Ivan Applegate, George Nurse, and Chief Old Schonchin. They arrived at the Lost River camp on December 22, and it was quickly ascertained that the mood among many of the Modoc braves there was clearly hostile. Though Meacham was warned that the atmosphere in the camp was tense, he boldly rode in, dismounted from his horse and demanded an audience with Captain Jack. Told that Jack was in his wickiup, Meacham climbed to its entrance and descended into the darkness of the interior. Inside, he impressed Jack with both his courage and his speaking ability, qualities prized by the Modocs. Jack agreed to meet in council the next day.

During formal talks on the 23rd of December, Frank and Toby Riddle acted as interpreters. It soon became apparent that there was dissension within the Modoc leadership. Fiery militant Curly Headed Doctor advocated killing everyone in the negotiating party. His views began to prevail and the Riddles warned Meacham. He in turn quickly dispatched secret word to a patrol of soldiers who had escorted the negotiations party as far as Linkville, a small community located just south of Upper Klamath Lake (today it is the city of Klamath Falls). Unfortunately, the soldiers had been spending their idle time at the local saloons and were in poor shape when word arrived that they were needed at the Lost River camp.

Meacham had sent strict orders to the soldiers that they were to remain outside Jack's village when they arrived. They were simply to be ready to put mild pressure on the Modocs to return to the Klamath Reservation. If the Indians resisted, the soldiers were to provide protection for the negotiators. But instead of standing ready outside the camp, the inebriated soldiers charged in wildly. Captain Jack and his people quickly scattered. Taking to canoes, they paddled furiously for the Lava Beds at the southern end of Tule Lake where they hid in the natural fortifications.

The next move was Meacham's. He persuaded Mary, Captain Jack's sister, to go to the Lava Beds and talk with him. While there, Mary convinced the Modoc leader that he should return to Lost River and complete the negotiations with Meacham. In the talks that ensued, Meacham persuaded Jack to return to the Klamath Reservation. In exchange, Jack made Meacham promise that other Indians on the reservation, particularly the Klamaths, would not ridicule him for surrendering. On December 28, 1869, Captain Jack and his people made the fifty-mile journey back to the Klamath Agency.

For a while it appeared that Captain Jack and his band would be able to live in harmony with their fellow tribesmen under the leadership of Old Schonchin and with their historical enemies the Klamaths. Unfortunately, peaceful coexistence lasted only a short time. By early 1870, Jack's people began to suffer a series of humiliating experiences. The Klamaths ridiculed them for surrendering. They were denied the use of some reservation land, and the Klamaths even began to charge the Modocs for cutting wood.

In an attempt to resolve the conflict between the Modocs and the Klamaths peacefully, Captain Jack made repeated appeals to Captain O.C. Knapp at Fort Klamath. Unfortunately, Knapp ignored him. In fact, Knapp considered Jack to be a nuisance and did not even bother to investigate his complaints. Finally, in disgust, Jack and 371 Modocs left the reservation and headed south back to Lost River. The date was April 26, 1870.

In the meantime, significant changes had taken place in the Lost River Valley and the Tule Lake Basin. Assuming that the Modocs had been permanently removed, a number of white settlers had moved in. New arrivals along Lost River and the northern shore of Tule Lake included the William Boddys, Abe Ball, Nicholas Shira and his family, William and Richard Cravigan, the Brothertons, Henry Miller, the Bybees, the Colwells, George Nurse, and the Dennis Crawley family. [15]

When Captain Jack and his 371 Modocs arrived back in the Lost River Valley the newly arrived white settlers viewed them with alarm. Soon the whites were filing reports with the Oregon and California Indian Superintendencies, claiming that the Modocs had taken to small-time racketeering by demanding tribute from the settlers in return for being left alone. They claimed that Modoc men would walk unannounced into their homes and that they stole food and various household goods. The Modocs were also accused of stealing hay and of turning their stock loose to graze in cultivated fields.[16] But these reports were not substantiated, and in fact there was evidence to suggest that the Modocs were relatively well behaved. One settler, who was interviewed, said "I have lived near the tribe for ten years, and did not consider that there was any danger to settlers from them; [and] the parties whose hay was taken had agreed to pay the Indians for cutting hay on lands claimed by them and had failed to do so ..."[17]

A report filed by Captain James Jackson on August 27, 1871 confirmed that the settlers' claims were exaggerated.

> The Modocs are insolent but as far as [we] could ascertain no one has been hurt or seriously threatened. Reports on Captain Jack are very conflicting - he carries around with him letters from prominent citizens of Yreka testifying to his good conduct and good faith with the whites. Many of the settlers in the district where he roams are opposed to having him molested.[18]

These facts did not stop local settlers in their campaign to get rid of the Modocs. In January of 1872, a petition was sent to Superintendent Meacham and General Edward Canby, who was in charge of military affairs for the Pacific Northwest. It was signed by forty-six citizens and said:

> We the undersigned citizens of Lost and Link river, Klamath and Tule lake country, after suffering years of annoyance from the presence of the Modoc Indians ... make this earnest appeal to you for relief ... Their long continued success in defying its authorities has emboldened them in their defiant and hostile bearing ... in many instances our families have become alarmed at their threats to kill and burn, until we were compelled to remove them for safety across the Cascade mountains.[19]

Another petition was sent to Oregon Governor L.F. Grover and signed by sixty-five settlers who asked for his help in forcing the Modocs back on the reservation.

> Our reasons for this request are these: We have been harassed and bothered for the last four years by this renegade band of lawless Modoc Indians. They are extremely saucy and menacing in their repeated threats against settlers and their stock; they set up claim to our homes; they frequently draw guns and pistols on

inoffensive citizens; they recently fired at the house of citizen Ball; they watch the men leave their houses and then go to the house and insult the female inmates of our sacred homes; they boast defiance to the authorities, etc.[20]

Alfred Meacham tried his best to ameliorate the situation at Lost River. In spite of the citizens' petitions, he became convinced that the best solution was to secure reservation land within the area of Lost River for Captain Jack and his people. In a report sent to General Canby and to the Indian Bureau in Washington, Meacham said:

> The Modocs cannot be made to live on [the] Klamath Reservation, on account of the ancient feuds with the Klamaths. They are willing to locate permanently on a small reservation of six miles square, lying on both sides of the Oregon and California line, near the head of the Tule lake ... I would recommend that they be allowed a small reservation at the place indicated above ... [21]

But Meacham's request was refused by the Indian Bureau out of fear that the new reservation would be used as a base by the Modocs for harassing the local settlers.[22] Meacham was soon removed as the Superintendent of Oregon and he was replaced by T.B. Odeneal.

The appointment of T.B. Odeneal as Indian Superintendent was unfortunate, and it represented another fateful step in a long list of blunders committed by the Indian Bureau. Odeneal was impetuous. He viewed the lack of action in the Modoc case as unacceptable, and he was anxious to have the matter done with. But government bureaucracy grinds slowly, and he received cautious messages from the Indian Bureau in Washington, D.C. On April 12, 1872, F.A. Walker, Indian Commissioner, sent Odeneal the following memo:

> You are instructed to have the Modoc Indians removed, if practicable, to the reservation set apart for them under the treaty concluded with said Indians October 14, 1864 ... If they cannot be removed to or kept on the reservation, you will report your views as to the practicability of locating them at some other point ...[23]

It almost appeared as if Indian Commissioner Walker would accept Meacham's original recommendation for a reservation on Lost River (although, following in the tradition of government policy, Walker probably had in mind moving the Modocs to Oklahoma, which at that time was declared "Indian Territory"). However, Odeneal consulted local employees of the Indian Bureau, including Ivan Applegate, for their opinions. Applegate replied:

> In regard to moving the band to [the] Klamath reservation and protecting them from the Klamaths, I give it as my opinion that the place is not only practicable, but is really the only policy that can be adopted with any hope of success ... The white settlers are very much opposed to establishing a new reservation for this band of desperadoes, and their determined opposition would keep up a continual conflict.[24]

It should be mentioned here that the Applegates were later accused of protecting their own interests when they collectively opposed the Lost River Reservation. They had settled on land in the Clear Lake area and their residency suggested a conflict of interest.

Ivan Applegate cautioned Odeneal to be prudent in his dealings with Captain Jack, and to select the right moment to take action.

> It is reasonable to believe that they will not come on to the reservation peaceable while their present leaders are in power ... I feel confident that in winter they could be removed quite easily by the troops stationed at Fort Klamath [also] The proposition to arrest the leaders is one worthy of serious consideration ... but under present understanding between the Department [and the Indians] ... the arrest would no doubt be regarded by the Indians as an act of treachery on our part. [25]

A little more than a week later, Applegate reported to Odeneal that he had met with Captain Jack concerning his return to the Klamath Reservation. Jack gave the following reply:

We are good people, and will not kill or frighten anybody. We want peace and friendship. I do not want to live upon the reservation, for the Indians there are poorly clothed, suffer from hunger, and even have to leave the reservation sometimes to make a living. We are willing to have whites to live in our country, but we do not want them to locate on the west side and near the mouth of Lost River, where we have made our winter camps. The settlers are continually lying about my people, and trying to make trouble.[26]

Odeneal ignored Captain Jack's feelings and on June 17, 1872 issued an arrest order for the leaders of the Lost River band of Modocs. He wrote to Indian Commissioner F.A. Walker explaining his decision.

The leaders of these Indians are desperadoes, brave, daring and reckless, and their superior sagacity enables them to exercise full and complete control over the rest of the tribe. They have for so long a time been permitted to do as they please, that they imagine they are too powerful to be controlled by the Government, and that they can, with impunity, defy its authority ... They must in some way be convinced of their error ... by such firm, decided action as will leave no doubt in their minds to the fact we intend that they shall be obedient to law and faithful to proper management.[27]

At his Portland, Oregon office, General Edward Canby received word of Odeneal's action, and he quickly expressed his concern. The garrison at Fort Klamath was undermanned, and he was afraid that Odeneal might persuade the officers at Fort Klamath to raid Captain Jack's village without careful planning. As a consequence, General Canby ordered Major John Green, Fort Klamath's military commander, to scout the Modocs and report back to him. Major Green took his time and finally left on September 9, 1872. The Major attempted to make contact with Captain Jack, failed and soon returned to Fort Klamath.

In the next two months, Odeneal became more impatient. Finally, in November he moved from Salem to Fort Klamath and on the 25th presented to Lieutenant Colonel Frank Wheaten, who had come to the fort from Camp Warner to assist in handling the Modoc problems, the following statement:

Sir;
I am here for the purpose putting the Modoc Indians
upon this reservation ... You are directed to remove
the Modoc Indians to the Klamath Reservation,
peaceably if you can, but forcibly if you must.[28]

Odeneal made one last attempt to meet with Captain Jack, but
he was rebuffed. Jack told one of Odeneal's agents: "Say to the
Superintendent that we do not want to see him or to talk with
him. We do not want any white men to tell us what to do. I am
tired of being talked to, and am done talking."[29]

The die had now been cast. Odeneal and Major Green
conferred and mutually decided to send a patrol of soldiers,
under the command of Captain James Jackson, to arrest Jack
and other leaders of the Lost River band. It was a monumental
error. Jackson's patrol was small. There were only three officers
and thirty-six enlisted men, and they carried with them only
three days' rations of food. Only one day later, the folly of
Odeneal's decision and Major Green's order became apparent.
Captain Jackson's patrol started one of the most costly Indian
wars in western American history.

Gathering storm over the Lava Beds. *(Photo by author)*

CHAPTER 6

THE MODOC WAR

November 28, 1872 was cold and rainy. Captain James Jackson and his men must have left Fort Klamath with mixed emotions. The excitement of possible battle coursed through their veins, but the biting weather of the Klamath Basin quickly dampened their spirits. It was an omen of things to come.

November 28 was also a fateful day for Tule Lake rancher Henry Miller. In a meeting with the Lost River Modocs, he had assured them that he was unaware of any plans by the army to move into their territory. Furthermore, Miller told them that if he did become aware of troop movements, he would warn them immediately. Several days later, Miller paid for this promise with his life.

There were two principal Modoc camps at the southern end of the Lost River Valley. On the west side of Lost River, between Stone Bridge and Tule Lake, was Captain Jack's village. On the east side of the river was a village under the direction of another young Modoc leader, Hooker Jim. To the east, extending in an arc southward along the shores of Tule Lake, was a series of settler cabins. Soon they would all be engulfed in bloody war.

As Captain Jackson and his troops passed the small community of Linkville, just to the south of Upper Klamath Lake, word of the patrol's mission spread among the white citizenry. A group of civilians quickly organized their own-armed band and headed off toward Lost River Valley. Along the way they recruited additional help. By the evening of November 28, the armed citizens included A.J. (Jack) Burnett, W.J. Small, George Fiocke, and Henry Dunca—all from Linkville—plus Charlie Monroe, Jack Thurber, and Lost River farmers Dennis Crawley, Dan Colwell, and William S. "Dad" Bybee. Oliver Applegate was appointed the group's leader. Captain Jackson and his men spent the same evening in complete misery. They later reported that it was cold, wet and foggy. With miles between their camp and Fort Klamath, they found that the romance of fighting Indians was quickly dying.

Early in the morning of November 29, Captain Jackson and his men broke camp and by daylight arrived at Captain Jack's village. At first, the soldiers attempted to arrange a meeting with the Modoc leader, but the situation quickly deteriorated into a violent confrontation. Modoc men ran for their rifles, and the soldiers began firing indiscriminately at moving figures. Captain Jack and his people fled their village and headed south to the shores of Tule Lake. Taking to the water in canoes, they paddled some thirteen miles to the jumbled rock of the Lava Beds. At the village, the soldiers burned the wickiups. One sick Modoc woman was alleged to have been left behind and was burned to death in the conflagration.

Meanwhile, on the east bank of Lost River, the white civilians under Oliver Applegate entered Hooker Jim's village. In a pattern similar to the conflict just experienced by the army on the west side, fighting broke out quickly. The civilians did not fare as well as the soldiers, though, and in the first skirmish, settler Jack Thurber was killed. The ferocity of the Modocs' resistance routed the civilians and they beat a hasty retreat to Dennis Crawley's cabin, located about a mile to the north. There, they set up fortifications.

In the confusion of launching an attack on the Modoc villages, no one had thought to set up a communications network among the local settlers to warn them of conflict. As a result, a number of unsuspecting whites were killed. Settlers Joe Penning and William Nus were riding toward the Modoc villages to investigate gunfire when some of the Modoc men from Hooker Jim's band ambushed them. Penning was wounded and Nus was killed.

Hooker Jim's band then swung around the eastern shore of Tule Lake. They avoided Dennis Crawley's cabin, well aware that the white men who had earlier attacked their village had fortified it. Continuing east, they attacked William Boddy's cabin, killing Boddy, two stepsons, Richard and William Cravigan, and Boddy's son-in-law, Nicholas Schira.[1]

The next day, November 30, the carnage continued. W.K. Brotherton and his two sons were killed. Then Henry Miller—the man who had promised the Modocs he would warn them if the army planned to attack—was gunned down; so too was John Schroeder, a neighbor of the Brothertons. Hooker Jim and his men continued on around the eastern side of Tule Lake and by the time they reached Louis Land's ranch, at the lake's southeastern corner, they had killed another five men. These included Robert Alexander, John Tober, a man known as Follins, Christopher Erasmus and Adam Schillinglaw, a cowboy at the Land ranch.[2] All told, at least fourteen settlers were killed during the first three days of fighting, the result of a hasty and imprudent decision on the part of Indian Superintendent T.B. Odeneal and Major John Green.

Amid the bloodshed, there were individual acts of humanity. At the very time that Hooker Jim and his braves were wreaking havoc along Tule Lake's eastern shore, pioneer settlers Pressly Dorris, A.W. Watson, and John Ballaout were out looking for stray stock. They encountered Scarfaced Charley, a member of Captain Jack's band, and he warned them that their lives were in danger.[3] Thanks to the warning, the three men were able to avoid the renegade Modoc band.

After Hooker Jim's final attack on settlers near Land's ranch, his band moved west along the southern end of Tule Lake. They joined Captain Jack in the Lava Beds and settled into an ideally protected area that became known as the Stronghold. This fortification soon earned the respect of both the civilian and military personnel who had previously held the Modocs in contempt. In a review of the Stronghold, one report said:

> The military engineers ... are emphatic in their opinion that no man versed in military tactics could have selected a fortress in the Lava Beds better adapted to the ends of defense than this same stronghold. Where nature has not fulfilled the requirements of the situation, the Indians have piled up the lava, and so remedied every apparent defect. It is a fact that no soldier could have climbed within fifty yards of the stronghold while the Indians were in possession without looking into the muzzles of guns, and nothing but a gun could be seen. The ingenuity of the Modok (sic) has surpassed all understanding.[4]

On December 1, 1872, Captain Jackson regrouped his soldiers and established a headquarters at the Crawley cabin. That evening, he was informed of the terrible price paid by settlers along Tule Lake. As the gravity of the situation sank in, it became apparent to Jackson that a full-scale military operation would be necessary to punish the Modocs responsible.

Gradually the world beyond Tule Lake and the Klamath Basin became aware of the outbreak of war, but the information available was frequently inaccurate. On December 3rd, the *Weekly Oregon Statesmen*, published in Salem, announced an "Uprising of the Modoc Indians in Southern Oregon." In describing the conflict at Lost River, the paper said:

> The battle was a desperate one, lasting about two hours. One soldier was killed and four wounded. Two citizens, Wm. Nus and Thurber alias "Jack of Clubs" were killed; nearly all the women and children, some of the warriors and a number of horses were captured ... The women captured say that among the number killed were the four desperate chiefs. Capt. Jack, Black Jim, the Doctor and Scar-faced Charley, who have been the cause of all the insubordination of their followers, but about this, excepting the last one named, there is some doubt.[5]

A week later, the success of the Modocs in resisting the soldiers was still not known. The *Weekly Oregon Statesmen* reported: "The first news we had were (sic) the most direct and we think the most reliable. If that were true, there was a fight in which the Modocs were greatly worsted."[6]

There were many stupid mistakes and tactical blunders during the early stages of the Modoc War. One such incident involved the Hot Creek band of Modocs, who had a small village near Pressly Dorris's ranch on the west side of Lower Klamath Lake. When the Hot Creeks heard about the fight involving Captain Jack's and Hooker Jim's bands, they immediately went to the John Fairchild ranch for advice and protection. Fairchild and Dorris convinced the Hot Creeks that the safest thing to do was to leave immediately for the Klamath Reservation. Accompanied by Fairchild and Dorris, the Hot Creeks began their trek north. In the meantime, the citizens of Linkville had received information about the carnage at Tule Lake. They were already arming themselves when they received word that the Hot Creeks were headed their way. Fortunately, several Linkville citizens warned Fairchild and Dorris that a vigilante group was headed south. A number of the Hot Creeks were familiar with English and they too became aware of the impending danger. That evening, under the cover of darkness, the Modoc band fled south and joined Hooker Jim and Captain Jack in the lava beds. In time, some members of the Hot Creek band became among the most militant of the Modocs in the Stronghold.

As the final weeks of December faded into January of 1873, the United States Army slowly began to mobilize. The officers exuded confidence that the Modocs would be quickly captured. They had evidently accepted, with complete faith, Ivan Applegate's report to T.B. Odeneal, which had included Applegate's opinion that the winter months would play to the Indian Bureau's favor. After an interview with Major Green, Commanding Officer of Fort Klamath, one reporter said: "All he wants is plenty of provisions and a snow storm and he can get Captain Jack."[7] General Edward Canby, in charge of all military operations in the Pacific Northwest, echoed the same theme in a report he sent to military headquarters at the Presidio, in San Francisco.

> I do not think that the operations will be protracted. The snow will drive the Indians out of the mountains, and they cannot move without leaving trails that can be followed. It will involve some hardships upon the troops, but they are better provided and can endure it better than the Indians. In this respect, the season is in our favor.[8]

Not long after Canby's statement, the Modocs attacked an army supply wagon train coming from Fort Bidwell, and re-enforcements had to be sent to Land's Ranch, on the southeastern side of Tule Lake, to improve protection.

Several weeks later, the military headquarters was moved from the Crawley cabin at Lost River to the Van Brimmer ranch. Situated at the southwestern corner of Lower Klamath Lake, the new headquarters was separated from Tule Lake and the Lava Beds by the narrow spiny formation known as Sheepy Ridge.

The Van Brimmer ranch had been established by Dan, Clinton, and Ben Van Brimmer in 1864. The first building on the ranch was a heavily fortified cabin designed to protect the Van Brimmers from Indian attack. Not only were the walls of the cabin made of thick logs and the door solidly built, but also the cabin was constructed over Willow Creek. There was a trap door in the floor of the cabin and its occupants were assured of a continual supply of water in case of Indian attack.[9] The Van Brimmers never had to use their fortified cabin for defense, but the army soon found they were in need of some protection from the Van Brimmers. With a sharp eye for business, the Van Brimmer clan was soon capitalizing on the army's presence by selling hard-to-get food to the soldiers. They charged exorbitant prices. It was reported that a single egg cost $.50. Colonel William Thompson remembered with bitterness his experience at the ranch: "Until our departure, I spent a considerable portion of my time in studying human villainy with the Van Brimmers as a model." [10]

The press did not ignore the mounting expenses of the war, even in its early stages. An editorial in the *New York Herald* noted:

> The Modocs under the redoubtable Captain Jack, have immortalized themselves. They have not only put "hors de combat" some four or five hundred of Uncle Sam's regulars and volunteers in a fair Indian fight - fair for the Indians - but have also laid a train to burst open the iron bars of our good old Uncle's Treasury and deplete it to the amount of millions. How lucky it was for the Oregon speculators in army stores and supplies, and in Indian blankets, brass buttons, knick-knacks, and haberdashery, that the regulars were defeated in this first pitched battle . . .[11]

The *San Francisco Chronicle* added credence to the Herald's observations when on January 30, 1873 it reported the presence of Colonel Alvan C. Gillem in Yreka, supervising the purchase of supplies for the military operation. The *Chronicle* stated:

> The most astonishing thing he [Gillem] has observed is the sudden and unprecedented rise in produce of all kinds within the past twenty-four hours. Grain, which went begging a week ago at $1 a bushel, is held to-day, since the Quartermaster got here, at twelve cents a pound. Freighting and other things have gone up 200 per cent, and in fact there seems to be a general desire on the part of our patriotic citizens to make the harvest as abundant as possible.[12]

For nearly a month and a half, the soldiers and Modocs were at a standoff. The army was frustrated by the lack of developments and the military command was changed several times. From Captain James Jackson it had gone to Major Green, the commander of Fort Klamath. Then it was passed to Lt. Colonel Frank Wheaton. When Wheaton assumed command in late December, the army headquarters had been moved to the Van Brimmer ranch. It was from here that Wheaton launched a disastrous first attack on the Modocs at the Lava Beds.

Wheaton's plan was to trap the Modocs in a two-pronged assault. One detachment of soldiers was to attack from the east side of the Lava Beds, the other from the west. On the day the assault was launched, January 17, 1873, the winter weather was some of Tule Lake's worst. It was terribly cold and with low-lying fog covering the valley floor. Though the Modocs could not see any better than the soldiers, they did have the advantage of being intimately familiar with the great mass of lava that covered the area. As the soldiers advanced, Modoc sharpshooters picked them off. With courage failing and better judgment taking hold, the army withdrew.

The January 17 battle was a costly one for the army. In their attempt to defeat a band of Modocs that numbered between fifty-five and seventy men, the casualties ran high. At least thirty-seven regular soldiers and volunteers were hit by Modoc bullets and twelve of them died.[13] The battle had been far from a surprise attack. The Modocs were well aware of troop movements in the area. The day before the major assault, they had attacked a detachment of soldiers on the eastern flank. So many soldiers were wounded there that fortifications had to be set up at a lava outcropping northeast of the Stronghold. It became known as Hospital Rock. On the day of the attack itself, the Indians could easily hear the soldiers as they attempted to pick their way through the lava in the thick fog. The Modocs had a psychological edge as well. They knew many of the soldiers by name and could yell out words of derision to individual men.

The battle of January 17th was soon front-page headlines in the nation's major papers, and the war was turning into one of the biggest media events of the decade. The reporters sent to cover the events were an unusual lot. From the *San Francisco Chronicle* came Robert D. Bogart, who referred to his assignment as an "expedition" and himself as the "Chronicle's War Correspondent." Actually, many of the stories Bogart cabled to the *Chronicle* were second hand accounts.[14] It was Bogart who captured top prize for sensational journalism when he suggested that many of the early pioneers in the Klamath Basin were guilty of causing the conflict. In particular, Bogart went after the Applegates, claiming that it was their desire for power and land that had precipitated the war.[15] His attack intensified a long standing feud between California and Oregon. Each state claimed that the other was responsible for the current Indian troubles. Bogart and the *Chronicle* were soundly scolded for their sympathies with the Modocs and the attack on the Applegates. The *Weekly Oregon Statesmen* said: "The shameful lying of certain newspaper correspondents, acting in the interest of Capt. Jack and his band of murderers, certainly is without parallel in the history of Christian nations."[16] After the Modoc War was over, Bogart was arrested by the United States Navy and charged with embezzling $30,000 while he was a Navy paymaster.[17]

In addition to Robert Bogart, Alex McKay—a surveyor from Yreka—covered the war for the *San Francisco Bulletin* and H. Wallace Atwell represented the *Sacramento Record*. However, the most colorful reporter was Edward Fox from the *New York Herald*. He had served in the British Army, and at the time the Modoc War broke out he was the *Herald's* yachting editor. Fox's flair for bravado and his British charm caught the eye of the *Herald's* editor and he was asked to go to California to cover the unfolding events. Of the reporters who traveled to the Lava Beds, Fox's stories were generally the most comprehensive. He also had a streak of daring and he actually wrangled himself into attending a negotiations session at Captain Jack's headquarters. While there he took notes, shook the hands of several of the prominent Modoc leaders, and observed that Captain Jack was ill. He then retired to a sleeping area and spent the night. The next day he returned to the military headquarters to write his story. Of Fox's feat, the *Yreka Union* said:

> Fox has placed the *Herald* in the van, and distanced all competitors in the race for news! It is, no doubt, intended by the *Herald* office, which planned, and Fox, who executed this move, that it shall rank only second to Stanley's search for Livingstone in Central Africa.[18]

Needless to say, the *Herald* was pleased with the comparison.

In addition to the reporters, two photographers and a sketch artist covered the Modoc War. Eadweard J. Muybridge, who had become famous for his photographic studies of animals in motion, was hired by the United States government to do a photographic documentary of the war. Louis Heller, a freelance photographer from Yreka, who actually spent considerably more time at the "front," joined him. Heller's name was later lost in historical obscurity, overshadowed by Muybridge's reputation. Photographs taken by both men—which included pictures of the battle sites, the army camp, principal military and Indian leaders, and of soldiers and friendly Indians posed in mock battle— provided valuable information for students of the Modoc War. Sales of Muybridge and Heller photographs were brisk during and after the conflict. A number of Heller's pictures were done with a stereo camera. The three-dimensional appearance of the photographs, when viewed through a stereopticon, were startlingly lifelike.[19] Interpretive evidence was also provided by William Simpson, an artist and war correspondent working for the London Illustrated News. Simpson's realistic drawings of key battles, made from his own observations and the testimony of participants, added even greater dimension to the public's understanding of the events of the Modoc War.

Six days after the January 17 debacle, when the Army's military plan for taking the Modocs was shown to be total folly, Lt. Colonel Wheaton was informed that he was being replaced by Colonel Alvan Gillem. On January 30, while Wheaton was waiting for Gillem's arrival, Secretary of War William Belknap ordered that hostilities with the Modocs be suspended pending the arrival of a government appointed Peace Commission.[20]

The idea for a Peace Commission came out of Secretary Belknap's concern that the costs of the Modoc War were becoming prohibitive. A negotiated settlement seemed to be a wiser and cheaper approach. The men Belknap appointed to the commission included Alfred Meacham, Jesse Applegate, and Samuel Chase, the acting Indian agent for the Siletz tribe, located on the Oregon coast. [21] General Edward Canby, Commander of the Columbia Division of the U.S. Army's Department of the Pacific, was to coordinate the activities of the Peace Commission.

General Canby had been named Commander of the Columbia Division in 1870. Headquartered in Portland, Canby had anticipated that this assignment would be less hectic than those of his prior military career. His military service had included action in the Seminole Indian War, the Mexican-American War, and the Civil War. During the War Between the States, Canby had been responsible for leading the Union ground attack at Mobile, Alabama.[22] When Canby was assigned the Northwest command, his biggest headache was maintaining a full strength force of 1,225 soldiers. Fighting Indians and maintaining peace in the Northwest had grown unpopular, and in 1871 alone Canby lost nearly 20 percent of his men to desertion.[23]

General Canby's attitude towards the Indians of the frontier was compassionate. He felt that in conflicts such as the Modoc War, justice must be fairly applied. In order to avoid a repeat of the poor decisions originally made by Indian Superintendent Ordeneal and Major Green, Canby decided to personally assist the Peace Commission in their efforts to negotiate with the Modocs.

On February 7, Colonel Alvan Gillem arrived in the Tule Lake Basin and took command of the armed forces surrounding the Lava Beds. Not long after, General Canby and members of the Peace Commission arrived, and Gillem moved the army command headquarters to the John Fairchild ranch on Lower Klamath Lake.

Almost from the day that Secretary Belknap announced the formation of the Peace Commission, it came under attack, particularly by the Oregon press. On February 11th, the *Weekly Oregon Statesmen* printed an editorial, which in part said:

> We have no objection to the personnel of this commission, but the whole project of settling the Modoc difficulties through a "Peace" Commission is, in our judgment, a mistaken and foolish one ... In the name of all murdered men, the outraged settlers, and the people of the State of Oregon, we protest against the object of their appointment.[24]

During the ensuing weeks, the Peace Commission recruited the help of a number of old friends of the Modocs, including Elijah Steele and A.M. Rosborough. Frank and Toby Riddle, along with another mixed-marriage couple, Bob and Matilda Whittle, were asked to act as interpreters.[25] Several meetings were arranged with the Modoc leaders, but very little was accomplished.

While the Peace Commission was attempting to contact and negotiate with the Modocs in the Lava Beds, General Canby was developing a military plan of action to encourage the Modocs to negotiate. Dubbed the "Compression" or "Constriction Plan," it involved gradually increasing the pressure on the Modocs by bringing in more men and equipment and by slowly tightening the ring of army personnel around the Stronghold. One of the first parts of Canby's Constriction Plan was to move the army headquarters from the Fairchild Ranch back to the Van Brimmers', bringing it in closer proximity to the Lava Beds. At the same time, Major C.E. Mason moved his troops from an encampment on Jesse Applegate's ranch at Clear Lake to Scorpion Point, seven miles east of the Stronghold near the shore of Tule Lake.

When the military headquarters was moved to the Van Brimmer ranch, a number of bizarre incidents took place. The heavy increase in military activity necessitated hiring a large number of civilians as teamsters, packers, scouts and stockmen. Aside from hauling the huge amounts of equipment needed to maintain the army, these civilians had no real commitment to the campaign. They willingly bartered with various Modocs that wandered into the camp and security was so lax that Modoc brave Bogus Charley boldly walked in and stole an entire can of gunpowder from under the noses of the soldiers and civilians. Even more incredible was the report that Modoc women would sneak into the military section of the camp, sleep with the enlisted men, and in exchange for their sexual favors receive ammunition and food which they took back to their men in the Lava Beds Stronghold.[26]

The farcical events at the Van Brimmer ranch had their darker moments. In one incident, Modoc women visiting the camp were told that a large pile of firewood that had been recently collected was going to be used to burn Captain Jack alive when he was captured. The statement was made in jest, but it may have caused a crucial turn in negotiations with the Modoc leaders. Evidently during the first days of March, negotiations with Captain Jack had been going well—so well in fact, that on March 10 Elijah Steele led a group of wagons toward the Lava Beds thinking that Jack and his people were going to surrender. But Jack may have been informed about the firewood story and aborted the rendezvous. When Steele arrived at the prearranged location, Jack did not appear. [27]   The Modoc leader may have also changed his plans because of a meeting he was reported to have had with Charles Blair of Linkville. Not long before, a grand jury in Jacksonville, Oregon had indicted Captain Jack, Hooker

Jim, and several other Modocs for the death of the settlers along Tule Lake. Blair was reported to have told the Modocs in the Lava Beds that "the object of the peace commission was to get possession of the Indians indicted for murder ... and have them hanged."[28]

Negotiations were at a stalemate. While there was a lull in the war, a new element was added to General Canby's Constriction Plan. On April 1, 1873, Colonel Gillem moved the army head-quarters from the Van Brimmer ranch to an area on the western fringe of the Lava Beds. It was situated at the foot of a lava ridge that would become known as Gillem's Bluff. The army was now camped only three and a half miles from the Stronghold. In addition, on April 7, Major E.C. Mason moved his camp from Scorpion Point to Hospital Rock. The Modocs now faced soldiers on both their northeastern and western flanks.

For the average soldier, the shift of camps was merely another episode in a long, bleak, and often demoralizing campaign. Second Lieutenant Harry DeWitt wrote a friend about the campaign, saying:

> You make the remark in your letter that I must be leading a very rough life. You never guessed so closely to the truth in your life. I am leading as rough a life as it is possible for one to lead.
>
> I have been in this country now five months; with very slight prospect of getting out for at least six months to come. During that time I have marched a couple of hundred miles on foot and three or for times as many on horseback. I have fought and marched for thirty-three consecutive hours, without anything to eat and without an overcoat, when the weather was intensely cold. I have been in the saddle twenty-four consecutive hours, during which time I had nothing to eat, and during the same week, I was obliged to go to the same length of time without food and to pass the night in a dirty little log cabin in the heart of the Modoc country with nothing to cover me but my overcoat—afraid to build a fire on account of the Indians and the thermometer indicating the freezing point.
>
> We have all adopted the precaution of discarding all insignia of rank and it would be difficult matter to tell

us from enlisted men. I wear a private's uniform, no straps or stripes, and a white broad-brimmed hat. I have discarded boots and taken to government gun boats. Altogether I feel ragged ... I doubt if you would consent to dance the German with me in my present garb![29]

At the time that Colonel Gillem began to move his troops to the proximity of the Lava Beds, important developments were taking place in the Modoc camp. Though Captain Jack had failed to meet Elijah Steele on March 10, he was still contemplating surrender. Jack thought it might be possible to negotiate for a reservation in the Yainax area along the Sprague River. This was within the vicinity of the band of Modocs under Chief Old Schonchin that had remained on the Klamath Reservation. However, Jack met with strong opposition from Hooker Jim and his followers. They were fearful that if Jack surrendered, they would be captured and punished for their attack on the Lost River and Tule Lake settlers. The Hot Creek Modocs, who had fled the irate citizens of Linkville, also counseled against surrender. Jack was accused of being weak (it was reported that several Modoc braves wrapped a blanket around him and accused him of being a "woman"), and the inflicted shame caused him to announce a new course of action. Since the Modoc leaders did not favor surrender, Jack suggested that they kill the members of the Peace Commission.

Why Captain Jack chose this plan is difficult to determine. Erwin Thompson, whose book *Modoc War - Its Military History and Topography* provides a comprehensive analysis of the war's developments, suggests that it was the act of desperate men, who felt they had nothing to lose. "They were surrounded by hundreds of troops ... and many of the Modocs had been indicted for murder in Oregon . . ."[30] Walter Palmberg, writing in his strongly pro-Modoc book titled *Copper Paladin*, says the decision to attack the Peace Commission was not an act of violence "but rather an attack against what the commissioners represented."[31] Finally, Jeremiah Curtain, who wrote a detailed study of Modoc culture, felt that Captain Jack decided to attack the Peace Commission because his "ponies were captured by the troops, in spite of General Canby's promise of total suspension of hostilities. That act so aroused the chief that he determined to kill the peace commissioners, who he now thought to be planning treachery in place of peace."[32]

Even before formal negotiations began with the Modocs, there was uneasiness among some members of the Peace Commission. Two members of the original commission, Jesse Applegate and Samuel Chase, resigned. Both men were unhappy with the war's developments. The Reverend Eleazer Thomas, a fifty-eight year old minister from Petaluma, California, and Klamath Indian Agent Leroy S. Dyar, replaced them. General Canby also became a permanent member.

The Peace Commission held a brief but unsatisfactory meeting with the Modocs on April 2. Then a week later, a formal meeting was arranged for the 11th of April. At 11:30 A.M. on that day, Canby, Alfred Meacham, L.S. Dyar, and the Reverend Mr. Thomas left the army camp at Gillem's Bluff. They traveled east a short distance to an army wall tent that had been erected so that the negotiators would be protected if it started to rain. Frank and Toby Riddle (Toby would later be also known as Winema) accompanied the Peace Commissioners, but they were apprehensive. They knew these Modocs well and in previous negotiations they had overheard the whispers of several Modoc men who were plotting revenge. The Riddles felt that the commissioners were in danger, but General Canby refused to listen to their warnings.

When the April 11 meeting was arranged, it was agreed that the Peace Commission was to meet with six unarmed Modocs. However, when the commissioners reached the tent, they were met by eight men, all well armed. The Modocs present included Captain Jack, Schonchin John, Hooker Jim, Ellen's Man, Black Jim, Boston Charley and Bogus Charley.[33] Several other Modocs, including Scarfaced Charley, Sloluck, and Barncho, were hidden in the brush nearby.

General Canby knew that Captain Jack had an attraction to flashy uniforms, so in order to impress him, Canby appeared in full military dress. He also took with him a box of cigars.[34] After a brief greeting between members of the Peace Commission and the Modocs, Canby distributed the cigars. Several clumsy attempts were made to begin negotiations, but the atmosphere was tense and the Modocs seemed nervous. Suddenly, at a few minutes after noon, a quick signal was passed among the Modocs and they attacked the peace commissioners. Captain Jack shot Canby, and Boston Charley fired a bullet from his rifle into the Reverend Mr. Thomas. Alfred Meacham began a hasty retreat, walking backwards so that he could train a derringer on those intent on killing him. He stumbled and fell, one of the Modocs took aim and a bullet struck a rock next to him. A fragment from the bullet creased his forehead, knocking him unconscious. In the meantime, L.S. Dyar was able to escape by menacing Hooker Jim with a derringer and then running as rapidly as he could toward the army camp. Jeff Riddle also made a hasty retreat, but his wife Toby remained behind, hoping to save some members of the Peace Commission.

Before abandoning the carnage around the peace tent, the Modocs stripped the clothes off Meacham, Thomas and Canby as souvenirs of battle. They started to scalp Meacham but had only partially removed his hair when Toby Riddle intervened. She shouted to the Modocs that the soldiers were coming, which was not true, and the warriors quickly abandoned Meacham and headed back toward the Stronghold.

The impact of the assassinations of General Canby and Eleazer Thomas was immediate. The soldiers at Hospital Rock and Gillem's Bluff were stunned and angered. When the news reached the American public, sympathy for the Modoc cause quickly disappeared. Never before had an American general been killed in a western Indian battle. The press now cried for swift retribution. Their editorial pages were filled with indignation and rage.

> For a whole year, the remarkable spectacle has been presented of a great and powerful Government negotiating with a mere handful of paupers and murderers, seeking to make terms of peace with them as if they were a nation of equal dignity ... The inane Indian policy of which we have heard so much sentimentalism has at last born bitter fruits.
>
> *- The Chicago Tribune* [35]

> Peace policy and the Indian Bureau have accomplished the bitter end, and offered as martyrs to the cause lives of General E.R.S. Canby, commanding the District of the Columbia, and the Rev. Mr. Thomas of Petaluma, Cal, Presiding Elder of the Presbyterian Church.
>
> *- The New York Herald* [36]

And now the telegraph flashes to us the result of the
awkward manner in which the government has been
compounding murder and crime in the region of the
Lava Beds, and with those fiends in human shape, the
Modocs ... One of the bravest and most able officers of
the United States Army has been deliberately
murdered in cold blood ... who [was] at the very
moment engaged in carrying out the foolish and fatal
"peace policy" so strenuously upheld by Eastern
philanthropists towards these banditti of the plains ...
If when they committed slaughter and depredations
upon whites they would be immediately pursued by
our troops and shot at sight, there would be no more
Indian scalping parties visiting the pioneer settlements
of the west.

- *The Boston Globe* [37]

The sacrifice of Canby and Thomas to the folly of the
maudlin humanitarianism which has given the so-
called Quaker Policy to the country, will, we may hope,
bring some compensating benefits. It may possibly
suggest to the sympathetic souls, who are shocked at
the bare idea of an Indian's being hurt, and who
instinctively seek for a justification, or at least an
excuse for every outrage committed by an Indian, in
some superstitious outrage previously perpetrated by
white men on him, that something else than morning
prayers, psalm singing, and the distribution of tracts
may be necessary to secure and maintain harmonious
relations between the "noble red man" and his pale-
faced brother!

- *The Yreka Union* [38]

When General William Tecumseh Sherman, who was in charge
of the Indian "pacification" program in the West, was asked for
his reactions to the attack on the Peace Commission, he
responded that General Canby's death "was a terrible sacrifice to
the Quaker Policy."[39] Later, when a newspaper reporter asked
him if "this act of Indian treachery was unparalleled," Sherman
replied: "No Sir. Treachery is inherent in the Indian character."[40]
General Sherman was clearly angry over both the progress of the
war and the death of his friend, Edward Canby. The day after the
killing of the peace commissioners, he sent a cable to Colonel
Gillem, stating: "The President ... authorizes me to instruct you to

make an attack so strong and persistent that their fate may be commensurate with their crime. You will be fully justified in their utter extermination."[41]

Taking Sherman's orders to heart, the army spent the next two weeks attacking the Stronghold. Using mortars and howitzers, they bombarded the Modoc fortifications. But when they finally penetrated the Stronghold, they discovered it was empty!

A search for the Modocs began. On April 26, Captain Evan Thomas took a sixty-six-man patrol on a scouting expedition south of the Stronghold. When the soldiers had gone as far south as Sand (Hardin) Butte, they stopped. There they dismounted and broke out rations for lunch. Their actions were careless and foolish. Some of the men took off their boots to cool their tired feet. [42] Meanwhile, Captain Thomas left his men and began to climb to the top of Sand Butte. His purpose was to signal the headquarters at Gillem's Bluff to let them know that the patrol had arrived safely. Suddenly, a well-armed band of Modocs launched an attack. Apparently Thomas had marched his men near the relocated Modoc headquarters, and the patrol had been under continual surveillance since they had left Gillem's Camp.

The attack on Thomas's patrol was a terrible rout. First Lieutenant Wright attempted to organize his men into a disciplined formation, but he was severely wounded. Other men, including those barefooted, turned and ran. When the battle was over, both Captain Thomas and Lieutenant Wright lay dead with at least twenty-one others. More than two-thirds of the patrol had been either killed or wounded.[43]

Meanwhile, President Ulysses Grant had appointed Brevet Brigadier General Jefferson C. Davis to replace the slain General Canby as Commander of the Columbia Division of the United States Army. On May 2, Davis arrived at Gillem's camp and assumed command of the troops. Under General Davis, the military organization at the Lava Beds underwent a major transformation. It was Davis's opinion that the attack on the peace commissioners and the carnage at the Thomas-Wright battlefield were the result of poor strategy and lax discipline on the part of the officers and enlisted men. He tightened the command by demanding that his troops be alert at all times. Troop strength was increased and he initiated an aggressive program of patrols around the Lava Beds.

General Davis's order for better preparation paid off. At daylight on May 10, a band of Modocs attacked an army patrol at Sorass Lake (today known as Dry Lake), located about twenty-five miles southeast of the Stronghold. The army's sentries alerted the soldiers before the Modocs reached the main section of the camp and for the first time in the Modoc war, the army won a significant battle.[44] The battle at Sorass Lake may have been the turning point in the war. The Modocs lost an important leader, Ellen's Man. It was their first major setback and later reports claimed that this broke their spirit.[45]

Gradually, the army gained control of the entire Lava Beds region. It continued to apply pressure whenever a group of Modocs was spotted, and by May 14, most of the Indians had fled from the Tule Lake Basin. A number of Modocs, including many of the Hot Creek band, moved into the hills southwest of Lower Klamath Lake. Knowing that the army would soon catch up with them, they sent a message to John Fairchild that they wanted to surrender. Fairchild and his wife climbed to a ridge on Mahogany (Fairchild's) Mountain. They returned with sixty-three Modoc men, women and children. Soon after, Hooker Jim also surrendered.[46] Fairchild kept the Modocs at his ranch, under his protection, until General Davis arrived on May 22. Taking charge, Davis made assurances to the Modocs that soldiers seeking to avenge the death of their comrades would not harm them.

At the encampment of the surrendered Modocs, a number of the main leaders of the Hot Creeks and Lost River bands approached General Davis. No doubt seeking to save their own skins, they offered their services in helping to locate and capture Captain Jack. Those who volunteered included Bogus Charley, Shacknasty Jim, Steamboat Frank and Hooker Jim. Most of these men had been involved in the killing of white settlers at Tule Lake. Now the perpetrators of the Modoc War were offering to help capture the one man who had originally wanted to negotiate a peaceful settlement.[47] Davis agreed to allow the four men to assist in hunting Jack down. Before the amazed eyes of soldiers and Indians alike, each man was outfitted with a Springfield rifle, and then left with a military patrol.

Meanwhile, after the debacle at Sorass Lake, Captain Jack and about twenty of his followers moved east. They traveled through the Clear Lake Hills and were moving north to a favorite camp on the slopes of Bryant Mountain. Before reaching the camp, their scouts warned them the army was on their trail. In an attempt to avoid capture, Jack and his people crossed Lost River and began to head east to Steele Swamp.

As part of his effort to capture Jack and the few remaining members of his Modoc band, General Davis had sent out three squadrons of men. On May 20, one of the squadrons bivouacked at the Peninsula at Tule Lake, while the other two moved to Jesse Applegate's ranch just north of Clear Lake. Eight days later, on the 28th of May, the turncoat Modoc scouts discovered that Jack and his people were camped out at Willow Creek, on the east side of Clear Lake. On the 29th surrender appeared certain, but a Warm Springs Indian scout accidentally fired his rifle and the Modocs ran away. The next day, Scarfaced Charley, Schonchin John, and twelve other men and their families gave up.[48] Finally on June 1, 1873, Captain Jack found he could no longer elude his captors and he too surrendered.

The army and their Modoc captives moved back to the Peninsula campsite at Tule Lake. There, General Davis planned to have a quick trial for the Modocs and hang them. Though Davis's plans had little room for an honest trial, he did attempt to add some sense of judicial decorum to the proceedings. He brought in two of the bitterest survivors of the bloody November 29 attack on white settlers to testify against the Modoc prisoners. The two witnesses were Mrs. William Boddy and Mrs. Nicholas Shira. When the two women were confronted with Hooker Jim and Steamboat Frank, they attempted to kill both men. However, General Davis disarmed the women, cutting his hand when he took a knife away from Mrs. Shira.[49]

While General Davis was preparing a case against the Modocs, he had a scaffold built on the Peninsula so that the guilty parties could be properly hanged after the trial. However, on June 5 he received a telegram ordering him to halt the proceedings. The government needed time to determine who had jurisdiction in the matter: the military or the civilian courts. Davis received another telegram on June 9, informing him that the Modocs were to be tried in a military court at Fort Klamath.

In the meantime, the bloodbath of the war was not quite over. On June 8, John Fairchild was driving a wagon with seventeen Modoc prisoners east across Lost River. There were men, women, and children in the wagon. Some of the men were crippled because of wounds received early in the Modoc War. Fairchild was suddenly confronted by several men on horseback who chased him away and then proceeded to kill at least five of the unarmed men. Evidence indicates that the killers were members of the Oregon Volunteers under a Captain Hiser. Sadly, no action was ever taken against these men. [50]

Several days after the attack by the Oregon Volunteers, General Davis left the Peninsula with his Modoc prisoners. For the last time Captain Jack made the sad sixty-mile journey past his lost homeland and north to Fort Klamath. When General Davis delivered his charges to the fort, the War Department ordered that only the Modocs responsible for killing General Canby and the Reverend Mr. Thomas were to be tried. Those singled out included Captain Jack, Schonchin John, Boston Charley, Black Jim, Sloluck and Barncho. Hooker Jim and other members of the band who had been responsible for the killing of white settlers on November 29 and 30 were not included. They had been spared because of their cooperation in tracking down Captain Jack. Between July 1 and July 9, 1873 a military commission tried the six Modoc men and found them all guilty. They were sentenced to be hanged. Later, Barncho and Sloluck had their sentences commuted to life imprisonment, but they were not told until the day they were scheduled to be executed.

On October 3, 1873, Captain Jack, Schonchin John, Boston Charley, and Black Jim were led to a sturdy scaffold built on Fort Klamath's grounds. At 10:20 a.m. Captain George B. Hoge dropped a white handkerchief, signaling the release of the floor on the scaffold. Eight minutes later the four men were pronounced dead.[51] Reflecting on the execution, the *New York Herald* stated:

> In the death of the four Modoc captives upon the same gallows-tree a series of horrible crimes has been expiated ... It brings before us the Indian question ... neither tears nor wringing of hands will avail naught while the Indian, converted into a demon, defies civilization, and the land he encumbers is wanted for the plough.[52]

There was a grisly aftermath to the deaths of the four Modocs. Pieces of the rope used to hang Jack were sold to spectators, and Lt. George W. Kingsbury had some of the pieces mounted on cards that were imprinted with "The Rope That Hung the Chief of the Modoc Indians, Captain Jack. Oct. 3rd 1873."[53] Some of these cards he sold, and others he gave away to friends. Locks of Captain Jack's hair, which had to be trimmed in order to insure a better fit for the hanging rope, were sold for five dollars each. Other Modoc souvenirs picked up after the hanging included bows, pipes, and other personal items.

The most gruesome souvenirs were anatomical. After the bodies of the men were cut down, they were taken to a surgeon's tent. There the head of each man was severed and preserved for shipment to Washington, D.C. The heads were addressed to the Surgeon General's Office.[54] This was not an uncommon practice in the 1800s. The government had a vast array of bizarre, curious, and famous bodies and body parts, all carefully cataloged.

The head of Captain Jack may not have been the only part of him shipped off. Jeff Riddle, the son of Toby and Frank Riddle, claimed that Jack was mummified and displayed at a sideshow in Washington, D.C.[55] This allegation has been contested, but it has been documented that Captain Jack's skull was still in the possession of the Smithsonian Institute in the mid-1980s.

After the execution, the remaining 157 members of Captain Jack's band were taken in wagons to Yreka. On October 17, they were loaded on a train for Fort McPherson, Nebraska. From there, they were moved to Indian Territory in Oklahoma where they were given a two-and-a-half square mile tract of land on the Quapaw Reservation. In a report filed by Captain M.C. Wilkinson, which described the Modocs' arrival in Oklahoma, he stated:

> On the cars, in the old hotel-building used for them at Baxter, I found them uniformly obedient, ready to work, cheerful in compliance with police regulations, each day proving over and over again that these Modocs only require just treatment, executed with firmness and kindness, to make them a singularly reliable people.[56]

But on the Quapaw Reservation, they lived in terrible squalor, and disease took a heavy toll. On May 10, 1884, the *Linkville Star* reported:

They have dwindled down numerically, year by year, until now but 97 are borne upon the rolls of the agency. The change of habits, particularly that of climate has worked upon them fearfully. Nearly all adult deaths have been from consumption in a lingering form.[57]

In 1910, a few surviving Modocs of Captain Jack's band were allowed to return to the Klamath Reservation. The reaction of local citizenry was decidedly mixed. Several weeks before their arrival, an article in the *Klamath Republican* said:

The expected arrival of a number of Modoc Indians at the Klamath Indian Agency ... has revived memories of the incidents that led to the exiling of the Modocs from their former haunts ... Now it is understood that a number of them are on their way here, and when they arrive they will receive their allotments the same as though they had never rebelled against the government ... There are only about sixty members of the tribe left ... Their exile from their former homes for the past thirty-two years is deemed by the government sufficient punishment for their obstreperous conduct.[58]

With the execution of Captain Jack in October of 1873 and the exile of his people, a sad and infamous chapter in the history of the Tule Lake Basin was finished. The displacement of the Modocs had been costly in terms of lives lost and dollars spent. During the six months of the Modoc War, at least sixteen settlers and sixty-eight soldiers lost their lives. Another seventy-five military personnel had been wounded. The Modocs lost approximately sixteen men. To subdue the fifty-five to seventy warriors who holed up in the lava beds required a force of over 1000 men. [59] The cost in dollars was staggering for the time. Including maintenance of the regular army, the Oregon and California volunteers, and the large civilian support team, the government spent nearly three quarters of a million dollars. [60] The cost to purchase reservation land along Lost River, so desperately wanted by Captain Jack, would have been a fraction of that amount.

The principal leaders of the Modoc War: Kientpos (Captain Jack) and General Edward Canby. *(Photos courtesy National Park Service)*

Army Headquarters at Gillem's Camp, located on the southwest shore of Tule Lake. *(Photo courtesy National Park Service)*

Soldiers assembled for inspection at Gillem's Camp.
(Photo courtesy National Park Service)

Scouting for Modocs near Captain Jack's Stronghold.
(Photo courtesy National Park Service)

Newspaper correspondents writing reports from the "front."
(Photo courtesy National Park Service)

Canby's Cross, located in the Lava Beds National Monument. Site where Captain Jack killed General Edward Canby on April 11, 1873. *(Photo by Author)*

Clear Lake, located due east of Tule Lake. It is the major source of water for Lost River. Near this site Captain Jack and his small band of Modocs were captured on June 1, 1873. *(Photo by author)*

CHAPTER 7

LINKVILLE, SETTLERS AND IRRIGATION

The tumultuous removal of the Modocs in 1873 opened Lost River, Tule Lake, and the Klamath Basin to expanded settlement. Farms and ranches began to dot the countryside, and local geographic features were labeled with the names of some of the earliest and most notable white settlers. The springboard for this settlement was Linkville, which had been founded by George Nurse in 1867.

Nurse was involved in a variety of enterprises. He had dabbled in gold mining, and when Fort Klamath was established he became a supplier and trader there. Interested in expanding his merchandising enterprises, he entered into a partnership with Edgar Overton. Together they built a cabin in 1866 next to the Link River, which joins Upper Klamath Lake with Lake Ewauna.[1] The site they chose was unique geographically. The Link River is one of the shortest in the world, less than a mile long. At times, when Lake Ewauna was at high water level and when there was a stiff wind blowing northward, the river actually flowed in reverse, back into Upper Klamath Lake (today, because of a dam at Upper Klamath Lake's outlet, this phenomenon is no longer possible).

The land on which Nurse and Overton built their cabin was not only situated on the Link River but was bordered on its eastern and western sides by hills that descended to the broad, flat valley of the Lower Klamath Basin. It was a region that seemed well suited to both farming and ranching. It was also on the route linking Fort Klamath with Yreka, to the southwest and near a fork in the Applegate Trail. Traffic on these roads helped to maintain Nurse and Overton's meager trade, and they supplemented their income by operating a ferry across Link River. Gradually other buildings appeared at the site, and the infant community became known as Linkville.[2]

Linkville became a rendezvous point for many of the earliest settlers in the basin. Dennis Crawley came to the little town in 1867, where he joined in a partnership with H.M. Thatcher and planted several acres in grain. Their intent was to sell the crop to the military at Fort Klamath. However, the business venture failed and their partnership dissolved. Crawley moved south to

Tule Lake, where he built a cabin near its northern shore. It was the same cabin that had been the headquarters for the army during the early stages of the Modoc War.

In 1868, the Langell family passed through Linkville and moved twenty-five miles east to farm along Lost River. The valley that they settled in was soon named after them.[3] Several years later Stephen and Delilah Stukel moved to Linkville, where their son Joseph was born in 1873. In 1877, the Stukels acquired property on the east side of Lost River at the foot of what is now known as Stukel Mountain.[4] James M. Poe was another early settler who visited Linkville and then moved east to take up farming just beyond Olene gap. The land around his farm became known as Poe Valley.

In November of 1872, there were 40 permanent residents in Linkville, but the number rapidly changed after the outbreak of the Modoc War, when it more than doubled. The town was filled with frightened settlers, soldiers on leave, and freight handlers who hauled tons of supplies to the battlefront at the Lava Beds. During this time, Linkville developed notoriety as a hotbed for anti-Modoc sentiment. Soldiers, saloonkeepers, miners, and settlers alike called for the extermination of the tribe. On at least two occasions, the townspeople sent vigilante groups after Modoc bands they heard were in the area.

After the war, the town's atmosphere was more sedate and in 1874 its population was large enough to cause the Oregon State Legislature to designate Linkville as the county seat for Lake County. However, two years later, the county boundaries were redrawn, and the county seat was moved to Lakeview. [5]

During the next fourteen years, Linkville experienced steady if modest growth. In 1880, the town boasted 250 people, and in 1882 it was once again designated as a county seat, this time for Klamath County. Two years later, Linkville's first newspaper, the *Klamath Weekly Star* was established, and a gristmill was constructed next to the Link River, just north of town. By the spring of 1886, there were "seven stores, four saloons, three hotels, three blacksmith shops, a brewery, three livery and feed stables, a flouring mill, saw mill, sash and door factory, harness shop, butcher shop, U.S. telegraph office, four doctors, four lawyers, and one newspaper."[6] Near the end of that year, the

Klamath Weekly Star announced that 600 people were now residing in the town, a figure that was probably a bit exaggerated.

In January of 1887, the residents of Linkville applied to the state legislature for incorporation but they were turned down. Two years later, application was again made, and a charter was granted on February 25, 1889. In taking this action, the Oregon State Legislature said: "Inasmuch as improvements are very much needed in the town of Linkville, and said town is greatly in need of municipal government, this act shall take effect and be in force from and after its approval by the Governor."[7]

Meanwhile, some of the residents in Linkville were unhappy with the name of their town. They felt that it should be called something more befitting a town destined to become a major commercial center. The name "Klamath City" was heavily promoted, but on April 10, 1891, the *Klamath County Star* reported:

> Isa Leskeard, who has been in Portland most of the time since last summer, thinks the name of this town should be Klamath Falls. The name advertises the fact that there are falls here, thus giving the town an advantage fully recognized as such by other towns similarly situated ... "There is [Leskeard said] a great deal in the name of a town situated by a heavy cataract," and [the *Star*] is inclined to think so, too.[8]

In December of 1891, the United States Post Office was petitioned to change the name. On March 11, 1892 the change was approved and Linkville became officially known as Klamath Falls.[9]

By the turn of the century, industry had come to Klamath Falls. She boasted of lumber mills, agricultural processing facilities, and a great variety of smaller businesses serving the city and surrounding communities. But the town lacked an efficient transportation system. Most supplies shipped from the metropolitan centers of California had to follow a twisting road through the Siskiyous and Klamath Mountains to Laird's Landing. At this site, located at the southern end of Lower Klamath Lake, the goods were loaded onto steamboats and hauled north to Linkville. Material shipped to and from the north had to be freighted over a dusty, bumpy road to Bend, or west to Ashland and Roseberg.

Residents of the Klamath Basin heavily lobbied several major railroads to build lines into Klamath Falls. The Southern Pacific was interested in the project, but it wasn't until 1909 that the SP completed a line into the city from Weed, California. It took another seventeen years to complete the tracks northward to Chemult and Eugene.[10] By the 1920s the Great Northern also indicated an interest in constructing a rail line, but it wasn't finished until the early 1930s. The changes brought about by the railroads were significant. Markets for the products of Klamath Falls greatly improved, and the new prosperity caused the population to jump from 4,801 in 1920 to 16,093 in 1930.[11]

The railroad did not solve all of Klamath Falls's transportation problems. With the influx of automobiles and trucks, a fast, efficient road system was desperately needed. This was finally achieved in 1936. The *Klamath Herald* proudly announced the event:

> Twenty years of effort on the part of this community comes to a successful conclusion [with the] dedication of the Oregon section of the Weed-Klamath Falls highway ... For that long Klamath has been working on a short, fast route to the metropolitan centers to the north and a connecting link between The Dalles-California highway and the Pacific highway.[12]

In the years since the 1930s the population of Klamath Falls has stabilized, but the surrounding area has continued to grow. Today there are more than 17,000 people living in the city limits and the greater metropolitan area has a population of about 47,000. Klamath Falls is the hub for much of the commercial and social activities in the basin. To some degree, this has been to the detriment of businesses in the smaller towns, but the city provides the underpinnings for much of the region's economic prosperity.

Klamath Falls was not the only factor in the growth of the basin. Beginning in the late 1800s, a number of prominent landowners also helped effect change. One of the first was Jesse D. Carr of Salinas, California. Carr had been made aware of the potential for ranching and land development in the Tule Lake and Clear Lake regions through a chance meeting with Jesse Applegate. Applegate was obviously a persuasive talker, because by 1872 the two men were in partnership running cattle at Clear

Lake. Carr was to later remark "Applegate induced him to make application for some swamp land at Clear Lake, which he secured without seeing the property."[13]

While negotiating for land at Clear Lake, Carr acquired his first property along the shores of Tule Lake. There he purchased the estates of Henry Miller and William Brotherton, both of whom had been killed in the Modoc War. By November of 1878, the scope of Carr's enterprises in the basin was impressive. He had "500 breed horses, 500 stock cattle, 6,000 sheep and 5 dogs."[14] Fourteen years later, Carr owned and controlled most of the land between Tule Lake and Clear Lake. This included 3,882 acres in Klamath County, Oregon and 18,962 acres in Modoc County, California.[15]

Jesse Carr rarely visited his holdings, relying instead on a series of foremen to run his ranch. The men he selected must have had great skill and foresight, for Carr's ranch became famous for its high quality breeding stock. Under a carefully managed program, Durham bulls were brought in from South Carolina and mixed with other strains more common in the west, including Angus and Hereford. According to legend, Carr's Durham bulls were confined at The Peninsula, at the south-eastern end of Tule Lake. Since this volcanic formation was only connected with the eastern shore line by a narrow neck of land, it made an ideal location for confining the bull herd.[16]

Though Carr's ranching operation was carefully managed, it was not exempt from the hazards of inclement weather characteristic to the basin. The *Klamath County Star* reported in February 1890 that the severe winter had caused the loss of some 1500 to 2000 head of cattle, including over 200 of Carr's prize Durham bulls.[17] This was not Carr's first major loss of stock. Back in 1878, he lost 6,000 sheep due to extreme weather conditions.[18]

By the early 1900s, the Carr Land and Livestock Company owned a total of 40,000 acres in the Clear Lake and Tule Lake Basin area. The operation was managed by William Carson Dalton. Then on December 11, 1903, Jesse D. Carr died. His land holdings in the Tule Lake Basin region went to his daughter, Jesse Carr Seale. In 1906, the Reclamation Service purchased all of the ranch land at Clear Lake. Meanwhile, Jesse Seale formed the Tule Lake Land and Livestock Company and sold one-third interests to William C. Dalton, the ranch manager, and John Franks, her financial advisor. Later, Dalton acquired both Jesse Seale's and John Frank's shares of the company, and today the property is owned and managed by Robert A. and Elizabeth Dalton Byrne.[19]

The person who had the greatest impact on the Tule Lake Basin during the late nineteenth century was J. Frank Adams. Adams was born March 3, 1855 in Hangtown (Placerville), California. In 1872, seventeen-year-old Frank Adams migrated to Butte Valley, south of Linkville. There he worked as a cowboy and broke horses at the Fairchild ranch for the military during the Modoc War.[20]

In 1879, Adams settled on a piece of property on the northeast side of Lost River, near the northern shore of Tule Lake. There he raised cattle and horses, including registered Percherons. These large draft horses were used throughout the basin for farming and construction projects.

Adams's greatest contribution was not as a rancher, but as a promoter of irrigation land development. Soon after he arrived in the Lost River and Tule Lake Basin area it became apparent to him that farming in the region would be greatly enhanced by irrigation. The annual growing season in the Tule Lake Basin averaged only 95 days, and the yearly rainfall 9.4 inches.[21] Adams realized that if the land could be irrigated its potential was unlimited. He was also aware that several irrigation projects were already in operation in the Klamath Basin, and that they were successful in encouraging settlement and increasing farm output.

In 1878, a year before Adams started his ranch in the Tule Lake Basin, a group of citizens in Linkville incorporated the Linkville Water Ditch Company. They dug a canal from the Link River, near its headwaters at Upper Klamath Lake, and ran it into the Linkville townsite. The canal was a success. It provided a year-round water supply and made it possible for residents of Linkville to irrigate small garden plots. In about 1884 the Linkville Water Ditch Company was purchased by Irishman William Steele. He immediately embarked on an expansion program, running the canal east toward the community of Olene. Steele's canal opened about 4,000 acres of land to irrigation.[22] Its success whetted the appetite of others in the basin and soon several groups were developing plans for ambitious irrigation projects.

Dan and Clint Van Brimmer were also among those who believed that irrigation could bring major changes to the basin (This was the same Van Brimmer family that had been so sorely disliked by soldiers camping on their Willow Creek ranch during the Modoc War. Now they had an opportunity to redeem themselves). They settled on land to the south of Lost River, in the vicinity of Stone Bridge. Like other settlers in the area, they discovered that crop production was inhibited by the lack of sufficient seasonal rainfall. This was frustrating because the volume of water in Lost River was more than adequate for all of the needs of local farmers. The problem was that the normal level of Lost River was lower than that of the surrounding land, and if a dam were constructed it might cause flooding of much of the Lost River Valley. Recognizing these problems, the Van Brimmers conceived a plan to bring water east from White Lake. This body of water was actually an extension of the northeast end of Lower Klamath Lake. Only a small rise separated it from the Lost River valley as it entered the Tule Lake Basin. In 1882, the Van Brimmers began construction on a canal. As they progressed east from White Lake, they dug an eighteen-foot deep cut through the low divide separating Lower Klamath Basin and the Lost River valley. The project took four years and in 1886, the completed canal began delivering water to some 4,000 acres of land on the west and south sides of Lost River. In order to pay for construction costs and maintenance of the system, the Van Brimmers charged a fee of $1.00 per acre per year.[23]

The Van Brimmers had been supported by J. Frank Adams in their efforts, and when the initial canal proved successful, Adams began construction on his own canal on the east side of Lost River. In an agreement signed with the Van Brimmer brothers, Adams tapped into their canal and ran water across Lost River in an eight-foot wide wooden flume. The water was then channeled into a six-mile long canal system.[24] Naming his irrigation project the Little Klamath Ditch Company, Adams was able to supply irrigated water to farmland on the east side of Lost River, just north of Tule Lake.

The irrigation projects maintained by J. Frank Adams and the Van Brimmer brothers ran into a snag during the winter of 1887 to 1888. An unusually dry winter had lowered the level of White Lake dramatically, leaving the canal system without water. The Van Brimmers had hoped that underground seepage from Lower Klamath Lake would maintain a constant level in White Lake, but this didn't materialize. To alleviate the problem, Adams proposed a plan to cut a channel between the two lakes. Amid a great deal of skepticism, Adams began construction. It was a difficult task, because the area between the two lakes was filled with tough, fibrous tule reeds; so tough that they were almost impossible to cut with a knife. It took Adams two years to complete the project. It was successful, however, and for the next ten years a steady supply of water was provided for the Van Brimmer and Adams canals.[25]

Meanwhile, the success of the small channel dug between Lower Klamath and Lake White Lakes encouraged J. Frank Adams to expand his Little Klamath Ditch irrigation company. In December 1902, he purchased for $2500 a half interest in a dredge that had been working south in the Fall River Valley of Shasta County. He wanted it for work on Lower Klamath Lake. To haul the dredge north, he hired twenty-four wagons, one hundred and six horses and twenty men. The dredge was taken in pieces to Keno, west of Lower Klamath Lake. There, a twenty-eight-foot wide by sixty-foot long barge was built and the dredge was reassembled on its deck. Construction was completed on June 18, 1903 and by July, the dredge was in use, cutting a larger channel between Lower Klamath and White Lake.[26]

While his dredge was working on the channel, Adams was also enlarging his water delivery system in the Lost River Valley. He increased the capacity of his east side canal network by building a new flume across Lost River. It was thirty-two feet wide, 540 feet long and three feet deep. It more than tripled the water carrying capacity of the old flume. [27]

With the completion of the new flume and wider channel between Lower Klamath and White lakes, Adams began to approach neighboring ranchers and farmers, seeking to expand his system. One of his company's largest contracts was negotiated with the Jesse D. Carr Ranch. On January 4, 1904, he entered into an agreement to irrigate approximately 10,000 acres of Carr land at the north end of the Tule Lake Basin.[28]

Several years later, the federally sponsored Klamath Reclamation Project bought out the Adams and Van Brimmer systems. The cut from White Lake to Lost River Valley was sealed and water from Upper Klamath Lake and a diversion dam on Lost River was tied into the two canals. It was fortunate that the Klamath Project came when it did, because the water coming from White Lake was highly alkaline. If the land had remained under the old Van Brimmer and Adams system, it might have been severely damaged.

Today there is still ample evidence of the work done by J. Frank Adams and Dan and Clint Van Brimmer. The two main canals serving the lower Lost River Valley and the northern end of the Tule Lake Basin follow much the same course that they did when they were initially constructed in the 1880s. Even the Van Brimmer cut from White Lake is still visible for all but the last quarter mile of its run from White Lake. Perhaps the most significant contribution of the Van Brimmers and J. Frank Adams is that they proved, conclusively, that irrigation was possible in the basin. Based on the evidence produced by their efforts, a series of new communities would soon spring to life, and one of the United States' most complex and unique irrigation projects would be developed.

The city of Klamath Falls (formerly Linkville) in 1907, looking east across Lake Ewauna. *(Photo courtesy Klamath County Museum)*

Klamath Falls in 1908 looking southeast toward Olene Gap and Stukel Mountain. *(Photo courtesy Klamath County Museum)*

Klamath Falls in 2002, looking southeast toward Mount Stukel. *(Photo by author)*

CHAPTER 8

MERRILL, ACTIVITY ON TULE LAKE, AND WHITE LAKE CITY

J. Frank Adams's involvement with irrigation projects and dredging operations continued for another decade, but increasingly his interests turned to real estate. In 1889, he acquired from Benjamin Van Brimmer 152 acres of land on the north side of Lost River, near Stone Bridge. Two years later, on April 20, 1891, Adams and his wife Fannie sold the land to Nathan and Nancy Merrill for $3,000.

The Merrills' acquisition of the Van Brimmer land was not without careful thought. Nathan and Nancy Merrill were well aware of the success of J. Frank Adams's canal and knew that in time it would attract additional settlers. What the region lacked was a town. Klamath Falls was twenty miles by road, and it required nearly two days for basin residents to make the round trip journey for supplies.

In April of 1894, the Merrill's hired Antone Castel to survey 80 acres of their land for a townsite. Castel drew an ambitious plan that included two major thoroughfares for a business district, one running north and south, and the other paralleling Lost River. His map included neatly arranged residential streets, and sites designated for a school and park. In May, Nathan and Nancy Merrill "dedicated the streets and avenues of Merrill for use of the public forever," an act duly recorded at the Klamath County Court House on May 28, 1894.[1] They then set about establishing an economic base for their town. The construction of a flour mill was their first project.

One of the principal crops in the Lost River Valley and Tule Lake Basin was wheat, but it was costly to haul the harvest to Klamath Falls to have it milled into flour. The Merrills approached J. Frank Adams with their plans, and he began to solicit donations from local farmers for the construction of a mill.

Meanwhile, the Merrills talked to Thomas Martin, the owner of a flour mill in Klamath Falls. When Martin was informed that Adams had already raised $3,500 and that men were in the process of hauling rocks and timber for the foundations of a mill, he agreed to finance one himself. However, he stipulated that Adams and the farmers along Lost River give up any plans for a rival mill. All parties reached an agreement and in August 1894 Thomas Martin's flour mill was complete at the Merrill townsite.

Nathan Merrill's real estate transactions in developing his town were done with wisdom and care. He realized that a permanent community was dependent upon a healthy economic base. Consequently, Merrill actively recruited businesses to locate at the townsite, and he offered some of the earliest establishments free land. For example, Merrill donated the property on which the Martin Flour Mill was constructed. He also helped supervise the construction of the first residence, which housed Frank Brandon, who managed the mill. Brandon was soon joined by his mother, a brother, and two sisters. They were among the earliest citizens of the town.

During the summer of 1894, Nathan Merrill offered to give James O'Farrel a corner lot if he would move his general store from the community of Gale, located three miles to the north. He also offered the same deal to James Stoby of Gale to transplant his blacksmith shop.[2] By 1895, the town was beginning to take form. It had its own twenty by forty-foot school house and its first post office.[3] Merrill later reported to the *Klamath Morning Express* that there were "only two or three buildings the first two years," but the foundations for community development had been laid.[4]

In carefully measured steps, the little town took on definition. It was aided by civic-minded leaders who actively promoted the town's growth. On May 18, 1903, Merrill was officially incorporated in Klamath County, Oregon, and the town's first board of directors included Frank Brandon, George Tory, H.E. Smith, W.P. Rhodes, and George Offield.[5] Offield would later be elected mayor and serve a total of twenty years as leader of Merrill.[6]

Each year heralded a significant development in Merrill. In 1904, the Merrill School District proudly reported a total enrollment of 56 students, with 13 on the honor roll.[7] In 1905, the city's growth was impressive enough to draw the attention of the *Klamath Republican*, which gave high marks to the city on its development.

The writer had an occasion to visit the town of Merrill last week and was greatly pleased and surprised at the flourishing condition of the metropolis of the southern part of the county.

The town of Merrill has had a wonderful growth the past summer. The number of new buildings and the grade and quality of them is equal if not superior to those of any town in the county. Merrill now has three good sized hotels and they are crowded all the time.

One drawback which the town has had since its birth has been the lack of good water. This, however, has now been remedied by the residents digging a deep well, which has resulted in a beautiful supply of pure cold water. The town sports an electric light and water system.

Many of the ranchers living in the surrounding country are building residences in town and intend moving there for the winter.[8]

Representatives of the city, with whom the reporter talked, got a little carried away in their enthusiastic predictions for the town's growth. The article concluded by saying: "The town of Merrill is working to increase its population to 1000 during the next year. This seems to be ... an impossibility, but an acquaintance ... [says] they mean business and that there is no such thing as impossible."[9]

The reporter was correct. In 1906 the population was closer to 200 than it was to 1000 but the *Klamath Republican* still assessed the city as healthy and growing.

Merrill now has two general merchandise stores stocked with everything the citizen can wish for his home, one furniture store where the home can be furnished from top to bottom at prices that compare favorably with those of the metropolitan cities, three well equipped hotels doing an excellent business - so much so that they are not sufficient for the needs of the town, an up-to-date restaurant building is now being fitted up with lodging rooms in connection, two cigar and confectionery stores, two blacksmith shops, one drug store, one butcher shop, the only creamery in the county, two livery barns and a big feed barn under course of construction, four saloons, bank, doctor, newspaper, very large and fine opera house, harness shop, shoe repair shop, millinery store, flouring mill of fifty barrel daily capacity, a real estate firm and is represented by most of the leading fraternal societies as well as churches. A large capacity brick yard was recently established and a large brick bank building is to be constructed.[10]

The next year, the town's future seemed even brighter when, on February 14, 1907, it was announced that the Board of Directors of the California Northeastern Railroad planned to build a fourteen mile line to Merrill from Midland (which is located just to the south of Klamath Falls).[11] The excitement was short-lived. Financial backing didn't materialize and it wasn't until the end of the 1920s that the first rail line reached the town.

By 1909, Merrill was known as the "Flour City" because of the large business done by its mill. With a population of nearly 300 people, it was the second largest town in the Klamath Basin. The Klamath Falls *Morning Express* reported with enthusiasm that: "This is a new town, but the second in size in the district, having more than doubled in two years. It has a creamery, planing mill, flour mill, shingle mill, three churches, school, bank, two hotels and other town necessities. A transmission line gives electric light and power."[12]

It was an exciting and heady time for Merrill. The prediction of 1000 residents was still a long way from reality but now it seemed closer than mere newspaper hype. Then, two years later, the first of several disasters struck; putting a temporary damper on development.

On April 1, 1911, a major fire swept the city. It destroyed almost an entire block, including the Martin Brothers general merchandise store, the Mascot Livery Stable and Ritter's Shoe Shop.[13] At the time, the city's volunteer fire department was not well equipped, and citizens were hurriedly organized into a bucket brigade. They lined up from Lost River to the site of the fire, a block away, and handed buckets back and forth. The fire destroyed most of a block, but their efforts saved the rest of the business district from going up in flames.

Though the financial loss from the town's first major fire was in excess of $40,000 (a considerable sum at the time), new buildings were soon constructed, and fifteen months later the residents were occupied with a new task. The city decided that it was time to end the dust churned up from their dirt roads. Cinders were acquired at the Lava Beds and hauled by barge across Tule Lake and up Lost River. When the boats reached Merrill, they were tied up at the city's dock, and the cinders were loaded aboard wagons to be spread on all of the town's streets.[14]

During the next eight years, the city of Merrill watched with pleasure as the Tule Lake Basin continued to grow. Homesteaders were moving onto land reclaimed from Tule Lake, and in the northeastern corner of the basin a new community known as Malin was founded. Then in 1920 a second major fire struck the city. On May 7th, the *Klamath Record* reported:

> Merrill suffered a disastrous fire at three o'clock Thursday morning when the Merrill Opera House, the Frazier Pool Hall, the Hartelrode restaurant and the old Murphy building, next to the warehouse of the Merrill Mercantile establishment were entirely consumed. The opera house belonged to John Houston of Klamath Falls. The building occupied by the pool room belonged to Frank Bloomingcamp ... The Anderson store across the street west of the pool hall was scorched and plate glass windows broken. The bank, garage, and furniture store across the street south of the fire suffered a similar loss.[15]

Once again the city bounced back, but the next year, in 1921, a major fire struck for the third time. The *Klamath Daily Record* recorded the event.

> A fire that started in Dewey's confectionery store at Merrill shortly before 4 o'clock Sunday morning destroyed the store, Offield and Ratliff's meat market, Murray's barber shop, city hall, fire house, Wrights new pharmacy, and damaged the post office building. The flames were checked at the Riverside Hotel only after a hard fight.
>
> The fire was not discovered until it had gained good headway and the hose was rescued from the fire hall

just in time to save its being consumed by the flames, which probably meant the saving of the balance of the town.[16]

The city was rebuilt and for the next three decades Merrill was spared major disasters. By the 1930s, improvements in the city's volunteer fire department, under the leadership of Ben Faus, helped it earn a high degree of respect from other communities in the Klamath Basin.[17]

Merrill's economic growth was aided by the completion of the two railroads through the city in the early 1930s. The Southern Pacific was the first to complete a line. The Merrill siding, though, was constructed on the south side of Lost River, and about one third of a mile from city center. The Great Northern (today the Burlington Northern) came through several years later, but built its siding just three blocks north of Front Street (Highway 39).

The 1930s also marked the beginning of Merrill's largest yearly social event. In 1934 the annual Klamath Basin Potato Festival was inaugurated, and each year since then it has celebrated the end of the potato harvest. Activities include a community dance, city parade, coronation of a queen, exhibits, and a Harvest Ball.[18]

During the 1940s, World War II touched the lives of nearly every Merrill citizen as their sons and daughters left to serve in the armed forces and in jobs that supported the war effort. At the close of the decade, the town had another brief brush with disaster, when on November 29, 1949 the elementary school burned down. It had been built out of brick in 1911 and for many years housed classes for grades from one to twelve. Later, when a new high school was constructed on Front Street, it also served elementary level students.[19] In a tradition of rebirth, begun back in 1911 with Merrill's first major fire, the school was soon rebuilt and the new building was dedicated on January 25, 1951.[20]

The decade of the fifties was a bright and prosperous era for Merrill. Its population nearly made the magic 1,000-mark, and its businesses were well patronized by basin residents. However, by the 1960s growth leveled off and a number of Merrill's retail outlets began to disappear. The shopping centers of Klamath Falls had lured many residents away from local businesses that were not able to offer the variety of goods found in larger stores. Other changes also took place. The students of Merrill and Malin attended Lost River High School and by the late 1970s declining enrollment and a reorganization of the school district saw the closure of Merrill's junior high school.

Today, as the Tule Lake Basin's oldest town, Merrill has an air of maturity and wisdom. Its quiet tree-lined streets are unpretentious. The pace of life is slow but not backward. Its role as a town is much broader now. Though its business community is smaller than it once was, it remains viable. The town is a comfortable home to many older residents who are content to stay rather than cope with the frenzy of larger cities, and it has become a bedroom community for commuters to outlying areas, including Klamath Falls. In many ways it matches the style of town founded by Nathan and Nancy Merrill back in 1894.

In the 1890s, another important family arrived in the Tule Lake Basin. M.L. Coppock, his wife Alice, and their two daughters, Margie and Blanche, moved north from Watsonville, California in 1898. Coppock had been a nurseryman there and he was seeking a region of the country that offered greater opportunities for both farming and hunting. Through inquiry, they found they could homestead land on The Peninsula at the southeast end of Tule Lake. The section of land they choose was located south of Prisoner's Rock and was known at the time as the Sand Strip.[21] In 1899, Coppock moved his family into a small cabin. Two years later, in 1901, the Coppocks barged lumber down from Merrill and built a five-room house. Here two additional children, Charles and Irene, were born.

Coppock selected an ideal location for farming. The land was fertile and in a sheltered area between Prisoner's Rock and Scorpion Point. It was on the western side of a huge bay (soon named Coppock Bay), and the even temperature of the water helped to keep frost from forming on vegetables and fruit grown on the Coppock farm. The Coppocks became famous for the fruits and vegetables that they grew, and people traveled from as far north as Klamath Falls to buy apples, peaches and pears.[22]

In addition to his skills as a farmer, Milo Coppock was well known for his ability as a hunter and trapper. His ingenious methods for hunting waterfowl were legendary. At one time, he trained cattle to feed in the marshland around his homestead. He then used them as a blind to get within shooting distance of ducks and geese that had landed in the lake or among the tule reeds near the bank.

His hunting and trapping expeditions often took him some distance from his homestead. During the bitterly cold and snowy winter of 1906 he joined with trapper Arthur Crawford and traveled some thirty-five miles southwest to Medicine Lake. Because of the weather and poor hunting, the men ran out of supplies sooner than expected and they began an arduous trip back to Tule Lake. On the way they became separated. Crawford was forced to turn back because of heavy snow and died before he could reach shelter at Medicine Lake. Coppock struggled on until he reached the Lava Beds. Working his way east and north along the edge of Tule Lake, he finally returned to his homestead. There he met his wife, but because of his ragged condition she did not recognize him. According to legend she leveled a gun at him, ordering the gaunt stranger to leave. It wasn't until he spoke that Mrs. Coppock realized this mere skeleton of a man was her husband. [23]

The Coppocks witnessed many changes in the Tule Lake Basin while they occupied their Sand Strip homestead. With the development of Merrill and Malin as community centers for local residents, boats began to regularly ply the waters of Tule Lake. One of the most popular was a boat known as the "Fairy," which transported passengers between the two communities and made excursions across the lake.[24] Gravel quarried from the Peninsula was barged north to be used on roadways, and the Coppocks made frequent trips on the lake to ship their produce to market. For several years, they lived in a houseboat at the mouth of Lost River while their children attended school in Merrill.[25]

Pleasure boat excursions were popular on Tule Lake, often taking passengers as far south as The Peninsula, Coppock Bay and the Lava Beds. Though most of the trips were scenic and uneventful, several courted disaster. The Klamath Falls *Evening Herald* of October 4, 1911 reported:

> Great excitement prevailed in the Malin colony Sunday ... seventeen persons were lost on a gasoline launch ... Tule Lake was stormy, and high waves and whitecaps were rolling up. The party was expected back before sunset, but when darkness set over the stormy waters and there was no sign of the launch, several relatives and friends of the excursionists were running around on the shore, shouting and calling in the darkness, in vain. The launch (had) broke(n) down when the party

reached about the middle of the lake, and the waves were drifting the helpless vessel towards the peninsula. A merciful high wave threw the boat away up on the dry shore with all excursionists safe. The men of the expedition started on foot in search of help, and late in the evening secured from a ranchman the necessary wagons to take the "castaways" home. It is next to a miracle that no lives were lost. [26]

After the Reclamation Service began to drain Tule Lake in 1907, commercial and private boats gradually began to disappear. Yet even in 1917, the southern end of the lake was still navigable. An indication of the depth of the water in Coppock Bay at the time can be still seen on the eastern side of Prisoner's Rock (also known as The Petroglyphs). There Milo Coppock's son, Charles, painted an American flag while standing in a small boat that he had rowed from his home. The flag was a statement of his patriotic support for the United States' involvement in World War One. Soon after he painted the flag, Charles ran off to enlist in the Marine Corps.[27] Though painted in 1917, the flag is still clearly visible and is located twenty to twenty-five feet above the lava formation's base. The Coppock family continued to run their farm on the Sand Strip until 1923, and then sold their property to Hugh Williams. The Coppocks moved to Merrill, where Mr. Coppock died the next year, on May 3, 1924.[28]

Not all settlers in the Tule Lake and Lower Klamath basins were as successful as J. Frank Adams, the Merrills and the Coppocks. It was not uncommon for individual farmers and ranchers to work a piece of basin land for several years and then be driven out by crop failure or loss of stock. At least one town suffered a similar fate. In 1905, amid expectations for quick growth, a town sprang up at the northern end of White Lake and was named White Lake City. But the hopes of its residents and investors were dashed several years later when the projected development and rush for land did not occur.

White Lake City had its origins in a string of unusual events. In 1903, J. Frank Adams's dredge completed the widening of the channel from Lower Klamath to White Lake. This larger channel provided a steady supply of water for the Van Brimmer canal and made it possible for barges and boats to travel between the two lakes. The result was that land around the lake became more attractive for commercial development.

Meanwhile, rumors began to circulate that land on the Klamath Indian Reservation would be opened to white homesteading. The origin of the rumor seemed to be based on a precedent established by the federal government in the 1890s when it opened a section of Indian land in Oklahoma, known as the Cherokee Strip, for white settlement. In 1905 Bert Hall, a recent resident of Denver, Colorado, was on a fishing trip in Southern California. There he met an individual who informed him of the rumor related to the Klamath Reservation. Hall was in transition, having sold a business in Denver, and was now looking for a new location. The rumor sparked his interest, and he saw an opportunity to strike out on a new business venture. Hall met with the man a second time and gave him some money as payment for property in a prospective town.[29]

The rumor had spread to other parts of the country as well and by the fall of 1904, the Oklahoma and Oregon Townsite Company was organized. The name "Oklahoma" was included to suggest that the Klamath Reservation land rush would follow a pattern similar to that in Oklahoma, where towns sprang up overnight. Representatives of the company arrived in Klamath Falls in September. They quickly discovered they had been misinformed about the land openings on the Klamath Reservation. Faced with the possibility of returning the advance money they had received for the townsites, the representatives of the Oklahoma and Oregon Townsite Company looked around the Lower Klamath Basin for available property. On September 15th, the *Klamath Republican* reported on their activities:

> J.E. Loy, President, L.G. West, Secretary, and F.T. Cook, Treasurer of the Oklahoma and Oregon Townsite Company, have been in the city for the past two weeks looking for a site on which to lay out a town. (They) claim to be incorporated with a capital stock of $75,000. They have secured an option on 350 acres of land belonging to C.N.F. Armstrong, on Lower Klamath Lake, south (east) of Merrill. The purchase price is to be $10 an acre.

> The stated object and purpose of this company is to build a city in Klamath County. Their plan is to sell certificates of stock at $15 per share, $10 to be paid when the stock is issued and $5 to be paid on notice from the secretary, or before May 1, 1905. Each

certificate holder will be entitled to one lot in the town for each share of stock he holds, and his pro rata of the profits derived from the sale of the reserved lots. No person can purchase more than three shares from the company.

The town is to be opened on or before May 1st, 1905, or during the Lewis and Clark Exposition, to be held at Portland beginning May 1st, 1905 ... They believe that this mutual plan, together with the great natural advantages should give the town from 5000 to 10,000 population from the start.[30]

In the spring of 1905, the land was surveyed by Donald J. Zumwalt and recorded in Klamath County on May 16. The Oklahoma and Oregon Townsite Company printed up hundreds of brochures and began a nationwide advertising campaign for the new "boom town" on the Oregon-California border. Town lots were sold for $15 apiece and transactions accelerated when it was rumored that the McCloud Railroad would be routed through White Lake City. Thanks to slick brochures and fast-talking salesmen, the company made over $12,000 during the first few months of its operation. A letter to the editor of the *Klamath Republican*, dated September 28, 1905, illustrated some of the promotional hype.

Many strangers have been within our gates during the past few months and after careful survey of our favored Klamath basin (they) predict its great future.

We all know the place in commerce occupied by the Sugar Beet. The Sugar Beet King of Colorado tells us there are no better conditions in the world for the growth of this necessary article than exist here in Klamath country ... If currant (sic) reports are true we will soon see the first ten miles of the Government canal construction work begun.

Strangers continue to appear on the streets of Whitelake City, all with the same comment, "what an opportunity for business."

Signed: Whitelaker [31]

During the next five years, a few buildings were constructed at the townsite, including "two grocery stores, a hardware store, a butcher hop and a newspaper (office)."[32] At its peak, the town had about 200 inhabitants.

Bert Hall, who had been lured to Klamath Falls by the rumor of free Indian land, was one of White Lake City's biggest investors. He spent more than $5,000 on a building that housed a newspaper he founded called the *White Lake City Times*.[33] Later, when a history of White Lake City was being compiled, Hall was quoted as saying: "If you mention White Lake ... please say that I was one of the suckers, not one of the promoters."[34] Five years after it was founded, The *Klamath Republican* reported on January 20, 1910: "This new metropolis bore the euphonious name of White Lake City ... more recently having been christened "Lemon City." There are no more disgraceful pages in the annals of Klamath County than those bearing the history of the rise and fall of this piece of fraud."[35]

By 1919, White Lake City was deserted. Most of the former residents moved to nearby Merrill or to Klamath Falls. On March 9, 1955 the Klamath County Commissioners officially removed White Lake City from its register of townsites, ending its brief life as a basin community.

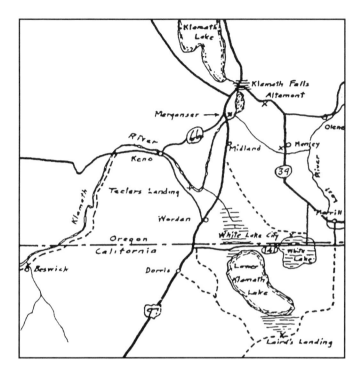

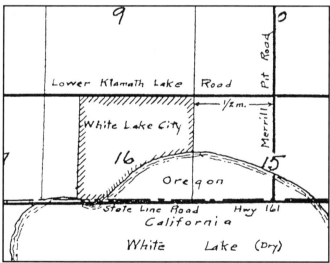

Maps showing location of White Lake City, Oregon.
*(Devere Helfrich, Klamath Echoes, No. 15,
Klamath County Historical Society)*

Cut made by J. Frank Adams linking   Lower Klamath and White lakes. *(Photo courtesy Klamath County Museum)*

Steamer "Klamath" at the Merrill, Oregon landing in1906.
(Photo courtesy Klamath County Museum)

Top and bottom: two views of Tule Lake circa 1900 to 1904, prior to reclamation. *(Photos courtesy Bureau of Reclamation)*

The boat "Fairy" on Tule Lake in 1918. It carried both passengers and freight. *(Photo courtesy Louis Kalina)*

A swim in Tule Lake. *(Photo courtesy Bureau of Reclamation)*

M.L. Coppock home on the "Sand Strip" at the southern end of Tule Lake. *(Photo courtesy Herald and News)*

Flag painted on Prisoner's Rock in 1917 by Charles Coppock. At the time the water level of Tule Lake was four feet below the bottom of the flag. *(Photos by author)*

Merrill, Oregon in the early 1900s—between fires!
(Photo courtesy Klamath County Museum)

Merrill, Oregon at Main & Front Streets in 2002.
(Photo by author)

CHAPTER 9

MALIN - BOHEMIANS IN THE WEST

The measured growth of Merrill and the boom and bust of White Lake City did not end efforts to build communities within the Tule Lake Basin—nor did it end J. Frank Adams's enthusiasm for projects that supported growth and change. In March of 1907, he joined in partnership with Charles L. Moore, E.P. McCornack, Alexander Martin and his son, Alexander, Jr. and Rufus S. Moore to form a corporation to promote land sales and settlement, principally in the area around the northern end of Tule Lake. Formally incorporated on August 27, 1907 as the Lakeside Company, their first purchase was 6,500 acres of land from the Tule Lake Land and Livestock Company. They paid $90,000 for the property, which amounted to about $14 an acre.[1] The land, owned by Jesse Carr Seale, the daughter of Jesse D. Carr, was located at the north end of Tule Lake and ran from a mile west of Adams Point to about a mile and a half east of Bevins Hill (now called Turkey Hill). Much of the property was already supplied by irrigation water from the Adams canal, and the federally sponsored Klamath Reclamation Project was in its early stages of construction. Reclamation Bureau plans included draining Tule Lake and building a system of canals that would link the area with Lost River and Upper Klamath Lake. The directors of the Lakeside Company knew that the combination of available irrigation water and the fertility of the soil would lure people to their property.

In preparing the land for sale, the Lakeside Company reserved 160 acres at the base of Bevan's Point for a town site, destined to become the community of Malin. The rest of the property was divided into farm plots that were generally 40 acres in size. At the time, this was thought to be the average amount of land necessary to support a farm family. Most of the farm lots were to be sold for $1600, at $40 an acre.[2] Once the land was mapped, surveyed and divided, the company began to promote its sale. Two years after incorporation, the Lakeside Company made connections with its greatest source of customers, a Czechoslovakian community headquartered in Omaha, Nebraska. Once again J. Frank Adams would play a major role in basin settlement.

The Czechoslovakians living in Omaha, Nebraska comprised one of many communities of immigrants who had come to the United States to start a new life, free from the political unrest of their homeland. Though some of the people in the Omaha community were second-generation, most were recent arrivals to the United States. Their roots in Europe could be traced to Russia and Czechoslovakia, where ethnically they identified themselves as Slovaks, Moravians, and Bohemians (In the United States the Czechs were often called Bohemians, a term which ignored the fact that many came from the two other principal regions of Czechoslovakia: Moravia and Slovakia). In their native country, they read brochures printed by American railroad companies which offered reduced rates for transportation to the mid and far-west, and railroad land for sale that could be transformed into productive farms. They also received letters from friends and relatives attesting to the availability of jobs and the fertility of the American soil. The Czechs emigrated to the United States by the thousands. Some became farmers, while others moved to American cities to take up trades learned in Czechoslovakia that included carpentry, cabinet making, tailoring, bricklaying, blacksmithing, and shoemaking.

In 1908 an agricultural magazine called *The Hodspodar*, published in Omaha, Nebraska for Czechoslovakian immigrants, advocated that a colony of Czechs be established in the far west. Response to the article was enthusiastic and the Bohemian Colonization Club was organized. Each person who joined paid an initiation fee of $10 and another $10 per month to finance the search for a colony site.[3] Under the direction of *Hodspodar*, the Colonization Club sent scouts to western Canada, the western United States, and Mexico to look for suitable land.

One of the men sent out by the Bohemian Colonization Club was Frank Klabzuba. He traveled to Canada in early 1909, where he looked in the provinces of Alberta and British Columbia for possible sites. Then he heard about land available in Butte Valley, south of Klamath Falls, that was owned by the Southern Pacific Railroad. Deciding that the prospects were worth the trip, he arrived in Butte Valley on March 15, but found the land unsuitable. Klabzuba went on to Klamath Falls. There he met C.S. Moore, who suggested that he contact J. Frank Adams of the Lakeside Land Company. Klabzuba took a stage to Merrill where he contacted the Adams ranch. The next day, J. Frank Adams took him on a tour of the company's property, and he was soon convinced that this was an ideal location for a Czechoslovakian settlement.

In the meantime, another scouting party sent out by the Colonization Club had arrived in Northern California. The men in this group included Vac Vostroil, Frank Zumpfe, and A.J. Sobotka. Like Frank Klabzuba, they had read the Southern Pacific Railroad advertisements for land in Butte Valley and were on an inspection tour. Klabzuba received word of their presence and traveled to Weed, California to meet them. He convinced the three men to accompany him to Klamath Falls. They were met by Will Adams, one of J. Frank Adams's sons, and were taken out to inspect the Tule Lake land. After their tour, Vostroil, Zumpfe and Sobotka agreed with Frank Klabzuba that this would be an ideal spot for colonization. However, the men concurred that they were obligated to continue their search and then return to Omaha as soon as possible with a report.[4]

A month later, the Czech scouting parties began to return to Omaha to announce their findings. As each report was made, the leaders of the Bohemian Colonization Club listened with care. Weighing the information, they decided that the land owned by the Lakeside Company property had strong possibilities and they passed this information on to club members. In August of 1909, nearly seventy men prepared to leave for the Klamath Basin and Tule Lake.

Meanwhile, an advance party left Omaha and arrived in Klamath Falls the first week of September. Their purpose was to conduct a final inspection of the Lakeside property and to make arrangements for major segments of the club membership to look at the land and consider purchase (no member had an obligation to buy at a site selected by the club and could opt out if they so chose).

On September 7, 1909, *The Evening Herald* of Klamath Falls published an interview with J. Frank Adams. In the article, Adams stated that "Arrangements have just been completed for the colonization of the Lakeside tract by 160 Bohemians with their families." He went on to say that the colony had intended to start from Omaha on the first of August, "but their departure has been delayed until the 16th of this month."[5]

On Saturday, September 25th, sixty members of the Colonization Club arrived by train. Their journey had taken them from Omaha to Sacramento and then north to Klamath Falls. They were met by J. Frank Adams, who had arranged an assortment of stage coaches and wagons to transport the Czechs to the settlement site. It was a gala event, replete with formal greetings, press coverage, and a photographer to record the festivities. *The Evening Herald* proclaimed with enthusiasm:

> Saturday night there arrived here sixty Bohemians, making a total of seventy-five that have come here during the past month. Anyone who reaches the conclusion that they are not a thrifty, up-to-date, progressive aggregation will change their minds if they have occasion to meet any of them. They are practical farmers. They have adopted modern methods in finding homes in the West, and every move that has been made savors of the practices followed by large corporations seeking to enter upon a policy of expansion.[6]

The *Herald* also interviewed A.J. Balaun, the chairman of the Bohemian Colonization Committee, who discussed the purpose and character of the people seeking a settlement site.

> Our club was organized for the purpose of finding homes in the West for the members. Only Bohemians [Czechs] can belong to it. We will, of course, be glad to have Americans or any other nationality for our neighbors. We are not going to isolate ourselves. All we want is to be a community of law-abiding citizens. Nothing less will satisfy us. We propose to become part of the community in which we may locate and always take an active, intelligent part in its affairs. Our people are progressive, up-to-date farmers, and will prove a valuable addition to the population of any county. We will pay our bills and obey all laws, and so conduct ourselves as to merit the esteem and confidence of our fellow citizens. That is the standard on which we seek homes among you, and future events will go to show that every principle will be lived up to.[7]

Adams transported the Czechoslovakians to Merrill, where they spent the night. The next morning they were taken out to the Lakeside Company property, which began about six miles east of

Merrill. On the last leg of the journey, the sixty potential settlers passed the shimmering waters of Tule Lake on their right. To their left was the Adams canal and around them were scattered farm plots that were already under irrigation. It was obvious to many of the Czechs that the land was productive, and it didn't take long for many of them to decide that this would be an ideal site for their colony. At noon, the party stopped and ate lunch at Bevans Point (today known as Turkey Hill). From the elevated vantage point, the men began to pick out land they wished to purchase. That evening, they returned to Merrill where they spent their second night. The next day the Czechoslovakian colonists drove back to Klamath Falls where about one third of the members filed for deeds.[8] On September 30, 1909, the *Klamath Republican* reported:

> With the closing of nineteen contracts by the Lakeside company for land in the Lakeside tract ... the colonization movement in Klamath County has started. It is expected that fully forty out of the sixty who came here will settle this tract ... The land purchased by the Bohemians is all under irrigation, and with these thrifty people in control of it, doubtless in the near future it will be one of the '"show" places of the county ... To J. Frank Adams is due the credit for bringing this condition of affairs about.[9]

The Czechs busily went about gathering their families and moving on to their newly purchased property. But in spite of the highly touted value of the Tule Lake land, the first wave of settlers found it to be anything but hospitable. The winter of 1909-1910 was unusually cold. All but one of the families had to winter over in tents and crudely built shacks. Only the Frank Zumpfe family had any type of permanent dwelling. They had purchased part of the land once owned by Jim Bevans and it included his old ranch house. Throughout the first winter, the Zumpfes were continually hosting families in need of shelter.[10]

Though the Czechs had a difficult first year, they were well treated by the Lakeside Company and their neighbors, J. Frank Adams and William C. Dalton. Adams personally supervised a majority of the 40 to 60 acre land purchases, and he extended liberal credit terms. Frequently he required no down payment and deferred installments until after the first crops came in. During the lean winter and spring months, Adams delivered butchered hogs, cured hams, and sides of bacon to the Czechs.

The new settlers were able to borrow wagons and other equipment from Adams and William C. Dalton while they built their homes. Some of the Czechs were given work on the Adams ranch and on the spread managed by W. C. Dalton for the Tule Lake Land and Livestock Company. Others went to Klamath Falls to work on the railroad. Though Adams and Dalton never asked for compensation for their help, every Czechoslovakian family paid their debts once the crops came in.[11]

The land settled by the Czechs was fertile and productive, but it had to be cleared and leveled before farming could begin. One of the most difficult tasks for the settlers was the removal of great stands of sagebrush, some as high as ten feet. Most of the clearing had to be done by hand, though later Adams developed a mobile brush remover that resembled a large steel-tined rake on wheels. During the early years, large piles of sage brush could be seen burning day and night throughout the northeastern end of the basin.

Preparation of the land was not the only problem the Bohemians faced. Once the ground was tilled and the crops planted, there was always the risk that a heavy wind would blow away the seed or that a late spring frost would kill the young plants. Predators were also a problem. Great flocks of birds would swoop into a field and clean out planted seed within a matter of hours. Jackrabbits by the thousands ravished the crops, nibbling young, tender blades of wheat to the ground. In addition, the weather was a constant problem. Not all of the farmers used the Adams canal to irrigate their land, relying instead on seasonal rain. Many found that dry farming wasn't suitable to the Tule Lake Basin because of the sporadic shift from wet to dry years.

The Czechs at least found a solution to the jackrabbit problem. They discovered that Klamath County was offering a bounty of five cents for each set of ears taken from a killed rabbit. With this incentive, they organized large-scale hunts and killed jackrabbits by the thousands. Not only did this help reduce the destruction of their crops but it also provided badly needed food for the dinner table. Rabbit meat became a common commodity not only for human consumption but for the chickens, dogs, and cats of the Czechoslovakians as well.

In general, life was hard for these early pioneers of the Tule Lake Basin. Rudolph Paygr, the first child born in the Czechoslovakian colony, remembered his mother telling him "she cried for a week after seeing the land of sagebrush and the loneliness." Paygr also remembered his mother said she saw "snow filter through the cracks of the house" and "buckets of water freeze solid during the night."[12]

Agnes Drazil vividly remembered her first years in the basin:

> I was afraid of the new country we came to. I would have gone home but there was no money. It was all in the land. I couldn't ask for things I needed in the grocery store. I didn't know the words, but I knew how to work. I helped grub sagebrush and later helped to harvest the crops. I had nine children and when I came in from the fields I didn't know what to do first, milk the cow or feed my family or clean the house.[13]

In spite of the hardships, the hardworking Czechoslovakians made their farms prosperous. Only a handful failed and returned to their former homes. Gradually their crops improved and they experimented with potatoes, beets, wheat, oats, rye, and hay as well as a variety of garden vegetables. Some raised beef and dairy cattle. Their hard work paid off and could be seen in the neat, well-built farm homes and sturdy barns that began to appear on the Lakeside land.

During the summer of 1910, a move was begun to settle the 160-acre town site that had been established by the Lakeside Company. Walter W.S. Adams, the brother of J. Frank Adams, constructed the first commercial building. The two-story structure housed the Pioneer Grocery Store downstairs and a hall upstairs for meetings and dances. It was also used as the community's first school.[14]

One year later, an effort was undertaken to attract some kind of industry or major business to the town site. In July of 1911, R.M. Osborn, head of a large dairy cow operation in San Luis Obispo, was asked to visit the community. He had been traveling through the area, looking at potential sites for a dairy and cheese factory.[15] Although the Czech community was not selected by Osborn, they capitalized on his idea and in the early 1920s built their own cheese and produce facility.

When the residents of the area that would soon be called Malin celebrated their second year as a settlement in the fall of 1911, they also faced a dilemma. As more children were born into the community, and new colonists arrived from the outside, they struggled to maintain a balance between the customs of Czechoslovakia and the infusion of American society. On September 7, 1911, the *Klamath Republican* discussed how the Czechs were going about solving this problem.

> With the rapid growth of the Malin colony and the constant arrival of more families from the East and Middle West, the colonists have felt the need of a means of perpetuating the native language. Arrangements have been made for a Bohemian school, to instruct the growing generation in the language spoken by their parents. That they will also be taught the language of their new land is shown by the fact that a school house has just been finished, and the fall term will open early this month.[16]

The Lakeside Land Company's town site grew slowly during its first years. Between 1910 and 1911, Walter Adams's store was joined by the Bohemian Hall (also known as the Sokal Hall) and the Malin School, which was built for $2,000 and situated about two blocks east.[17] To improve commercial trade and transportation, a dock was constructed in 1912 on the shore of Tule Lake (which lapped the southern edge of the town). For a while, goods and passengers were able to travel west to Merrill and south to The Peninsula and the Lava Beds. But the United States Reclamation Service was already beginning to drain the lake and the dock was only temporary.

In February of 1913, a new commercial business was opened and came to be known as The Kalina Store. Its owners, Alois and Marie Kalina, were destined to become major leaders in the development of the town site.

Alois Kalina (who went by "A" Kalina) and Marie Podlesak were both from the Bohemian section of Czechoslovakia. He was born in the town of Chotutice on February 9, 1880, and she was born in Spule on October 21, 1883. Alois had been unhappy with the heavy control exercised by both the military and church. He left Czechoslovakia in 1904. The next year, he and Marie were married in Vienna, Austria. Soon after the wedding they left for the United States and settled in Chicago. There on September 18, 1905 their first child, Vaclav, was born.[18]

In Czechoslovakia, Alois had been trained as a watchmaker and machinist, but once in the United States he engaged in many different occupations. For a while he worked in an iron foundry that made dragline shovels for the Panama Canal. Next he was involved in door-to-door sales, and finally, with Marie as his partner, he went into the saloon business. Alois dispensed the beer and Marie prepared food that was offered free during lunch hours to attract customers.[19]

The Kalinas were not satisfied with life in Chicago. When word spread among the Czechoslovakian community about the efforts of the Bohemian Colonization Club, the Kalinas decided to join. Alois was among the first sixty-six to travel to the Lakeside property at Tule Lake, and he purchased 40 acres at a site about three quarters of a mile east of the present town of Malin. The Kalinas tried farming for four years, but soon became tired of struggling with the land. They sold their property and moved to the town site. There, on February 13, 1913, Alois and Marie opened The Kalina Store, which sold general merchandise.

The Kalinas were good and generous business people. They freely extended credit, and when their customers were short on cash, they accepted eggs and farm produce in exchange for goods. Over time, Kalina became a powerful force in the community, and his contributions could be found in many areas. When a name was being solicited for the town, he suggested that it be called "Malin." Later, when queried about his choice, he said: "I named the town for a co-operative town in Czechoslovakia, a town surrounded with fruits and vegetables, green and beautiful. It was my dream that our little town here would be like it."[20] Another reason for Kalina selecting the name "Malin" was that horseradish was Malin, Czechoslovakia's main crop—which also grew well in the soil surrounding the new town.

Believing in the future of Malin, Kalina purchased a sizable number of blocks within the city limits. Some of the land he would later sell, but he also generously donated six blocks to the city for a high school, two blocks for a grade school, one lot for a jail, and two lots for a Presbyterian church.[21] At each step in Malin's growth, the Kalinas were present and played a major role.

Alois Kalina was the primary force behind the installation of the first telephone lines in 1915. Three years later, he joined with four other men and built the Malin Milling Company, which processed locally grown grain into flour. In the same year, he made plans to expand his commercial business. Construction was started on a new building, located across Broadway Street from his original store. The impressive structure was made out of native lava rock and was completed in 1920. It housed a bank and a general store that offered hardware goods, groceries, clothing, prescription drugs, and stationery.[22]

In 1919, an effort was initiated throughout the Klamath Basin to promote the construction of a system of permanent all-weather roads. An organization known as the Good Roads Association traveled around Klamath County promoting road improvements and asking citizens to support a two-percent increase in property tax evaluation. When the association held a meeting in Malin in April, Alois Kalina was present. During the discussion period after the presentation, he pointed out that "the people of Malin are always in favor of good roads and do not object to taxation for that purpose." But Kalina added that he thought "it is now time to quit talking about good roads and go to building them!"[23] Three years later in 1922, the first all-weather road was completed between Malin and Klamath Falls.[24]

The 1920s was a decade of prosperity and growth for both Malin and the Kalinas. In 1921, a drive spearheaded by Alois Kalina was successful in bringing electricity to the town. In the same year the Malin Cheese and Produce Company was founded, which provided both jobs and an economic base badly needed by the town. In addition, a high school was constructed, and by the mid-1920s Malin was graced with a church, two brick schools, a flour mill, cheese factory, post office, bank, dance hall, theater, blacksmith shop, various stores, a hotel, and several saloons. By the 1920s the Kalinas could also boast of their own growth, for their family now consisted of four children: Vaclav, Louis, Emma, and Rudolph. As soon as they were old enough, each child was put to work in the family business.

The year 1922 was a milestone for Malin. Its population numbered 151, which was exactly one more person than the minimum required by the State of Oregon for incorporation. Alois Kalina traveled to the county court house in Klamath Falls and personally paid the incorporation fee. The vote for incorporation was held on February 18, 1922, and the proposal received nearly unanimous approval. On February 22nd Malin was officially incorporated. Kalina was elected mayor, a position that he held for the next twenty-five years.[25]

As each year passed, new businesses were added to the community. In 1923, Tom Shannessy founded the town's first newspaper, The Malin Progress. Through a bit of complicated maneuvering, the paper went through several owners and finally ended up being published in Klamath Falls. By then it had "the distinction of being the only co-operatively owned farmers' paper in the Pacific Northwest."[26] A review of the articles published by the *Malin Progress* indicated it was a scrappy little paper, willing to take on the government, utilities, or any other organization that seemed to be working against the interests of farmers. In the 1930s, Malin was served by another paper, *The Malin Enterprise*, but it soon died, a victim of the Depression and low circulation.

In the late 1920s, Malin's Czechoslovakian heritage and its continued interest in Czech culture saw the town selected as the site for the Grand Pacific Sokol Festival, held between July 3rd and 5th, 1928. Sokol was a form of team calisthenics started in Czechoslovakia by Dr. Miroslav Tyrs. Dr. Tyrs believed that being physically fit was fundamental to a country's strength. His basic premise was that "not a glorious history, but (an) active energetic present is (the only) guarantee of a Nation's future."[27] Many Czech communities in the U.S. continued to practice Sokol and the festival in Malin hosted teams from throughout the west.

Malin also benefited from the opening of Tule Lake land to homesteading. The first eight homestead allotment periods, between 1917 and 1937, were concentrated at the northern end of the basin. Many were in the Malin area. This boosted commercial trade in town, and Malin and Merrill shared the honor of being the community centers for the early homesteaders.

Progressive change continued in Malin in the 1930s and 1940s, even under the burden of the Great Depression and World War II. In 1930, the Great Northern Railroad reached the town, and for nearly twenty years it contributed to the community's prosperity. The railroad siding at Malin became a distribution point for farm products and a receiving station for equipment and goods needed by farmers. However, after World War II, the economic impact of the railroad in Malin began to decline. With improved roads and modern trucks, farmers could ship their products directly to markets hundreds—even thousands—of miles away. Today the railroad only plays a minor role in the city's business community, and Malin is no longer a major distribution point for farm products.

The 1930s and 1940s brought other changes to Malin. In 1931, the city sank a deep well and constructed a municipal water system rated as best in the basin. In 1932, a sewage disposal plant was added, and eleven years later in 1943, the community started a fund to build a park. Construction began on both the park and a swimming pool in 1948. When completed, the "Malin Park and Recreation District" was the first park district established in the State of Oregon and had the first public swimming pool in Klamath County.

The period after World War II was a time of change for Malin. One by one the original Czechoslovakian settlers stepped aside, turning their farms and businesses over to their children. In 1947, Alois Kalina announced that he was retiring as mayor, after twenty-five consecutive years of service. When he was asked what he planned to do after such a long tenure, he replied modestly, "I'm going to take it easy."[28]

Though Alois Kalina would soon leave Malin and move to Portland, three of his four children remained to continue the family business and pursue their own interests. Only Rudy left. He moved to Eugene, where he owned and operated a soft drink bottling company. Louis Kalina bought the Malin Mercantile from his parents in 1947and named it Kalina "Food Market and Hardware." In 1951 he moved the hardware portion of the store two blocks up Broadway. Emma remained in the old stone building and ran a retail clothing business. In 1960 the Food Market was sold. As for Vaclav, he became involved in two business ventures: selling insurance and developing an entertainment center for the community.[29]

Vaclav Kalina's venture into the entertainment business began in 1924 when he purchased an old school from the Klamath County School District. The building was moved onto Broadway Street and was remodeled into a dance hall and movie theater. It was the era of silent films, and they became so popular in the basin that Vaclav showed feature movies at least three times a week in Malin, and once a week at the community center in Merrill. In 1930, he built a new movie house in Malin to accommodate the equipment needed to show "talking pictures." For the next twenty-five years, The Broadway Theater was popular among local residents. Riding on the crest of public interest in film entertainment, Kalina purchased the Marcha Theater in the city of Tulelake in 1948. But then in the mid-1950s, television came to the basin and it had a chilling effect on the movie business. In 1958, Vaclav sold both movie theaters; since that time, both have only been opened on occasion.

Vac Kalina may have been known for his movie houses, but he became famous throughout southern Oregon and Northern California for the big-name entertainment he featured in the Broadway Hall. Through skill and perseverance, he was able to get Malin included in the road circuit for the "big bands" of the thirties and forties. The likes of Phil Harris, Harry James, the Dorsey Brothers, Lawrence Welk and many others played to packed houses. People came from as far away as Alturas, Weed, and Lakeview. In 1940, the old converted school could no longer accommodate the crowds, so Vaclav tore it down and built a new Broadway Dance Hall next to his movie theater. For years it was the multi-purpose center for the community. All forms of entertainment took place there including dances, concerts, plays, and musicals. The smooth, well-varnished floor was used as a roller skating rink, and the building also hosted weddings, parties, and graduation ceremonies.

In 1984 Louis and Vaclav Kalina were still in Malin, carrying on the tradition established by their father. Louis had turned the hardware business over to Denny, his son, a number of years before, but he continued to work at the store and took an active part in running the business. Though Vaclav had long since stopped showing feature movies, he still ran his insurance company and dabbled in entertainment. There were no regularly scheduled groups performing in the Broadway Hall, but he did open the building on weekends for roller-skating, and occasionally for parties and dances. Both Louis and Vac were involved in a lifetime of community service and were part of the leadership that helped the city celebrate its 75th Anniversary on July 14th and 15th, 1984. Several of their children and grandchildren have remained in Malin, and there is little doubt that the Kalina tradition will continue for years to come.

Malin in the 1980s is a stable community. Hopes that it would become a major metropolis have long since disappeared, and local business establishments have been winnowed down to a small but healthy number. Yet, since its inception in 1909, Malin has maintained a spirit of unity unlike any other town in the region. The sense of "community" transcends Czechoslovakian heritage to include all people who have become residents. In 1959, Malin celebrated its fiftieth anniversary with a large celebration. Though it had a strongly Czech theme, residents from a variety of ethnic backgrounds helped plan and participate in the festival. It is a tradition that has continued through the 75th Anniversary Celebration.

What is the origin of the spirit of Malin? Clearly it is rooted in the common bond that created the Czechoslovakian colony in 1909. But it is also rooted in a willingness by its residents to reach out and support other members of the community. The spirit is still very much alive. It can be seen in the town's neat, tree-lined streets, in its well-kept homes, in the popular community park, in its swimming pool and public library. It can be seen when crisis befalls one of its citizens. For example, when a fire struck Buddy and Yvonne Booe's restaurant in July of 1981, local merchants, farmers, and townspeople raised $60,000 to help them rebuild. Another fund drive began almost immediately to help a family whose home had been destroyed by fire.[30] This unique bonding that can be seen in so many elements of life in Malin has created a community that will remain viable for years to come.

First major group of Czechoslovakian settlers gather on Bevans (Turkey) Hill in September, 1909 to survey land offered by the Lakeside Land Company. *(Photo courtesy Vac Kalina)*

Malin, Oregon in its infancy. *(Photo courtesy Vac Kalina)*

Malin Mercantile, later "Kalina Food Market and Hardware" under construction. *(Photo courtesy Tulelake-Butte Valley Fair, Museum of Local History)*

Above: The original Kalina "stone" building.
Below: Downtown Malin today. *(Photos by author)*

CHAPTER 10

RECLAMATION - A NEW LOOK FOR THE BASIN

No federal statute has had as great or as profound an effect upon the Klamath and Tule Lake Basins than the Newlands Reclamation Act. Authored by Francis G. Newlands, Representative from Nevada, and signed by President Theodore Roosevelt on June 17, 1902, this law stipulated that money collected by the government from the sale of federal lands in sixteen western states was to be placed in a fund designated for irrigation projects. In addition, land reclaimed from swamps and lakes under the Newlands Act was to be opened to homestead entry.[1] As a result of this law, the Klamath Project, an ambitious scheme involving three lakes, two major rivers, and an interconnecting network of man-made canals, was created. When the project was completed it was able to deliver a reliable and controlled source of water to hundreds of farmers in the Klamath and Tule Lake Basins, and reclaim large tracts of land submerged under Tule and Lower Klamath Lakes, opening them to farming.

In order to understand how the Newlands Act was applied to the Tule Lake Basin, it is necessary to review the unusual nature of the region's drainage system. As discussed in Chapter One, the source of Tule Lake's water begins only six miles to the east at Clear Lake, which is about 400 feet higher in elevation. Water flows into the Lost River at the north end of Clear Lake and then travels in a great irregular arc seventy miles north, west and then south before entering the Tule Lake Basin. During its course, Lost River travels through the Langell, Poe, and Lost River valleys. Each is broad and flat and without diversion dams or pumps, making canal irrigation of the surrounding fields impossible. The earliest farmers had to depend upon the unreliable seasonal rains to water their crops.

The geographic configuration of the areas through which Lost River flows is of particular importance. There is only a slight difference in elevation between the Langell, Poe, and Lost River valleys, and the plain running between Olene Gap and the Klamath River. During normal weather cycles, Lost River is placid, even sluggish. But during years of heavy snow and rainfall, the river, prior to reclamation, would overflow its banks.

Over time it cut a natural slough westward to join the Klamath River.

The concept of utilizing the unusual features of the Lost River drainage system did not begin with the Newlands Act. The first known effort was in 1868 when the Langell family moved to the valley that was later named after them. They began to re-channel Lost River, and their efforts led to the reclamation of nearly 4,000 acres of swamp land for farming and ranching.[2] In the 1870s, James Poe did much the same thing ten miles to the west and downstream from the Langells.

In 1871, the first large-scale project was formally envisioned. Jesse D. Carr and Jesse Applegate developed a plan to dig a canal between the Klamath and Lost rivers to irrigate about 350,000 acres of land in the basin. Due to the lack of sufficient funds and the Modoc War, the project was not carried out.[3] Then, within a six-year period, several irrigation projects were undertaken. The Linkville Water Ditch Company constructed the first in 1878. A headgate was constructed on the east bank of the Link River at a site near the outlet of Upper Klamath Lake. From there, a small canal was constructed that led to the town of Linkville, providing water for town lots. Later William Steele expanded the system. A larger canal was dug and it ran water southeast into the plains area between Linkville and Olene. Steele died in 1888 and the irrigation system was taken over by a group of investors, who formed the Klamath Falls Irrigation Company. They built an enlarged ditch known as the Ankeny Canal and provided water for about 4,000 acres of land. Meanwhile, in 1882 the Van Brimmer brothers cut a narrow channel east from White Lake to irrigate 4,000 acres of land in an area south and west of Lost River. In 1884 J. Frank Adams expanded the Van Brimmer system to the opposite side of Lost River. He constructed a large wood flume to carry the water over the river, and tied it into a canal designed to irrigate farmland at the southeast end of the Lost River Valley.

The irrigation projects developed by Steele, the Van Brimmers, and Adams were relatively small. They were immensely important, though, because they demonstrated that irrigation could make the land highly productive. What was needed was greater capital to finance a comprehensive system. The Newlands Act provided such a base.

In 1902, federal engineers were well aware of the potential for irrigation and reclamation in the Lost River and Klamath River drainage systems. But before the Newlands Act could be applied, a number of steps had to be taken. There were at least four privately owned canal systems in operation in the basin and they would have to be bought out. Water rights, currently held by California and Oregon, and riparian rights owned by settlers had to be obtained. Finally, there had to be documented support from local farmers and ranchers.[4]

In October of 1902, Frederick Haines Newell, the first director of the Reclamation Service, toured the Klamath Basin. He was impressed with its potential for reclamation and when he returned to Washington, D.C. he ordered several preliminary surveys. Engineer John G. Whistler conducted the first in October of 1903, and H.E. Green did another survey during the same year. In 1904, T.H. Humphreys completed an additional survey. The reports from all three engineers were in agreement. An irrigation and reclamation project would function well in the Lost River, Tule Lake, and Klamath Basin areas.[5]

Meanwhile local farmers and ranchers circulated petitions in support of reclamation. Leadership in this effort included both J. Frank Adams and William C. Dalton. The petition circulated stated:

> Resolved, That we, the citizens and land owners in the Klamath Basin in public meeting assembled for the purpose of considering the matter of requesting the Federal Government to construct irrigation works, are in favor of such construction by the Federal Government under the provisions of said act of Congress.[6]

In November of 1904, Reclamation Service Director Frederick Newell returned to the Klamath and Tule Lake Basins on another inspection tour. At a meeting held in Klamath Falls and attended by a large number of farmers and ranchers, Newell outlined the steps necessary for the project to be carried out. These included resolving all conflicting and vested water rights within the planned system; securing the rights to the shoreline of Lower Klamath and Tule lakes; convincing the states of California and Oregon to deed to the federal government all rights and title to the two lakes; enacting laws in both states permitting the lowering or raising of the lakes' water levels; and passing legislation in Congress permitting the Secretary of the Interior to order the draining of the lakes, thereby destroying the ability to navigate them.[7]

One by one, each step outlined by Newell began to fall into place. In January of 1905, the Oregon legislature deeded title to their segments of Tule Lake and Upper and Lower Klamath lakes. This act was followed in February by similar legislation passed in California, which relinquished ownership of Clear Lake, as well as its segments of Lower Klamath Lake and Tule Lake.[8] In addition, Congress passed legislation which gave the Reclamation Service power to end navigation on the four lakes.

Not all steps in the acquisition process went smoothly for the Reclamation Service. The first rough spot was with the Klamath Canal Company, which had been formed in May of 1904 and had acquired irrigation rights to much of the area targeted by the government. There is good evidence to suggest that the formation of this corporation was for speculative purposes rather than for serious construction. On the surface, the company gave every indication that it intended to build its own irrigation system. In a prepared statement to Poe Valley residents, the Klamath Canal Company's president said: "Our company claims it can offer a better proposition than can be offered by the government because it is a well known fact that private work can be done for much less than public work."[9] The Reclamation Service challenged the actions taken by the Klamath Canal Company, and for the next five months the two factions were caught in a web of litigation. Though basin residents were anxious for the project to begin, some elements of the community urged that the resolution of the Klamath Canal Company controversy be done with care. In an editorial, the *Klamath Republican* stated:

> The Klamath Canal Company has certain rights and these should be recognized. Because it may be considered to be in the way of the Government enterprise in a measure is no reason that it should be branded as a brigand and hounded and driven from the community; neither should those who espouse its cause, under the idea that it has some rights, be classed as outlaws.
>
> *The Republican* believes that if the Government plan of irrigation is carried out as is promised, and within the time approximated, that it will be better for the people

of Klamath County than any other system. But it does not believe it right for the Government to confiscate, injure or damage the property or rights of the Klamath Canal Company, or any other local institution, or person, without making due reparation.[10]

In January of 1905, the Klamath Canal Company announced it would proceed with its own construction, in spite of government efforts to block them.[11] Then in February the situation seemed to improve, and the company indicated an interest in selling out. The *Klamath Republican* reported:

The good news is authoritatively stated that a deal is practically consummated by which all differences are settled between the Government and the Klamath Canal Company.

Telegrams are now passing back and forth in the arrangement of the final terms of settlement. The same deal will include the interests of the Little Klamath Water Ditch Company, the Ankeny-Henley Ditch and all other water rights in the Klamath Basin.

The exact terms of the deal with the Klamath Canal Company have not been definitely settled, though there is scarcely a doubt that the matter will be amicably consummated before the next issue of the *Klamath Republican.*[12]

The matter was not "amicably consummated" as the *Republican* had hoped. The government offered the Klamath Canal Company $150,000 to purchase their irrigation rights, but the company wanted $500,000 (best estimates given at the time said that the company's irrigation rights were actually worth about $50,000).[13] The Reclamation Service then secured an injunction against the company, preventing them from taking water from any portion of Upper Klamath Lake and from the Link and Klamath rivers. Finally, in May of 1905, the company agreed to sell.[14] The Reclamation Service also concluded negotiations with other landholders and irrigation companies. When the proceedings were finally concluded, the government acquired the following holdings: the Klamath Falls Irrigation Company (Ankeny Canal) for $47,530.65, the Klamath Canal Company for $150,000, the Little Klamath Water Ditch Company (Adams

Canal) for $100,000, the Jesse D. Carr Land and Livestock Company (25,000 acres of land around Clear Lake), and the acquisition of the right-of-way for the Keno cut from Thomas McCormick for $10,000.[15]

There were several other rough spots that had to be dealt with. One involved confusion over estimated construction costs. Under the Newlands Act, the federal government underwrote reclamation projects, but the users were to pay the costs for the construction of the system serving their area. The problem was that most of these projects took years to complete, and it was difficult to determine what the actual construction cost would be. As a consequence, the fee assessed was usually an "estimate" of costs. This left many farmers feeling uneasy. Would they be assessed more when the project was completed? Why were there going to be differences in fees between sections in a project? Why couldn't the fee be established at a fixed rate? Would there be help for people who could not afford to pay the fee? To the first question, the government answered that the fee estimate would be all that the farmer would be charged. If the costs proved to be higher, the government would absorb them. But the answers to the other questions were not as easily resolved, and they were an area of contention until the end of the 1920s.

Two other problems developed during the sixth year of the Klamath Project's operation. In February of 1910, Secretary of the Interior Richard A. Ballinger announced that the Klamath Project would not expand its service into the Yonna Valley. This area was located north and slightly west of Bonanza, Oregon. The rationale was that the construction costs would be too high and that not enough people had signed up. This action brought a stinging rebuke from the *Klamath Republican*. In an article entitled "Farce Enacted by the Federal Government," the paper said:

> If ever there was a farce committed against the people of any section there certainly is one shown in the operations of the Reclamation Service in the Klamath Project during the past five years. Secretary Ballinger has now announced that the entire upper project is to be abandoned and practically everything except that covered by the gravity system in the lower project, thus reducing the acreage to about 138,000.

In the eyes of the world the government has simply
been playing horse with the people of this country and
it would look as if the land owners of the upper
country were fortunate in getting free from the grasp of
the government before they were burdened with
further expenses which they would be unable to
liquidate.[16]

In answering the *Republican's* charges, Secretary Ballinger
pointed out that the construction costs for the Upper Project
would run from $50 to $65 an acre, which was up to twice as
much as the rest of the Klamath Project. In addition, less than 60
percent of the land was under subscription. He also pointed out
that throughout the rest of the system, construction costs were
running from $5 to $15 more than original estimates, and that
the government was not in a position to absorb such costs.[17]
However, the issue was resolved in May of 1910. The rate of
subscription (people pledging to pay construction costs for
irrigation water) was up appreciably and the Reclamation Service
decided to go ahead with the Upper Project.[18]

The controversy over actions taken by Secretary of the Interior
Richard Ballinger did not end with the resolution of the Upper
Project issue. He was earning himself a reputation for supporting
private interests over federal wilderness protection, and for less
than enthusiastic support of expanding the federal reclamation
program. In Washington, D.C., Chief Forest Ranger Gifford
Pinchot was appalled at Ballinger's willingness to sell to private
companies land that had been set aside for federal protection by
former President Theodore Roosevelt. Ballinger fired Pinchot for
his criticism, and the Secretary became highly unpopular among
conservationists. Gifford Pinchot was not the only one critical of
Ballinger. Reclamation Service Director Frederick Haines Newell
was concerned about the Secretary's seeming lack of support for
expanding the federal reclamation program. In the bitter
acrimony that developed, Ballinger tried to get rid of Newell by
asking Congress to pass a bill placing the Army Engineering
Corps (today known as the Army Corps of Engineers) in charge of
all reclamation projects. The bill failed, Ballinger was eventually
dumped from the Taft Administration, and Newell remained at
the helm of the Reclamation Service. This action allowed the
Klamath Project to continue on schedule.

The actual construction of the Klamath Project took place in three major stages. The first involved diverting water from Upper Klamath Lake and the Link River by means of a head-works and tunnel just to the north of the city of Klamath Falls. A main canal leading from this tunnel would join a complex system of canals to serve farms as Far East as the Poe Valley and south through the Lost River Valley to Tule Lake. In the second stage, a dam was to be constructed at Clear Lake to impound floodwaters and regulate water taken from Lost River for irrigation purposes, and a series of irrigation canals were to be constructed to serve farms in the Langell and Poe Valley regions. Finally, the third stage called for the draining of Tule Lake and Lower Klamath Lake and opening land there for homesteading.[19]

On December 29, 1905 bids were opened in San Francisco for constructing the first phase of the project. This involved building the headgates and tunnel at the south end of Upper Klamath Lake and then constructing the "A" Canal to carry water east and south into the lower basin region.[20] The second phase began in September 1908. A dam at Clear Lake was built, more than doubling the lake's capacity from 10,000 to 25,000 acres and was completed in January of 1910.[21]

Meanwhile, work was begun on draining Tule and Lower Klamath Lakes. At Tule Lake, the draining process took place in phases. The first involved controlling the flow of Lost River into Tule Lake. Building a diversion dam four miles southwest of the town of Olene and digging a canal west to the Klamath River accomplished this. When completed in 1912, this system shut off most of Tule Lake's supply of water, sending it instead into the Klamath River drainage system.[22] Denied a steady flow of water, the level of Tule Lake began to recede through evaporation.

The second phase involved an ambitious but not overly successful plan to drain the waters of Tule Lake through a series of fractures in the lava at its southern end. The legend that Tule Lake had an underground drain had been in existence for years, but in 1907 several events occurred which prompted the Klamath Project to take the notion under serious consideration. The rain and snow in 1907 had been unusually heavy. Tule Lake's level was up considerably and farmland on its northern shore was flooded. Then, over a two-week period, local residents noted a two foot drop in the lake. William C. Dalton and J. Frank Adams conducted an investigation. As they searched the southern end of the lake, they discovered water flowing into several openings in the lava near Scorpion Point, on the western side of Coppock Bay. On December 5, the *Klamath Republican* reported the events that then transpired.

> This morning J. Frank Adams and wife, W.C. Dalton and wife, Chas. Beardsley, John Colwell and Fred Pope started for the place armed with picks and crowbars. They reached the spot about ten o'clock this morning and proceeded to work to see if anything could be done to increase the flow.
>
> The result is that after about five hours' work, clearing away the debris and prying open the rocks, a body of water measuring at least 200 second feet is rushing straight down into a gorge, the depth of which it is impossible to determine.[23]

When Adams was queried by the paper concerning why the drain had not been seen in prior years, he explained:

> The crevice in the rocks has been covered with soil and debris for years. The lake has not been high enough to reach the open space ... until this spring, when the waters washed away the accumulated soil and debris leaving the hole through which the water is now pouring. As soon as the lake goes down past the opening the whirlpool will disappear, unless artificial measures are taken to make a cut to a lower level.[24]

Adams and Dalton's discovery excited many local residents. There was even talk of deepening the Van Brimmer channel from White Lake and using the Tule Lake outlet to drain Lower Klamath Lake.[25] Meanwhile, a party consisting of Mark Howard, William Duncan, Elmer Hoyt, Tom Norton, and Jess Roberts made a proposition to the Reclamation Service. If the government would furnish the tools, they would be willing to work for one year in an attempt to drain Tule Lake by further opening the holes along the shoreline of Scorpion Point. They asked to be rewarded with 160 acres of reclaimed land if they were successful, and if they failed they would donate their time and labor.[26] Instead of accepting the offer, the Reclamation Service embarked on its own experiments to increase the lake's drainage.

In 1908, Reclamation Service engineers loaded equipment onto several barges and headed towards the southeastern end of Tule Lake. Near Scorpion Point, they began to blast a series of trenches and vertical holes out of the lava rock. At one site "a trench fully 70 feet long, 20 feet wide and 15 feet deep ... was dug."[27] Several other trenches and holes, varying from ten to eighteen feet deep, were also excavated. Records of the Klamath Project show that between April 13 and June 26, 1908, the flow of water into the series of excavated holes was at a rate of about thirteen second-feet.[28] This was far less than had been indicated by the *Klamath Republican* one year before. By December additional work increased the rate to thirty second-feet and this volume continued until July of 1909 when it tapered off as the lake level became lower.[29]   In 1915, the Klamath Project brought in several pumps to further speed the draining of the lake, but the amount of water moved into the surrounding lava beds was insignificant and the plan was soon abandoned.[30] Though some drainage was achieved through the Scorpion Point project, in reality it had little impact on the lake's water level. The most effective means was diverting Lost River into the Klamath River drainage system, allowing the water of Tule Lake to evaporate.

While the draining of Tule Lake was in progress, construction on the main irrigation canals east and south of Klamath Falls was well under way. In 1907 the main "A" and "B" canals were completed, allowing water to flow as Far East as Olene. Offshoots from this canal were also constructed. In 1909, the "C" Canal was completed which took water south through the Lost River Valley to Merrill. Eventually a whole matrix of canals crisscrossed the entire area around Lost River. The water was carried by ditch, pipe, and flume around the contours of the land as well as over and under various creeks, streams, rivers, and roadways.[31]

With the diversion of water away from Tule Lake and with the minimal drainage from its southern end, the lake was reduced in size from 98,600 to 68,000 acres between June 1907 and the fall of 1919.[32] To help facilitate further reductions, as well as to improve the efficiency of the Klamath Project's irrigation network, additional construction took place. In 1921, the Link River Dam was built. Located at the southern end of Upper Klamath Lake, it was designed to regulate the lake's outflow, facilitate storage of irrigation water, and generate electric power. The dam was actually constructed by the California-Oregon Power Company (today known as the Pacific Power and Light Company), under guidelines established by the Reclamation Service. The power company was to receive income from the generation of electricity, but the Reclamation Service controlled all rights to water and water flow.

Also in 1921, the Lower Lost River Diversion Dam was constructed. Since renamed the Anderson-Rose Diversion Dam, this facility moved water from Lost River into the "J" Canal. This canal provided water for the area south of Malin, and later it would be extended further south to become the major source of irrigation water for the Tule Lake Basin. When the Lower Lost River (Anderson-Rose) Diversion Dam was built, there was a historical loss, however, because it was constructed on the stone outcropping of Natural Bridge. This famous ford became the dam's foundation and is now hidden under its cement structure.

In the teens, while the program to drain Tule Lake continued, preparations were made to open reclaimed land for homesteading at the northern end of the Tule Lake Basin. The year 1917 marked the first of eleven homestead offerings that continued until 1949. Each coincided with the completion of new segments of the Klamath Project, and represented the ultimate goal of the Newlands Act—providing average American citizens the opportunity to own land that might otherwise be beyond their reach.

By the 1920s the impact of the Klamath Project's efforts to drain Tule Lake could be clearly seen. In 1923, records show that only 2,000 acres of water remained out of the 98,600 acres when the project began.[33] In the same year, the Klamath Project continued to expand its irrigation program by building the Malone Diversion Dam on Lost River, eleven miles north of Clear Lake. The Malone Dam was designed to provide irrigation water for the Langell Valley. During 1924 and 1925, Gerber Dam on Miller Creek was built. Originally designated as Horsefly Reservoir, Gerber Dam provided further control over the Lost River drainage system. Also in 1924, a diversion dam was built on Miller Creek, eight miles below Gerber Dam, to provide additional irrigation water.[34]

While the draining of Tule Lake involved a rather complex program, this was not so in the draining of Lower Klamath Lake. This large lake received most of its water from the Klamath River and small streams, including Willow Creek. In 1908, the California Northeastern Railroad was constructing a line north from Weed towards Klamath Falls (later this section became part of the Southern Pacific). As the railroad approached the Lower Klamath Basin, it was faced with a dilemma. It could either follow the twisting contours on the basin's western side or build a causeway across the northwestern end of Lower Klamath Lake. To do so, however, would end water travel from the lake north to Klamath Falls. Several steamship companies threatened a lawsuit if the railroad commenced construction on the causeway. However, since the federal government owned Lower Klamath Lake and it was under the jurisdiction of the Reclamation Service, the right to end navigation on the lake was in the hands of the government. Based on this power, an agreement of mutual benefit was worked out between the railroad and the Reclamation Service.

The California Northeastern would be allowed to build its causeway, which in effect was a dike. This would cut off Lower Klamath Lake's main source of water and it would evaporate, allowing more land to be reclaimed. The project was completed in 1912 but pressure from the Fish and Wildlife Service, and concerns about supplying water for irrigation caused the construction of a gate through the causeway at Ady, Oregon in 1914. This linked the Klamath River with the Klamath Straits. Later the irrigation system was further expanded through the construction of the North and "P" canals, which took water to the northern and eastern ends of Lower Klamath Basin.

Reclamation efforts at Lower Klamath Lake were not as successful as they were at Tule Lake. Though the northern end of Lower Klamath Lake proved suitable for farming, its southern end was heavy with alkali. In addition, windstorms blew up great clouds of dirt and alkali dust, sending it north to Klamath Falls. On windy days, the skies were darkened and choking dust filtered into homes throughout the basin. To make matters worse, the water remaining in Lower Klamath Lake became brackish and pungent. A water-borne strain of botulism spread throughout the lake, killing thousands of migratory birds. The directors of the Klamath Project and representatives from the Fish and Wildlife Service began an urgent attempt to find a solution. Finally, part of Lower Klamath Lake was reflooded. The problem with botulism remained, however and a solution was not found until the late 1930s.

The draining of Tule Lake was not without its own problems. When the lake was drained, 37,000 acres of land were set aside to be used as an evaporation sump. However, during the 1930s, much of the 37,000 acre plot was not underwater and consequently much of it was leased to farmers.[35] As farming increased in the basin, the demand for irrigation water also increased, and so did the volume of excess water flowing into the Tule Lake Sump. Gradually the sump began to fill to near capacity, and the leased land under cultivation was threatened with flooding. To make matters worse, this process was occurring during a dry year. The situation caused Klamath Project officials to worry. What would happen during a wet year? Would the sump be able to handle the increased volume of water? Most agreed that it would not.

While Klamath Project officials worried about too much water in the Tule Lake Sump, Fish and Wildlife Service personnel had opposite concerns. There was an insufficient amount of fresh water coming into the sump and it was creating a botulism problem similar to that at Lower Klamath Lake. Its presence was taking a heavy toll on migratory birds and threatening to substantially reduce the total population of birds using the Pacific Flyway.

Reclamation engineer J.R. Iakisch finally developed a solution to these problems in late 1938. Iakisch proposed that the size of the Tule Lake Sump be reduced from 37,000 to 17,000 acres. This would allow more area to be opened for leased farming. To control the water level of the smaller sump area, as well as to provide circulation of fresh water for migratory birds, the report advocated the construction of a pumping station and tunnel on Tule Lake's west side. Because Tule Lake was lower in elevation than Lower Klamath Lake, the water would have to be lifted some sixty feet and then carried through a tunnel under Sheepy Ridge. Once the water reached Lower Klamath Basin, it would then be used for irrigating fields at the basin's north end and supplying fresh water for the Lower Klamath Lake Sump to the south. As with the Tule Lake Sump, the addition of fresh water would help prevent outbreaks of botulism, providing a measure of protection for waterfowl.[36]

Between 1940 and 1941, the Klamath Project constructed a tunnel through Sheepy Ridge and built a pump house on the west side of the Tule Lake Sump. In May of 1942, Pumping Plant "D" began operation, making the Iakisch plan a reality. Today it is still an integral part of flood control, wildlife management, and irrigation for both the Tule Lake and Lower Klamath basins.

During the first thirty years of the Klamath Project, there were seven directors. T.H. Humphreys, D.W. Murphy, and W.W. Patch supervised the major phases of the Project's construction between 1905 and 1912. J.G. Camp and J.B. Bond then followed them. The two directors with the greatest longevity—until the end of World War II—were Herbert D. Newell and B.E. Hayden. Newell was project director from March 3, 1919 until November 11, 1929. Under his leadership, the project widened and deepened much of the water delivery system. Succeeding him, B.E. Hayden served as project director through the Depression and into the period of World War II. Hayden's skillful leadership was at times hampered by the Depression. In November of 1932 "all project construction stopped due to lack of funds" and during the same month a year later, similar action had to be taken.[37]

By the mid 1930s, Hayden found it easier to manage the Klamath Project as additional funds became available. The Project was also given assistance by the Civilian Conservation Corps. Beginning in 1935, Camp Tulelake, located on Hill Road near the base of Sheepy Peak, and Camp Klamath, located north of Merrill, provided men to work on canal maintenance, repair, and construction.[38] Several key improvements were made on the Klamath Project during the 1930s, including enlarging the capacity of the Lost River Diversion Channel and increasing the height of Clear Lake Dam.[39]

In the Tule Lake Basin, one of the primary benefits of the Klamath Project was the opening of reclaimed land to homestead entry. Between 1917 and 1949 there were eleven different sections of the basin opened for homesteading. Each of these openings was based on several factors: the rate at which Tule Lake was receding; the installation of delivery canals, laterals, and drains by the Reclamation Service; and the length of time required to advertise an allotment, process applications, and draw names.

Homesteading at Tule Lake will be discussed in detail beginning with Chapter Eleven, but it is germane at this point to mention that in the period immediately after World War II, the Klamath Project was heavily involved in the basin as the last three major homestead allotments took place. Although most of the system of canals, laterals, and drains was in place prior to the war, some sections had not been used and were in need of repair. One of those was the "M" Canal in Coppock Bay. Originally dug in the 1930s, its earthen sides had gradually collapsed. The

Klamath Project revitalized and enlarged this portion of the system, and later added the "N" Canal.

With the close of Tule Lake Homesteading at the end of the 1940s, the Klamath Project was essentially complete. There had been hope within the Bureau of Reclamation that the irrigation and homestead program could have been expanded into areas of Upper and Lower Klamath Lake but concern for the protection of migratory birds on the Pacific Flyway led to the passing of the Kuchel Act in 1964. The law in effect stabilized the project and the service area has generally remained the same since that time.

Today, more than eighty years after it was initiated, the Klamath Project remains a monument to human ingenuity. When traced on a map, the interconnected latticework of dams, pumps, canals, lakes, and rivers is a marvel to behold. Some water is delivered to the most unlikely places. For example, in the east, the Lost River system provides water for all of the Langell Valley area but today the demand is so high there that in normal years, little water flows beyond Harpold Dam. So where does water for the rest of the Lost River system (including Tule Lake) come from? The primary source for the Klamath Project is Upper Klamath Lake and the Klamath River. For instance, much of the water for the Poe Valley is channeled from Upper Klamath Lake via the A, B, E, and F canals. Water for the Lost River Valley and Tule Lake comes from the A, B, and C canals and from the Lost River Diversion Channel, which moves water from the Klamath River east to the Lost River Diversion Dam.

The water delivery system within a specific area is even more fascinating. Perhaps the most intricate operation is found in the Tule Lake Basin. Water that is released from the Lost River Diversion Dam flows down Lost River to the Anderson-Rose Diversion Dam. Here the water is shunted into the "J" Canal. This canal sweeps in an arc along the eastern side of the Tule Lake Basin. At carefully measured intervals, smaller canals and then laterals take water to individual fields. It is then used on crops through flood irrigation or sprinkler systems (which is the most common method used today). The excess water percolates through the soil and collects in drain canals. This water is then pumped back into the main system to be used again. The sum result is that water throughout the Tule Lake Basin is recycled several times before arriving at the Tule Lake Sump. Here it is pumped to the Lower Klamath Basin where the process begins once more.

Today the role of the Klamath Project has changed somewhat. Many of the areas served by canals constructed by the Bureau of Reclamation are now under the jurisdiction of individual irrigation districts. Each district maintains its own canals and assesses construction and user fees on individuals who are tied into the system. But the Klamath Project remains a viable part of the program. It still owns and operates several of the dams, and all of the irrigation districts are subject to regulations established by the Bureau of Reclamation. The Klamath Project also serves one other vital role. As water flows through the system, it passes through two states, three counties, and at least two federal jurisdictions (the Bureau of Land Management and the National Fish and Wildlife Service). Were it not for a single agency managing the project, there would be a bureaucratic tangle of monumental proportions! The Klamath Project has successfully straddled the delicate balance between public and private sector interests. Its achievements are an example of the positive and progressive use of government.

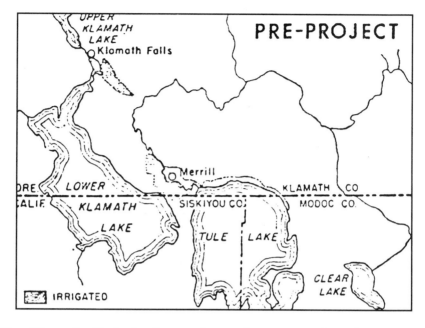

The Klamath Project: Comparison of pre-project and present irrigated areas. *(Courtesy Bureau of Reclamation)*

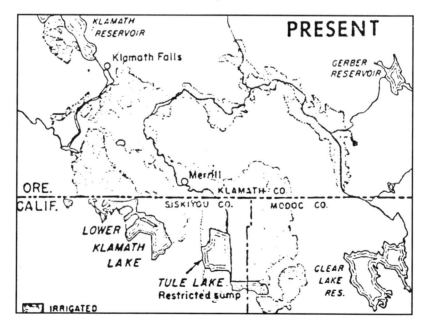

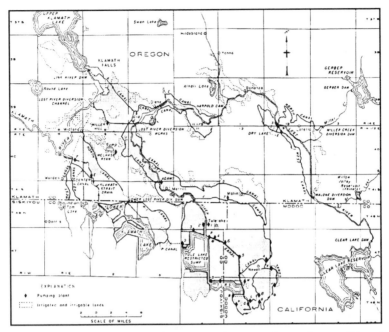

Map showing the Klamath Project's canal system. *(Courtesy Bureau of Reclamation)*

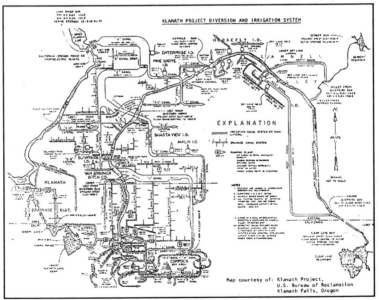

Detailed map showing the canal and water distribution system of the Klamath Project. *(Courtesy Bureau of Reclamation)*

Headgates at the southern end of Upper Klamath Lake under construction for the main or "A" Canal. *(Photo courtesy Bureau of Reclamation)*

Horse-drawn Fresno Plow excavates the "A" Canal in November 1908. *(Photo courtesy Bureau of Reclamation)*

On November 15, 1908 a large hole was dynamited in the lava rock at the southern end of Tule Lake in an attempt to increase the outflow of water. *(Photos courtesy Bureau of Reclamation)*

Klamath Project irrigation water is carried by flume over Lost River at Olene Gap. *(Photo by author)*

Wheel lines distribute water on fields in the Tule Lake Basin. *(Photo by author)*

Pumping Plant "D" located at the west end of the Tule Lake Sump. *(Photo by author)*

The tunnel linking the Tule Lake Sump with Lower Klamath Lake nears completion, circa 1941. *(Photo courtesy Bureau of Reclamation)*

CHAPTER 11

HOMESTEADING RECLAIMED LAND
IN THE TULE LAKE BASIN - THE FIRST WAVE

In the spring of 1916, a new era began in the Tule Lake Basin. On May 24th, A.P. Davis, Director and Chief Engineer of the Reclamation Service, authorized the opening of 4,000 acres of land at the northern end of the Tule Lake Reclamation Project. Each homestead was to be 80 acres in size and $21,000 was to be spent on surveying the land and installing irrigation laterals (small canals) to service each unit.[1] This was the first of eleven homestead periods sponsored by the Reclamation Service, and it represented the initial fruits of nearly ten years of work reclaiming the land once under the waters of Tule Lake.

The Evening News of Klamath Falls was one of the first newspapers to announce the land opening. In its Friday, January 5th, 1917 issue it said:

> Four thousand and nine hundred acres of fertile land around Tule Lake will be thrown open for home-steading this next spring. This became known when J.G. Camp, manager of the Klamath Project, received orders from the interior department to give notices to all leasees of land about Tule Lake that their leases would be canceled in about 90 days.[2]

When comparing the *Herald* article with Davis's memo, there was a 900-acre discrepancy in the amount of acreage to be opened. This was not due to error. Klamath Project officials did not know exactly how much land would be offered in the first homestead allotment. The Newlands Reclamation Act required that all land opened for homesteading be under irrigation, and Project officials were uncertain as to how many farm units could be serviced given their present budget. When the allotment was opened in April of 1917, about 3,000 acres, or 35 homestead units, were actually made available.

The public was made aware of the Tule Lake homesteads primarily through official notices published in local newspapers in the west. Those interested in filing for one of the 35 units made application to the United States Land Office in Lakeview, Oregon.

When the filing period closed on April 23rd, 1917, nearly 180 applications had been received. On the day of the deadline, the *Evening Herald* reported:

> A large number of Klamath Falls and Klamath county people are taking advantage of the opportunity to secure the land, while many have come from outside points.

> The applicants include men from all trades and professions: lawyers, bankers, dentists, farmers and many others. Among the applicants are fifteen women. Only single women or married women not living with their husbands are permitted to file. Only Americans or foreigners who have taken out their first naturalization papers are permitted to file on the lands.[3]

The drawing was held on Wednesday, April 25th, and three days later, a complete list of the winners was published. It was reported that among the 35 names drawn, "fifteen ... live in Klamath Falls, seven in Merrill, five in Malin, three in Weed, one in Hood River, one in Medford, one in Ashland, one in McMinville ... and one in Oroville."[4]

In many ways the first homestead allotment was an experiment for the Klamath Project and the Reclamation Service. At the close of the drawing, a number of questions were raised. How much time was needed to prepare irrigation service in an area that was to be homesteaded? When should public notices be issued? How long should the filing period be? How many farm units should be offered during each allotment? What qualifications should there be for applicants? It would take more than ten years to resolve all of these issues, and many of the answers came through trial and error.

The second homestead allotment was not held until 1922. Part of the delay was due to the Reclamation Service's limited budget, brought on by World War I, but it was also due to pressure from veterans' organizations and the Klamath Falls Chamber of Commerce. They urged that preference be given to applications from military veterans, particularly those who had served in the World War. After careful consideration, the Reclamation Service concurred and rendered a decision that allowed veterans a preferential filing period of ninety days. If homestead units were still available after the deadline, then non-veterans could apply.

On September 22, 1922, the Department of the Interior and Reclamation Service issued Public Notice #13, advertising the opening of 174 units of Tule Lake land.[5] In a memorandum, Klamath Project director Herbert D. Newell described the potential homesteads:

> The lands for which water will be available are of comparatively smooth topography, free from brush, trees and stones ... The soil is of a sedimentary character, generally it is slightly sandy ... The country is adapted to the growing of forage crops and grain. Alfalfa does well on the adjacent lands; potatoes have been successfully grown ... likewise there are good gardens of the hardier vegetables ... Most of the land could be put in good condition for irrigation for around $10 per acre. It is likely to cost from $15 to $30 an acre more to secure a good stand of alfalfa ... The nearest railroad station is Klamath Falls, distance, 30 miles from the land. There is a state highway between Klamath Falls and Malin. The maximum summer temperature is about 100 degrees; the minimum winter temperature is about -15. While the variation in temperature is not as great as in many places, the winters are long and the growing season rather short.[6]

Application requirements in 1922 were very simple. The applicant had to be an American citizen, or had to have completed his or her naturalization papers, and during the 90-day preference period, one had to prove that he or she had been honorably discharged from the armed services. The only other requirement, for veteran and non-veteran alike, was that the homesteader had to "establish, maintain and occupy a residence on his drawn land for a minimum one year period of 'proving up' before clear title to his land was obtained."[7]

Unfortunately, the 1922 homestead allotment did not go smoothly. The request for applications was sluggish, particularly after the applicants discovered that the Klamath Project construction fee to be assessed for each acre of land was to be $90. For an 80 acre farm, this meant that the homesteader was obligated to pay the Reclamation Service $7200 over a twenty year period of time.[8] With the uncertainty of crop yield and expenses related to equipment, land improvement, and home building, many potential homesteaders were frightened away. The other major problem with the 1922 homestead was that there were no requirements for applicants to have had farm experience, or to have the financial backing necessary to get into farming. As a consequence, the failure rate among homesteaders was much higher than expected.

Collectively, these difficulties led to loud protest on the part of veteran's organizations and after only 54 homesteads were awarded, the allotment period was ended. For the next five years, further homesteading at Tule Lake was suspended while issues over construction costs and application requirements were tied up in litigation.

The battle lines were primarily drawn around the issue of construction costs. Prior to the 1922, private landowners and homesteaders were charged $45 per acre. In 1922, the Reclamation Service doubled the assessment to $90. In many ways, the rationale for the new fee was reasonable, but it caught basin residents by surprise. When George J. Walton, a Merrill banker, publicly challenged the Reclamation Service's increase, he received a reply from Morris Blen, Acting Director of the Reclamation Service, and E.C. Finney, First Assistant Secretary of the Interior.

> Reference is made to your letter of September 23 [1922] asking for a statement of the reasons and items responsible for the difference between the charge of $90 per acre for the lands to be included in the present opening ... and the $45 per acre for the "Marginal Lands in Oregon" included in the contract approved July 6, 1913 ... [T]he "Estimate" ... include[d] no charge for drainage, permanent improvements and lands [ditch-rider's quarters], telephone system, operation and maintenance during construction, and a portion of vested water rights ... It is also to be noted that under the supplemental contract of June 23, 1920, the district assumed responsibility for an additional expenditure of $225,000 for canal lining and flume construction ... The larger part of the difference, however, is due to the fact that the original plan ... was based [on using] the "D" Canal. [It] is an old private canal purchased and enlarged by the Reclamation service and the plan at that time was

merely to extend a few of the existing laterals to cover all the land down to the Oregon-California border. When construction was recently undertaken to supply [the new] lands, it was found necessary to build an entirely new system known as the "J" Canal.[9]

The explanations by Blen and Finney did little to mollify the homesteaders and their advocates. In 1925, the veterans in the Tule Lake Basin formed an American Legion Post. One of the major reasons for its creation was to give homesteaders a forum from which to voice their complaints over the construction cost issue. Soon after, they were able to recruit a powerful ally, Klamath Falls attorney Joseph H. Carnahan. His melodious but threatening tones filled the offices of the Klamath Project. Letters and legal briefs flooded the offices of the Reclamation Service, the Secretary of the Department of the Interior, and key congressmen. Finally, the stalemate was broken and the Reclamation Service agreed to reduce the construction fee to $45.

The American Legion and Carnahan then addressed the issue of homesteader qualifications. In a series of meetings with officials of the Klamath Project, and based on the Reclamation Bureau's own studies, a new set of requirements for homestead application were issued. Each applicant was required to have $2,000 in cash and assets. Veterans were still to receive 90-day preference and each person filing had to clearly show farming ability.

The rift between the homesteaders and the Reclamation Service appeared to be on the mend, but then the issue over construction costs returned to haunt both sides. In preparation for the third homestead period, planned for January of 1927, the Klamath Project announced that the construction fee would be $51 per acre. Once again the Legion and Joseph Carnahan complained, and this time their position was strengthened by an unexpected development. The federally sponsored Land Bank refused to make loans on Tule Lake lands until the construction fee was reduced to $40. Hearing this, Carnahan advocated a $37.50 fee, and in a statement given to *The Evening Herald* he said:

> No one can make a go of it on Tule Lake land at the price put on it by the department, and the price is economically and morally wrong and unfair. It was

never contemplated that there should be a $51 per acre construction charge and in putting that on the land the department has wrecked the whole scheme of land settlement on Tule Lake.[10]

Carnahan's reasoning was rooted in the original intention of the Newlands Act of 1902. Reclaimed land was to be made available to those who, under normal circumstances, would not be able to purchase farm acreage. A compromise was finally reached and all parties involved agreed upon a $45 construction fee. The five-year hiatus was over, clearing the way to resume homesteading in the Tule Lake Basin.

Public notice for the 1927 homestead was first issued on January 22. One hundred and forty-five units were to be made available, comprising slightly more than 8,000 acres of reclaimed land. It was the largest single homestead allotment in the history of the Klamath Project. The public notice included the new qualifications for applicants.

Ex-service men have a preference right of entry, but selection of applicants will be made by an examining board on approved qualifications of industry, experience, character, and capital, of which the applicant must have at least $2,000 or its equivalent in livestock, farming equipment, or other assets.[11]

The results of the 1927 homestead were far different than they had been in 1922. At the conclusion of the entry period, every homestead had been filed on, and in subsequent years, the number of homesteads abandoned was far less. One of the primary reasons was that the new applicants were far better prepared to farm the land they received. In October of 1927, the Reclamation Bureau's publication *New Reclamation Era* gave a clear indication why the success rate was so much higher.

Eighty-six of the applicants approved up to June 15, 1927, possessed an average capital of $5,600. Fifty-three of them were soldier entrymen. The smallest amount of capital possessed by any approved applicant was $2,200, and 8 applicants have more than $10,000. Of the 86 applicants 52 were from towns on the Klamath project. A considerable number will not change their address through securing these farms, which are adjacent to Malin, Oregon. Approximately 90 per cent of the applicants came from Oregon, Washington, and California.[12]

With the success of the 1927 homestead under their belt, the Reclamation Service conducted two additional allotments during the 1920s. Both, however, involved considerably smaller tracts of land. On March 20, 1928, Public Notice #22 was issued, declaring that nine homestead units were available for those who met the following requirements:

> Each applicant must possess health and vigor and have at least two years in actual experience in farm work and farm practice. He must have at least $2000 in money free of liability or the equivalent thereof in live farm stock, farm implements or other assets deemed by the examination board to be as useful to the applicant as money.[13]

All nine units were taken, with the approval process apparently running smoothly. This paved the way for the final homestead allotment of the 1920s. It was an important one, in particular because for the first time since 1917, there were more applications than farm units available. On February 6, 1929, the Klamath Project announced the availability of 28 homestead units, and by the time the filing period was closed, a total of 94 applications had been received. The nearly three to one applicant ratio was proof that the Tule Lake Basin was gaining respect as a suitable area to farm. The number of applicants was also a vindication for nearly every party involved in the struggle to develop an adequate list of applicant qualifications and a fair assessment of construction costs. From 1929 on, the ratio between applicants and available homestead units steadily increased. In 1948, a whopping 5,063 individuals applied for 86 farm units!

The 1929 homestead period also started a tradition for determining the winners among qualified applicants. Each name was written on a slip of paper, which was folded in half and deposited in a fishbowl. The names were then randomly drawn, often in the presence of a good number of those who had made application. As the number of applicants increased, the fishbowl was no longer able to hold all the names and a large pickle jar was pressed into service. Its presence became an institution at each of the later homestead drawings.

In looking at the statistical elements of homesteading between 1917 and 1929, one cannot help but wonder what it was like for the 282 single and married people who came to "prove up" their land in the Tule Lake Basin. Fortunately, several of the early homesteaders recorded their experiences. One of the most vivid descriptions comes from Marie and Karl Gentry, who were among the original 54 who homesteaded in 1922.

The Gentrys were introduced to the Tule Lake Basin through an obscure article published in the Sunday edition of the *Portland Oregonian*. The brief article, buried next to the classified section of the paper, simply stated:

> Approximately 10,000 acres of tule lands under the Klamath irrigation project will be opened to entry on October 27 ... This land will include 174 farm units for which ex-service men will have the preference right of entry.[14]

Karl Gentry had been raised on his family's farm in Kansas. Later he left and served in the military. He saw action in the Philippines and during World War I went to France with the 18th Army Engineers. After the war, he worked for the highway department in the State of Oregon. His wife Marie was originally from Everett, Washington. She had gone to high school in Edmonton, Alberta, and later returned to the United States and found a job teaching in Mayville, a small community in eastern Oregon. It was there that she met Karl. He had been helping construct a new road that went through the town. They were married in 1921.

The Gentrys bought a home in Lake Grove, Oregon, a suburb of Portland. Karl was working in construction, and they had recently been blessed with the birth of a son. On Sunday morning, September 24, 1922, Karl had been leisurely leafing through the pages of the *Sunday Oregonian*, when the simple article on homesteading caught his eye. He had always wanted to own a farm. He discussed with Marie the possibilities of acquiring a homestead, and they decided that it would be in their interests to travel to the Tule Lake Basin to investigate the land offering.

The Gentrys left Lake Grove during the last week of September. They traveled in an old "turtleback" Ford. The car only held two people. A small trunk-like affair on the back (the "turtle") carried their belongings. Their journey took them south on old Highway 99 through the Willamette Valley, then to Roseberg, Medford and Ashland. There, they turned east onto the Green Springs Mountain Road. This graveled highway took them over a twisting, climbing route as it ascended toward the summit near Green Springs Mountain. On the steepest parts of the grade, the Gentrys had to turn their car around and back up the hills. It was the only way they could keep gasoline flowing to the engine from its gravity fed tank. When they arrived in Klamath Falls, they immediately talked to several local merchants about the Tule Lake land. Those they approached were extremely pessimistic. They claimed it was common knowledge that the land was not productive and was subject to frost year-round. The land was so poor, the merchants said, that it could only grow alfalfa.

The next day, the Gentrys drove southeast toward Merrill. Just outside of town they stopped and talked with a farmer they encountered. He echoed the Klamath merchants' views, claiming that Tule Lake was unsuitable for farming. Then, to their amazement, he tried to sell them his own place. The Gentrys quickly declined, noting that the land's white powdery appearance showed evidence of having a high amount of alkali that would severely limit the types of crops that could be grown.

Karl and Marie continued south to the Tule Lake Basin, and as they passed the farms along its northern fringe, they immediately realized that the people they had talked to in Klamath Falls and Merrill were wrong. The soil was obviously fertile and the farms on private and leased land around Malin were doing well. While inspecting the crops in a number of fields, the Gentrys met J.W. Taylor and his wife. Taylor was the assistant engineer for the Tule Lake Basin portion of the Klamath Project. In his conversation with the Gentrys, he spoke with enthusiasm about the potential for the area, claiming "the soil was considered comparable in richness to that of the Nile Valley."[15]

The Gentrys moved on and crossed over to the west side of Lost River. There they met Lewis Kandra, Sr. who was raising grain on land he had leased from the government. Kandra had set up a temporary camp for the harvest season, and he invited the Gentrys to spend the night there. That evening he talked with them about the potential for farming in the Tule Lake Basin. He spoke highly of the soil's productivity and the changes that had been brought about by irrigation. He was so confident in the land's potential that he flatly told the Gentrys that if they acquired a homestead and then failed, he would buy them out. Then he added that he doubted that would happen.[16]

Based on the conversations with Taylor and Kandra, Karl and Marie Gentry decided to file for a homestead plot. Though the land was supposed to be awarded to individual applicants through a drawing, so few people applied in 1922 that the Gentrys were actually able to pick the land they wanted. They did so the morning after their conversations with J.W. Taylor and Lewis Kandra. Driving back across Lost River, they carefully surveyed the land and then chose a 60 acre plot one-half mile south of the Oregon-California border and about three miles north of the present city of Tulelake.[17]

That afternoon the Gentrys returned to Klamath Falls, planning to drive to Yreka the next day to officially file for the land they had selected. They checked into their hotel and were soon treated to an event they would always remember. The sky suddenly turned very dark. A thick cloud of dust, ash and smoke had blown into Klamath Falls from Lower Klamath Lake. As the dust storm swirled through the city, Marie Gentry remembered: "The streets were as dark as night and ash sifted into everything in the hotel. One could write in the ash dust on the furniture and even the restaurant food was gritty."[18]

At the time that the Gentrys were staying in Klamath Falls, dust storms had become a regular occurrence. When the Reclamation Service drained Lower Klamath Lake between 1910 and 1920, the receding water exposed large areas of fine peat and chalky alkali dust. The powerful fall winds picked up the loose debris and sent it billowing toward Klamath Falls. To make matters worse, some farm machinery, very likely a steam tractor, had ignited a section of peat dirt in the old lakebed. The fire had been burning out of control for months, and the smoke and cinders joined the gray brown dust in assaulting the city. One storm was even severe enough to cause the temporary closing of the schools in Klamath Falls.[19]

The next day the skies were clear and the Gentrys proceeded to Yreka where they filed for the land they had chosen. Then they returned to their home in Lake Grove, and Karl Gentry anxiously waited for the spring of 1923 so that he could return to Tule Lake and begin farming. Marie Gentry was not as enthusiastic. Her first impression of the Tule Lake Basin was that: "It was just a vast emptiness ... I wouldn't have given it away for a nickel. There was dust, dryness, no trees and nothing green."[20] But she returned to the Tule Lake Basin and joined her husband in putting their roots deep into the land.

For the Gentrys and other 1922 homesteaders, life was Spartan. There were no roads, no telephones, no electricity, no indoor plumbing or running water. During the winter, when the ground was wet and oozing with knee-deep mud, the only time that anyone could travel by car was when the temperature was well below freezing. During the fall, when it was dry and the crops harvested, great dust storms blew up. Clothes had to be washed early in the morning in the hope they would be dry before the windblown dust of the afternoons re-soiled them. Dishes were always turned upside down so that one wasn't greeted by a bowl of dirt when it was time for a meal. The water from shallow wells smelled of methane gas and discolored clothing washed in it. In fact, when the irrigation canals were filled in the spring of each year, the homesteaders took to washing their clothes there because the water was so much softer and cleaner.

Some of the homesteads had been previously farmed by leaseholders, but most had not been scraped and tilled for flood irrigation. It was a tedious chore to properly level a piece of land so that water would flow evenly between the rows, particularly since all work was done with draft horses. In addition, there were virtually no buildings on any of the farm units. In essence, everyone had to start from scratch including preparing the soil, building shelter, and putting in roads.

The new homesteaders were mostly single men, with a scattering of married couples like the Gentrys. Out of common need, they banded together to provide mutual assistance. They leveled the land and built each other's first houses—crude shacks, really. It would take most of the homesteaders several years of successful harvest before they were able to afford to build more substantial housing.

What the homesteaders lacked in amenities had to be compensated with patience and ingenuity. Because the methane-tainted water was not pleasant to drink, they traveled to Malin where Alois Kalina kindly gave them free access to his deep well. The water was drawn into large barrels which had spigots attached near the bottom. It was a chore that most homesteaders had to do at least once a week.

During all but the winter months, food preservation was a continual problem. Meat butchered during the summer had to be immediately shared with neighbors because it would rapidly spoil. To keep items such as milk, eggs, and butter, many of the homesteaders rigged up simple evaporation coolers. A wooden box was placed in a large pan partially filled with water. A burlap sack was draped over the box. The burlap absorbed the water, and the water than began to evaporate. The process cooled off the box and helped preserve its contents.

The early homesteaders had to cope with problems unforeseen when the Reclamation Service first surveyed and plotted the farm units. Roads were practically non-existent. To travel from one location to another in the basin, one often blazed his own path. However, once the land was homesteaded and under cultivation this was no longer possible. To build a road between homesteads, which were often only 40 to 60 acres in size, robbed both owners of precious land, particularly when they had already used some of their farmland for a house and barn. Sometimes the problem was made more acute when a new water-carrying lateral had to be dug, using up more land, or even isolating a section from the rest of the farm. In the early years, the Reclamation Service could provide some help when such losses took place. There were times when land adjacent to several homesteads was either unclaimed or vacated, and a variance was allowed give the adjacent owners pieces of the land. This was particularly true when new canals had to be added or laterals changed.

When it came to growing crops, the homesteaders had only limited information on what was suitable for the basin. They could look to their neighbors in the Lost River Valley and to the Czech community in Malin for suggestions. Even the Reclamation Service was able to offer some advice, having established several experimental farms. But for the most part it was trial and error. Success was predicated both on what crops were able to survive the climate and what the market would buy. Alfalfa was the first crop grown but experimentation and diversification quickly followed. Netted Gem potatoes proved particularly profitable, but there was always the risk that frost would kill the vines before maturity. Other crops grown in the 1920s included onions, horseradish, and cereal grains.

Another difficulty for the early homesteader was orienting oneself to the absurdity of artificially drawn state and county lines. Beginning in 1922, most of the homesteaders settled in California, separated from their neighbors to the north by an invisible line that marked the southern Oregon border. To make matters worse, the boundary line that separated Siskiyou and Modoc counties further divided the Californians. The end result was a nightmare of competing government agencies that inhibited basin growth and frustrated even the most patient of the settlers. Licensing automobiles presented particular problems. If you were a resident of the State of California, you were required to have California plates on your automobile, and the state would only register a vehicle if the owner had a California address. The problem was that there were no California post offices in the Tule Lake Basin. The circular, no-win situation was finally resolved when an enterprising individual nailed a mailbox to a tree on the California side of the border and created the fictitious town of Straw. Mail was routed to Merrill or Malin in care of "Straw, California" and this seemed to satisfy the bureaucrats in Sacramento. Until the townsite of Tulelake was opened in 1931, the Straw mailbox was a frequent receptacle for mail, particularly California license plates![21]

The 1920s was a time of pioneering in the Tule Lake Basin, but it was also a time of developing community consciousness. Recreation for the homesteaders in the early days was simple and community-oriented. Dances were the most popular form of entertainment. The gatherings were both big and small, held in living rooms and barns. But no matter the size, they gave the basin residents an opportunity to socialize and develop lasting friendships. This bonding was important, particularly as the need arose for public action on schools, roads, utilities, and the establishment of a new town site. The homesteaders of 1917 to 1927 worked hard to make their farms productive, but this was not enough. Now they had to come to grips with the needs of the greater community and become an active force in shaping its future.

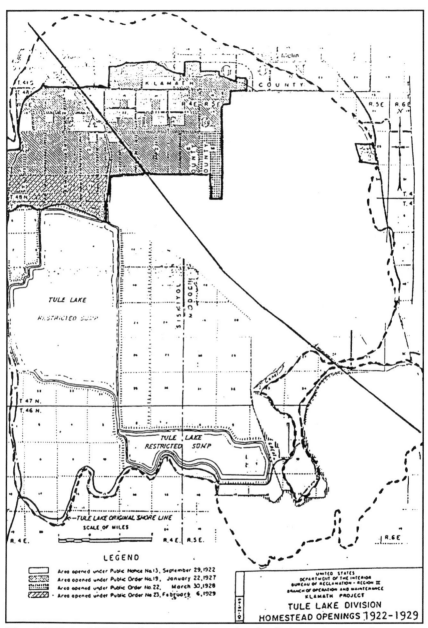

The 1922 to 1929 Tule Lake Homestead allotments are shown in the shaded area in the upper left-hand corner of the map. *(Courtesy Bureau of Reclamation)*

Above and below, typical first homes for the 1920s homesteaders.
(Photos courtesy Portia Aikens)

The Ganger family homestead their land in 1928. Sheepy Peak is in the background. *(Photo courtesy Bill Ganger)*

The Ganger home being moved to a new site on their homestead. *(Photo courtesy Bill Ganger)*

CHAPTER 12

CHANGES IN THE BASIN AND
A DEVELOPING SENSE OF COMMUNITY

From a contemporary standpoint, it is difficult to imagine a community without electricity, running water, telephones, indoor bathrooms, all-weather roads, schools, fire and police protection, and modern transportation. The strength that yesterday's towns and cities possessed was a concentrated power base, a group of citizens that could be tapped when a need arose. But for people living in the country, where the population was spread out over great distances, developing a power base was much more difficult. This was the essential problem facing the Tule Lake homesteaders of the 1920's. There was an immediate need for a great many things, from dealing with the Reclamation Service on construction costs to securing decent roads, electricity, telephones, and good water. The American Legion and supporters, such as Joseph Carnahan, were able to help the homesteaders on some issues, but there was a need for a local organization to take charge. Thus was born the Tule Lake Community Club.

The Tule Lake Community Club was organized during the first months of 1928. Its president was H.A. Knight, the secretary ws Joe Spence, and its mailing address was Malin, Oregon. The club's by-laws stated that its purpose was: "To promote the social and economic welfare of the community; to provide a suitable place where the people of the community may meet, and to encourage cooperation and good fellowship."[1]

This mild description belied the tenacity of this group. The *New Reclamation Era* of July 1928 came closer to the mark when it said, "The purpose of the organization is to have somebody authorized to speak for the community as a whole."[2] And speak they did. When an issue confronted the homesteaders, the club's officers were perfectly willing to barrage the offending party with speeches, personal meetings, and letter writing campaigns that directed correspondence to every politician conceivable on the local, county, state, and federal level. From school needs to roads, bridges, utilities, railroads and the location of a town site, the club waded in without fear. At times they were frustrated in their efforts, but in the end they won most of the battles.

The first big fight, and one of the most important, was over schools. It came about soon after the homestead of 1922. Previous settlement in the Tule Lake Basin had been, for the most part, on the Oregon side of the border. Consequently this was where all the educational facilities were located, save one. The exception was the Carr School, which was located on the eastern side of the basin, just inside California. However, it was more than five miles away from the nearest 1922 homestead, too far to be of help to most families.

When the homesteaders began to explore the possibility of establishing their own school, they ran into a bewildering array of obstacles. First, they discovered that the boundary between California's Siskiyou and Modoc counties ran right up the middle of the Tule Lake Basin, creating two different educational jurisdictions. Second, they found out that the State of California had a law that stipulated that local taxes were to be used to build and operate schools. Third, when they tried to set up a taxing district, they were told that it was not possible because most of the homesteaders did not own the land yet. The Newlands Reclamation Act required a "proving up" period, a length of time often spanning several years when the homesteader had to "prove" to the Department of Interior that he or she was capable of farming the land, and that it was not their intent to quickly turn around and sell the property for profit. Fourth and finally, the homesteaders found themselves victims of geography. Lost River flowed right through the middle of the homestead land, cutting it into eastern and western halves. It was a frustrating problem, because sitting right across the Oregon border were perfectly good educational institutions. In any event, children who were California residents weren't able to attend (at least legally).

In an attempt to solve the problem of schools, California residents on the east and west side of Lost River established their own school districts. Both began with local homesteaders pledging money for the construction and maintenance of a school. Not only did they raise the money, but they also constructed the buildings as well. Generally county funds paid for the teacher.

On the east side, each person contributed $9.00, plus their labor, and the first school was built just to the south of the

California-Oregon border on a homestead owned by Bert Lund. Homesteader Marie Gentry remembered that:

> [The] one room school building led a vagabond life. It served several years on the Lund place. By then another homestead land opening had occurred and after much arguing and some discontent, it was moved to a corner of the Dick Walsh place, he being one of the newer homesteaders. The following year it was moved to a corner of the Clyde Moore place ... [3]

By 1927, the number of children enrolled in school had increased to the point that a new, larger school had to be built. Because there was still no tax base, twelve families obligated themselves for $1200 to the Swan Lake Lumber Company of Klamath Falls to purchase the necessary building materials. The new school was erected on the Moore homestead at the site where the smaller school had originally been moved. It consisted of two large rooms, separated by a large folding partition. The new building, known as the White School (because of its color), soon became a community center for east side farmers and their families. On weekdays it was an educational center. At night it was frequently the site of community meetings, and dances were held there nearly every weekend. On Sundays a Presbyterian minister from Merrill conducted services in the building.[4]

In order to pay off the debt on the White School, the homesteaders conducted a number of fund raising activities. Dances and talent shows were held, and food was auctioned off. By the time the note was due to the Swan Lake Lumber Company, only $700 had been collected. Concerned about the financial obligation encumbered by the families who had signed the promissory note, the homesteaders requested help from the Tule Lake Community Club. The club immediately swung into action and on May 29, 1928 it sent a letter to Herbert D. Newell, Director of the Klamath Project, asking for some kind of aid from the Reclamation Service. The letter summarized the basic problems related to the school issue, especially those encountered in trying to set up a tax district.

> It will be at least three or five years before the [school] district can be bonded, and at that time we will have an attendance of several hundred pupils. It seems as though we are not able to bond the district at the present time due to the fact that there aren't enough

homesteaders having a patent to their land ... when a
school building is built by popular subscription some
of the people will help and others won't, making it a
burden on those who are public spirited enough to
help.[5]

The letter went on to ask for Newell's help in securing the use
of Reclamation Service money to build a bridge over Lost River.
The rationale was that the bridge would not only link the two
communities together but also enable children from both sides to
attend the same school. Newell was not able to provide the
homesteaders with help in either area.

The club then sought help from the superintendent of the
Siskiyou County Schools. In response to their request for
financial aid to pay off the debt on the White School,
Superintendent L.S. Newton said:

I fully realize the true conditions in the Tule Lake
district, but under the school laws of the State of
California it is impossible for me to do the thing you
have mentioned in your letter. The only way ... to raise
funds in this state is by special tax or bonds, and the
valuation of the Tule Lake district is very little ...[6]

Ultimately a solution was found. It turned out that
Superintendent Newton was up for re-election in the fall. While
campaigning for votes in the Tule Lake Basin, he was told that
there was absolutely no support for his candidacy. Surprisingly,
several days later some county school money was "unexpectedly"
found and the loan on the White School was paid off![7]

Families on the west side were also in need of a school for their
children. Like the east side parents, they felt the easiest solution
was to build a bridge over Lost River. Then both sides could pool
their educational resources. But the refusal of the Klamath
Project to spend money on a bridge thwarted this idea. When help
was requested from Superintendent Newton, he stated: "The only
solution that I can see would be to establish another school on
the west side."[8] And so that is what the "westsiders" had to do.
They organized the Westside Welfare Club and were able to get
enough donated funds to build a 30' by 40' building. The facility
was named the Winema School and it opened for its first session
in September of 1928.[9]

The two school districts helped homesteaders on both sides of Lost River develop a unique identity. A friendly rivalry developed between the "Eastsiders" and "Westsiders," and it remained long after a bridge was finally completed over Lost River.

The elusive bridge over Lost River caused one of the most annoying and hotly contested disagreements between the homesteaders and the Reclamation Service. The homesteaders believed that up through 1928 they had tried the "friendly" approach. Now they were going to go on the assault. On December 12th, the Tule Lake Community Club issued the following resolution:

> Whereas, on the Tule Lake Division of the Klamath Project, in the $90 per acre construction charge there is included an item of $15,000 for the construction of a bridge across Lost River, somewhere between the river pumps and the lower dikes, to facilitate the operation and maintenance of the irrigation and drainage systems, and also, in case of breaks in the protective dikes, to permit the rapid disposition of draglines, and

> Whereas, the present development of units around this area, together with those to be opened soon, it appears that the construction of this bridge is vitally needed now, and

> Whereas, this bridge can be made to serve the Bureau of Reclamation fully and also provide a greatly needed means of travel in the division,

> Now, therefore, be it resolved at this meeting of the Tule Lake Community Club that we go on record as strongly favoring the building of this bridge as soon as possible ...[10]

But the Reclamation Service rejected the Community Club's resolution. In a letter sent by Klamath Project Director B.E. Hayden to Fred McMurphy, the new club secretary, Hayden said: "I am today in receipt of a letter from the Chief Engineer stating that he has discussed this matter with the Commissioner and the Chief Law Office of the Service, Mr.Dent, and that their decision is that the Service cannot construct the bridge requested by your club."[11]

Feathers ruffled and angry over what they believed to be insensitivity on the part of the Reclamation Service, the Community Club began to write to every politician connected, even in the remotest way, with the interests of the Tule Lake Basin. Among those approached for help were Senator Hiram Johnson and Representative Harry L. Englebright, both of California. Tule Lake was in Englebright's congressional district and he became the club's strongest advocate. But when Englebright asked Elwood Mead, Commissioner of the Bureau of Reclamation, to release funds for the bridge, he received a rather terse reply. "A bridge at this location is not needed in connection with the construction or operation and maintenance of the Klamath Project. This being the case, federal funds could not properly be used for the construction of the bridge as desired by the Tule Lake Community Club."[12]

Mead challenged the accusation made by the club that money had been set aside for bridge construction by saying: "Little significance can be attached to the fact that the estimates, prepared when the project construction charge was fixed, included a bridge across Lost River. In making such estimates, many items are included which are later found not to be needed."[13]

When Englebright again pressed Mead for action, he received another firm response dated June 19, 1930: "We are unable to see how the construction of a bridge across Lost river at a cost of $18,000 or more from the Reclamation Fund, to be charged to the Tule Lake homesteaders, can be justified by project needs."[14]

The battle raged on for another year and a half. Finally, several years after the Tulelake town site was established in 1931, a bridge on East-West Road was constructed ... with state and county funds.

Back in 1929, when the bridge issue was just beginning to heat up, the Tule Lake Community Club became involved in a number of other important issues. They successfully lobbied the Reclamation Service to set aside land for a town site (though it took congressional action to finalize the town site designation). In the same year, they convinced the Southern Pacific Railroad, which was constructing a main line through the basin, to build a siding at the site of the proposed Tulelake community.

In 1930 the club took on the California Oregon Power Company, which was charging 9% higher rates to its customers on the California side of the Tule Lake Basin than it was to its Oregon customers. An appeal was made to the Railroad Commission of the State of California (which at that time handled issues related to utilities) and in July the Community Club was advised that the California Oregon Power Company "has indicated that (it) desire(s) to make an adjustment in (its) rates."[15]

Also in 1930, the club was successful in having a local homesteader appointed to the Klamath Project's Selection Board. It was the job of this body to review all homestead applications and oversee the drawing of winners for farm units. The Community Club felt that it was appropriate to have a local person serve on the board. When Project Director B.E. Hayden was first approached on the issue, he was reluctant to appoint someone from Tule Lake. Hayden told the Community Club:

> Personally, I would like to see someone down there on the Board if it were as convenient for the operations of the Board as having members closer at hand. You may not be aware of the fact that all members of the Board serve without compensation and are called upon to spend considerable time in examining papers ... I doubt if any of your people down there would care to serve on the Board without compensation and mileage.[16]

The club disagreed with Hayden's conclusions and persisted in its request. In March of 1930 Hayden changed his mind. A fourth position was added to the Review and Selection Board, and the Community Club was asked to nominate a person for that position.

The string of successes chalked up by the Tule Lake Community Club helped set the stage for an era of change and development in the basin. The decade of the 1930s was witness to three periods of homesteading: the establishment of the central basin's first town; the gradual appearance of such amenities as decent roads, electricity, and telephones; and the introduction of a host of federal programs designed to put depression ravaged individuals back to work.

On September 30, 1930, Public Notice #26 announced the fifth major homestead allotment in the Tule Lake Basin. Twenty-four farm units were offered, and 162 individuals made application.[17] The requirements developed in the late 1920s to qualify as a potential homesteader were in effect for the 1930 allotment. However, the gradual economic stranglehold of the Great Depression was already putting a hardship on those who applied. The most difficult requirement was related to personal worth, which stipulated that an applicant must have $2,000 in either cash or free-and-clear assets. To meet this requirement, some applicants, including Edgar M. Mitchell, sought individuals who were willing to financially back them. Mitchell had been working for the Bureau of Reclamation, dredging out canals, when the new allotment was opened for application. A friend of his from Malin, Frank Victorin, signed over $2,000 worth of milk cows and Mitchell was one of the 24 fortunate men whose names were drawn. Several years later, Mitchell paid back Victorin, and he went on to develop a highly productive and valuable farm.[18]

In general, change, though significant, came gradually to the basin in the 1930s. Crude rural roads still mired vehicles during rainy months, and residents continued to rely on freezing weather to make the ground hard enough to drive on. Hardship bred both ingenuity and just plain foolishness. Some enterprising travelers took to driving their trucks and cars on the roadbeds of Southern Pacific and Great Northern railroads. By keeping their vehicles slightly off center to miss the rails, they could bump along from one solid patch of ground to the next without being trapped in the mud. The risks were obvious. A driver could either meet a train head on or be overrun by one as he struggled to reach the next road crossing. There was also the chance that the car would be ruined as it bounced from one tie to the next.[19]

The lack of good roads was not the only problem facing the basin. By 1932, the Great Depression had begun to clearly affect individual lives. Even so, the residents had an obvious advantage over individuals living in cities and towns because they could grow their own food. The Depression generated a strong sense of community among Tule Lake farmers. Every effort was made to help those who were destitute. When the banks began to fail in the early 1930s, one local hay farmer used $700 in cash that he had hidden to help out several needy families. He hired them to do odd jobs around his farm and in return paid them in $20 bills at the end of each week.[20]

With President Franklin Roosevelt's election in 1932, a variety of federal programs designed to put the unemployed to work began to filter into the basin. One of the most important was the Civilian Conservation Corps. Men recruited to work at Camp Tule Lake and Camp Klamath spent most of their time working on Bureau of Reclamation projects. In Klamath Falls, a chain link fence was installed along the A Canal to prevent young children and the unsuspecting from falling in and drowning. CCC crews spent long hours cleaning debris from canals and laterals. They built roads on Klamath Project levees, and killed off noxious weeds. In addition, most of the men were on standby, ready to fight local forest and range fires. In 1936 when a section of the embankment along the J Canal gave way, CCC men quickly plugged the break and then strengthened the canal's earthen sides. In the same year, a break in the dike along the Tule Lake Sump flooded 1,400 acres of grain. A CCC crew from Camp Tule Lake not only repaired the dike but also assisted in harvesting some of the fields of grain endangered by the flood.[21]

The CCC also embarked on a large-scale project at the Lava Beds National Monument. It was a significant development, because the park was new and it was relatively unknown to the general public. It had been more than sixty years since the Lava Beds had made national headlines as the scene of the Modoc War. In the intervening years, only a few homesteaders and tourists visited the area each year. Even in the second decade of the twentieth century, groups visiting the Lava Beds were infrequent enough to be featured in local papers, and their trips were treated more as "expeditions." For example, the *Klamath Republican* reported on May 25, 1911:

> The party consisting of J.F. Goeller, John Shook and J.C. Rutenic, who left here two weeks ago for the lava beds, returned Saturday night in Mr. Goeller's launch. While they report severe weather and considerable hardship on that account, they are full of praise of the points of interest, historic and natural.[22]

A month later, the *Republican* reported on another party's visit to the Lava Beds:

Saturday evening Mr. and Mrs. Nelson Rounsevell left this city for Merrill with Henry Rabbes in his Brush runabout. There they met Mr. and Mrs. Carey Ramsby of this city and Mr. and Mrs. Edward Martin of Merrill. The following morning the party ... boarded the gasoline boat Crystal, and made the trip of thirty miles to the lava beds in 2 1/2 hours. A stop of four hours was made at Jack's stronghold, and during the day Canby Cross, Gilliam's Camp and other points of interest on the battlefield were visited by the party. A number of cannon balls, fragments of shells, rifle balls and other relics were found on the field. On the return trip the Crystal reached Merrill at 8 o'clock.[23]

In 1916, efforts were begun to establish the Lava Beds as a federal reserve. Advocates of this effort believed that its unique geologic features, its historical significance, and the wildlife that inhabited the region should be protected ... particularly in light of the increasing number of people who were going through the Modoc War battlefields, picking up souvenirs, and destroying evidence that would be useful in understanding the history of the period.

On November 21, 1925, President Calvin Coolidge officially declared the Lava Beds a National Monument. For the next eight years the site was under the jurisdiction of the National Forest Service and only modest improvements were made. Roads remained poor. Guy Merrill ran the only popular facilities in the area. He operated a restaurant and several tent cabins near Merrill Ice Cave during the 1920s. Visitors interested in seeing the miles of lava caves that snaked through the area frequented the modest resort, and many were also inclined to sample a bit of Prohibition-period moonshine that found its ways into the camp!

On June 10, 1933, the jurisdiction over the Lava Beds was transferred to the National Park Service. Gradually a comprehensive plan was developed for park improvements, including new roads, trails, signs, camping and picnicking areas, cleared pathways into selected lava caves, and living facilities for full-time and summer staffs. Best estimates suggested that the completion date for the plan was at least a decade away. Then in 1937, the Civilian Conservation Corps expanded its program in the Tule Lake Basin by building a new facility at the site where Colonel Alvan Gillem had established his military camp during the Modoc War. Unfortunately in preparing the ground for the new CCC camp, which was to be called Camp Lava Beds, most of the physical evidence of the army's encampment was bulldozed away. In spite of this faux pas, the CCC did an enormous amount of good in the Lava Beds. Many of the dreams outlined in the plans of 1934 were realized. One newspaper article, summarizing the work of the CCC in the Lava Beds, reported:

> Civilian Conservation corps activities have placed the development of this monument at least ten years ahead of what it would have been without CCC labor ... Improvement of roads within the monument has been a major project in making different sections of the monument more accessible to the motoring public ... Parking areas have been provided ... and trails into lava caverns have been substantially improved by gravel and stone steps.
>
> CCC enrollees have devoted many days to the development of camping facilities at the main campground near Indian Wells. It is now equipped adequately with tables, benches, stoves, and fireplaces.
>
> Valuable project training in carpentry was derived by enrollees in the construction of a new office building for the national park service technical agency on duty with the Lava Beds camp. The building, regarded as one of the most stable structures of its kind, was almost entirely built by CCC members, who also applied attractive coats of brown stain to the exterior.[24]

Residents in the Tule Lake Basin watched the developments at the Lava Beds carefully. Not only were they encouraged by notions that more tourists would be drawn to the area, but they were also hopeful that some of the CCC labor might be put to work on roadways in the basin itself. But for the most part, this didn't materialize. One glimmer of hope came when the State of California and Modoc County decided to build a new highway through the basin linking Alturas and Canby with Merrill and Klamath Falls. The "Old Alturas Highway" followed the edge of the rim rock along the eastern side of the basin. It was narrow, twisting, dusty and inconvenient for most of the homesteaders who resided several miles to the west. The new highway was to parallel the Southern Pacific tracks. The road was completed but it was not blacktopped for several years more, making travel through the basin tedious and slow.

In the final third of the 1930s, the Reclamation Service conducted its last homestead allotment of the decade. Limited funds for new construction had delayed the homestead opening, as had considerations for individuals who did not have the required capital to qualify. Even more important, the delay had come about because of the uncertainty as to how much more basin land would be made available for homesteading. The American Legion, local homesteaders, and some officials in the Bureau of Reclamation wanted to open an additional 20,000 acres at the southeastern end of the basin by reducing the size of the Tule Lake Sump. But their plans ran into two snags. The United States Biological Survey, which ran the bird refuge at the Tule Lake Sump, strongly protested, and the engineers at the Bureau of Reclamation were concerned about flood control. There had already been one break in the sump's levee and increased farming was dumping more water into it every year. A solution was finally found in the study done by J.R. Iakisch, described in chapters ten and nineteen.

Meanwhile, preparations were made to announce the opening of 5,100 acres of land located to the east of the intersection of the Southern Pacific and Great Northern railroads. On September 9, 1937, Public Notice #35 was issued, announcing the availability of sixty-nine farm units. When the October 2 deadline passed, over 1,300 individuals had applied.[25] So famous had the productivity of the land in the basin become that the ratio of applicants to farm units was now nearly nineteen to one ... a far cry from the 1922 homestead entry when farm units had gone begging.

The 1937 homestead allotment included a number of new procedures for processing applications. Preference was still given to veterans, but a rating system was now to be applied to the traditional requirements of farm experience, capital, industry, and character. Minimum qualifications in each of these categories remained, but an individual applicant could earn more points if he or she exceeded the minimum. For example, in the area of farming, a person had to have at least two years experience, but a much higher rating was awarded if the applicant had continuously worked on an irrigated farm during the last three years. In the areas of industry and character, points were awarded on the basis of the number and quality of letters of recommendation. Finally, points were also awarded for the amount of assets or capital a person possessed. The minimum was $2,000 in cash or assets, but a higher rating was awarded for those with $10,000 or more.

There were protests over the rating system, particularly the practice of awarding higher points for individuals with $10,000 or more in capital. It was alleged that it favored the wealthy over the poor and critics pointed out that this violated one of the basic tenets of the Newlands Act. Criticism was also leveled at the rating system used for character and industry. Since each applicant picked his or her own character references, every letter was filled with glowing reports about the person's qualifications. As a result, character references were not an accurate way of determining farming capabilities.

In addition to the rating system, the procedures for processing each application were complex. First, an examining board carefully reviewed each applicant's filing form and his or her letters of recommendation. These were then rated and point values assigned. Then a personal interview was arranged with the applicant, with at least one member of the examining board present. The results of the interview were also rated. Finally, the points earned on the application and interview were totaled. Homesteads were to be awarded on the basis of the rating scores, and if the number of individuals with equal ratings exceeded the number of farm units available, their names were to be drawn in a lottery.[26]

Though on paper the new system for awarding farm units seemed to be prudent and fair, when it was put into actual practice it was a nightmare. Processing and evaluating 1,308 applications was tedious. So too were the endless interviews with those who passed the first screening. When it was finally over and the sixty-nine homesteads were awarded, the Bureau of Reclamation carefully studied what had transpired. Several key decisions were made. First, the emphasis on seeking applicants with strong farming background would continue. Second, a rating system would be employed again, but it would be modified so as not to discriminate against applicants who met the minimum requirement for capital. Finally, personal interviews would only be conducted for a limited number of individuals.

Actual implementation of the new screening procedures had to be delayed for a period longer than anticipated. The Klamath

Project completed the next construction phase in the early 1940s, but because of U.S. involvement in World War II, orders were issued to halt any further homestead allotments "for the duration."

Meanwhile, other changes had taken place in the Tule Lake Basin. Out of the rich bottom soil of the reclaimed lake, a new town was born. In its youth, its streets were filled with saloons and rooming houses, and its nights were punctuated with lusty brawls. Later, with maturity, it became an important community center. The story of the development of this community, destined to be called "Tulelake," is chronicled in the next chapter.

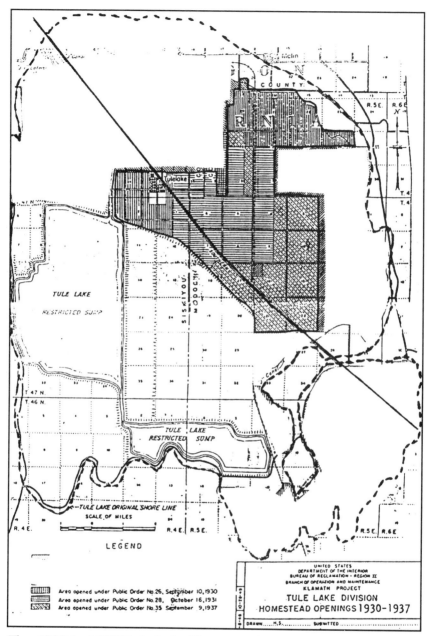

The 1930 to 1937 Tule Lake Homestead allotments are shown in
the shaded area in the upper right-hand corner of the map.
(*Courtesy Bureau of Reclamation*)

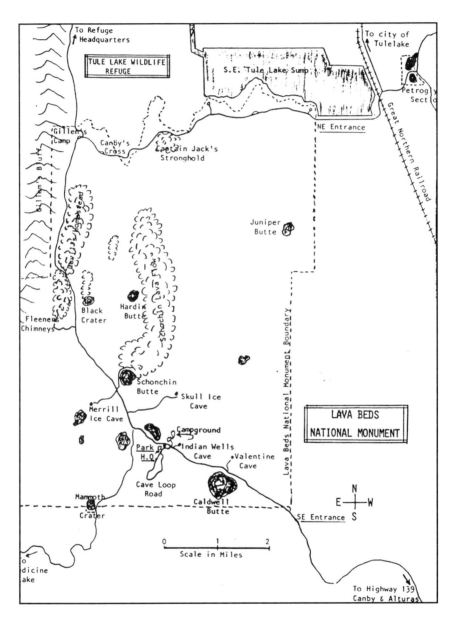

Map of the Lava Beds National Monument.
(Map drawn by author)

Camp Lava Beds, built in 1934 by the Civilian Conservation Corps. The buildings shown were used to house CCC recruits while they worked on road building and trail improvements in the Lava Beds National Monument. *(Photo courtesy Bureau of Reclamation)*

Site of Camp Lava Beds as it appears today. The ring of rocks in both photos dates to the Modoc Indian War and was used as a horse corral by the soldiers at Gillem's Camp. *(Photo by author)*

Sign at southeastern entrance to the Lava Beds National Monument. *(Photo by author)*

A new visitors center will be constructed in the summer of 2002, replacing the smaller structures shown above. *(Photo by author)*

Civilian Conservation Corps recruits at Camp Tule Lake line up for inspection in 1937. The camp was located at the base of Sheepy Peak, on the western side of the Tule Lake Basin. It was used as an Italian and German prisoner of war camp during World War II. *(Photo courtesy Bureau of Reclamation)*

Camp Tule Lake in 2002. *(Photo by author)*

Road construction on Hill Road, which runs parallel to Sheepy Ridge. *(Photo courtesy Bureau of Reclamation)*

CHAPTER 13

TULELAKE: A NEW TOWN ON THE LAKE BED

When the Reclamation Service opened the 1922 homestead in the Tule Lake Basin, preliminary plans were also drafted for the creation of a town site. Tentatively it was to be situated in the central portion of the basin, but its establishment was held in abeyance until such time as population size and economic climate were appropriate.

It was not until seven years later, in 1929, that serious plans for a permanent community were undertaken. Its creation emanated from several important developments. First, the homestead allotments of 1927, 1928, and 1929 had gone well, and the economic predictions for the future of the basin were on the upswing. Consequently, it was realistic to consider the possibilities of a community that would attract a permanent commercial and residential population.

Second, the Southern Pacific Railroad had completed a main line south from Klamath Falls through the Tule Lake Basin to Alturas. A number of sidings had been established in the basin during construction, including ones at Hatfield, Homestead, and Stronghold.

Third, the Tule Lake Community Club—which had already championed the establishment of schools, decent roads, mail service, and a bridge over Lost River—now lobbied the Bureau of Reclamation for proceeding with plans for a town. In February 1929, the club sent the Klamath Project Director, Herbert D. Newell, a formal request for assistance. Newell readily agreed to help, and assembled supportive documents including letters from local merchants and community groups, statistics on farm output, information related to the completion of the S.P. line, and reference to plans made by the Great Northern Railroad to run its own line through the basin.[1] Based on the material provided by Newell, the Bureau of Reclamation announced in the summer of 1929 that a "Government Town Site" was to be established at a location three miles south of the Oregon-California border, next to the Southern Pacific line.

The Tule Lake Community Club was pleased with this announcement, but it was disturbed that there was no railroad siding located at the proposed government town site. Some members feared that the railroad might try to establish a town at the existing siding at Stronghold, five miles to the south. Any such plans by the railroad might lure businesses to the Stronghold location—businesses which otherwise might establish themselves at the government site.[2] The club immediately laid out a battle plan. They drafted several letters requesting the construction of a siding, and sent them to the State of California Railroad Commission, the Bureau of Reclamation, and the Southern Pacific Railroad. While waiting for replies, the Community Club sent a form letter to every business that had expressed even the remotest interest in establishing an outlet in the basin. The form letter read:

> We have been informed that you are or were interested in building a warehouse for your business on Tule Lake, at the Proposed Government Townsite. We are very glad to learn of this and would like to inquire if you would still be interested, if a siding can be secured at an early date.[3]

The club had hoped that if they could arm themselves with enough positive replies that these could be used as leverage if the railroad was reluctant to put in a siding. This was not necessary, though, because in early August they were assured by G.W. Boschke, Chief Engineer of the S.P., that construction of a siding at the Government Town Site would begin within a matter of weeks.[4]

Over the next two years, the interminable snail's pace of government bureaucracy saw further plans for the Tule Lake townsite develop in miniscule increments. In the interim, several buildings were constructed on the Southern Pacific right-of-way including a small depot, several potato cellars, and a sheet-metal clad building that housed the town site's first major business: the Siskiyou Tractor and Implement Company. The builder and owner was Earl Ager who quickly became one of the community's visionaries and strongest promoters.

Earl Ager had owned a successful grocery business in Yreka. When it was announced that the government was planning to establish a town in the Tule Lake Basin, he traveled there to look at the prospects. Upon his arrival in the summer of 1929, Ager climbed to the top of a Southern Pacific boxcar, which had been left at the newly constructed siding, and surveyed the surrounding land. As his eyes followed the fields of yellowing grain and green-vined potato plants to the surrounding hills, he recognized the enormous potential for retail growth in the basin. Consequently, he arranged a long-term lease with the Southern Pacific Company and financed the construction of a large metal warehouse. There, Ager sold Case tractors and later obtained a franchise from International Harvester.[5]

Though Earl Ager was in business by the winter of 1930, the Reclamation Service still dragged its feet on opening the Tule Lake Town Site for actual sale. Continual prodding by the Tule Lake Community Club, the American Legion, and men like Ager, finally spurred the Bureau into taking action. In the summer of 1930, J.W. Taylor, engineer and local homesteader, was hired to survey the land and lay out the streets, blocks, and individual property lines. The land he surveyed was mostly planted in grain and contained only one lonely cabin, which was occupied by Mr. and Mrs. L.J. Horton.[6]

While Taylor was completing his survey, the Reclamation Service formulated plans for selling the town lots. It was determined that all sales would be by auction, and that notices of the sale would be sent to newspapers and government offices in a broad radius throughout the West. Two hundred and nine lots were to be initially offered, with additional property held in reserve for the construction of a school and city park. Adjacent land would be opened for town expansion if future growth warranted such action. Public notice of the sale was issued on March 17, 1931 and Wednesday, April 15th was selected as the date for the auction.

As the day approached for the government sale, preparations took on a festive air. The Klamath Falls *Evening Herald* observed:

> If the interest being shown in the Tule Lake auction sale is a criterion, a large crowd of purchasers as well as others who wish to view the auction of a town being sold under the auctioneer's hammer, will attend the sale which will begin at 11:00 A.M. Wednesday.[7]

Arrangements were made for a special auction-day excursion train for both spectators and those interested in purchasing lots. Round trip tickets from Klamath Falls were offered for a dollar. Members of the Tule Lake Community Club made plans to sell chicken luncheons, and a dance was scheduled to be held at the townsite Wednesday evening.[8]

On the day of the auction, *The Evening Herald* estimated that more than 500 people were in attendance. At 11:00 a.m., J.W. Taylor, who had been assigned the job of auctioneer, climbed onto the back of a truck and commenced the sale. The truck moved from one lot to the next, and Taylor verbally announced its appraised value, which represented the minimum bid allowed. The base for residential property ranged from $65 to $120 per lot, and commercial property was appraised as high as $500. At the close of a round of bidding, Taylor struck his gavel on the wooden frame of the truck, announcing the sale of a parcel of land. By the end of the day, 121 lots had been sold, ranging in price from $65 to $530.[9] Another nine lots were offered for sale the following Saturday, and the remainder were sold off over the next twelve months. In 1936, 1941, and 1948, the Bureau of Reclamation held three additional auctions. These led to the city expanding south and westward.

Almost overnight, the new city of Tulelake took on many of the characteristics of a wild-west boomtown, exhibiting spirited growth and "cuss worthy" hardship. In describing the first year, *The Evening Herald* of Klamath Falls said: "Houses, cabins and tents arrived from every direction almost overnight, drawn by teams, tractors and hauled on trucks. Dust was ankle deep ... and not one drop of water for human consumption (was) closer than Malin or Merrill."[10]

One of the first sets of buildings to arrive was the "Havlina Camp." Originally it was a hunting resort situated on the League of Nations tract, south of the townsite. The conglomeration of wood frame structures was brought into town by the Havlina brothers and set down in an irregularly shaped block bordered by Main Street, Modoc, A Street, Second, and B Street. Three of the buildings fronted Main, and during their years of use, housed a variety of businesses including several cafes, a pool hall, *The Tulelake Reporter*, and an auto repair and tire dealer.[11] Behind the Main Street buildings were cabins, principally for migrant workers, and shower and toilet facilities.

Also during the first year, Fred Taylor established a lumberyard on Modoc Street, about 100 yards north of Main, next to the Southern Pacific right-of-way. The town's first post office was located here, marking an important step in basin development. Betty Taylor was the first Postmaster. No longer did residents on the California side have to depend on such spurious locations as "Straw" for delivery of license plates and other material that required a California mailing address, nor did they have to travel to Malin or Merrill for routine mail service.

The post office at the Fred Taylor Lumber Company also had another important role. Its postal cancellation stamp was given the name "Tulelake," the first "official" consolidation of "Tule" and "Lake" on record. As discussed in Chapter One, the reason for the single word spelling has been lost over time, but most likely it was done to try to separate Tulelake, the town, from any association with Tule Lake the—well—"sump" (since there wasn't all that much of a lake left by the 1930s). In later years, even the consolidated name caused confusion about the nature of the town and its setting. For example, in 1941 a Mrs. Grace M. Hilgert of San Mateo wrote to the Postmaster of the city, stating: "I am seeking information regarding recreational, vacation, and general living conditions at Tule Lake, contemplating a vacation at said place. Will you be so kind as to give the facts regarding renting cabins, housekeeping apartments or small houses in that locality near the lake ..."[12] Sarah Welsh, secretary of the Tulelake Chamber of Commerce at the time, patiently wrote to Mrs. Hilgert, explaining that the city was not "a lake shore recreational area" but instead, a farm community and a popular area in the fall for bird hunters.[13]

One of the most important additions to the new townsite came in 1932 when local members of the American Legion, Post 164, built a meeting hall on the corner of D and Second streets. The imposing one-and-a-half-story building became the community center for Tulelake and hosted everything from Legion meetings to dances, entertainment, and social gatherings. Its construction epitomized the community spirit of basin residents. The dedication of the building had its humorous moments. The building contractor misjudged the completion date, and the roof was not fully installed on the day of the formal ceremony. Invitations had already been sent to Legion members, dignitaries, and representatives of social and fraternal organizations in Oregon and California, urging them to attend the gala opening. With the lack of a comprehensive phone system, and to the extent to which plans had already been made, it was virtually impossible to put off the date. Naturally, the elements of nature had been waiting to taunt the confidence of the promoters of the event, and on the day of the ceremonies there was a healthy storm! Malcolm Epley, editor of the Klamath Falls *Herald and News* vividly remembered visiting the new building:

> I ... recall we waded through mud across a field from the train to the Legion hall. Anticipated progress had not been made ... but it was the only place for our meeting, so we went ahead despite the rain coming in the room.[14]

The storm didn't dampen the community's enthusiasm and a sizeable crowd turned out to dedicate the Legion Hall. With umbrellas over their heads, they patiently listened to a variety of speeches, while two children were kept busy with mops trying to keep water off the new hardwood floor.[15]

Throughout the 1930s, new businesses appeared on Tulelake's two main commercial streets, Main (which was known as Third Street until 1939) and Modoc. In 1935, Clyde Barks built a two story hotel and retail store complex on the southwest corner of Main and B streets. Other buildings on the same side of the street included the Marcha Theater, and an eatery built by Joe Frydendall and Pete Bergman known as the "Shasta Lunch." Later, the building would become a hardware store. Across the street were several taverns and a clothing store. Other establishments soon followed, including the Tulelake Hotel, located on Main Street, to the east of Modoc Avenue.

One of the most enduring institutions was a grocery and general merchandise business operated by Earl and Dorothy Ager, which was originally situated in the Clyde Hotel. In 1932, Earl had lost the Siskiyou Tractor and Implement Company due to the impact of the Depression and a hard frost that killed off many of the local crops. Farmers were unable to make payments on equipment they had purchased and the implement business went under. Ager's building was taken over by the Martin Brothers of Klamath Falls, with whom he had been friends, and used for grain storage. For several years, Earl was employed by the Martins to manage the building, and then in 1935, he left to open a grocery business. Later, another farm implement dealer acquired the building.

Meanwhile in 1933, Dorothy Frydendall came to Tulelake to work for her brother at the Shasta Lunch. Her arrival was rather unceremonious. She had driven down from Portland with a cousin and when they arrived it was pitch dark. In attempting to find her brother's house they got lost and ended up in Malin, where they had to repeatedly ask for directions to get to Tulelake. The confusion caused by the dark, coupled with dusty roads created a surrealistic nightmare. As they groped their way along, Dorothy muttered to herself, "Of all places to live!"[16] Late that evening they finally reached her brother's home, and soon after, she was put to work at the cafe. Gradually, her impressions of Tulelake mellowed. It was while she was employed at the Shasta Lunch that she met Earl Ager. In 1934 they were married, and the next year they opened a grocery store in the Clyde Hotel.

The Agers did well and five years later, in 1940, they constructed their own building on the northeast corner of Main and Modoc. Known as "Earl's," it became the town's centerpiece. Its five departments offered everything from groceries to general merchandise, and its ice cream and cafe counter became the daily gathering place for the town's inhabitants. The store's slogan—"Meet me at Earl's"—was more than a mere advertisement. People came there to work out business deals, to socialize, and to find missing children, husbands, and wives. Ager's phone at the cafe counter was constantly ringing, with callers looking for friends, business associates or relatives. "At times ... more telephone messages than milk shakes" were dispensed "to the constant scores of farmers, buyers and businessmen who milled around the fountain, perch(ed) on the stools and talking ... while they nurse(d) a ten cent cup of coffee."[17] The store was once described as the "Wall Street of western barley, the crying wall of the potato industry, the place for a can of Libby's or a Coke, a porterhouse or a pleasant chat."[18]

At one time, the Agers considered removing the soda fountain because it was not very profitable. But when apprised of the plans, patrons complained. Some even threatened to do business at another grocery store in town, and the Agers changed their minds. Maintaining the fountain became part of their philosophy of giving "$2.00 worth of service with every $1.00 purchase."[19]

The success of the Agers' grocery business was one of the many examples of development in Tulelake in the 1930s. The city's first newspaper, *The Tulelake Wave* was founded in 1933. Several years later it was replaced by *The Tulelake Reporter*. Though it changed ownership several times, the paper retained the same name until it went out of business in the mid-1980s.

The town's first house of worship was the Tulelake Community Presbyterian Church, which soon joined with the Legion Hall in hosting many of the town's family oriented social functions. Together, the two institutions led the drive for many of the city's improvements.

One of the most important developments was in the field of education. The city's first school building was the White School, brought into town in 1931 from the Clyde Moore homestead. It was placed on a large piece of property bordered by Second Street and East-West Road that had been reserved by the Bureau of Reclamation for schools. One year later, the facility was filled to capacity and temporary classroom space had to be found elsewhere. The first building utilized was the one that housed Joe Frydendall's Shasta Lunch on Main Street. The cafe occupied one half of the building, and an elementary class was moved into the other.[20] Several months later, the class was moved to the Community Presbyterian Church, and remained there until Tulelake Elementary School was completed in 1933. The next year, a three-room high school was built and in 1936 its capacity was expanded when voters approved bonds to build additional classroom space.

Tulelake continued to experience growth throughout the 1930s, but it soon became apparent that the town's commercial interests were divided into two distinct groups. One was made up of the tavern and bar owners, who reaped healthy profits from liquor sales and gambling. The other was made up of grocery and retail owners whose clientele primarily consisted of basin residents. The "Liquor Element," as the tavern owners were called, wanted Tulelake to remain a wide-open town, catering to the entertainment interests of migrant workers, "out-of-towners," sportsmen, and local "hellraisers." But this direction was opposed by many of the city's residents. They were willing to tolerate, even frequent the saloons and gambling halls, but the "unsavory" elements that were attracted to town, and the nightly fights and street brawls, were giving Tulelake a bad name.

The real and imagined violence in Tulelake intimidated those who came to town or lived nearby. There was no local police agency and the only law enforcement was provided by the Siskiyou County Sheriff's Office, which was located over 100 miles to the southwest. One basin resident remembered that for reasons of safety, individuals who were either doing business in town or were attending a dance at the Legion Hall made sure that they had left town by eleven o'clock at night. Another man in business in town during the 1930s claimed that he had to sleep with a shotgun nearby for his own protection.[21]

In November of 1935, the Tulelake Chamber of Commerce, with Earl Ager as president, appointed a committee made up of Perry Wilson, Luke McAnulty and Leland Otey to look into the possibility of incorporating the city "before the townsite got shot up, or burned down."[22] California law required that a town must have a minimum population of 500 in order to incorporate. At least on paper, Tulelake was reputed to have had the minimum population--though it had been suggested that the count was taken during planting and harvest seasons, when the town's ranks included a sizeable number of migrant farm laborers.

Support for incorporation was not universal. The "Liquor Element" expressed concern that such a move might threaten their businesses, as a city government could exercise control over their operations. In 1936, plans went ahead for incorporation. In April, a petition was circulated in town. Most members of the "Liquor Element" wished to remain anonymous; consequently, there was little open opposition to the effort. On October 3, 1936, the petition for incorporation was filed with the Siskiyou County Board of Supervisors. It included a lengthy list of reasons for incorporation, including needs for a water and sewer system, street improvements and lighting, fire and police protection, and the creation of a taxing district to finance city operations.[23] The petition also included a list of businesses in Tulelake, which indicated the phenomenal growth that had taken place in the city during its first five years. These included:

Seven restaurants	Three auto garages
Fifteen potato cellars	Three warehouses
Six liquor establishments	Five service stations
Four farm machinery agencies	Three tourist camps
Two welding shops	Two hotels
Two barber shops	Two lumber yards
Two dry goods stores	One theater
One hardware store	Steam plant
Electrical contracting shop	One plumbing shop
Chevrolet agency and showroom	Blacksmith shop
Plymouth Agency	Shoe shop
Bank of America	Fuel Yard
Two churches	Telephone exchange
Drug store	Southern Pacific Depot

One beauty shop	One dentist
Siskiyou County Library branch	One attorney
California Oregon Power Co.	Branch County Jail
One newspaper publishing and printing plant	One Post Office (3d class) Small water dist. system
Grammar School having an attendance of 178 students	High School having an attendance of 116 students.[24]

Ten days after the petition was mailed to Yreka, the "icing" on the incorporation drive was provided by a major disaster in Tulelake. On the afternoon of Tuesday, October 13th, a fire broke out in the second story of a rooming house in the Al Powers business block, located at the southeastern corner of Main and E streets. The town lacked any organized fire protection, and the blaze soon spread to several saloons and gambling centers, including the Silver Mint beer parlor and restaurant. In a bizarre series of events, residents of the rooming house and customers of the saloons pitched in to save much of the buildings' contents, including furniture and cases of beer and hard liquor. A great pile of merchandise was stacked in the middle of Main Street, and when it became obvious that the fire was out of control, the customers seated themselves on an assortment of chairs, beds, and couches to watch the conflagration. In the process, they quenched their thirst by looting the great store of alcohol piled in the street.[25]

The few fire hoses available in town proved inadequate to fight the fire, and an emergency call was put out to the volunteer fire department in Merrill for assistance. When the volunteers arrived, they found that their hose couplings did not match the hydrants in Tulelake, and that the irrigation ditches next to the town were dry. A local welder was summoned and the hoses were welded to the hydrants, but then, to add to the comedy of errors, it was discovered that the amount of hose available was not long enough to reach the fire![26] By that evening, most of the block was reduced to glowing embers and the drunken spectators threatened to become an unruly mob. Since the town had no police force, an appeal for help was telephoned to the Siskiyou County Sheriff's Office. When the sheriff got on the phone, he was reported to have said; "All right, I'll be over first thing in the morning."[27]

On the morning of Wednesday, October 14, the unruly mob had dispersed, nursing hangovers from the drunken spree of the night before. The Powers block lay in ruin, but the fire proved to be a catalyst. Motivated by the inability of the town to deal with the disaster, virtually all opposition to incorporation disappeared.[28] With the blessings of the Siskiyou County Board of Supervisors, an incorporation election was set for Friday, February 26, 1937. During the final week of campaigning, *The Tulelake Reporter* printed a flyer emotionally appealing for support:

> Tulelake can get a loan and possibly a grant from WPA funds for a water system if it is incorporated. A YES VOTE in the election Friday will pave the way ...

> Last year six little girls in the Tulelake section were attacked by degenerates, one little child contracting a loathsome disease from the brute and was ruined for life. Fathers and mothers of Tulelake, your child may be the next victim. Help protect your child and your neighbor's child by VOTING YES for incorporation.

> Siskiyou county will on March 3 get $10,330 as the county's share of state liquor tax. If Tulelake was incorporated about $1500 of that amount would come here ...

> A madam from one of the vice houses in Klamath Falls has paid Tulelake several visits the past sixty days, presumably with the idea of bringing in "girls" and opening the first den of a redlight district. If residents of Tulelake don't want that kind of trash cluttering up their back streets then they should VOTE YES on incorporation Friday.[29]

On the day of the election, the ballot was divided into two parts. The first dealt with the town's status, the second with the formation of a city government that included a five-man council, a city clerk and a city treasurer. There were eight candidates for the city council positions, including: Clyde H. Barks, hotel owner; Everett L. Booth, implement dealer; Byron A. Crumb, auto camp proprietor; Harry E. Dicus, carpenter; Lawrence J. Horton, farmer; George Rieben, high school principal; Ernest C. Robinson, mechanic; and Charles K. Weise, real estate broker. Two candidates ran unopposed: E.H. McElroy for city clerk, and Charles Coats for city treasurer. When the ballots were counted, eighty-seven had voted in favor of incorporation, and only eight were opposed. Booth, Rieben, Horton, Weise, and Barks won seats on the city council.[30]

The ballots were kept in Tulelake until Sunday evening, February 28th, and then taken to Yreka by Floyd Boyd, Ed Gresham, Alex Clements, and Ed Davis. There at 12:01 A.M. on Monday morning, the Siskiyou County Board of Supervisors held a special session in which they officially certified the election results.[31] The four Tulelake men then hurriedly drove to Sacramento where they received the official seal of Frank Jordon, California Secretary of State, which was dated March 1, 1937— 9:45 a.m.[32] Tulelake was now officially incorporated—well, almost. Amid all the drama and haste of getting the new city charter approved by Siskiyou County and the State of California, the four representatives had neglected to bring an official map of the city with them. The error was not discovered until 1940 when Tulelake tried to hold a bond election for water and sewer improvements. The state refused to allow the election because of the missing map. The problem was quickly rectified with the help of Siskiyou County—but in a technical sense, Tulelake had functioned for three years without actually being a city![33]

With official certification of the February 26, 1937 election out of the way, representatives of Tulelake immediately embarked on a campaign to bring improvements to the city. The week after the election, a committee composed of Hyman Wechsler, Clyde Barks, Jack Carlisle and Charles Coats was formed to help organize a volunteer fire department. They drove to Merrill to meet with Ben Faus, Merrill's fire chief, and discuss the necessary procedures for establishing a volunteer fire district. Four months later, on June 10th, the Tulelake Volunteer Fire Department was officially organized and consisted of twenty-one members. Weschsler was elected president, Floyd A. Boyd, chief, and Jack Metz, assistant chief.[34]

Eighteen days after the official organization of the Tulelake Volunteer Fire Department, they had their first run. The department's minutes of June 28, 1937 read:

> About one o'clock in the morning, the siren blew. This was our first fire. It was at the L.J. Horton home here in town. The boys did a good job in extinguishing the fire with only a small loss. This home would have been completely destroyed had we not been organized to tackle the job.[35]

On July 1st, the department went on its second run, this time to put out a fire in the framework of the city's water well. In recognition of the fire department's organization and achievements, the city council agreed, on July 22nd, to purchase a fire truck from the Howard Cooper Corporation of Portland, Oregon for $2,250. The model ordered was reported to have been the "latest thing out."[36] Mounted on a Chevrolet truck, the engine was fully equipped with "hoses, pumps, axes, ladders, wrenches, collapsible buckets, shovels, fire truck siren, flash lamps and other items."[37]

When the fire truck arrived on September 4, the *Tulelake Reporter* recorded the momentous event:

> An air of festivity pervaded Tulelake Saturday, September 4, 1937 when the long looked for and badly needed fire equipment arrived in town ... Saturday morning the truck, under the escort of the Oregon State Police, left Klamath Falls for Merrill where it was met by the Merrill Fire Department and escorted to the Merrill city limits. At Merrill the Tulelake party and twenty or thirty automobiles joined the procession and ... it proceeded to the state line where Patrolman Ed Washburn took charge ... The parade entered Tulelake at the noon hour amid the tooting of siren, horn and other noise making.

> The paraders toured up and down the streets, finally leaving the truck at the far end of Main Street ... After the fire wagon had reached that point, a small outhouse, that had been hauled to a vacant lot across from the theater and stuffed with tar paper, was set afire and the siren sounded. [This brought] the apparatus pounding [down] the street. Reaching the scene, the fire laddies went through their paces and demonstrated their ability to cope with any fire that occurred.[38]

That night, the engine had its second official test. A drunk at the city jail had started a fire in his bedding and it was promptly extinguished. Five days later, the truck and crew were called out on another run. This time they went to the Tulelake carnival grounds where a trailer house was on fire. Due to the firemen's rapid response, only a small loss was incurred.

The next week, the fire department had its first major call. A railroad car loaded with baled hay was on fire near the Southern Pacific Depot, threatening several nearby buildings and a whole string of rail cars. The department's effort limited losses to $500, and it was praised for its accomplishment by officials of the Southern Pacific Company.[39] In later years, the skill of the department became known statewide, and its services provided concrete proof of the benefits of incorporation.

One of the last major hurdles in the 1930s for the town of Tulelake was obtaining a reliable source of drinking water. The only local source of good water was at the Kalina store in Malin, which was made available for free to anyone who came to town. In addition, as a gesture of good will, the Southern Pacific Railroad brought in tank cars of water, filled at its rail yard in Perez, 30 miles to the south. These were placed at sidings in Tulelake and Stronghold where people filled buckets and fifty-five gallon steel drums to take to their homes.

There were several fundamental problems with water drawn from basin wells. Its high iron content stained nearly everything it came in contact with, it had a highly sulfurous odor, and it was loaded with methane gas. Other than just being "downright nasty stuff to drink," local water could be dangerous. One of the standing jokes in town was to tell visitors that the water in Tulelake was so volatile that it would burn. As expected, the visitor would reply with scoffs. A milk bottle would then be ceremoniously filled half full of water, shaken, and a match dropped in. Sure enough, the air above the water ignited with a loud "pop." There were other stories about pockets of methane gas catching the foolish and unwary. For example, at the Chevrolet Garage on northwest corner of D and Main (today used by the Tulelake Basin School District as a bus garage), a man was warned not to smoke while in the bathroom. He ignored the warning, lit up a cigarette while using the facility, and ignited a sizeable pocket of gas. The explosion blew open the bathroom door and singed the occupant—confirming that Tulelake's water could indeed be considered a fire hazard![40]

Incorporation of Tulelake in 1937 gave the town the ability to coordinate the search for a good source of water, but it took sixteen years of effort to bring about success. The city first asked the Bureau of Reclamation for help, but this was denied. Then the city began a fundraising drive to drill a well. Community rummage, craft and bake sales were held, along with dances and solicitations for individual contributions. In 1938, a test well as drilled and by the end of the year, a shaft had been sunk more than 1900 feet without hitting bedrock. In 1940 the search for the elusive "good water" continued with the passage of a bond issue (*after* the city officially recorded its map with the State of California) to sink a new well and construct a comprehensive water delivery system. By January of 1941, the well had been deepened to 2,200 feet and on the 23rd, amid great celebration, the new well's water was turned into the city's mains. Unhappily its quality soon deteriorated and the elusive "good water" was not yet to be found! Tulelake limped along on using its tainted water supply for the remainder of the 1940s. Several schemes were suggested to resolve the problem. One was to tap into a spring at Bryant Mountain and pipe water to the city. Another involved an ambitious plan, suggested by city councilman E.L. "Roy" Coyner, to separate the methane from the water, and then sell both to city customers—the water for drinking and the gas for cooking and heating.[41] Coyner's plan might have had possibilities, but there was never enough capital available to invest in the equipment needed to give it a try.

By 1950, the city's water situation reached a crisis stage as Tulelake's population exceeded 1,500 and the old well's production declined. On May 24th, the Outdoor Store on Main Street suffered major fire damage. In fighting the blaze, the fire department nearly depleted the deep well's water supply. There was a backup shallow well pump standing by, but, had it been used, it would have put contaminated water into the city's system.[42] The city then decided to sink a new well, but ran out of money before getting any positive results.

In 1951, the shaft in the deep water well was sunk to 2,254 feet but *The Tulelake Reporter* expressed the general feelings in town when its headlines read "IT'S SOFTER, SMOOTHER, SWEETER; BUT MOST FOLK CAUTIOUS OVER NEW WATER."[43] Initially the new water received good reviews. One local resident said, "I can't get my wife away from the wash tub; she just keeps on washing and washing."[44] And a local merchant commented: "We served Tulelake water all afternoon in the cafe; not a single customer complained or even noticed it."[45] But not everyone was satisfied with the results. The Valley Camel, which sold bottled water, reported no drop in customers, and in fact one woman called to ask for the service because the new water had killed her goldfish![46] The fish may have been an omen, because it wasn't long before the same problems with gas, mud, and iron plagued the city once again.

Finally in 1953, the city sank a new well nearly 3,000 feet deep, with miraculous results. The water was clean, pure, and for a while it actually "artisaned" from the well, flowing on its own into a storage tank at the city's corporation yard on the west end of town. From there, the water was pumped to a large silver water tank erected next to the city hall and near Highway #139. With "TULELAKE" written in large black letters on its side, the tank boldly proclaimed that the long battle for decent water was over. The same well is still producing potable water today, and its delivery system covers both the city and much of the northern and central basin.

Tulelake had to struggle for other improvements, including the installation of an airport. Lacking its own funds, the city hoped that through appeals to the state and federal government, plus a little "tactical maneuvering" on its own part, an airport could be constructed. Several sites were contemplated for an airstrip. One proposed site was located about six miles south of town near Stronghold. The other proposed location was on the east side of the Peninsula. The airport campaign began with the Tulelake Chamber of Commerce writing to the Civil Aeronautics Administration asking for help in establishing an emergency landing field. The letter said in part: "A pole has been set and wind indicators mounted, and we would greatly appreciate it if you would advise us in any way to secure proper airport markings, and have the temporary field designated on your maps for the convenience of both civil and defense pilots."[47]

While waiting for a reply, the chamber wrote Tide Water Oil Company, asking for a wind sock for use at its local airport. The company responded by saying: "We are pleased to advise you that one of these wind socks is being shipped to you direct and should reach you within the next few days."[48] But then the chamber's plans went awry. R.W.F. Schmidt from the Civil Aeronautics Administration wrote to say that: "Before such a field can be established in our records it will be necessary for a field inspection to be accomplished by a representative of this office."[49] Before the inspection took place, World War II broke out and plans for Tulelake's airport were put on hold.

In the late 1940s, the airport campaign was renewed, and attention was focused on Bureau of Reclamation land to the east of Newell. The site was rapidly being emptied of barracks that once housed more than 18,000 Japanese-Americans and Japanese resident aliens who had been incarcerated there during World War II. The large firebreak in the middle of the Japanese section of the former internment camp was an ideal location for an airstrip. In 1950 Congressman Clair Engle, from California's Second Congressional District, was asked for help. Engle approached the Bureau of Reclamation, requesting that the site be deeded to the city of Tulelake. However, the transfer of ownership was complicated by the fact that the proposed airstrip was in Modoc County and Tulelake was in Siskiyou County. By the summer of 1950, Engle's work was effective and a unique arrangement had been worked out. Tulelake was given ownership of the land, and money to build a 3,500-foot cinder landing strip was provided jointly by the federal government and Modoc and Siskiyou counties.[50]

Although Tulelake was able to solve many of the major obstacles to becoming a viable city, there were some problems that seemed insurmountable. Foremost was the town's continual battle with obscurity. Its two basin neighbors, Merrill and Malin, earned a certain notoriety that at least stirred recognition when their names were mentioned. Merrill was known both because Oregon Highway #39 passed through its downtown section, and because of its annual Potato Festival. Malin became famous for its Czechoslovakian heritage. But Tulelake struggled to find some form of recognition. The "Liquor Element" made the earliest efforts. However, the campaign to make the town the "Little Reno" of Northern California didn't float well with the town's populace. After incorporation in 1937, the city primarily sought to emphasize the recreational advantages of the basin and its fame in producing potatoes and horseradish. Still, gaining recognition remained difficult. For example, the Chamber of Commerce had to fight in the 1940s to get Tulelake listed on maps, to have its name included on city mileage signs, and to get the media to correctly identify its location. In one classic example, a motion picture photographer for Paramount News visited the Tule Lake National Wildlife Refuge in 1941 and took pictures of the birds there. However, when the newsreel was run, it was labeled Tule Lake, Oregon and the story implied that it was located next to Klamath Falls. The Chamber of Commerce was incensed, and in a letter told Paramount Pictures:

> Your news pictures ... will be shown in thousands of theaters in the largest centers of the United States. We

feel that there is a strong possibility that your erroneous caption of the film may mislead many hunters who desire to take advantage of the sport here.

And ... the unkindest cut of all is that through the incorrect titles, Tulelake stands to lose the most valuable advertising that it is possible to obtain.[51]

Paramount apologized for the error, but it was not until the homestead drawings of 1946 to 1949 that the town was able to bask in "positive" national headlines.

Though "Tulelake" did not become a household word, the growth pattern of the city, both in terms of people and businesses, followed a continual upward swing throughout the 1940s. From 1942 to 1945, the city became an unusual crossroads beneficiary of World War II. In the spring of 1942, a huge camp was constructed to the east of the Peninsula at a site designated as "Newell." It housed more than 18,000 Japanese Americans and Japanese resident aliens, who had been incarcerated as a direct result of war-bred racial hysteria along the west coast (see chapters Fourteen to Sixteen for a complete discussion of Japanese internment in the Tule Lake Basin). While the camp was being constructed, the city of Tulelake was filled to capacity with construction workers. They were subsequently replaced with families whose husbands and wives were employed at the camp. Tulelake merchants not only served the needs of these new residents, but they also did a thriving business with the camp itself.

In 1944, through a rather strange twist of events, the city and basin were the recipients of several hundred prisoners of war. Basin farmers had been desperate for seasonal workers, whose ranks had been substantially reduced because of the draft and war-related industry. The Tulelake Growers Association requested help from the federal government, and arrangements were made for Mexican nationals to be brought in, but the labor shortage remained critical. Consequently, an appeal was made to bring in Italian and German prisoners of war, held at Camp White in Medford, Oregon. The first group of POWs to come into the Basin was Italian. They were used to refurbish the CCC camp on Hill Road, to the west of the city of Tulelake, at the base of Sheepy Ridge. As many as 400 German POWs were subsequently brought in to work the fields. Some were housed at the CCC camp, while others lived in tents put up in a large vacant area that is today Tulelake's city park.[52]

Long-time basin resident John Staunton was a teenage boy when the POW camp was in operation. He remembered frequently seeing German soldiers trucked by his farm and shouting "Heil Hitler" as they were being taken to the Lava Beds. There they had been assigned to tear down the CCC camp. Apparently many of the nails the Germans pulled from the dismantled buildings were bent into triangles and secretly strewn along the roadways. Staunton noted "You couldn't travel anywhere in the basin within getting a flat tire!"[54]

The German POWs were under constant guard, but among the younger prisoners relations with basin residents were generally cordial. One son of a homesteader remembered his family's interaction as being:

> a friendly type situation. My father would take out, depending on what time of year it was or what they wanted, a case of beer, soda pop, or coffee. He would pay them, too, so they earned a total of about $1.25 a day. The guards would set aside their rifles in the ditch and they'd go out and work too! My dad paid them the same wages right along with [the prisoners].[54]

Later the Army put an end to such fraternization, but it was a unique situation. Some basin residents were even the recipients of gifts from the Germans, including a number of paintings made while the Germans were at the CCC camp.

After the war, the city continued to grow. Many new businesses appeared as merchants anticipated an economic boom brought about by the Bureau of Reclamation opening additional homestead land at the southern end of the basin. In the fall of 1945, work was begun on the city's largest and most elaborate hotel, the Sportsman. Its construction was financed by William Seigler, John Melin, Rafael Moresco and James Horn, and it featured a lunch counter and restaurant, bar, and gambling casino. Until 1948, when a new sheriff ended open gambling in town, the Sportsmen was the town's most palatial night spot, offering slot machines, poker, Black Jack, and roulette.

In 1947, the basin's increased population led to the construction of a larger Presbyterian church, which was joined in the next two years by a Catholic church and a chapel for members of the Church of Jesus Christ of Latter Day Saints (Mormons). The last year of the decade was also a proud moment for basin residents. One of Tulelake High School's graduates, Hugh Wilson, Jr., received an appointment to the military academy at West Point.

The decade of the 1950s represented both the zenith of Tulelake's growth and the beginning of its decline. During the first half of the decade there were still the traditional battles to be won and noble causes to be fought. One of the important issues in the early 1950s was establishing a fairground in the Tule Lake Basin. Basin youth living on the California side of the border who were involved in 4-H, or were interested in showing animals that they had raised, had to travel to county fairs in either Cedarville or Yreka. Both were more than 100 miles away.

Soon after the end of World War II, a drive was begun by the Tulelake Chapter of Rotary to establish a local fair. Chet Main, a 1938 homesteader, spearheaded the effort. Initial efforts were dampened when, in 1948, California Governor Earl Warren declared a moratorium on the creation of new fair districts. However, through intensive lobbying by Main and other members of Rotary, support was secured from the California State Legislature and the town was given a "Junior Show" designation. Negotiations were then undertaken to receive full county fair status, which included convincing the Bureau of Reclamation to deed land at the southwest end of town for a fairgrounds. At times success seemed uncertain as the state initially balked at providing money for fair buildings when title to the fairgrounds was not assured, but finally by the end of 1952, all details were worked out and the Tulelake-Butte Valley Fair achieved official status. The first fair board included Chet Main as president, Bill Hagelstin as Vice President, plus Pete Bergman, Vern Hemstreet, Arnold Criss, and Webb Staunton. The first fair manager was Sam Kellett. Bill Whitaker, who helped design and landscape the fairgrounds, replaced him the next year.[55]

During the first year of the fair, in September of 1953, members of the fair board were exuberant that their lengthy efforts had finally paid off, but the weather managed to add a touch of humility. There had not been time to plant grass and on the opening day a strong wind came whipping through the grounds, blowing down booths and covering everything with dust. Chet Main remembered walking by several stands where the proprietors soundly denounced him for the weather. With a twinkle in his eye he admitted that there were certain things beyond the control of even the most dedicated planner in Tulelake.[56]

Tulelake of the 1950s was still, in many ways, a young town, eager to celebrate a major addition. For example, on Saturday, March 4, 1950, over 3,000 people attended a nighttime festival to witness the turning on of eighteen mercury vapor lamps, the city's first major street lighting system. *The Tulelake Reporter* described the event:

> Over 3,000 people, including several hundred visitors from six neighboring communities, crowded into Tulelake Saturday night for the city's Big Lite Night ... one of the most successful celebrations held here in several years.

> Mayor W.R. Moore threw the switch at 6:46 p.m. A faint glow appeared in the 18 lamps arched over Main street from the highway to East-West road where the making of a parade was slipping into line. The lights reached their full brilliance in about 15 minutes, casting a soft, blue veil over the business area.

> Led by the V.F.W. color guard, the three-block long parade started off with a boom ... provided by [the] Tulelake High School band. Merrill's High School drill team came next followed by the local Cubs, then the long assortment of 1950 model cars bearing the "big brass," then commercial floats, fire trucks and a lone rider astride a stout mount.[57]

The early 1950s also heralded the creation of the city's park. The site had originally housed the German POWs, and then after the war, temporary government housing had been constructed there to provide shelter for returning veterans and their families. In November of 1950, the housing program was terminated and, for several years, the fate of the park block was debated. Finally, in the summer of 1952, the Kiwanis Club promoted the idea of developing the park and promised to provide swings and other playground equipment. A brief squabble developed between the Kiwanis and the 20-30 club over the development of the park, but in 1953 the issue was resolved, and the Otis Roper Park was graded, grass planted, and playground equipment installed.

Amid the excitement of growth, tragedy befell Tulelake. Hugh Wilson, Jr., who was the pride of the basin when he became a West Point "plebe" in July 1950, was killed in a plane crash in Arizona. He had been on a return flight to the Academy after spending the 1951 Christmas holidays with his parents. His loss was mourned, but his memory lived on through the publication of a small booklet that described the Modoc Indian War. Hugh had originally written the account as an entrance assignment to the Academy.

On a positive note, evidence of the city and basin's continued growth in the early 1950s was reflected in the Tulelake Basin Unified School District's enrollment of 1952, which reached a record 737 pupils.[58] Continued healthy student enrollment through the second half of the 1950s led to the construction of a new, larger high school in 1957. It was located on the southeast corner of Main and G streets, across from the fairgrounds. The close proximity of the two facilities was to allow the mutual use of building space and grounds for school and fair activities.

Though the completion of Tulelake High School was new cause for celebration, significant growth in the town was essentially over. In fact, there were clear signs that the character and direction of Tulelake were changing. Some of the changes were subtle and at first appeared to be part of the growth of the city. For example, the American Legion Hall on the corner of D and Second streets, once the center for community activities, was torn down and its lumber used to build a Baptist church on the same lot. The stately building that had at one time been the site of countless meetings, dances, strategy sessions, weddings and the last homestead drawing had become less frequently used and a financial burden to the local chapter of the American Legion. Even the Legion itself had lost its steam. As the post war years drifted by, the Legion's original membership began to focus its energies in other organizations, from church groups to community service clubs. Facing dwindling membership and the expense of maintaining a large, aging building, the Legion sold the hall and property and the famous structure disappeared.

Change also came to Earl's Market, Tulelake's daily social gathering place. Earl and Dorothy Ager sold the store in the mid-1950s, and Earl entered the arena of politics as a Siskiyou

County Supervisor. The new owner, who changed the market's name to Jock's, converted the building to strictly deal with groceries and sundries; a realistic move considering the unprofitability of the soda fountain. Local residents who sought a cup of coffee and a meeting place moved over to the lunch counter at the Sportsman's Hotel.

The disappearance of the Legion Hall and the transition at Earl's Market portended three decades of decline for Tulelake, both in terms of population and retail outlets. Why did Tulelake go from a boomtown of as many as 2,500 people to a community with slightly more than 800 residents? And why did it lose from one-third to one-half of its businesses? The change came about due to a combination of factors. In the heady years immediately following World War II, there was excessive optimism about the economic future of both the city of Tulelake and the surrounding farmland. Real growth continued until 1952, and then the upward curve flattened out. At first there was internal finger pointing, as merchants and town promoters searched for a reason for the economic downturn. During a March 1953 meeting of the Tulelake Chamber of Commerce, insurance man Paul Roger railed against his fellow businessmen:

> The merchants here blame the sales tax for this, they blame the lack of selection available in Tulelake, they blame everything except what is the real cause ... the businessman himself. What we lack here is ... service. Perhaps it's because we know each other too well—there's too much treating each other as "friends" and not enough of treating each other as customers ... [in addition] we don't do enough promotion and advertising to let people know what is available.[59]

In part, Rogers was correct. During the economic boom, a certain smugness had settled over the retail community, but in truth there were too many other factors to have stemmed the economic decline. Improved roadways and automobiles made Klamath Falls a short thirty to forty-minute drive away from the basin. Most local merchants were unable to compete with larger volume retail outlets found in that city. Farm mechanization was replacing seasonal workers, and the city became increasingly less crowded during the planting and harvesting seasons. After the final homestead period of 1948 to 1949, no additional land in the basin was opened for farm settlement. Gradually, the farming population declined. To survive the increasing expenses of farming, farmers who remained generally purchased farm units offered for sale by those who moved away or retired. Consequently, there was little to draw newcomers to the basin.

By the end of the 1950s, the impact was clearly seen. One by one, the smaller business in Tulelake closed their doors. The car dealers were among the first to go, followed by clothing stores, and other general merchandise outlets. By the 1970s, the only new businesses of significance were those related to farm services. One of the saddest losses was the Sportsman's Hotel. On Thursday morning, December 13, 1984 an electrical short started a fire that consumed the entire building.[60] Gone in a matter of hours was the town's major gathering place. Because of Tulelake's stagnant economy, it was doubtful that the hotel would be rebuilt. Instead, the town's people hoped that a restaurant with meeting rooms would be constructed on the site, but it seemed unlikely this would happen.

Another loss occurred on May 29, 1986, when the *Tulelake Reporter* published its last newspaper. Ed Davis had started the paper in 1934, and it was housed in a building located to the west of Earl's Market, on the corner of Siskiyou and Main streets. In 1945, it moved to the Golden Hotel building, where its offices remained until the paper ceased operation. The *Tulelake Reporter's* last owner was Fred Tate, who was unable to weather the economic slump and competition from another basin paper, the *Lost River Star*, published in Merrill.

Was the city of Tulelake's thirty-year decline and the loss of the Sportsman's Hotel and the *Tulelake Reporter* an indication that the city's retail community was destined to disappear? No, not unless all farming were to cease in the basin. Tulelake during the last thirty years has gone through a period of maturation. The brash young town that regaled in continual growth for two and a half decades is now a more mature and quiet town, where the retail community matches the existing population more evenly.

A drive down Main Street in the mid-1980s gives a false impression of Tulelake. There is a significant number of empty buildings, but these are vestiges of the boom years. In time, as these buildings are torn down or are converted to other uses, Main Street will take on a more enterprising appearance. Hope for the future is not dead either. City Clerk Joe Cordinier once jokingly said that "All roads lead to Rome ... and some lead to Tulelake," but there was a hint of seriousness in his statement.[61]

Cordinier believes that Tulelake needs to develop something unique to attract outside attention; something beyond the annual Tulelake-Butte Valley Fair and bird-hunting season. Malin has been enormously successful with its periodic Bohemian festivals, and Cordinier feels that Tulelake could possibly develop its own annual festival. One suggestion is to tie together the basin's wealth of waterfowl and wildlife with a yearly cultural celebration. Such a festival would emphasize the Tule Lake Basin's singular beauty and its unique blend of farming and wildlife management. The festival would cater to the interests of conservationists, bird watchers, artists, photographers, and sportsmen.[62]

The dreams of Joe Cordinier are not much different from those of the original founders of Tulelake. It was visionaries who built the town, and it will be those willing to become involved in molding Tulelake's future that will keep the community alive.

"Official Map" of the City of Tulelake in 1940.
(Courtesy Siskiyou County Court House, Yreka, California)

Aerial view of Tulelake in the 1980s. *(Photo courtesy Tulelake-Butte Valley Fair, Museum of Local History)*

First sale of lots at the Tulelake townsite, April, 1931. *(Photo courtesy Bureau of Reclamation)*

On October 13, 1936, a fire consumed much of the "Al Powers" block, including the Silver Mint Cafe. *(Photo courtesy Herald and News)*

Above and below, Tulelake in the prosperous days of the1940s and 1950s. *(Photo above courtesy Bureau of Reclamation; below courtesy Tulelake-Butte Valley Fair, Museum of Local History)*

Tulelake in 1938, looking north on Main Street. *(Photo courtesy Tulelake-Butte Valley Fair, Museum of Local History)*

Tulelake in 2002, looking north on Main Street. *(Photo by author)*

The City of Tulelake in 1949, looking south on Main Street. Note that the streets are not yet paved but the business district was thriving. *(Photo courtesy Bureau of Reclamation)*

Looking south on Main Street in 2002. *(Photo by author)*

CHAPTER 14

PRELUDE TO THE INTERNMENT YEARS
IN THE BASIN—WHY JAPANESE-AMERICANS?

Though there is considerable historical distance between the events of Pearl Harbor and contemporary American society, the surprise attack by the Imperial Government of Japan on the Hawaiian Islands on December 7, 1941 still remains one of the most important moments in American history. The attack's immediate impact was electrifying. The power of the American fleet in the Pacific was severely curtailed, most civilian and military officials were caught by surprise, and there was concern on the West Coast that the Japanese would launch an invasion at any moment. Yet the real impact of the attack on Pearl Harbor was unforeseen by most Japanese leaders. Instead of forcing the United States to capitulate its interests in Southeast Asia and to give up the Pacific to Japan, Pearl Harbor unified a divided country. Pacifists, members of the America First Committee, and other isolationistic groups who had counseled against American involvement in the war in Europe, disappeared. Instead the country committed itself to full-scale war in both Europe and the Pacific.

Though Pearl Harbor unified Americans, leading to a concerted effort to defeat Japan and Germany, it had a negative impact on an important segment of American society. On the West Coast there were more than 120,000 Japanese-Americans and Japanese alien residents. Because of their race and because of racial prejudice and self-imposed isolation, they could be easily identified. As frantic military and civilian personnel cast about for a reason for the swiftness and efficiency of the attack on Pearl Harbor, their attention quickly became focused on Japanese-Americans. It seemed obvious to civilian and military leaders that Pearl Harbor was the product of a well-orchestrated conspiracy on the part of the Japanese community living in the United States. In reality, their conclusions were rooted in war-generated hysteria and deep seated racism, rather than actual fact.

During the early stages of the war, every act perpetrated by Japan brought greater focus on the Japanese-American community. For example, on February 23, 1942, a Japanese submarine shelled a number of oil wells at Goleta, California. The actual damage was minimal (around $500) and the intent of the shelling was harassment, but psychologically, the shelling had a strong impact. To worried civilians and military personnel, this was further proof that an invasion was forthcoming. They also were convinced that the submarine had received information from on-shore spies, part of an espionage team that had made Pearl Harbor possible. To these people it was evident that the source of this spy network was the Japanese-American community.

An intense campaign was launched by West Coast public officials to deal with the Japanese-American community and to neutralize any part that they might play in supporting Japan launched an intense campaign. Leaders in this effort included General John L. DeWitt, commander of the Western Defense Command, California State Attorney General Earl Warren, and Congressman John H. Tolan. Their campaign led to President Franklin D. Roosevelt issuing Executive Order #9066 on February 19, 1942. The directive by the President read in part:

> WHEREAS the successful prosecution of the war requires every possible protection against espionage and against sabotage to the national-defense materials national-defense premises, and national-defense utilities as defined:

> NOW, THEREFORE, by the authority vested in me as President of the United States, and Commander in Chief of the Army and Navy, I hereby authorize and direct the Secretary of War and the Military Commanders who he may from time to time designate ... to prescribe military areas in such places and of such extent as he or the appropriate Military Commander may determine, from which ANY OR ALL PERSONS may be excluded ...[1]

General DeWitt implemented President Roosevelt's executive order by declaring the coasts of Washington, Oregon and California as military zones. Suspected enemy aliens, including Germans, Italians and Japanese (many of whom had already been arrested by the FBI and local agencies), were ordered to be removed from these regions. Soon after, DeWitt and other government officials decided to remove the entire Japanese-American and Japanese resident alien population as well.

At first, Japanese-American families were encouraged to move on their own to the interior of the United States. However, this plan did not work well. Many Japanese were reluctant to leave their familiar and well-established communities. Of those who did make the voluntary move, a significant number returned to the West Coast with reports of white hostility to their resettlement. The government then implemented the second phase of removal, which involved the involuntary uprooting of all Japanese residents from the West Coast. Temporary facilities were first established at racetracks and fairgrounds to house the Japanese until ten permanent relocation camps were built. The site selected for one of these ten camps was in the Tule Lake Basin.

The decision to intern Japanese-Americans who lived on the West Coast was a perplexing one, filled with contradictions. On the Hawaiian Islands, where the Japanese-American community made up a substantial percentage of the population, only a small number were incarcerated. Among other ethnic groups whose ancestors were at war against the United States—principally Germans and Italians—only a few individuals were detained and jailed (though to be fair, it should be pointed out that many Germans and Italians were harassed during the war). Why then were 110,000 West Coast Japanese interned? And why was Tule Lake selected as the site for one of the largest camps, one that would earn an infamous page in the history of internment? The answers come through an analysis of the history of the relationship between the United States and Japan and the history of Japanese emigration to the West Coast.

In July 1853, Commodore Matthew C. Perry forced Japan out of self-imposed isolation through gunboat diplomacy. With his formidable, well-armed "black ships," he sailed into Tokyo Bay. Using his position of military strength, Perry convinced the Tokugawa government to open Japan to American ships seeking supplies and shelter from Pacific storms. Japan soon entered into a series of trade agreements with a variety of foreign countries, and her new contacts with the outside world caused a frenzied program of modernization. As a resource-poor country, with finite boundaries and a growing population, Japan not only embarked on an ambitious program of foreign trade, but also began to dramatically upgrade her military strength. The power and efficiency of her military caught world attention in 1894 when Japan invaded Korea, and again ten years later when she defeated the Russian army at Makden in Manchuria and the

Russian navy in the Straits of Tsushima. Clearly Japan was a power to be reckoned with.

Meanwhile, Japan's age old problem of too many people and not enough land led the Japanese government to allow segments of her population to emigrate to other countries. This opportunity was particularly attractive to the second and third sons and daughters of poor farm families. With little chance of inheriting land or marrying into families of prestige, they had an uncertain future in Japan.

It was America's need for cheap labor and the dream of financial success that brought the Japanese to Hawaii and the West Coast of the United States. The greatest period of immigration was between 1890 and 1920, when more than 80,000 Japanese men and women made the trek across the Pacific.[2] Settling in Hawaii, Washington, Oregon, and California, they went to work in canneries, on the railroads, in farm fields, and on fishing boats. The pay was low and the hours were long, but with thrift, many Japanese workers were able to save enough money to buy their own small plots of farmland. The farms they developed were marvels in themselves. Incorporating Japanese farming techniques of soil chemistry, terracing, hybrid seeds, and fertilizers, marginal land was transformed into highly productive vegetable and flower growing farms. On the West Coast, the Japanese farm population was so successful that in some areas of California it controlled 50% of the truck farming and 70% of the flower growing market. Other Japanese became independent merchants and fishermen. In locations such as San Pedro, near Los Angeles, and to the north in Monterey, their fishing boats were found in large numbers.[3]

In the meantime, anti-Asian feelings in America were steadily growing. The first perception of a "Yellow Peril" streaming out of Asia to overwhelm the United States developed as a result of Chinese immigrants coming to the United States in the mid-1800s. They were lured first by the California gold rush and later by jobs offered by the railroad. But the Chinese suffered terribly from acts of discrimination and violence. When the Chinese were no longer considered desirable, the Chinese Exclusion Act of 1882 was passed, barring further Chinese immigration. Yet there continued to be a need for cheap labor on the West Coast, and the focus turned to the Japanese and a new wave of immigration began.

There were several clear differences between the immigration patterns of the Chinese and the Japanese. The majority of the Chinese men who came to the United States were sojourners who planned to make their fortune and then return home. Sadly, most were never able to earn enough money for their return passage, let alone strike it rich on the "golden mountain" of California. On the other hand, most Japanese left for the United States with the intent of putting down permanent roots, knowing that there was little future in Japan. Yet, no matter where they moved, the Japanese government still considered them to be part of Japan and these transplanted citizens were to be treated with courtesy and respect (much the same way that the United States felt about its citizens).

Though the early Japanese immigrants were treated relatively well by West Coast Caucasians, it may have been more out of curiosity than respect. By the early 1900s, those who came to America were encountering strong resistance and overt racism. For example, in February of 1905, a resolution was unanimously passed by the California State Legislature, which in part stated:

> Japanese laborers, by reason of race habits, mode of living, disposition and general characteristics, are undesirable. Japanese ... do not buy land [or] build or buy houses ... They contribute nothing to the growth of the state. They add nothing to its wealth, and they are a blight on the prosperity of it and a great and impending danger to its welfare.[4]

The next year, the Board of Education in San Francisco took action to exclude Japanese students from the city's public schools. Whereas racial segregation and exclusion was a long established pattern in the United States, it was not well accepted by the Japanese government, who took offense at the poor treatment of its present and former citizens. The San Francisco incident reached a critical stage when the Japanese government, flush from their victory over Russia, lodged a strong complaint with the U.S. government. Concerned about possible hostilities with Japan, President Theodore Roosevelt intervened. In 1907 he negotiated the Gentlemen's Agreement, in which Japan agreed to curtail immigration to the U.S. in return for fair treatment of its citizens residing in America. However, in the long run, the Gentlemen's Agreement did not achieve either objective.

Opposition to Japanese immigration and the presence of Japanese on the West Coast went through several phases. The first phase was sparked by labor interests who were fearful that Caucasian workers would be replaced by Japanese willing to work for lower wages. Leaders in the movement to exclude the Japanese included Mayor James D. Phelan of San Francisco, later a United States Senator. Phelan's slogan was direct: "Keep America American."[5] This was an interesting phrase, since all but Native Americans (Indians) were relatively recent immigrants!

In 1910, the anti-Asian movement was so strong that every major political party in California—Republican, Democratic and Socialist—had anti-Japanese statements in their platforms. In the same year, a drive was launched to restrict all Asian immigration to the United States. On April 10, 1910, a bill was introduced in Congress by Representative Hayes of California, which would have extended the Chinese Exclusion Act to include "Japanese, Koreans, Tartars, Malays, Afghans, East Indians, Lascars, Hindoos (sic) and all other people included in the Asiatic or Mongolian race."[6] In Japan, the reaction of the press to this action was tempered with reason. The *Daily Asahi*, published in Tokyo, said:

> The question of the naturalization of Japanese in America is one of the most important matters at the present time. The time is ripe for Japan to take a decisive step toward co-operating with the better element in America, as represented by ex-President Roosevelt. Such attacks on the Japanese as made by the Hayes bill, now before the American Congress are becoming wearisome, and are made only by the lower element of the American nation.[7]

Though Congress put off curtailing all Asian immigration, the racial feelings expressed against the Japanese residing in the U.S. continued. These feelings were intensified by foreign developments. Japan's victory over Russia in the war of 1904 to 1905 elevated her military status in the Pacific. By 1910 there was concern in the United States that the U.S. and Japan might go to war over conflicting naval interests. Even remote rumors made national headlines. One article put out on the national wire service in December of 1910 said:

It is persistently reported that a Japanese plot to mine Manila harbor and blow up American warships in the event of hostilities ... is emphasized by the discovery of quantities of high explosives in Japanese houses. General Duvall is supervising the search, but all requests for information have been refused.[8]

Between 1900 and 1930, the films of Hollywood aided in the perpetuation of the myth of the "Yellow Peril" as a threat to America. "Movie audiences were acquainted with Orientals almost solely as villains: sinister and inscrutable figures who lurked in opium dens by day and emerged under cover of darkness on errands of vengeance and treachery."[9] For example, in 1909 Hollywood produced "The Japanese Invasion." In the film a Japanese valet steals military secrets from an American officer, providing Japan with a battle plan for attacking the West Coast of the United States. In 1920, the American Legion released a film titled "Shadows of the West" which depicted Japanese as masterminding vegetable market and land acquisition operations in California.[10] Hollywood was not alone in its racist assault on Japanese-Americans. Novels, comic books, and pulp magazines of the time promoted the stereotypical "Jap": bucktoothed, bespectacled, and crafty.

In the teens and early 1920s, anti-Japanese feelings on the West Coast pressured state governments and Congress into passing a series of restrictive laws. In California, Oregon and Washington, as well as Arizona, Colorado, Delaware, Nebraska, Texas, Idaho, and New Mexico, alien land acts were passed by popular vote and barred land purchases by "aliens ineligible [for] citizenship."[11] These acts dove-tailed neatly into the Exclusionary Immigration Act of 1924. This federally sponsored bill not only halted further Asian immigration, but prevented alien Asian residents from becoming U.S. citizens. This law jeopardized the legality of land holdings of many Japanese in the U.S.. In order to preserve their property, many foreign-born Japanese, called the Issei (designating them as the first to come to the United States) transferred ownership to their American born children, who were called the Nisei (meaning the second group to live in America or the first American born generation). Those who were childless had to wait nervously to see if their state government would take action. Some states did and a number of the Issei lost their property.

In June of 1929, California Governor William D. Stephens articulated the sentiments of whites on the West Coast in a letter sent to Secretary of State Bainbridge Colby. The letter is especially interesting when contrasted with the resolution passed by the California legislature in 1905, for no longer were the Japanese considered shiftless and uninvolved with the economy of the state. Governor Stephens remarked in his letter that:

> The Japanese in our midst have indicated a strong trend to land ownership and land control, and by their unquestioned industry and application, and by standards and methods that are widely separated from our Occidental standards and methods, both in connection with hours of labor and standards of living, have gradually developed to a control of many of our important agricultural industries. Indeed, at the present time they operate 458,056 acres of the very best lands in California.

> More significant than these figures, however, is the demonstrated fact that within the last ten years Japanese agricultural labor has developed to such a degree that at the present time between 80 and 90 per cent of most of our vegetable and berry products are those of the Japanese farms. Approximately 80 per cent of the tomato crop of the state is produced by Japanese; from 80 to 100 per cent of the spinach crop; a greater part of our potato and asparagus crops, and so on.

> These Japanese, by very reason of their use of economic standards impossible to our white ideals: that is to say, the employment of their wives and their very children in the arduous toil of the soil: are proving crushing competitors to our white rural populations. The fecundity of the Japanese race far exceeds that of any other people that we have in our midst. They send their children for short periods of time to our white schools, and in many of the country schools of our state the spectacle is presented of having a few white children acquiring their education in classrooms crowded with Japanese. The deep-seated resentment of our white mothers at this situation can only be appreciated by those people who have struggled with similar problems.

But with all this the people of California are determined to repress a developing Japanese community within our midst. They are determined to exhaust every power in their keeping to maintain this state for its own people ... California stands as an outpost on the western edge of Occidental civilization.[12]

In the 1930s, Governor Stephens's comments were accentuated by a variety of fraternal and business organizations that took the position that the Japanese either needed to be severely controlled or removed from the West Coast. These groups included the American Legion, the Native Sons of the Golden West, the Grange, and the American Farm Bureau Federation.[13] Anti-Japanese expressions usually peaked during election years or as the result of global developments. One of the great periods of reaction came when Japan attacked China in 1937.[14]

With the surprise attack on Pearl Harbor on December 7, 1941, the long history of racism and discontent aimed at the Japanese community in the United States came to a head. In the eyes of many Caucasians, the movement to remove the Japanese now had legitimacy. They assumed Japanese-Americans had played a direct role in the Pearl Harbor tragedy. This became a paramount theme in West Coast mobilization and remained so even after exhaustive investigations discovered no such conspiracy.

Two months after Pearl Harbor, when President Roosevelt issued his executive order allowing the removal of Japanese-Americans and resident aliens from the West Coast, John H. Tolan, congressman from Oakland, California, commenced a series of hearings in San Francisco. Tolan's purpose was to "inquire further into the interstate migration of citizens," and to look into the "problems of evacuation of enemy aliens and others from prohibited military zones."[15]

During the Tolan hearings, members of the Japanese American Citizens League attempted in vain to proclaim the loyalty of Japanese-Americans and to defend their right to remain on the West Coast, but the congressional committee turned a deaf ear. Instead, what caught their attention was the testimony of those who vociferously wanted to remove the Japanese. When California Attorney General Earl Warren testified, he stated:

> We believe that when we are dealing with the Caucasian race we have methods that will test the loyalty of them, and we believe we can, in dealing with Germans and Italians, arrive at some fairly sound conclusions because of our knowledge of the way they live in the community and have lived for many years. But when we deal with the Japanese, we are in an entirely different field and we cannot form any opinion that we believe to be sound.[16]

Warren went on to testify: "I want to say that the consensus of opinion among the law-enforcement offices of this state is that there is more potential danger among the group of Japanese who are born in this country than from alien Japanese who were born in Japan."[17]

Warren's reasoning for not trusting Japanese-Americans was that "many of them were within a grenade throw of coast defense guns" as well as air fields, power lines, railroads and other vital facilities.[18] Warren did not mention in his testimony that many of the Japanese he made reference to had lived for years on the land he described. Because of racial discrimination against Japanese farmers, this had been the only land available to them as its quality was marginal. The land had become productive because of their hard work.

In further testimony it was implied that the Japanese had purchased land near airfields, oil refineries and other vital installations years in advance of the war because they were crafty and patient people, merely waiting for the inevitable conflict to begin. At that time, their farms would be used as staging grounds for attacks and crops grown in the fields would be made into the shape of arrows to guide enemy airplanes to key targets. Later it was shown that these charges were absurd. Even an extensive investigation by the FBI uncovered no evidence of espionage, but the absence of concrete evidence had no effect on the Tolan Commission.

During the time of the Tolan hearings, a number of important newspaper journalists took up the cause of removing the Japanese. Henry McLemore of the San Francisco Examiner made one of the strongest statements. He wrote:

Let them be pinched, hurt, hungry, and dead up against it. If making one million innocent Japanese uncomfortable would prevent one scheming Japanese from costing the life of one American boy, then let the million innocents suffer ... let us have no patience with the enemy or with anyone whose veins carry his blood. Personally, I hate the Japanese. And that goes for all of them.[19]

Westbrook Pegler, a columnist for the Scripps-Howard syndicate, stated: "The Japanese in California should be under guard to the last man and woman right now and to hell with habeas corpus until the danger is over."[20]

When the FBI and other government agencies came up with no evidence of a Japanese-American conspiracy on the West Coast, Walter Lippmann, a well-respected syndicated columnist, provided an answer. In an article entitled "The Fifth Column on the Coast," he wrote:

Since the outbreak of the Japanese war there has been no important sabotage on the Pacific Coast. From what we know about Hawaii and the fifth column in Europe, this is not, as some would have liked to think, a sign that there is nothing to be feared. It is a sign that the blow is well organized and that it is held back until it can be struck with maximum effect.[21]

The majority of Americans who spoke out in favor of Japanese removal and internment were not evil people but were victims of evil times. The sudden involvement of the United States in global war had generated genuine fear. It had acted as a catalyst for the years of lingering distrust of Asian Americans.

The first phase of Japanese incarceration took place within a matter of days after Pearl Harbor. The FBI swept through communities such as Terminal Island, near Los Angeles, arresting Japanese aliens that were suspected of having ties with the Japanese government. Most of them were sent to a high security prison at Fort Lincoln in North Dakota. Then, after President Roosevelt issued Executive Order #9066 in February of 1942, plans for the removal of the entire Japanese-American community on the West Coast were initiated. Government agents arranged for the use of racetracks and fairgrounds as temporary "assembly centers." Here, the Japanese were to be housed until permanent "relocation camps" could be built in regions inland from the West Coast. Ten sites were selected, located for the most part in the western regions of the United States. Two were to be built in California, two in Arizona, and one each in Utah, Colorado, Wyoming, and Idaho. There were also two camps to be constructed in Arkansas.

In addition, other countries in North and South America were also preparing to intern or remove their own Japanese communities. Canada was developing plans to move Japanese-Canadians to abandoned lumber and mine towns in eastern British Columbia and Alberta. In Latin America, Brazil, Uruguay, and Paraguay developed their own plans for detention, but fourteen other counties accepted help from the United States. The U.S. government offered to transport and detain any citizen of an Axis country deemed dangerous and over 2,000 Japanese from Latin America were shipped to the United States for the duration of the war. Most of them were interned at a camp in Texas.[22]

Responsibility for the removal of Japanese-Americans from the West Coast of the United States was under the direction of General John L. DeWitt of the Western Defense Command. In addition a new governmental agency, the War Relocation Authority, was formed to oversee the operation of ten permanent internment camps that were to be constructed. Because of the overlapping responsibilities of the army and WRA, many of their functions blended together. For example, the design of each relocation center (or internment camp) came from the army, and soldiers were used as security forces to patrol outside perimeters. On the other hand, the WRA assumed responsibility for coordinating the construction of the camps and supervising the internal activities once the Japanese arrived. Later, the WRA also coordinated efforts to resettle Japanese-Americans in the midwest and on the east coast.

On April 7, 1942, the removal orders were officially given. Members of Japanese communities in California, Oregon and Washington were required to register at city halls, schools, and churches. Removal notices were frequently posted just a matter of days before a selected departure date. Individuals were allowed to take with them only belongings that could be bundled together and carried. The government offered storage for household goods and other personal property, but supervision was poor and many of those who did place their belongings in government run warehouses returned after the war to discover their property vandalized or stolen. Some families were fortunate to find compassionate help from Caucasian friends who cared for their farms, homes, and personal possessions, but most were not so fortunate. Fearing they would never be able to return to their old homes, families sold their possessions, receiving almost nothing for them. The hardships of preparing to leave were compounded because the government had taken into custody personal savings deposited in Japanese banks operated in the United States. Insurance companies canceled automobile, homeowner, and life insurance policies. The federal government confiscated guns, cameras, short wave radios, and knives in the belief that they could be used for espionage purposes.

When the date came due for removal to the assembly centers, the Japanese gathered at predetermined loading points. Each person was only allowed two pieces of luggage weighing no more than 75 pounds each. These were opened and carefully inspected by local law enforcement officials. Tags were then issued bearing a pre-assigned family number. At the completion of the check-in process, the people were then loaded onto buses, streetcars, trucks and trains to be transported to the assembly centers. Here, they were housed in hastily cleaned horse stalls and livestock exhibition buildings until construction of the ten permanent camps could be completed.

Each of the ten permanent relocation centers was selected on the basis of criteria developed by the military and WRA. The sites were to be isolated from major population centers, and large enough to house from 5,000 to 15,000 people. Unfortunately, these criteria did not take into consideration human comfort. Eight of the ten sites were in semi-arid desert regions. Characteristic problems included wind borne dust loosened by bare-stripped earth, temperature extremes that plunged the mercury well below freezing in the winter and above 100 degrees Fahrenheit in the summer and barren, nearly treeless land-scapes.

The design of the camps and the rapidity of their construction contributed to less than desirable conditions. Each housing unit was a barrack, 100 feet long and 20 feet wide. Originally designed for soldiers living en masse, they were divided into four or five apartments, each heated by a coal-burning stove. Families were generally assigned one apartment, and single people were expected to join with several others. Most of the wood used to construct the barracks was green and when it dried the boards shrank, leaving gaping cracks in floors, walls, and roofs. Because of material shortages brought on by the war and the enormity of the internment camp projects, sheet rock and insulation material were not initially available.

The first to arrive found the inside of the buildings to be uncompleted. Only tar paper, used to cover the outside walls, prevented dust and moisture from invading the structures. Generally, the barracks were built in blocks, with 14 barracks per block, plus a 40-foot by 100-foot mess hall, and a 20 by 100-foot recreation hall. In the middle of the block were two buildings, one housing laundry facilities and the other toilets and showers. The toilet facilities caused embarrassment for early camp arrivers. Since the buildings were based on military design, there were no partitions between toilets nor in the shower facilities. Until stalls could be constructed, many Japanese internees, hoping to avoid others, waited until late at night to use the toilets only to discover that most of their neighbors were there as well! Other camp buildings included facilities for schools, warehouses, and compounds to house civilian employees of the WRA and military police. Barbed wire and guard towers surrounded all of the camps.

Each War Relocation Authority camp was given a name. They reflected local geographic features or the names of settlements nearby. Titles included Jerome, Rohwer, Granada, Topaz, Minidoka, Gila River, Amanche, Heart Mountain, Manzanar, and Tule Lake. In attempting to find a "generic" name for all the camps, the WRA had difficulty. Euphemisms such as "colony," "relocation center," "resettlement center," and "evacuation center" were used. However, some elements of the press (and later many members of the Japanese-American community) more accurately described them as—"concentration camps"—not in the same mold as the death camps of Nazi Germany, but clearly descriptive of sites of forced detention, surrounded by barbed wire and armed guards. Most of these camps were opened by the summer of 1942.

Soon after the removal of the Japanese from the West Coast, General John L. DeWitt wrote a 600-page report detailing the "evacuation" and the reasons for internment. For the most part, his report discussed the procedures used for processing the internees and described the facilities provided at both the assembly centers and relocation camps. However, it also included a rationalization for internment that was both misleading and inaccurate. For example, DeWitt stated that:

> [The] distribution of the Japanese population appeared to manifest something more than coincidence ... It was certainly evident that the Japanese population of the Pacific Coast was, as a whole, ideally situated with reference to points of strategic importance, to carry into execution a tremendous program of sabotage on a mass scale should any considerable number of them have been inclined to do so.[23]

Was there a high risk of sabotage by members of the Japanese American community? Not according to an investigation conducted by J. Edgar Hoover and the F.B.I. They were unable to find any evidence of conspiracy. Indeed, it was the feeling among some government officials that after the initial detainment of suspected German, Italian, and Japanese aliens (from December of 1941 to January of 1942) that the risk of internal problems on the West Coast had been minimized.

In attempting to substantiate his claim, DeWitt went on to say:

> There were many evidences of the successful communication of information to the enemy, information regarding positive knowledge on the part of our installations. The most striking illustrations of this are found in three of the several incidents of enemy attacks on West Coast points.

> On February 23, 1942, a hostile submarine shelled Goleta, near Santa Barbara, California, in an attempt to destroy vital oil installations there. In the vicinity of Brookings [Mt. Emily], Oregon, an enemy submarine-based plane dropped incendiary bombs in an effort to start forest fires. Similarly, a precise knowledge of the range of coast defense guns at Astoria, Oregon was in the possession of the enemy. A hostile submarine surfaced and shelled shore batteries there from the only position at which a surfaced submarine could have approached the coast line close enough to shell a part of its coast defenses without being within the range of the coastal batteries.

In summary, the Commanding General was confronted with the Pearl Harbor experience, which involved a positive enemy knowledge of our patrols, our naval disposition, etc.[24]

There were several incongruities in General DeWitt's attempt to link the Japanese-American community on the West Coast with the incidents he described. First, the sites shelled by the Japanese submarines were not secret. They were not only listed on common maps, but were easily photographed by tourists and foreign visitors. As for the attacks on Fort Stevens and Brookings, Oregon, these occurred on June 21st and September 9th, long after the Japanese had been interned. In addition, the implied notion that signaling was taking place between elements of the Japanese community and enemy submarines was baseless.

General DeWitt's lack of objectivity in dealing with Japanese-Americans was most clearly shown in testimony he gave on April 13, 1943 before the House Naval Affairs Subcommittee, when he said:

A Jap's a Jap. They are a dangerous element, whether loyal or not. There is no way to determine their loyalty ... It makes no difference whether he is an American; theoretically he is still a Japanese and you can't change him ... You can't change him by giving him a piece of paper.[25]

DeWitt's comments were tragic and unfortunately reflected the general sentiment of the time. The assumption was that race allied individuals, behaviorally and politically, with their ancestral home. This was particularly applied to non-whites.

So it was that by the summer of 1942, 110,000 people, two-thirds of whom were American citizens by birth, were behind barbed-wire. They had not been judged in a court of law as having committed a crime; they were there solely because of their race. More than 18,000 of these people were destined to live in the Tule Lake Basin. They lived there for up to four years, not as beneficiaries of reclamation, but as prisoners in a remote land; waiting, wondering what the future would bring them.

Map showing Assembly and Relocation and Centers for Japanese-Americans and Japanese Resident Aliens. *(Source: General John L. Dewitt, Final Report: Japanese Evacuation from the West Coast, 1942)*

Barracks under construction at the Tule Lake War Relocation Authority Internment Camp. *(Photo courtesy Bureau of Reclamation)*

CHAPTER 15

THE WAR RELOCATION CAMP AT TULE LAKE

The initial decision to use federal land in the Tule Lake Basin for an internment camp was made quietly. Even before the removal orders were issued on April 7th, the Bureau of Reclamation had been pressed into service. Joining with the Bureau of Land Management and Bureau of Indian Affairs, they were asked to identify suitable locations for internment camps. Among those selected was a 1,100-acre site on the eastern side of The Peninsula. An additional 3,575 acres were set aside for agricultural purposes related to the camp.

Though no official announcement had been made by the government concerning plans for the construction of an internment camp, by mid-April Tule Lake Basin residents were aware of such plans. On the afternoon of Saturday, April 11, 1942, a meeting was held in the town of Tulelake to discuss appropriate action. It was decided that several organizations, including the American Legion, the Grange, and the Merrill, Malin and Tulelake Chambers of Commerce would draft resolutions to be sent to Western Defense Commander General John L. DeWitt protesting the construction of a camp in the basin. The next Monday, the chamber met to discuss the contents of such a resolution. The Klamath Falls *Evening Herald* reported on the results of the meeting:

> The resolution as ordered by the group Monday noon will point out that the Tule Lake basin was settled by whites and has no orientals or negroes among its residents. It will voice the desire of the Tulelake chamber to maintain the present character of the population ... South-end residents and officials who attended the meeting pointed out in general discussion that the Tule Lake area was settled and developed by Caucasians and that it would be obviously unfair to deprive them of the rich farm land in favor of the Japanese ... They also pointed out that American-born Japs would be more apt to remain in the basin after the war.[1]

The rough draft of the resolution also recommended that the site for the camp be moved 90 miles south to the Madeline plains, located between Alturas and Reno. It was felt that this site was far enough away to insure that the basin would be not be later settled by Japanese internees, yet close enough to be able to use Japanese labor during harvest seasons.[2]

General DeWitt was not the only government official petitioned. On April 28th, California Congressman Harry L. Englebright responded to a letter sent to him by Tulelake Chamber of Commerce Secretary, Sara Welsh by stating:

> I want you to know I emphatically agree with your views in (sic) the subject, and have taken it up with officials of the War Department, the Agricultural Department, and the United States Reclamation Bureau; and when I have word from these agencies, I shall be pleased to communicate with you again.[3]

Englebright's efforts on behalf of the Tulelake Chamber were futile. Construction of the camp had begun on April 21st, the same day that the protest letter had been sent, and three weeks later, on May 11th, Secretary of War Henry L. Stimson put the issue to rest. In a letter to Congressman Englebright, Stimson clearly spelled out the government's position:

> The establishment of such projects will always be the subject of well meaning objection wherever located. Our experience has shown that so rarely has any local group approved of the establishment of the centers that it is impracticable and unwise to seek approval. The sites have been selected by the War Relocation Authority after survey and careful consideration of alternative sites. In the national interest it is essential that relocation go forward without delay. Time does not afford further search, and the accomplishment of the plan to establish a center on the area mentioned by you must go forward by reasons of impelling military necessity.[4]

In an attempt to reassure the congressman, the Tulelake Chamber of Commerce, and the basin residents, Stimson went on to say: "The project area is in a military area and when the Japanese arrive, it will have the status of a prohibited zone subject to Army control. An external guard of military police will assure full protection to nearby communities and to the Japanese themselves."[5]

Congressman Englebright also received correspondence from Commissioner John C. Page of the Bureau of Reclamation. In his letter, the commissioner explained to Englebright the process used to acquire the Tule Lake landsite.

> In the case of the Tule Lake camp the War Department arranged for the acquisition of land for the camp site and is supervising the building of the camp. The War Relocation Authority is arranging for the acquisition of lands for agricultural or other work programs and on completion of the camp will supervise its operation, except for the construction of any public works that might be undertaken ... In the case of the Tule Lake camp, the area is under the general control of the Bureau of Reclamation and this Bureau will be expected to supervise any work such as lateral construction and building of drain ditches.
>
> The camp and work area will be set up as a military reservation and the general public will be denied access to the area. Guards will be furnished by the Army and the Japanese residents of the camp area will not be permitted to leave the reservation or mingle with the local population. In an effort to be as self-sustaining as possible, and to reduce the cost of this program, the Japanese will farm such lands as can be made available to them but will not acquire any rights to the lands so farmed. It is fully expected that on the termination of the war the camps will be abandoned and the lands revert to their prior status.[6]

Though the Tulelake Chamber of Commerce tried to block the construction of the camp, the Army and WRA quickly put their plans into action. On April 17, only four days after the chamber had drafted its resolution, government agents were in Klamath Falls negotiating for the purchase of lumber. The event led to the first "official" government acknowledgment of plans for the camp and it was duly reported in the *Evening Herald* on Friday, April 17, 1942.

> The Tulelake Japanese reception camp became an actuality Friday morning when purchasing agents

visited various wholesale lumber dealers in Klamath Falls and bought 100,000 feet of lumber for immediate delivery to the campsite.

The "no comment" status of the U.S. Reclamation Service changed immediately when the actual purchase of lumber was learned, and B.E. Hayden, superintendent of the Klamath Project, admitted ... that the camp was to be started "at once."[7]

Two construction companies from Medford, Oregon—Fort J. Twaits and Morrison-Knudson—were awarded the contract to build the camp. Originally, it was to be constructed in Coppock Bay, near the southern base of The Peninsula. Here on Saturday, April 18, equipment and supplies were delivered. During the next two days, more than 500 workers were brought in by the Twaits and Morrison-Knudson companies to begin work. However, after two days of construction, soil conditions and poor drainage made it apparent that the original site was unsuitable for the camp's location. Rainy weather made the ground mushy and a site for a sewage disposal plant could not be found. As a consequence, the camp was moved a mile northeast.

The new site, running due east of The Peninsula toward Horse Mountain, was described by the Bureau of Reclamation as "cheap pasture." The porous soil consisted of coarse sand, scattered with the shells of freshwater snails. It had been a broad beach area that separated Tule Lake from Coppock Bay to the south. Little time was lost in the construction schedule. Buildings already erected at the old site were converted to housing for construction workers, and lumber and other materials were quickly shifted to the new location.[8]

Faced with a one-month completion date, work on the camp reached a frenzied pace. This put a strain on local farmers and merchants as clerks, laborers and farm workers left their jobs to join the construction crews. An *Evening Herald* article complained:

"Gone to the Jap camp" has become a by-word with farmers in the south end of the basin.

Farm laborers are fading out of the spring seeding picture like fog before the sun. Potato sorting crews too are answering the call for help on the government project and store managers are losing clerks.

Farmers faced with the necessity of irrigating land before seeding grain and potatoes are running double shifts by themselves, chasing water night and day. Coupled with the call to the armed forces, defense work and federal projects, the drain on farm labor in the basin is beginning to pinch.[9]

While the camp was under construction, General John L. DeWitt designated Portland, Oregon as the first major city for removal of Japanese-Americans and Japanese resident aliens. The April 29th edition of the *Oregon Journal* was published with a page-wide, boldface headline which read "PORTLAND TO BE FIRST JAP FREE CITY: Next Tuesday To Find Town Sans Nippos." The word "Jap," freely used by the press at the time, was a repugnant racial slur, yet there were no letters to the editor in complaint. Save for the protests of a very few willing to risk the label "Jap lover," the city was strangely quiet. Perhaps they agreed with the implication of the *Journal's* headline, that Portland was ridding itself of a great plague. The article itself was surprisingly mild.

Hundreds of Portland and Multnomah county Japanese and Japanese-Americans today began registering for evacuation to the Pacific International Livestock exposition center by noon May 5.

"By noon Tuesday, Portland will be the first city in the nation completely evacuated of Japanese," said Ernest Leonetti, manager of the war-time civil control administration in Oregon.

Many of the Japanese being "assembled" here probably will be sent to the Tule Lake section near Klamath Falls.

That the whole registration and evacuation is being carried on in an "orderly and democratic manner" was revealed by Leonetti in announcing that Japanese who haven't disposed of household goods may have them tagged, picked up and stored for the duration.

Japanese also will be given free transportation to the assembly center by volunteers, Leonetti said, if they have no means of travel.[10]

By late May, the camp's first stage of construction was nearly completed. Because the project was destined to become a city of nearly 20,000 people, the WRA and Bureau of Reclamation decided to name the site "Newell." It was chosen to honor "the memory of Frederick Haines Newell, original director of the Bureau of Reclamation."[11] Soon after, the United States Postal Service recognized the townsite name, and a branch office was opened there. Letters sent from the camp bore the "Newell" cancellation.

On Sunday, May 24, the camp was opened for inspection to the general public. In describing the project, the *Evening Herald* marveled at the speed of its completion.

The possibility of constructing over 1,000 buildings within 30 days' time was far fetched and yet, through perfect coordination of 3,000 men, including engineers, administrative workers, carpenters and laborers, the job has been done.[12]

The great sprawling camp was an impressive one and one-half square miles in size. Its west side was bordered by the Canby-Hatfield Highway (now Highway #139). Running parallel to this road, from north to south, was the military compound, camp jail and detention center, motor pool, WRA administration center, camp hospital, housing for civilian employees of the War Relocation Authority, and maintenance and warehouse area. Also paralleling the camp on the west side was the Southern Pacific Rail Line. It had already funneled thousands of boxcars of supplies into the camp, and later antiquated passenger trains would disgorge thousands of internees sent to Tule Lake.

Approximately one-quarter mile east was a broad strip of open land. At the north end was the main entrance to the camp, with a guard station conspicuously located in the center of the entry road. Only one other building was present in this "no-man's land," a fire hall. Several months later it was joined by a large complex of structures built to house the camp's junior and senior high schools.

Further to the east lay the main compound encompassing the living quarters for the Japanese. It consisted of seven gigantic wards, each divided into nine blocks. A block consisted of sixteen barracks, a mess hall, recreation hall, men's and women's toilets and showers, and laundry facilities. A year later another three wards were added to the complex, providing housing for more than 18,000 Japanese in all. Though the interior of the barracks was not quite complete, the internees at Tule Lake were fortunate. Unlike several other camps, some of the sheet rock and insulation was installed before the winter months. The coal supply was ample so keeping the buildings warm was not a difficult problem, though they were by no means comfortable. The monotony of row upon row of black, tar papered barracks was depressing, as were the evenly spaced guard towers and barbed wire fence that ringed the entire area. It must have been sobering, even to the curious visitors who came to see the internment camp on May 24, 1942.

On May 27th, the first internees arrived at Tule Lake. There were 447 men and women in the group. They were volunteers from the assembly centers at Portland and Puyallup, Washington. They had come to assist in preparing the camp for the first major group of residents.

The advance party found the nearly completed camp to be barren and bleak, but a concerted effort was made by acting WRA Project Director Elmer Shirrell to ameliorate the situation. He insisted that his staff treat the internees with friendliness and cordiality, and he made a strong effort to soften the impact of a camp surrounded by barbed wire, guard towers and military personnel.[13] Working together with the advance group, he established an orderly procedure for processing new arrivals. Each family was to be met by a representative of the advance party, who would help them check in and then take them to their assigned barrack.

On June 2nd, the first major contingent arrived and by the 6th, nearly 1,500 people had moved into the camp. The new residents had left their homes and assembly centers with a mixture of sadness and anticipation. Shuji Kimura, who had lived with his parents on a farm outside of Seattle, wrote of his emotional departure.

> The 18 car train was drawn up on the siding along the packing house from which we used to ship our peas

and lettuce, and the place was full of people. There was a tremendous lineup of trucks loaded with baggage. Along in the middle of the afternoon, it began to rain. We wondered how everyone could get all the baggage, duffel bags, and blankets into the two baggage cars but it was easily done.

We didn't feel so bad about leaving with all the excitement ... But soon when six p.m. came and the train began to move, and we saw old Mr. Ballard waving his hat at us, his coat collar turned up against the rain, mother began to cry. I couldn't see through my tears either. I saw the Main Street Crossing—there were more people waving. The train began to go faster and the berry rows, the rhubarb, the lettuce fields, the pea field began to slip past our window like a panorama. My throat hurt, but I couldn't take my eyes from the familiar fields and pastures slipping so quickly away.

An hour later, toward sunset, the sun came out again. We saw it shining over the Puget Sound. The country was no longer the familiar scenes of our valley, and we did not feel so badly. It felt good to relax and close my eyes. I felt at peace as the train rolled steadily southward. So ended the world I had known since boyhood and a new world of the evacuee began for me.[14]

What the Kimura family and hundreds of others discovered when they arrived at Tule Lake was that the facilities, at best, were Spartan. Each person was provided with an army cot, straw-filled mattress, and wool army blankets. Nothing else was in the assigned apartments, save a naked light bulb and a cylindrical coal burning stove. There were no chairs, tables, shelves, cabinets or partitions.

In many ways, those who came during the first month were fortunate. Great piles of scrap lumber, left over from construction, dotted the grounds of the camp. It was relatively easy for internees to find choice pieces of wood that could be turned into furniture, shelving, bedroom partitions, and even wooden sandals known as "getas." Convenient barrack quarters near mess halls, recreation facilities, laundries, and toilets could be found. The internees in the first wave assumed positions of leadership in Block Councils and other political organizations. They also secured the best jobs that included work as truck drivers, block managers, mess hall cooks, internal camp security officers, firemen, typists, and supply clerks. The pay was only $16 a month, the same as an army private, but the work gave people a more meaningful way to occupy their time at the camp.

Friction between the first wave of settlers and new arrivals developed between June 16th and 26th when more than 4,000 internees from the Walerga Assembly Center, located near Sacramento, were shipped to Tule Lake. There was anger and jealousy when the Walergans discovered that the internees from the Pacific Northwest had taken the best jobs and housing.[15]

Other developments contributed to a rising tide of tension at the camp. Ignoring all advice to the contrary given by camp director Elmer Shirrell, the Army implemented a strict program of mail censorship. This incensed the internees. Simultaneously the quality of food served in the mess halls declined substantially. This had been caused by a number of factors including: poor menu planning on the part of the WRA; improper food preparation due to the inexperienced help in the mess halls; and food shortages caused by the continuing arrival of new internees. The culmination of these factors led to at least one mess-hall strike and to accusations that the WRA was hoarding food for personal gain.[16]

Conditions in the camp helped intensify the division between the generations of Japanese. A considerable number of the Issei, who had been born in Japan and who had come to the United States prior to 1924, spoke little English and they found themselves pushed aside by the American born Nisei, who took the best jobs. In their own communities, the Issei had held respected positions as the elders of the community; now they had lost much of their status. They were angry with the brash young Nisei who seemed to show contempt for the old ways, and they were also angry at a country that had not only denied them citizenship but had taken away everything they owned, including their freedom. Many Issei refused to work and spent idle hours with their friends, complaining about the system.

In early August, tension in the camp focused on a major labor dispute that involved crews working an adjacent farm plot known as the League of Nations. Here most of the camp's produce was being grown. There was resentment over a variety of conditions, including the low wage scale, the pressure placed on workers to get the harvest done before the first frost, and the fact that they were being bossed by Caucasians who had less farm experience than they did. On August 15, the protest took the form of a general strike, which lasted two days. It was brought to an end after a number of promises were made by the WRA to improve food distribution and work conditions. But the end of the strike was only a lull in a continuing battle between factions of internees and the camp's administration.

Meanwhile, a combination of unfortunate events was giving the internment camp at Tule Lake "bad press" in the outside world. At root, the causes were directly related to the racial animosity the country felt toward the Japanese. It was not lost on whites, particularly residents of the Klamath and Tule Lake basins, that the internees at the relocation camp looked like the enemy their sons had been sent to fight on islands in the Pacific. The terrible hurt of war struck home every time one of them was wounded or killed. Unfortunately, what many residents did forget was that the enemy in Europe, a Caucasian enemy, was equally guilty, but the inability to distinguish a German from a Swede or an Irishman directed their emotional feelings toward dislike for a country and not for a race of people.

Bad feelings about the WRA camp were not just rooted in racism. The mere fact that a sparsely populated region of southern Oregon and northern California had to contend with a new city of more than 15,000 people (later it would grow to over 18,000) was enough in itself to generate resentment. A population that size, even if it is contained behind barbed wire, puts a strain on services and the availability of goods. One local resident wrote a letter to the editor of the Klamath Fall *Evening Herald* complaining:

> [I] have talked to many restaurants, taverns and store keepers in regard to the shortage of soft drinks in Klamath Falls. They all tell me the same story. Two local bottlers send the Japanese center at Tule Lake the pop and if and when there is any left the Americans, who have been steady customers for years and years, get it. Days and days and the pop distributors say "We have none, the Japanese colony takes most of it."

> Why on God's green earth should the yellow man get first choice and the American dealers and the public get second best? The war and these Japs will not be with us forever and a day of reckoning will come from these bottlers to answer to. Right now a move is on foot to establish a bottling house for pop that will refuse to furnish the Japanese pop. If this condition keeps up it will wreck the people's morale that the Japs in this country get first choice and the rest of us second choice.[17]

A number of farmers in the basin were unhappy because they had lost their leases on prime farmland in an area to the northwest of the camp known as the League of Nations. It had been taken over so that the camp could grow its own food; but it also meant that whites who had been farming it before lost an important source of income.[18] On the other hand, the camp was an economic boon for the basin. It provided employment for many local residents, and the city of Tulelake was the recipient of a great deal of business from employees of the WRA.

The discontent expressed by local residents towards the camp, and the resentment of camp internees toward the outside world became a vicious circle. Each act of defiance by the Japanese at Tule Lake, from demonstrations to work stoppages, was further proof to whites that the Japanese were disloyal. Each newspaper article and public speech that made reference to the internees as "Japs" and a foreign enemy confirmed the feelings of the internees that they were unwelcome in their own country. For the camp's residents, their bitterness was increasingly transformed into action.

After the farm strike of August 15th to 17th, most of the internees turned a deaf ear to pleas from the WRA for workers to assist in harvesting sugar beets and potatoes in the Northwest. The war had caused an acute labor shortage, and harvesters were desperately needed to save the two crops. By October 1942, only 800 out of 15,000 camp residents had been hired. The small number not only reflected a camp-wide boycott but a growing fear among the internees that if they did cooperate with the WRA they would be branded an "inu." The word meant "dog" and was one of the most derogatory labels in the camp. Its English equivalent could be loosely translated to "Uncle Tom," "fink," or even "bootlicker." It implied that an individual had sold out. As tension and resentment increased at Tule Lake, "inu" became a powerful weapon, and the threatened label intimidated individuals into cooperation with the more radical elements.

Predictably, the farm labor boycott angered farmers and politicians in the Northwest. Charles A. Sprague, Governor of Oregon, stated: "I am shocked at reports of attitude expressed by these Japanese, many of whom, prior to internment, gave assurances of their desire to promote the welfare of the nation in any way they could serve."[19]

Among the 800 Japanese who did volunteer to harvest sugar beets and potatoes, experiences were mixed. One internee wrote to Camp Director Elmer Shirrell, saying:

> In appreciation of swell treatment I have had in Tule Lake project, I wish to personally thank you. I'm one of the groups who have come to Idaho to work ... You can bet I'll do my darndest to help in the harvest here. People here are very reasonable ...[20]

But another Tule Lake internee wrote from Weiser, Idaho:

> Guys around here are pretty prejudice against Japs. Although we have an 8 o'clock curfew every night, except Tuesday, when it is eleven. They slapped a 12 o'clock noon curfew on us for Sunday. We had to eat in town a couple of days and customers didn't like it so we can't even go into a restaurant now. It is pretty bad and most of the fellows wanted to go home, but we all decided to see how it becomes in a week or two.[21]

In the fall of 1942, several news articles helped fan the flames of white discontent concerning the internment camp. On September 30th an *Evening Herald* article announced that Japanese writing had been discovered on the east side of the Peninsula, covering an ancient Indian petroglyph with letters one foot high and extending about eight feet across the rock face. [22] In October, another article announced that the director of the California Fish and Game Commission had been given evidence that Japanese internees were illegally snaring ducks, pheasants, and geese along the shores of the Tule Lake sump.[23]

On the evening of October 14th, a propaganda broadcast by Radio Tokyo incensed the editorial staff at the *Evening Herald*. The next day the paper stated:

> We happened to tune in on a shortwave broadcast from radio Tokyo last night and wish to report the not very surprising fact that radio Tokyo lies.

> In a labored answer to President Roosevelt's Columbus Day speech, the Jap broadcaster mentioned the "brutal treatment of Japanese civilians in the United States." On the very day in which the War Relocation Authority was getting a local blast for coddling Japanese civilians, that remark by the nasal-voiced gent in Nippon brought a scornful guffaw from the listening circle that was very much in order.

> If there is just half truth in what we hear about the easy time the Japanese civilians are having, we would be happy to know that American prisoners in Japan are treated half as well.

> Over here we have been leaning over backwards to treat the Japanese civilians fairly - so far over, in fact, that the local population is getting hot under the collar about it. One wag suggests that the white population ought to move into the WRA settlement and let the Japanese do the work for awhile.[24]

At the time of the *Evening Herald* editorial, Elmer Shirrell and his staff were being accused of lax management of the camp. There were charges that the number of military police at Tule Lake was inadequate and that Japanese-American truck drivers violated fuel conservation regulations by traveling at 40 to 45 miles per hour. Additional allegations suggested that the camp was supplied with an ample number of teachers while schools in the surrounding area were short-handed. It was also asserted that hams and bacon were freely available to camp residents, along with milk and other hard-to-get food, whereas none of these items were available to residents of the basin and Klamath Falls.[25]

In an attempt to halt the continued escalation of rumors and allegations, Elmer Shirrell invited the Klamath Falls Chamber of

Commerce to visit Tule Lake and ascertain for themselves the validity of the charges. In their summary report, the Chamber of Commerce said:

> As far as members of the committee can ascertain, the vast majority of rumors are unfounded and we recommend at this time that before any stories are repeated concerning the Japanese Relocation center the facts concerning these stories be fully determined and the stories be investigated. It is our belief that no good can come from idle rumors or gossip and we further believe that if there is any mismanagement or any acts being committed that are not for the general welfare these cases should be reported to the proper authorities only after, and we repeat, the facts have been ascertained.[26]

Unfortunately, the Klamath Falls Chamber of Commerce's report did not stem the tide of rumors nor soothe the uneasy relationship between the camp and the basin residents. However, Elmer Shirrell made repeated efforts to improve the camp's image. He invited local farmers, businessmen, and the Klamath Falls Rotary Club to visit the camp. He even extended an invitation to the national media in hopes that an accurate picture of life in a relocation center could be provided. One such event was reported by the *Evening Herald*:

> Newswriters and photographers of all prominent newspapers and motion picture news studios swarmed over the Tulelake Relocation Center of Japanese people this past week. Their mission was to observe activities of the big camp with its 16,000 Japanese population and other personnel, making it the 5th largest city in Northern California. They talked freely with young and old alike regarding living conditions, the schools and other matters.[27]

But the "media event" backfired. A number of the journalists were fed in the civilian section of the camp, located outside the internees' compound. According to Charles Palmerlee, a mathematics teacher at the camp, they were fed steaks, roasts and other food not normally provided for the camp population. Consequently, when some of the reporters returned to their newspaper offices, they wrote articles with references to the "coddling" of the Japanese at the expense of other Americans who were subjected to rationed food.[28]

The camp did not receive all bad press. Also reported in the papers were events such as "Japanese Women At Camp Newell Have Knitted 63 Shawls and Sent Them to Red Cross for Distribution to Servicemen."[29] Another account told of "thirty-five young Japanese Americans (who) volunteered for active service in the United States Army" and were guests of a farewell program "arranged by the Tule Lake Project Veteran's club and the Parent's club."[30]

There were also acts of kindness on the part of basin and Klamath Falls residents. Some people visited the camp with regularity and befriended people interned there. In Klamath Falls, Eugene Haynes, minister of the town's Congregational church, helped establish exchange visits between internees and church members. Kenneth and Winifred Lambie, who were members of the church and ardent supporters of the Fellowship of Reconciliation, an organization that sought non-violent solutions to world problems, provided help for some of the internees by purchasing clothing and other items requested by individuals.[31]

Rules and regulations related to the internees sometimes frustrated the efforts of those who sought to help them. For example, Winifred Lambie invited five Japanese women to attend the World Day of Prayer services at Klamath Falls' Episcopal church. After the invitation had been extended, she discovered that the church, located on the west side of Highway 97, was out of bounds for internees. The meeting was moved to the Lambie home, located on the east side of the highway, in order that the Japanese women could attend the prayer service.[32]

During the first year, many internees settled into a daily routine that helped them cope with both boredom and discontent. The daily regimen included breakfast in the block mess hall, school for the children, and work for adults who had joined one of many different details. Work opportunities were varied. The camp had its own shoe and clothing factories, construction and repair crews, hog production facilities, slaughterhouse, and fields under cultivation. The internees had their own internal police force, fire department and camp council, whose duty it was to help iron out complaints and problems with the camp's administration. Each block had a manager whose duties ran the gamut, including "nursemaid, janitor, messenger, complaint board, diplomat, tyrant, judge and jury."[33] Japanese doctors, dentists, and optometrists worked in the camp hospital. There were opportunities for individuals to work on the camp's daily paper, *The Tulean Dispatch*. All of these positions provided useful work to help pass the hours. For those who chose not to work, life between meals was spent idly socializing. Recreation opportunities spanned the range from traditional American games such as football, basketball, and baseball to Japanese pastimes including playing Go and Sumo Wrestling. There were youth and social organizations including Boy Scout and Girl Scout troops, and religious services were available for both Christians and Buddhists.

Many of the jobs and responsibilities assumed by the Japanese at Tule Lake had a positive impact. Before internment, most Japanese faced racial discrimination in their hometowns. They were denied access to the social structure of their community. Now in the camps:

> Japanese Americans were able to play all the social roles, not just those traditionally reserved for minority group members. Those in school became student body leaders, captains of athletic teams, and editors of yearbooks. Those with teacher training could teach; positions of some authority and community leadership were filled by others. And for some older people there was for the first time in their adult lives a time for leisure.[34]

Daily routine helped stabilize the camp's community but there were too many factors at play that would throw Tule Lake into a state of imbalance. The awkward, embarrassing and traumatic experience of being uprooted from homes and businesses had a clear psychological impact on each person. The adjustment to camp life and the demands placed on individuals as more and more people were sent to Tule Lake also destabilized people's lives. The camp's community was in a precarious balance between coping and open rebellion.

On the first anniversary of the WRA camp at Newell, *The Tulean Dispatch* published a book of essays and poems titled *A Tule Lake Interlude*. In carefully measured words, it summarized the feelings and experiences of the internees, particularly the

Nisei, at Tule Lake. In an essay called "Fleeting Impressions," Arthur T. Morimitsu reminisced:

> It is like a dream—the scenes so familiar, voices that echo in the distance, the cool breeze that sweeps soothingly over the firebreaks, the clangings of the mess hall bells, the chatters and shrill laughters of carefree children. The wiry grasses growing along the firebreaks and between the barracks, the purple hills in the distance, Castle Rock's [The Peninsula's] outline in the evening when the sky is light—like that of an Egyptian mummy; the sound of a phonograph jiving away in a laundry room, the stamping and shuffling of feet—jitter-bug session.

> One year in Tule Lake Project. A thousand and one events kaleidoscoped into a Dali-like impression: softball games along the firebreaks. The "Ohs" of the crowd as the batter takes a healthy cut at the ball. "Strike? Oh, you robber!"

> Dust. Dust. The weather of Tule Lake, as unpredictable as a woman in a millinery shop. Snow in May, Indian Summer in November—but all the year round, wind, wind, and more wind. Wind gentle as a baby's breath; strong enough to rattle the windows; wild enough to shriek between the telephone wires— whirling dust and papers like a miniature tornado— sending fine dust particles seeping through the windows; blanketing furniture and floor with a coating of white. Dust. Dust. Dust.[35]

Sada Murayama proclaimed his loyalty and his pride in poetry:

> I am a citizen –
> Let no slander
> Slur my status.
>
> In the other war,
> I stood with countless others
> Side by side
> To fight the foe.
> My arm was just as strong
> My blood fell

As bright as theirs
In defense of a new world
More precious far
Than any tie of land or race.

Steadfast I stand,
Staunchly I plant
The Stars and Stripes
Before my barracks door,
Crying defiance
To all wavering hearts.

I am a citizen –
I can take
The bad with the good.[36]

An anonymous young Nisei recorded some of the significant events during his first year at Tule Lake:

JUNE 21, 1942 - MOVING AGAIN: I've been here in Walerga for less than a month, but I'm packing up my worldly possessions to move again. I hope they'll put us in a place at least semi-permanent.

I hear Tule Lake is a barren desert and I wonder how long I could bear living in a place like that. My mind is numb towards any long range plans of the future. My only present concern is my bodily comfort.

JUNE 26, 1942 - SECTIONALISM: The whole picture is too generalized. The northerners regard us as rowdy and ill-mannered. Because we were tanned bronze under the naked sun in the assembly centers, we are called "California niggers." I can readily recognize a northern girl by her pale white complexion. It seems that they are more Americanized because they did not live in congregations of Japanese colonies back home.

What I resent most is that they came here first and got all the good jobs. But I feel as long as all of us are going to live here together there should be no room for petty differences.

AUG. 25, 1942 - DUSTSTORM: Today is no day for anyone to be outside. The sky is black and overcast. The wind is relentlessly blowing and churning up the loose ground and no nook or crevice is immune to the ubiquitous dust.

I came home from work and found the room gritty and filthy with grime. Powdery white dust had sifted through the edges of windows and settled on the bed, the shelves, the books and all my possessions.

NOV. 18, 1942 - FISH FISH FISH: Air is biting cold outside and the flimsy barracks quiver like Jello on a chill morning. It's a good thing WRA had the foresight of insulating these army barracks and installed coal stoves in each apartment; otherwise we'd freeze this winter. The G.I. blankets are itchy but nevertheless they keep us warm.

We had fish again today. It's fish, fish, fish, almost every other day. Issei love fish but I will go for hamburgers any day.

Tonight I toasted some bread on the stove to avert "starvation." I'm dreaming of a thick juicy tenderloin smothered with raw onions.

DEC. 1, 1942 - NOSTALGIA: We walked home slowly and weary between the dark rows of barracks reminiscing the "civilization" we left behind. We thought of the pink salmon sparkling in the sun, the hardness of the sidewalks, the sophomore hops, the favorite hot dog stand, The Big Game, the splotches of golden poppies on the green hills of Moraga, the thundering clatter of trolleys on Geary and the kindly old professor in his dark office in Wheeler Hall.

I slipped in between dust-ladened blankets quietly so as not to awaken my father who snored and creaked in an army cot nearby.

FEB. 18, 1943 - DECISION OF A LIFETIME: The army is in the process of registering all male citizens to find out where their loyalty lies.

"What the hell," says a guy, "we have to plan our future courses according to how we were treated in the past. All our lives, both our parents and we have been kicked around like unwanted dogs. We never got a chance. There is no future for us in America. Being pushed into camp such as this is evidence enough."

Although everyone is entitled to his or own conviction, down in my heart I hope people with sentiments like these are in the minority.

It is too much for me when some of my friends whom I have associated closely all my life talk like this. Evacuation was a tragic mistake. The effect is slowly warping everyone's minds to cynicism and defeatism.

I don't want to be bitter and cynical. I want to look ahead: to be far-sighted enough to look beyond my petty grievances, whims and desires. I have a lifetime to live in America and I'm not going to throw it away now. I realize that I'm making a decision of my life and my mind is made up. My conviction has always been the same.

FEB. 19, 1943 - UNSHAKABLE FAITH: This morning I strolled over to the Ad building and registered. The questions were simple. Questions 27 and 28 asked me if I were still loyal to the United States. I signed "yes" to both and walked out feeling relieved.

MAR. 4, 1943 - SIDE BY SIDE: A few of Washington's cigar smoking congressmen in their soft leather chairs are charging that we are being pampered and coddled. I certainly would like to have one of them live with me for a week and eat and sleep with us in our dingy barracks. I'd like to see him sit side by side with me in the latrine. It wouldn't be long before he'd start yelling about his constitutional rights.

MAY 12, 1943 - GOING, GOING, GOING: Joni Shimoda is leaving for Chicago tomorrow. Grace Asai, Stan Sugiyama, Roy Yokote, I and some of his close friends were invited to a farewell party tonight. It gives me an empty feeling to watch the fellows, whom I've become attached during my stay here, leave one by one. Riley leaves tomorrow. Art Morimitsu says he has no alternative but to volunteer for the Army to show his loyalty. He has applied for Camp Savage.

MAY 15, 1943 - THE OUTLOOK: Now that I have made my plans to leave the Project, I feel like staying here a little longer. Life here has made me soft and indolent. I'm clothed, sheltered and I don't have to worry about where my next meal is coming from. I feel as though I've become part of the dust.

It's funny ... I want to prolong this sort of life but if I procrastinate I'll be here for the duration and I don't want to be here when the war ends. My better conscience tells me that the sooner I re-establish myself in a normal American community, the better I would be prepared to meet the post-war future.

I must go out and make my living the hard way again. Yet doubt and fear disturb my mind. Will I be happy outside in a strange community? It makes me feel weary. I hope this will be the last time I'll have to move again.[37]

The anonymous author not only brought to life his personal impressions of Tule Lake, but he touched on the one event that brought about the biggest change at the camp—the distribution of a loyalty oath. It had been conceived with the best of intentions. The Army was seeking Japanese-American volunteers to form a military combat unit. The WRA was looking for a means to phase out the internment camps and allow the Japanese to resettle in the interior of the U.S. But its implementation had the very worst of results, and it transformed the basic character of the internment camp at Tule Lake.

Map of the Tule Lake War Relocation Authority Internment Camp, 1944. *(Courtesy Bureau of Reclamation)*

Above and below: aerial views of the Tule Lake Internment Camp taken in 1944 when the camp housed over 18,000 internees.
(U.S. Army Signal Corps photos)

The enormity of the camp can be seen in these panoramic photos of the Tule Lake Internment Camp taken in 1944. (*Courtesy U.S. Signal Corps*)

The Tule Lake War Internment Camp in 1943, looking west toward The Peninsula. *(Photo courtesy Bureau of Reclamation)*

Site of the Tule Lake Internment Camp in 1984. Much of the former barracks area is now part of the Tulelake Airport. Since this photo was taken, open land around the airport has been cultivated and the roadways that ran between the barracks are gone. *(Photo by author)*

An overview of the Tule Lake Internment Camp taken from the eastern side of The Peninsula in 1944. *(Photo courtesy Bureau of Reclamation)*

The same overview taken in 1984. The land formerly occupied by the camp is now the town site of Newell. Many of the buildings to the left were originally barracks housing the camp's military guards. *(Photo by author)*

CHAPTER 16

A NEW PHASE OF INTERNMENT - TULE LAKE BECOMES THE NATION'S SEGREGATION CENTER

During the initial phase of internment, between May and August of 1942, only Japanese-American college students and Japanese farm laborers were allowed to leave the camps. The War Relocation Authority and its director, Milton Eisenhower, had carefully monitored their movement to outside communities. On June 17, 1942, Dillon S. Myer took over the directorship and began to investigate the possibility of increasing the number of Japanese who could be released. As Myer stated: "I was fearful we would have something akin to Indian reservations to deal with if steps were not taken soon to move the Japanese-Americans back into the mainstream of American life."[1] The major concern in developing a policy for releasing Japanese-Americans was whether or not the general public was ready to accept them, particularly after the adverse publicity generated by Pearl Harbor. Though this consideration had clear racial overtones, Myer was genuinely concerned about the safety of the internees.

The first phase of Myer's program to re-integrate Japanese-Americans was implemented through a policy statement issued on July 20th. This announced that American-born Nisei, who had never studied in Japan, could leave the camps if they had a definite offer of employment. On October 1, a more comprehensive set of regulations related to leaves was developed in a cooperative effort with the United States Justice Department. Four classifications were developed:

1. Short-term leaves ... intended for ... evacuees who found it necessary to leave the center for medical consultation, property arrangements or other personal business.

2. Seasonal leaves ... designed to provide for widespread demand for agricultural labor.

3. Indefinite leaves ... granted ... only by the national director after four specific requirements were met:

    a. An applicant had to have a definite job offer or some other means of support;

    b. There must be no evidence either in the applicant's record at the center or in the files of the intelligence agencies indicating that he might endanger the national security;

    c. There had to be reasonable evidence that the applicant's presence would be acceptable where he planned to live;

    d. The applicant had to agree to keep WRA informed of any change of address.[2]

Although the regulations drafted by the WRA and Justice Department provided a means for releasing Japanese-Americans, the policy statement itself was cumbersome and highly restrictive. Myer felt that a more expedient method had to be found. The opportunity came in mid-January, 1943, when the United States Army decided to organize an all-Nisei combat team. Its members were to be drawn from both the internment camps and Japanese-Americans living on the Hawaiian Islands. In order to speed the clearance for potential recruits, the Army decided to issue a special form to those who volunteered that included a statement of loyalty to the United States. An official public announcement was made on January 28, 1943 concerning the formation of the all-Nisei combat team. Three days later, President Franklin Roosevelt issued a statement concerning the decision.

No loyal citizen of the United States should be denied the democratic right to exercise the responsibilities of citizenship, regardless of his ancestry. The principle on which this country was founded and by which it has always been governed is that Americanism is a matter of the mind and the heart; Americanism is not, and never was, a matter of race or ancestry. A good American is one who is loyal to this country and to our creed of liberty and democracy. Every loyal American citizen should be given the opportunity to serve this country wherever his skills will make the greatest contribution—whether it be in the ranks of the armed forces, war production, agriculture, government service, or other work essential to the war effort.[3]

WRA Director Myer and the Army had hoped that this would not only inspire enlistments but that the accompanying loyalty oath would make it easier for American born Japanese to be granted leave status. However, almost from the inception of the loyalty oath there were problems.

First, it must have been naive on the part of the government to assume that Japanese-Americans would ignore the hypocrisy of President Roosevelt's message. As Roger Daniels stated in his book *Concentration Camps USA*, "if the President's message was true, many of the evacuated people must have asked why are we in concentration camps?"[4]

Second, the loyalty oath and its administration to the interned population was confusing and poorly handled. When it was first issued on February 10, 1943, it was entitled "War Relocation Leave Clearance." For Japanese who had no interest in leaving the camps, the oath did not seem to apply. Yet it was the intention of the WRA to have it administered to all internees.

Finally, there was the matter of the wording of the loyalty oath itself. Two separate questionnaires had been developed, and both had forty questions. One was to be administered to American born Nisei males and the other to women and foreign-born Issei men. On both questionnaires, items twenty-seven and twenty-eight were poorly written and presented unique problems in accordance with the internee's place of birth.

The two questions asked of Nisei men stated:

Question #27: Are you willing to serve in the armed forces of the United States, in combat duty, wherever ordered?

Question #28: Will you swear unqualified allegiance to the United States and faithfully defend the United States from any and all attack by foreign or domestic forces, and forswear any form of allegiance or obedience to the Japanese emperor, or any foreign government, power or organization?[5]

Some Nisei who read questions twenty-seven and twenty-eight readily agreed to answer in the affirmative. Among these men were individuals who joined the 442 Combat Team, which fought and was highly decorated for its gallantry in the European Theater of War. Their motto was "Go For Broke." However, for other Nisei men, these two questions were insulting. Their loyalty had already been questioned when they were placed in the WRA camps. They felt their country had turned against them. In addition, among the Nisei was a special group known as the "Kibei." Though they had been born in the United States, their parents had sent them to Japan for their education. Steeped in Japanese custom, suspected by many Americans of spying for the Japanese government, these bitter young men assumed a more radical anti-American stance when the loyalty oath was issued. Not only did they denounce the U.S. Government, but they also demanded to be repatriated to Japan.

The loyalty oath was equally troublesome for Japanese women and foreign-born Japanese men. Questions twenty-seven and twenty-eight had been slightly altered but they still did not apply to all respondents and they created a problem of choice for those who were asked to sign. The questions stated:

> Question #27: If the opportunity presents itself and you are found qualified, would you be willing to volunteer for the Army Nurse Corps or WAAC?

> Question #28: Will you swear unqualified allegiance to the United States of America and forswear any form of allegiance or obedience to the Japanese emperor, or any other foreign government, power or organization?[6]

The problems facing Issei men and women when they were asked to sign the loyalty oath were complex. The Immigration Act of 1924 denied them the right to apply for American citizenship, hence they were still citizens of Japan.[7] If they signed "Yes" to question twenty-eight they would become people without legal ties to any country. If they signed "No" they risked being deported. Because of the confusion this question caused and because the WRA was informed that it violated the Geneva Convention's regulation on treatment of enemy aliens, question twenty-eight was reworded to read:

Question #28: Will you swear to abide by the laws of the United States and to take no action which would in any way interfere with the war effort of the United States?[8]

But the rewording came too late and there were other complications that could not be adequately resolved. Some internees feared that by signing the loyalty oath, whether it be "Yes" or "No," the government would break up their families—particularly through the release program that allowed older children to attend school and obtain jobs in the east, and through the military draft. Further, there was general fear of the outside world. Radio broadcasts, newspaper articles, and pronouncements by myopic politicians convinced the internees that American society in general was hostile to their presence. They would rather stay in the relative security of the internment camps than risk being resettled.

The loyalty oath created major divisions within the camps between those who signed "Yes, Yes" to the two questions and those who signed "No, No." The "Yes-Yesers" castigated those who signed in the negative, and told them that they were making it more difficult for the Japanese to reintegrate into American society after the war. Signing "Yes," they said, was a pledge of loyalty and faith to a country that had imperfections but offered greater opportunity than did Japan. In return, the "No-Noers" angrily retorted that those who signed "Yes" were fools in light of years of racism and restrictions aimed at the Japanese in the United States. Cooperation with white-dominated America had led to nothing but internment. Those who signed "yes" were "inu"—sellouts to a society that did not care one whit about the Japanese living in the country, save getting rid of them and taking their land.

"Doubt and fear accompanied registration in all relocation projects."[9] Surprisingly though, most internees agreed to complete the questionnaire. Out of 78,000 who were eligible to register (those over 17 years of age), 75,000 completed the form. Out of that number, 65,500 answered "Yes" and 6,700 answered "No" to question twenty-eight. Another 2,000 responded "with qualifications" to the question. They were lumped with the "No" category by the government and were considered "disloyal." Finally, some 1,200 Nisei respondents volunteered for military service and about two-thirds were accepted.[10]

In analyzing registration at each of the ten camps, a marked contrast could be seen.

> At five camps everyone registered; at four others a total of only 36 individuals—10 aliens and 26 citizens —refused to register; but at Tule Lake almost a third of the camp population—3218 people (1,360 citizens and 1,856 aliens)—refused.[11]

Why did so many people at Tule Lake refuse to cooperate? Resistance was rooted in the turmoil that had existed since the summer of 1942, when camp factions from the Northwest and California clashed over jobs, political positions, and housing facilities. Tule Lake had a built-in tradition of dissent. Resistance was also due to a shift in camp administration. In December, 1942 Elmer Shirrell was replaced by Harvey Coverly, who barely had time to assume leadership before orders were given to administer the loyalty questionnaire. Confusion soon reigned.

On January 29, 1943 internees at Tule Lake were informed via *The Tulean Dispatch* that forms would be distributed for the purpose of military registration. It was not until six days later, on February 4, that they were told that the registration was not just for men interested in volunteering for military service. It would involve all individuals in the camp seventeen years of age and older and registration would be related to "leave clearance." When director Coverly was approached with a request to provide more information, he stalled, waiting to receive more detailed instructions related to the components of the questionnaire and the methods for its distribution.

Meanwhile, in the absence of concrete information about the nature of the impending registration, the evacuees began to draw their own conclusions.

> Formal and informal discussions centered on the injustice of instituting military service, on the discriminatory aspects of the proposed segregated combat unit, on the probability of forced resettlement as inherent in the program and on the dubious prospects of favorable employment opportunities on the outside.[12]

Members of the Japanese American Citizens League counseled fellow internees to be cooperative with registration, but their advice was met with derision and hostility. The JACL chapter at the camp had long been held in contempt because at the time the camp opened, its leaders had assumed key positions of political authority and taken the best jobs.

Delays in registration continued until February 9, giving the antagonists additional time to foment opposition. When the military registration contingent finally arrived, plans for administering the questionnaire were hastily made. Registration teams were to be organized, consisting of two teachers, one Nisei, and one Caucasian. Army personnel would accompany each team to sign up Nisei males for military service. Block managers were instructed to inform everyone over seventeen that they were to report to the first barrack of their block to fill out the questionnaire.

On the afternoon and evening of February 9th, Coverly and representatives of the Army met with block managers and other leaders in the camp. Unfortunately, these meetings were poorly handled. They were brief and impersonal. A prepared statement was read, with no real opportunity for questions or discussion from the audience.

On the morning of February 10th, registration was scheduled to begin but practically no one came. The camp's administration was shocked and frustrated, unsure about what to do next. Meanwhile:

> Reports began to circulate that many Nisei and Kibei were tearing up their birth certificates - a symbolic repudiation of their citizenship - when they learned that they were being asked to serve in the Army after having been subjected to the indignity of evacuation, confinement behind barbed wire, and the insults of the American press.[13]

As a result of the camp administration's bungled effort to circulate the questionnaire, there was a significant shift of power among the camp's political factions. The JACL leadership was repudiated, and its membership made scapegoats for all of the camp's ills. New leaders emerged from the ranks of disillusioned Nisei, alienated and militant Kibei, and angry and discontented

Issei. The power they held over the camp's general population was substantial. It was manifested through both psychological pressure as well as verbal and physical attacks on those accused of cooperating with the camp's administration.

By mid-February, the situation at Tule Lake was precarious. Those living outside the camp had occasional glimpses of the tension. In a letter written to Klamath Falls residents Kenneth and Winifred Lambie, a Japanese friend related:

> Please be patient and don't come to visit us just now. Wait awhile. People here have an aversion to blue eyes and blond hair ... None of our Caucasian teacher friends will visit us for fear we will be harmed. Suffice it to say, we are all fine and when I say O.K.—come. I won't write about this mess down here—for it will keep.[14]

Originally March 2 had been set as the deadline for registration at Tule Lake, but because so few had completed the forms by the last week in February, camp director Harvey Coverly extended the deadline to March 10. In an attempt to resolve some of the ambiguity related to the questionnaire, particularly items twenty-seven and twenty-eight, the Army posted a mimeographed statement in each mess hall. It was poorly written and merely served to antagonize the militant factions further. One section of the memo stated:

> Nisei and Kibei who answer "No" to questions No. 27 and 28, and who persist in that answer, cannot anticipate that the Army of the United States will ever ask them for their services or that they will be inducted into the armed forces by Selective Service.

> A "No" answer on question 27, accompanied by a "Yes" answer on question 28, is not regarded by the War Department as a proof of disloyalty in the individual, or as bearing on that question ... [but] these men have the minimum chance of being called into the military service.

> The "Yes" answer to both questions speaks for itself ... In case it is so filed, then they are liable to induction for general service elsewhere throughout the Army of

the United States, in the same manner as any other inductee within the country.[15]

Accompanying this lame and confusing attempt at clarification was a threat that those Nisei and Kibei men who did not complete the questionnaire would be violating both the Espionage and Selective Service acts and could be sentenced to 20 years in jail and fined $10,000. Later the FBI informed the camp administration that refusing to respond to the questionnaire was not a violation of either act. However, the damage had already been done.

Next, Coverly and the Army attempted to force the questionnaire issue by specifically ordering all Kibei men to register. Collectively they refused and when the Kibei openly demonstrated against registration, they were removed from Tule Lake and taken across the basin to an abandoned Civilian Conservation Corps camp (though the records are unclear, the detention facility was probably operated at Camp Lava Beds, since it was the closest CCC facility to the internment camp). The defiant Kibei were held there for several months, and then divided into smaller groups. Some were sent to other camps, and the rest returned to the Tule Lake compound.

When registration was finally over on March 10, 1943, 42% of the eligible Japanese resident aliens and 49% of the Japanese-American internees had either signed "No" to question twenty-eight or they had refused to answer it at all.[16] Now the WRA was faced with a problem. On one hand, they were committed to expediting the process of releasing "loyal" internees and moving them to the mid-west and east coast. On the other hand, they had to deal with those who had signed "No" and were therefore "disloyal." After weighing the alternatives, the WRA decided that the best solution was to move the "disloyal" to Tule Lake, since it had the highest percentage of "No" respondents. In the resettlement process, the other nine camps were to be gradually phased out of operation.

By the spring and summer of 1943, the program to move the "disloyal" into Tule Lake and the "loyal" out was well under way. For safety, the two groups were segregated within the compound, but this did not prevent jeering and derisive comments between the antagonists. When the shift was completed in September, friction between factions of "loyal" and "disloyal" was replaced by a new brand of tension. It was a familiar scenario, already played out once before when Tule Lake first opened. "Old Tuleans" viewed the "segregation center" (as Tule Lake was now called) as their turf. They saw themselves as the true resisters. To the "Old Tuleans" the newcomers from the other nine camps were outsiders who did not understand nor fit into the social organization of the camp. But the "Old Tuleans were hated by the newcomers partly because they were not considered genuine 'disloyals' (because they had not been faced with removal from other camps) and also because they had established themselves in the best jobs and apartments."[17]

To complicate the problem, the population at Tule Lake swelled to 18,000 people. Tension and overcrowding took their toll on the camp's morale. Vocal and physical scuffles were common, and the radical elements began to organize into groups that focused on open defiance against the camp administration and repatriation. Two of the most powerful groups were the Daihyo Sha Kai, roughly meaning "representative body" in Japanese, and the Sokuji Kikoku Hoshi-dan, or the "Organization to Return Immediately to the Homeland to Serve."

In July of 1943, Raymond Best replaced Harvey Coverly as director of Tule Lake. He took over leadership at an extremely difficult time. Labor strikes, physical intimidation, and beatings were becoming commonplace in the camp, particularly against anyone accused of being "inu," In order to improve camp security, Best approved the construction of a new double "man-proof" eight-foot high fence around the camp and the personnel at the army garrison was increased to 31 officers and 890 enlisted men. As a symbol of force, six obsolete tanks were lined up next to the military compound, in full view of the segregees.

Through the fall and winter of 1943, the camp was plagued by work stoppages and demonstrations. Then on November 1st, Dillon Myer, the National Director of the WRA, came to Tule Lake on an inspection tour. Hoping to impress Myer with the degree of discontent at the camp, the Japanese leadership organized a demonstration involving over 5,000 men, women, and children. They marched to the administration compound and surrounded both the administration center and camp hospital. Representatives from the demonstration demanded a meeting with Myer and for the next three hours discussed with him a series of demands they had drafted. These included an improvement in working conditions, food, and treatment by WRA employees. They also requested that Raymond Best be removed as director of the camp. At the end of the meeting, both Myer and the representatives spoke to the crowd outside the building. Soon after, the crowd dispersed. During the demonstration there were several altercations between whites and Japanese, and the chief medical officer at the hospital was beaten. At no time were the lives of Dillon, Best, or other personnel in the administration center in danger. But, as Dillon Myer described in his book *Uprooted Americans*, "outside tradesmen who had been in the center on business and some hysterical employees had left the center and given out wildly imaginative stories."[18] For example, Francis Biddle, Attorney General of the United States, received word that:

> Serious disturbances have recently taken place at a relocation center of the War Relocation Authority at Tule Lake ... Five hundred Japanese internees armed with knives and clubs shut up Dillon Myer and some of his administrative officers in the administration building for several days. The Army moved in to restore order.[19]

Later, testimony given to the Joint Fact Finding Committee on Un-American Activities in California, stated that:

> On Nov. 1, 1943, a delegation of spokesmen for the subversive Japs called upon Director Best and presented a series of demands which he was utterly unable to grant. Shortly thereafter all the caucasians working at the center, about 200 persons, were imprisoned for about 4 hours, while a mob of howling Japs, armed with daggers, swords and clubs, milled around outside the administration building, shouting obscenities at the caucasian women and loudly proclaiming their disloyalty to the United States.[20]

And the *San Francisco Examiner* printed an "eyewitness" account allegedly given by a WRA employee who resigned his position immediately after the incident.

> Japs began coming across the compound, between the hospital and the administration building. They came in droves, and they simply wiped away the low barbed wire fence which formed a deadline they were not supposed to cross.

One group of about a thousand, led by the Judo
boys—the strong arm boys who rule the camp by
intimidation—stopped by the hospital to have it out
with Doctor Pedicord.

And one nurse had her hair pulled and her faced
slapped.

Meanwhile, several thousand Japs—my guess is about
6,000 or 7,000—were outside the administration
building ...

I saw Japs walk up to the building with sacks full of
straw, and poke the sacks under the building. Later,
we learned that the straw was soaked in oil. And I saw
the Judo boys ostentatiously take up positions guarding every door of the building ...

The Japs outside stood stolidly by ... I know enough
about the Jap to know that he's most dangerous when
he's quiet. My knowledge wasn't any more comforting
when added to the fact that most of the Japs outside
carried knives—long, curved bladed beet knives or
butcher knives ...[21]

It was unfortunate that the accounts were embellished with such
lurid and inaccurate detail. Most Americans were all too ready to
believe them.

In an attempt to prevent a repeat of the November 1st demonstration, Raymond Best issued an order on November 4th
prohibiting public gatherings of evacuees in the administration
headquarters area, around WRA housing, and within the areas of
the camp where the hospital and warehouses were located. His
edict was printed in *The Tulean Dispatch.* The reaction among the
camp's general population was hostile. They were angry that the
demands presented to Dillon Myer were being treated with
contempt. At 8:15 that night, several of the segregees sneaked
into the motor pool and took a number of trucks. As they drove
toward the administration buildings, a crowd formed around
them and people began shouting "Get Best! Take Best!"[22]

At about the same time, a number of fights erupted between
Caucasian employees and roving bands of Japanese men.

Meanwhile, the military police was mobilized and at 10:00 PM the Army entered the camp, armed with both guns and tanks. It was reported that the soldiers fired six shots during the takeover but no one was hit. In spite of the gunfire and the roar of the tanks and other military vehicles, it was not until the next day that most of the camp's residents became aware that the army had taken over and that they were now under martial law.[23] For the next two-and-a-half months the camp remained under military rule and the WRA did not regain control until January 15, 1944.[24]

Though the news accounts of the November riot at Tule Lake doted on sensationalism, a few people attempted to appraise the situation in calmer tones. On December 15, 1943, the *Christian Century* magazine published a letter written by Howard D. Hannaford. In it, Hannaford, who had worked at the camp, attempted to explain the unique situation at Tule Lake and to compare it with the WRA program in general:

> The way many newspapers reported the recent happenings in Tulelake Center is likely to create wrong impressions regarding the nine relocation centers and to intensify opposition to the government's resettlement program for Japanese and Japanese-Americans. No effort was made to show that Tulelake was a different kind of center from the others and, while the main events were on the whole accurately reported, sensational trimmings distorted the story ...
>
> The majority of the people in Tulelake Center are not actively disloyal to the American government and ... many of them have no desire to go to Japan. The situation would be less complicated if Tulelake was actually and definitely the "disloyal camp" as it is termed in common parlance. However, it must be remembered that, although the motives in making the decision to go to Tulelake were far too complex to be correctly appraised without sympathetic consideration, the residents, with the exception of minor children, entered the segregation center voluntarily. Therefore, the group in Tulelake is distinctly different from those in the nine relocation centers ...

The problem of administration of the Tulelake Center remains a thorny one. All difficulties were not cleared up by the army's assuming control in spite of the confident expectations of many vociferous people in communities near the center. The trouble-makers are chiefly a group of bachelors, without stake in this country and fanatically pro-Japanese, who seem determined both to be non-cooperative with the center's administrative officers and to intimidate their milder fellow segregees into participation in their program. The number of agitators is proportionately very small, but it is difficult even for the army to identify all of them and more difficult to apprehend them, since no resident wishes to turn informer regardless of his personal opinion about recent events. A kind of passive resistance has developed. It has its humorous aspects. The colonel, properly guarded, goes to deliver an address to the people, as carefully arranged and advertised beforehand. No one comes to hear him and the colonel puts a curfew law into operation. Then a group of small children, carrying home-made Japanese flags, are sent out in their innocence to parade, contrary to regulations against demonstrations. So a puzzled soldier, unable to employ the means usually employed to break up assemblies of adults, "gently disperses" the children, as the reports phrase it!

Public agitation as to the agency of administration of Tulelake Center continues, many demanding permanent army control. There is no easy solution of the problem. As long as there are gentle old people and children in the center, social services, such as recreation programs, family counseling and education, must be continued. WRA is better equipped and more suitable than the army for such work. At the same time, as long as there is the possibility of agitators threatening the peace and security of both adminis- trators and segregees, then there is a need for a stronger police force than is provided in the usual WRA organization; in the present national manpower shortage is it difficult to recruit such a force from among civilians.

We should sympathize with those who bear the responsibility for solving this administrative problem and with the unfortunate people in Tulelake Center. At the same time let us also exert every effort to help the people of the Japanese race who are not in Tulelake, that they may again take their places in normal communities, and so find their faith in America justified and confirmed.[25]

For nearly a year, the climate at Tule Lake remained tense. Several incidents threatened to ignite another riot. On May 24, 1944 a soldier guarding one of the entrance gates got into an argument with James Shoichi Okamoto and shot and killed him. A composite report from witnesses, assembled several weeks later, gave the following information:

Shoichi James Okamoto ... 30 years old ... was driving Truck #100-41 at the order of the construction supervisor ... to get lumber piled across the highway from the old main gate, which is called Gate #4 ... (a) new sentry had just come on duty ... and was known as one of the tougher sentries. The sentry asked to see ... (Okamoto's security) badge. It is claimed Okamoto said words to the effect of, "Well, here's the pass." Perhaps this sounded cocky to the already irritated guard. The sentry ordered him off the truck ... Okamoto was apparently apprehensive by this time. When ordered out of the truck he had done so reluctantly and had left the truck door opened.

The sentry then ordered Okamoto to the back of the truck ... the sentry (then) struck Okamoto sideways on the right shoulder with a rifle-butt. Okamoto raised his right arm and moved his body slightly back to ward off any further blows. While in this defensive position, the guard stepped back one pace and from a distance of four or five feet fired without warning ... Okamoto fell with what seemed to have been a close-range stomach wound. How long a time elapsed before he was hospitalized is not known; some say 20 minutes. According to the attending physician and surgeon every possible means of treatment was administered ... In spite of the doctors' efforts, Okamoto died at 12:10 A.M. May 25, 1944.[26]

Camp Director Best skillfully handled the situation. He immediately had a letter of regret published and gave his blessings to a public funeral. The dead man's family was given assistance and he promised a thorough investigation into the shooting. Though Best was able to defuse a potentially volatile situation, the formal investigation was in the hands of the military. In July the sentry was found innocent of murder and transferred to another Army unit.

Violence was not confined to tension between soldiers and segregees. Dissension within the camp itself was a Kafkaesque nightmare. Japanese even remotely associated with the camp's administration were accused of being "inu" and risked verbal abuse and beatings. One internee commented: "Having inu around keeps everybody on edge. Everybody suspects everybody else and it has led to a great deal of hard feeling. It keeps people in a constant state of tension."[27]

On July 2nd, internal violence reached a peak when Takeo Noma, who had supervised the camp's cooperative stores, was murdered. He had been beaten, his throat slashed, and a pair of scissors stuck through his neck. It was reported that many of the internees felt that Noma deserved what had happened to him. He had been viewed as "Public Inu Number One" because of his close work with the administrative staff of the WRA.[28]

While Tule Lake was falling apart internally, the outside world continued its pattern of insensitivity toward the camp's Japanese internees—even in times of patriotic gallantry. For example, on July 27, 1944 the County Record of Alturas, California reported the death of Technical Sergeant Zentaro Akiyama, who had been killed while fighting with the 442nd Combat Team in Europe. The article stated:

> A family in the Tule Lake Center has been notified by the War Department that their Japanese American son was killed in action in Italy, the War Relocation Authority announced.

> The WRA said this was believed to be the first death of a Japanese American soldier whose parents are living at the Tule Lake Center.[29]

The article was like tens of thousands appearing all over the country that brought the tragic news of Americans boys killed in action. But it had one element that was unique to the Japanese community in United States—the wording of the headline. It stated "Son of Tulelake *Jap* Is Killed" (emphasis added). Whites who are old enough to remember World War II may argue that this critical observation is uncalled for. The word "Jap" was simply the term everyone used at the time. But to the Japanese of America it was a painful reminder that even when their sons were spilling blood in the world war, they remained second-class citizens.

By the fall and winter of 1944, the War Relocation Authority and Justice Department faced a thorny problem—what to do with Tule Lake and the increasing number of segregees who were demanding to be repatriated to Japan. By October 14, 1944 nearly 19,000 Japanese living in the United States had indicated a desire to repatriate, and most of the requests came from Tule Lake. By January 1945 the number of repatriation requests had grown to over 20,000.[30] The temptation among some government officials was to simply honor all the requests, particularly in light of past events at Tule Lake. But there were severe problems with this quick solution. A substantial number of the segregees at Tule Lake and other camps had renounced their citizenship and requested repatriation because of social pressure and because of anger over their treatment by the government. In testimony later given to government review boards, many reasons were given for renunciation. One Tule Lake segregee explained that the fear of verbal attacks on his family caused him to renounce his citizenship: "During the time of my hearing I was forced to (renounce) or else the "Pressure Group" (would have) continuously (spoken) evil of my family which I could not bear."[31]

Another camp resident gave anger as his reason:

> When the Western Defense Commander assumed the responsibilities of the West Coast, I expected that at least the Nisei would be allowed to remain. But to General DeWitt, we were all alike. "A Jap's a Jap. Once a Jap, always a Jap." ... I swore to become a Jap 100 percent, and never do another day's work to help this country fight this war. My decision to renounce my citizenship there and then was absolute.[32]

Fear based on rumors was a common reason for renunciation: "Everybody told me that I must renounce my citizenship of the United States, otherwise I will be forced to go outside of the camp to be murdered."[33]

Perhaps the strongest force was social pressure:

> Everybody around me renounced. At least they said they did. They wouldn't speak to me. They treated me like an outcast. I felt alone and powerless in a huge dark place. I was afraid. Aloneness and powerlessness got worse and worse. What else could I do but renounce?[34]

Fortunately, through the almost single-handed crusade of San Francisco lawyer Wayne Collins, and prudent reconsideration by the Justice Department, plans for wholesale repatriation were abandoned. A screening committee was established and gradually the sincere repatriates were separated from those who had been caught in the emotional tide. It was not an easy matter, and litigation for some Japanese-Americans and resident aliens who sought to remain in the United States continued until 1949.

The decline of Tule Lake's population accelerated through the fall and winter of 1945. On August 1, Tule Lake had a population of 17,341, by January 1, 1946 the number had been reduced to 7,269.[35] Of those that remained, some were waiting for hearings on requests to regain U.S. citizenship or resident alien status; some were waiting to be transported to Japan; and others either had no place to go to or were afraid to leave the camp. Gradually the reluctant were nudged out, the repatriates taken to other camps, and those seeking re-instatement were granted reprieves. Finally on March 20, 1946 the camp officially closed its doors. A government report described the events of that day:

> March 20, the intricate complex of detention and relocation ended at Tule Lake with the movement of 554 persons. The bare figures hardly convey the sense of the dramatic: 102 relocated, 60 of them released in the "eleventh hour," 450 to the Department of Justice internment at Crystal City (Texas) ... A survey of the empty barracks left no doubt that the center('s) residential area (was) closed ... as night fell ... the perimeter lights went off.[36]

So ended internment and segregation at Tule Lake. But the closing of the camp did not end its impact or its memory. Out of the more than eight thousand Japanese who repatriated to Japan, over 4,400 had been interned at Tule Lake. The ugly experiences of years of racial discrimination and the war had driven a precious commodity from the United States. The country had lost the skills of these talented Japanese resident aliens and Japanese-American citizens. For the rest of the Japanese-American community, Tule Lake and the other nine camps became symbols of the effects of wartime hysteria and racism. For a while, they sought to erase their memories, to forget their experiences, to put internment behind them. But since the late 1960s, Japanese-Americans have come out in great numbers to talk of their life as internees, to let the world know that it must not happen again.

Today the barracks that housed 18,000 Japanese-Americans and Japanese alien residents at Tule Lake are gone. They were given away to late 1940s homesteaders to be used for housing and farm buildings. Portions of the western section of the camp, which made up the military post, administration headquarters, civilian housing, and warehouses still remain. Collectively, they are part of an unincorporated town known as Newell.

Only a stone monument located along Highway 139, near the entrance to the old camp jail, commemorates the camp's existence. Dedicated on May 27, 1979, the monument's inscription reads:

TULE LAKE

May 1942.   March 1946.

Tule Lake was one of ten American concentration camps established during World War II to incarcerate 110,000 persons of Japanese ancestry whom the majority were American citizens behind barbed wire and guard towers without charge, trial or establishment of guilt. These camps are reminders of how racism, economic and political exploitation can undermine the constitutional guarantees of the United States citizens and aliens alike. May the injustices and humiliation suffered here never recur.[37]

From the Japanese American Citizens League comes a hymn of reflection and hope that brings this chapter to an appropriate end:

> There was a dream my father dreamt for me
>   A land in which all men are free -
> Then the desert camp with watch tower high
>   Where life stood still, mid sand and brooding sky
> Out of the war in which my brothers died -
>   Their muted voices with mine cried -
> This is our dream that all men shall be free!
>   This is our creed, we'll live in loyalty.
> God help us rid the land of bigotry,
>   That we may walk in peace in dignity.[38]

In 1984, cement platforms for the camp's shower and toilet facilities could still be found at the southern end of the former internment camp. Much of the area is now under cultivation and these platforms are gone. *(Photo by author)*

Monument commemorating Tule Lake Internment Camp.
(Photo by author)

Remnant of the original fence that surrounded the Tule Lake WRA Internment Camp. *(Photo by author)*

CHAPTER 17

THE LAST HOMESTEADERS

When the last Japanese internees left the Tule Lake WRA camp in March of 1946, it had been nearly ten years since the last homestead allotment. In March of 1942, Klamath Project Director B.C. Hayden had submitted to the Bureau of Reclamation a draft of an order that would have opened new land in the southeastern section of the basin. However, the Bureau decided to delay the allotment until the war was over in order to give the new veterans an opportunity to file.[1]

By April, 1945 the Klamath Project had received numerous inquiries from veterans concerning the availability of homestead plots in the Tule Lake Basin. Veterans returning from the war, particularly those who had originally come from the Klamath Falls and Tule Lake regions, were anxious to file for land. But Klamath Project Superintendent E.L. Stephens counseled that preparations should be done with care. Stephens's position was that there were still many servicemen on active duty and that the land should not be opened for application until as many men as possible were released from their military obligations. Stephens strengthened his argument by saying:

> I have discussed the matter with the County Agent, Representatives of the Veterans Advisory Boards and farm organizations ... they believe that there are over 500 men in the service who are sons of farmers in this community and who have been waiting for years for an opportunity to file on a homestead in the Tule Lake area. Very few of these men have returned, and it is the belief of these organizations that the lands should not be opened for entry until at least some of these men are returning home.[2]

The Bureau of Reclamation concurred with Stephens's reasoning and the land opening was delayed for a year and a half.

In preparation for opening the new homestead allotment, the Klamath Project carefully analyzed its past selection policies. It began by reviewing the different criteria that had been used for determining qualified applicants. The Project's study noted that qualification requirements had gone through a number of developmental stages. In 1917 one only needed to have been an American citizen or an alien who had taken out naturalization papers. In 1922, veterans were given first preference but little else was required. By 1927, each person had to have $2,000 in assets and produce clear proof of farming experience. Finally, in 1937 a rather complex rating system had been developed that involved an assessment of one's character, industry, farming experience and assets. As mentioned in chapter twelve, the rating system became a center of controversy, particularly over the points awarded for a person's assets. Critics suggested that the 1937 homestead drawing was the "rich man's" allotment, although this was not actually true.

At the conclusion of their review, the Project recommended the following criteria be used for screening individuals who applied for homesteads:

1. $2,000 minimum in assets or capital, with verification through various forms, including a bank statement.

2. Two years of farming experience with supporting affidavits.

3. A medical certificate declaring the applicant's ability to operate a farm.

4. Letters of character reference.

5. Proof of World War II military service.

6. Male and female veterans would receive equal consideration.

7. To avoid speculation, the homesteader would be required to farm his unit for five consecutive years before he/she would be given free ownership.

8. Persons applying had to currently own less than 160 acres of land.[3]

In further refinement of policy, the Klamath Project decided against holding initial interviews with those who applied. This was done to speed up processing of what was anticipated to be a large number of applications. Instead, the winnowing process would go through several stages. First, all applicants were to be screened for proper military service, farm experience, capital and character. If a person was challenged, then he or she could appeal to the Board. Next, the remaining names would be placed in a container and a drawing of names equal to twice the number of farm units available would take place. The order in which the names would be drawn would determine an individual's opportunity to select a homestead or position on an alternate list. The first person drawn, provided he or she passed a second screening, would have first pick of a homestead, and the process would continue until the final unit was awarded. Slots vacated by persons who were found unqualified during the second screening would cause everyone to move up one notch, in the order of their drawing.[4]

With the mechanism for selection in place, the Klamath Project then met with representatives of the Bureau of Reclamation and Department of the Interior to establish an opening date for homestead applications. Initially, July 1, 1946 was selected, but last-minute details had not been worked out and as a consequence the public notice was not issued until August 1. When it was published, the notice announced the availability of 86 farm units located in the central-eastern section of the Tule Lake Basin. The deadline for applications was to be September 15th.

In preparation for the homestead allotment, the Project also formed a Selections Board, whose job it was to screen applicants. The Board was to be made up of five members who represented the interests of veterans, farmers, the basin community and the Bureau of Reclamation. Members selected by the Klamath Project to serve on the board included: Nelson Reed, a businessman from Klamath Falls and a veteran of World War I; Robert Norris, Vice Commander of the Merrill, Oregon American Legion Post, farmer and World War II veteran; Fred E. McMurphy, veteran of World War I, farmer in the Tule Lake area, and former officer of the Tule Lake Community Club; Lockie McLeod of Dunsmuir, who was selected from outside the Klamath Basin area to add impartiality to the Board; and finally, E.L. Stephens, Superintendent of the Klamath Project.[5]

When the announcement was made by the Bureau of Reclamation that the period of application would only last a month and a half, the Board protested, claiming it was too short.

Board members also pointed out that the deadline was on a Sunday, precluding normal mail delivery. The Board failed to secure an extension from the Bureau of Reclamation. However, it was able to arrange with the Klamath Falls post office to sort and deliver all applications received by 2:00 PM, Sunday, September 15, so that last minute applicants would have an equal chance.

The public notice advertising the homesteads was distributed over much of the United States. Word was spread through government publications, newspapers and even church groups. As the applications began to arrive, they represented a cross section of World War II veterans. Some applicants, like Philip Krizo, Laurence Hartley and Bob Pillared, were local men who had waited with anticipation for the opportunity to file for their own land. Others, like ex-Army Air Force pilot Vernon McVey, became aware of the Tule Lake lands by accident. Three days before the filing deadline, McVey had been investigating the availability of reclamation land in Arizona at the Gila Project. While there, he crossed paths with his former agronomy professor, Ian A. Briggs. Briggs, now an official with the Bureau of Reclamation, told him of the homestead opening at Tule Lake, but expressed sympathy for McVey because the filing deadline was only several days away. Undaunted, McVey immediately obtained the necessary application papers. By Saturday morning he had finished all the paper work and had made arrangements with a friend to fly him to Klamath Falls. McVey beat the 2:00 PM Sunday deadline by only a few minutes. Some applicants were less frenetic about filing. Walter Hulse, from La Habra, California had been looking at some land in Grants Pass, Oregon. On the way home, he stopped in Tule Lake to investigate the homestead allotment. Hulse decided to file and hold off purchasing any property until after the drawing.[6]

When the September 15 deadline had passed, the Selection Board had received 2,150 applications for the 86 farm units. The tedious process of sorting out qualified applicants then began. It was done with care and compassion. As the Board reviewed each completed form, many of the statements made by individuals were simple and straightforward. "It has been my sincere desire to return to farm life since my discharge from the Navy, but due to inflated prices of farm land, I have not been able to find anything suitable," said one man.[7] Another stated: "Any consideration that can be given me in helping me to fulfill my desire to return to farm life will be greatly appreciated."[8] Others expressed idealism and hope: "I believe this will be the chance of a lifetime to become independent and to develop a farm which will compare in productiveness to any other in that region."[9]

One of the individuals who survived the initial screening was a Japanese-American war veteran who had been wounded by shrapnel while fighting in the Italian Campaign. He stated in a letter to the Selections Board:

> I have made out this application with the sincere hope that I will receive the same consideration that others will get. The fact that I am of Japanese descent should not be of issue but in the past other agencies have passed up qualified people of my race simply because of the difference in skin color. I sincerely hope that the members of this Examination Board show no discrimination due to race.[10]

The Board added his name to the list, but he was not among the 172 finalists whose names were drawn.

During the initial screening process, the Selections Board waded through nine documents for each applicant. These documents included three character references, three farm experience testimonials, an affidavit of military service, a statement corroborating capital assets and a certificate of medical examination.[11] When the Board was done, 858 out of 2,150 applicants had been rejected. About 200 of those appealed to the Board but only 13 rejections were reversed.[12]

In early December, the Selections Board completed their work and 1,305 names were prepared for drawing. Each person's name was assigned a number that was typed onto a small slip of paper and then placed inside a gelatin capsule. The capsules were in turn placed in a three-gallon pickle jar, which had been fitted with an axle and crank. Before the actual drawing, the jar was to be turned numerous times in order to thoroughly mix the capsules.

Wednesday, December 18, 1946 was selected as the date for drawing names, and it was to be done at a public meeting held at the Klamath Falls National Guard Armory. A combined effort by the Klamath Falls *Herald and News*, the American Legion, and the Klamath Project helped draw national attention to the event.

On the day of the drawing, the doors of the Armory were opened at 9:00 AM and a capacity crowd filed in. Those in attendance included both local residents and applicants who had come from many parts of the United States. They seated themselves in folding chairs that surrounded a boxing ring located in the center of the armory. Lois Stewart of the *Herald and News* described the audience:

> These weren't the grizzled veterans of the first World War. These were kids hardly old enough to scrape stubble off their chins. Kids who looked pink and scrubbed, their hair tousled in rumpled curls and all sporting a gold discharge button in the lapel of their jackets, the glitter of the emblem absolutely eclipsed by the grin on their faces.[13]

At 10:30, a carefully planned program began with introductory remarks by George Conner, who represented the Klamath Falls Civic Committee. Mayors Ed Ostendorf of Klamath Falls and Ralph Fawcett of Tulelake followed him. Klamath Falls radio stations KFJI and KFLW broadcast the program. Through network hookups, it was heard by listeners in all of the west coast states.[14] Other dignitaries who made introductory remarks included Nelson Reed of the Selections and Examining Board; Howard Dayton, commander of District No. 2 of the American Legion in California; Raymond Best of the Bureau of Reclamation; W.C. Ryan, representing Governor Earl Snell of Oregon; and Lawrence Carr of Redding, California. Carr represented the California State Veterans' Affairs Council and California Governor Earl Warren. In his presentation, he stated:

> Here a grateful Nation is rewarding its men whose sacrifices so recently brought us this greatest of victories. This Nation, however, is not merely giving some veterans a chance to become owners of valuable public land. You are being given an opportunity to become self-reliant, independent, American farmers.[15]

When the last introductory remarks were out of the way, the drawing began. The Klamath High School band played a fanfare and then the pickle jar, filled with the 1,305 gelatin capsules, was turned several times. Olney Rudd, a World War I veteran and homesteader from Tule Lake, stepped forward to draw the first capsule. Lois Stewart of the *Herald and News* reported on the tense anticipation that could be felt in the crowded armory:

> Even ... the newspaper people, the radio announcers, technicians and spotters, the clerks and the typists, were touched by the electricity which charged the air as anxious Tule lake homestead applicants, their families and friends, waited for the first drawing of the tiny capsule from the pickle jar.[16]

Rudd handed the capsule to Klamath Project director E. Layton Stephens, who cracked it open with a wooden mallet. Stephens retrieved the slip of paper inside and handed it back to Rudd. The audience was silent, only the creaking of several chairs could be heard. Station manager Dave Hoss of KFJI Radio moved a microphone close to Rudd so that listeners from Canada to Mexico and east to Denver could hear him read the first number. It was number 128. When it was matched with a list of names monitored by Bureau of Reclamation official Ten Broeck Williamson it was found to be Robert L. Smith, a resident of Banks, Oregon. Though the audience broke into applause, Smith was not there to receive congratulations. Instead, he was working his parents' farm near Forest Grove, Oregon.[17]

Rudd then retrieved the next capsule. It belonged to Gerwin McCracken of Arlington, Virginia. As each number was drawn and matched with the winning applicant, the name was written on a chalkboard. It wasn't until the fifteenth name was called that a local resident was drawn. It was Ernest M. Lindsay. It was reported that the crowd broke into pandemonium by "stomping, whistling, shouting" when Lindsay's name was announced.[18]

The individual whose number was in the nineteenth capsule drawn captivated the audience. He was Elmer Metz, Jr. of Wellington, Kansas. Orin Cassmore, writing for the *Reclamation ERA*, described the scene:

> "Feeling lucky," he had just blown into Klamath for the drawing and was staying with his brothers at their Tule Lake machine shop. Elmer was honeymooning and it may have been he was looking dreamily at Mrs. Marjorie Cook Metz, who is cute and almost 19; or he may have decided to get philosophical and resigned about his chances; but anyway he didn't recognize his number when it was called. Marjorie did, though. She punched him with her elbow. Then, she whirled in her

seat and shook him: "Elmer! Wake up Elmer! It's your number! Wake up, Elmer!" Elmer woke up. Elmer bounced to his feet with a whoop, beat himself on the chest and yelled out above the cheers; "That's ME! Elmer Metz. Folks, Here's Elmer!"[19]

The "luck of the draw" brought others into the spotlight. The thirtieth person drawn was Vernon McVey, the ex-Army Air Force pilot from Arizona who had filed his application at the last minute. The fifty-second person was Walter Hulse, who had passed over his opportunity to buy land in Grants Pass for a chance at Tule Lake. The fifty-eighth person drawn was ex-WAVE Eleanor Jane Bolesta of Everett, Washington. Married at the time to Charles Bolesta, a Marine who had been wounded in Guam, she was the first and only woman to be awarded a homestead in the 1946 drawing.

The sixty-ninth person drawn was Phillip Krizo, whose Czechoslovakian father had come to the Tule Lake Basin in 1912. The elder Krizo had purchased land from the Lakeside Land Company and farmed south of Malin. At the time, the waters of Tule Lake still reached most of its original shoreline. Then in 1927, he acquired a homestead. His son Phillip grew up in the basin, and when the United States became involved in World War II, he served as a radar navigator on P-61 night fighters in Italy and the China-Burma-India theater. Phillip and his wife, Barbara, were married during the war. When he returned to the basin in 1946, he opened a small electronics shop in the city of Tulelake. When applications were made available, Krizo filed for a homestead, but he had little hope of winning one. His reasoning was that since his father had won a homestead in 1927, the chances of such luck being repeated in the family were slim. On the day of the drawing he told Barbara, "I'm not going to go [to the armory in Klamath Falls] because there's not a chance in the world I'm going to win a homestead."[20] But she countered with, "I just have a feeling you're going to get one and we've just got to be there."[21] She was right and the Krizos were featured in both the Bureau of Reclamation's publication *Reclamation ERA* in February of 1947 and in the July, 1948 edition of *Pic Magazine*.

The eighty-sixth name drawn, the last the crowd believed would receive a homestead, was William E. Macy of Lakeside, California. With 85 names previously drawn, the odds that Macy would win a homestead were 1,220 to 1. Macy was not at the drawing but he later admitted that, "If I had been there I would probably have given up."[22]

The drawing took a total of three hours and at its conclusion the Examining Board began a second, in-depth screening of the names drawn. Their review took several days. The winners were interviewed and nineteen were called back for another round of questions. At the conclusion of the investigations, ten individuals out of the first 86 names drawn and one from the first ten alternates, were rejected. Nine were rejected because they failed to meet the farming experience requirement, one because he owned more than 160 acres of land, and one because he had not paid irrigation construction charges to the Bureau of Reclamation on land he already owned. Ten of the eleven appealed their rejection and when the hearings were completed in February of 1947, the Board only reversed its decision in one case.[23]

For those whose names were drawn from the pickle jar but rejected by the Examining Board, it was a bitter disappointment. Malcolm Epley, managing editor of the *Herald and News* and a regular columnist in his paper, wrote:

> A painful aftermath of the widely publicized home-stead drawing is the announced rejection of 10 of those whose names appeared among the first 86 drawn on that eventful day.
>
> Despite repeated notations in news stories and official statements that the 86 "lucky" veterans would be subjected to a full screening before certified as entry-men, undoubtedly many people got the impression that the drawing was final. The veterans themselves must have known better than that, but there is understandably bitter disappointment among those who have been rejected since the drawing.[24]

Certainly some of those who were rejected by the Examining Board had false hopes built on news articles. Elmer Metz, whose personality and exuberance had captivated the audience at the armory, was one of those declared ineligible. Not only had he been featured in articles appearing in the *Herald and News* but also in *Reclamation ERA* and *Life Magazine*. The *Life* article had concluded a feature on the Tule Lake homesteads with a statement that must have come back to painfully haunt Metz.

"Out [of the pickle jar] came the names of the lucky veterans, like Dale Sprout and Elmer Metz [who] are now established for life."[25]

The appeals hearings were concluded in February of 1947, and individuals on the waiting list filled the ten open slots. Several weeks later, on March 13th, the 86 finalized winners met at the Klamath Falls airport in the offices of the Bureau of Reclamation. The meeting began with Examining Board Chairman Nelson Reed making an introductory speech. He stated:

> This is what you waited endless months for ... Whether this Board chose wisely or not will depend on you from here on out ... Even though these lands of yours are some of the best in this country of ours, life will not be all smooth sailing. All of you at the start will be cursed with shortages of machinery and materials. Many of you and your wives will have to get used to living in a strange land. You will experience the usual troubles with climate, bugs and blights. [But] you will find yourself in a very friendly community where you will be judged by what you are and not who you were. Your next door neighbors will become your best friends. Their help and advice will be invaluable ... On behalf of this Board and the representatives of the Bureau of Reclamation, I am very pleased to welcome you to this country. After all, you are probably the only friends we made out of over 2,000 original starters![26]

As each person's name was called, in the same order as it had been drawn from the pickle jar, he walked to a map that had been posted at the front of the room. There he pointed to the desired homestead plot and then completed a series of forms related to stipulated agreements with the Klamath Project. These pertained to payment of irrigation construction charges, fees for irrigation water, and regulations related to living on and farming the land. It was estimated at the time that each of the 86 irrigated sites was worth between $15,000 and $25,000.[27]

Two additional homestead allotments in the 1940s completed the division of the Tule Lake basin into individually owned farm units. Both followed nearly an identical pattern to that established in 1946. In October of 1947, the Klamath Project opened forty-four units to filing, and a total of 4,066 made application.[28] Screening reduced this number to 2,757 and the names were drawn on March 15, 1948. Once again, one of the winners was a woman, Frances Jeanne Ivory of Redding, California, an ex-WAC lieutenant who had served in Africa and Italy.[29]

The final homestead allotment, centered mainly at the southeastern end of the basin in Coppock Bay, involved 86 farm units. The Klamath Project opened filing on August 27, 1948 and when the application period ended on December 20th, a whopping 5,063 men and women had applied. The Examining Board only declared 63 of the applicants ineligible. The drawing was scheduled for February 15, 1949 at the American Legion Hall in the city of Tulelake. As the day approached, the community took on a festive air. A large banner was stretched across Main Street, proclaiming "Welcome HOMESTEADERS," a souvenir program was printed, and the women's auxiliary of the American Legion provided refreshments for those who attended the ceremonies. The pickle jar had been brought down from Klamath Falls, and it was filled nearly to the brim with 5,000 capsules. The Legion Hall, which had served as the community center for Tulelake since it was built in the early 1930s, was packed. With each name drawn, the tension of the crowd was broken with cheers. Eighty-six names were drawn for those who would have the first opportunity to receive land, another eighty-six were drawn as alternates. By late afternoon the last capsule was drawn and the final homestead allotment concluded. All that was left for the Examining Board was to screen the winners.

Once again, the finalists trekked to the Bureau of Reclamation offices at the Klamath Falls airport to select their land. Most of the winners had carefully scouted out the homesteads they wanted and had listed several alternates if their first choice was taken. Many homesteaders received highly fertile land, others were not quite as lucky. Ralph Morrill remembered that he had previewed a soil expert's analysis of the unit he had tentatively selected. However, when he successfully acquired the land, he found the topsoil to be quite shallow and it was never as productive as claimed in the report.[30]

The condition of the land on one farm unit made it particularly difficult to give away, this in spite of the popularity of the 1949 homestead and the number of applicants. The unit consisted of 137 acres, one of the largest in the allotment. It was located south of Malin. Its major drawback was the high alkali content of its soil. The first twenty alternates refused the land. Finally, in late June of 1949, Earnest Lee Thacker of Hemet, California, number 107 in the drawing, accepted the property.[31] He officially became the last homesteader in the Tule Lake basin.

Unlike the first farmers in the Tule Lake Basin, the 1940s homesteaders were not faced with pioneering totally undeveloped land. Roads fronted each farm unit, all canals, drains, and laterals had been constructed, and community services were readily available in the city of Tulelake. Nevertheless, the first years were Spartan. Most of the farm units did not have electricity, running water, or telephones. The amount of leveling and soil preparation faced by individual homesteaders was mixed. Since the late 1930s, the Bureau of Reclamation had leased out large sections of the newly homesteaded land, particularly for growing grain. Consequently, some homesteaders had crops growing on their land when they gained acquisition. Others had to do considerable work to prepare their land for farming.

Robert Anderson, whose name was selected in the 1947 drawing, homesteaded on the eastern side of the basin, near the old shoreline of Tule Lake. The land was littered with volcanic rock, which had to be removed before farming could begin.[32] Bill Whitaker, a 1949 homesteader, whose land was at the southwestern end of Coppock Bay, found the same problem. He had to do a great deal of leveling in order to make the land irrigable. Whitaker estimated that he had to make nearly 18,000 trips back and forth across his land with a scraper so that it could be properly irrigated.[33] Both men spent years removing rocks from their fields.

In the years immediately following World War II, lumber, machinery, and other necessary supplies were difficult to obtain. Therefore it was not uncommon to find the 1940s homesteaders living in tents while they made arrangements for more substantial shelter. The ubiquitous Tule Lake wind was not a friendly neighbor during this time. It took delight in spreading dust over everything, and it made a concerted effort to send every tent in the basin skyward. Bob Anderson remembered with frustration and a wry smile that heavy winds repeatedly blew his tent down— with little respect for the time of day or the disposition of its occupants![34]

To help alleviate the supply shortage, the Bureau of Reclamation made arrangements to sell to the homesteaders surplus equipment from the Japanese Internment camp. In addition, to help offset the critical shortage of building materials, as well as to hasten the dismantling of the camp, each homesteader was declared eligible to receive one of the 20' by 100' barracks.[35] To obtain a barrack, the homesteader filled out a Bureau of Reclamation form which stipulated that the building was not to be sold and that it was to be used exclusively on the homestead. The form also absolved the Bureau from any liability from injury during the removal of the building. A $50 deposit had to be placed with the Bureau to insure that the site from which the barrack was removed was left clean.[36]

Once the forms were completed, the homesteader either dismantled the barrack and took the lumber to his property or contracted with one of several movers to truck the building to his farm. For a fee of about $150, the barrack was cut in half and then either loaded onto a lowboy trailer or onto a homemade rig that consisted of a double set of tandem axles attached by a long steel beam to a tractor. Into the early 1950s, barracks were transported all over the basin, and then hurriedly set down on stacks of wood or cement piers also brought from the camp. Often left in precarious positions, it was the job of the homesteader to lower the barrack onto a permanent foundation. According to Barbara Krizo, moving the buildings created a hazard for automobiles and farm machinery. Thousands of nails were scattered over the basin roads, shaken loose from the flimsy barracks, and there was an epidemic of flat tires.[37]

Though the barracks provided badly needed shelter for the 1940s homesteaders, their poor construction meant that their new occupants were just as uncomfortable in them as the Japanese had been. In between farming, though, most of the homesteaders either used the barracks as temporary housing or renovated them in a variety of ingenious ways. Some of the barrack halves were placed at right angles to each other in order to get away from the monotonous straight lines of a 100-foot long building. Others had completely new sections added on. Though the appearance of the former barracks have changed considerably from the tar paper buildings that once dotted the Tule Lake WRA center at Newell, the discerning eye can still pick out hundreds of them throughout the Basin. From Alturas to at least Klamath Falls, and from Lakeview to Yreka, there was hardly a community that didn't obtain at least one piece of equipment or building from the internment camp.

The 1940s homesteaders remember with both pride and wonderment the hardships they encountered during their first year. The Phillip Krizo family not only braved living in a one-room barrack but also had to suffer through their first winter with Barbara handicapped by illness and the responsibilities of raising their two-year-old daughter Dorothy Marie, and four-month-old son, David. Though they were one of the first in their section to have electricity, they had to haul drinking water from one of two tank cars located at Stronghold and Tulelake. When the rains set in, the Krizo farm turned into a sea of mud. At times there was as much as fourteen inches of water standing around their home. The driveway that led from their house to the county road went down into a ditch and then up the other side. Until they were able to install a culvert, they could only drive their car to and from their house when the ground was frozen. This often called for strategic planning. The Krizos would get up in the early morning, when the ground was frozen, drive off the farm and do their shopping in Klamath Falls. They would delay their return until late at night, when the ground was again solid so that they could return to their house.[38]

The ambitious nature and industry of the 1940s homesteaders surprised the Bureau of Reclamation. Originally, bureau officials had predicted that most of the new homesteaders would have to rent out their land for the first year because of the time necessary to start up individual farms—from securing equipment to determining suitable crops. In actuality, only 15% opted for leasing their land during the first year of production.[39] When Gerald Corcoran was asked why he decided not to rent out his land, he replied:

> Everybody trades work and equipment ... We figure that if somebody is willing to rent our land for $50-$60 an acre that means he figures he can add that amount to his costs and still make a good profit. Why shouldn't we get that extra money ourselves? All it takes is a little cooperation and we can get the crops in and still get our houses fixed up and everything going fine by the end of the year.[40]

The new homesteaders joined the "old timers" in growing the basin's staple crops, including Hannchen barley, alfalfa, clover, flax and potatoes. Like other waves of homesteaders before them, the newcomers were willing to experiment in hopes of generating even higher returns on their investment. Individuals dabbled in melons, strawberries, sugar beets, celery and carrots. But Tule Lake's infamous killer frosts took their toll on the more fragile crops and the long distance between the basin and central markets made it unprofitable to grow carrots, celery and sugar beets.

The *San Francisco News* had described the 216 men and women who homesteaded the Tule Lake basin in the late 1940s as being: "... the best possible type of young American youth. Intelligent, healthy, and strong, they are serious in their ideas about opportunities that have fallen to them through the luck of the lottery."[41]

For many of those people, the 1940s homestead was the fulfillment of their dreams, but for others the romantic notion of being an independent farmer quickly faded. The adverse weather with its bitter cold, blustery winds, crop-killing frosts, and short growing seasons took its toll. Some people lacked skills in business management and were not able to cope with the spiraling costs of farming. The remoteness of the basin from surrounding communities also had its effect, particularly on wives who either were not from farm backgrounds or did not share their husbands' love for the land. The combined impact of these factors saw a significant number of homesteaders leave the basin in the 1950s and 1960s. Frank King estimates that thirty years after the land-opening of 1949, only twenty remained out of the original 86.[42] When Phillip and Barbara Krizo reviewed the names of 1946 homesteaders still owning land in the basin, they found that only one-third were left.[43]

Though the number of original homesteaders has dwindled, the 1940s homestead period still represents the final phase of one of the most successful government projects in American history. Malcolm Malcolm Epley of the Klamath Falls *Herald and News* aptly described the essence of the final homestead period: "Tule Lake has proved to be a tremendous success as a reclamation project. The land is fertile, the water supply is ample, and the farmers, largely veterans ... have made the most of the great opportunities it offers."[44]

> This isn't charity. It's giving a chance to the people who can build this country up ... I know that the real wealth of this country comes from what you can grow on this land ...The future of this whole Klamath region

depends on setting it up with owner-operated farms, people who have a stake here ... [45]

For those who remained in the basin, their roots went deep into the land. Their hard work and dedication produced prosperous farms, and their unique blend of fierce independence and compassion for their neighbors became legendary. If Francis G. Newlands and Frederick Haines Newell, founders of the federal reclamation program, were alive today they would be proud of the achievements made in the nearly seventy years of homestead farming in the Tule Lake Basin.

World War I veteran Olney Rudd draws the winning names from the "pickle jar" in the 1946 homestead drawing. *(Photo courtesy Bureau of Reclamation)*

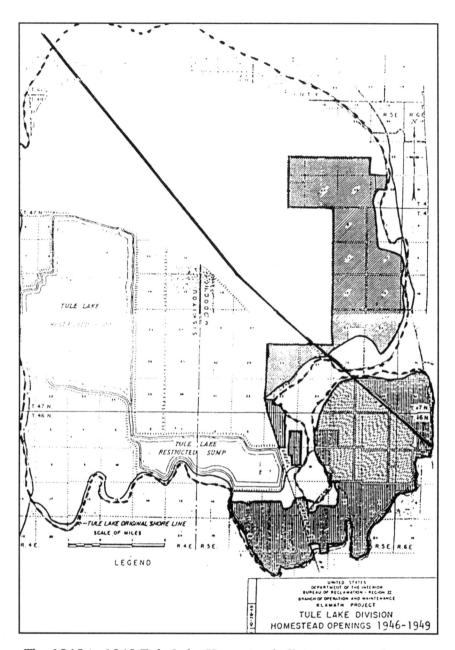

The 1946 to 1949 Tule Lake Homestead allotments are shown in
the shaded area in the lower right-hand corner of the map.
(Courtesy Bureau of Reclamation)

The Klamath County Museum, formerly an Oregon National Guard Armory, site of the Tule Lake Basin homestead land drawings of 1946 to 1949. *(Photo by author)*

The famous "pickle jar" from which names were drawn for the 1940s homestead period. It is now on display at the Tulelake-Butte Valley Fair, Museum of Local History. *(Photo by author)*

<u>Above:</u> Philip and Barbara Krizo are interviewed by newspaper and radio reporters on December 18, 1946. They were among the winners of the 1946 homestead drawing. <u>Below:</u> Inside the new Krizo home with Philip, Barbara, daughter Dorothy and son David. May 21, 1947. *(Photos courtesy Bureau of Reclamation)*

Left and right: Eleanor Jane Bolesta was the only woman to win a homestead in the 1946 drawing. *(Photos courtesy Bureau of Reclamation)*

Homesteaders at the site of the former Tule Lake Internment Camp in 1947 inspecting a partially dismantled barrack.
(Photo courtesy Bureau of Reclamation)

Above and below: Tule Lake Internment Camp barracks, 20 feet wide and 100 feet long were cut in half and trucked to homesteads. They were converted into homes, garages, shops and implement buildings. A number of these converted barracks can still be found in the Tule Lake Basin. *(Photos courtesy Bureau of Reclamation)*

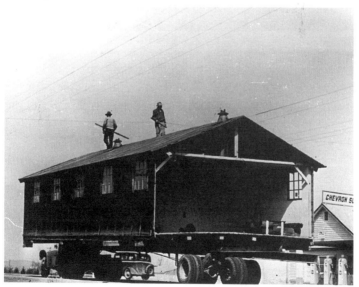

Frances Johnson stands between her "old" and "new" home on the homestead won by her husband, Gerald. *(Photo courtesy Bureau of Reclamation)*

A "completed" barrack home.
(Photo courtesy Bureau of Reclamation)

CHAPTER 18

NEWELL - A COMMUNITY IN TRANSITION

The post-World War II homestead allotments brought more than 200 farm units into production in the basin and a rapid influx of new people possessing similar background and interests. Though old residents openly welcomed the new homesteaders, it was only natural that the World War II veterans were drawn into their own social networks. These people lived next door to each other, many were close in age and they mutually shared the hardships of the first years in the basin. In addition, their farms were between six and ten miles from the city of Tulelake, where community leadership in political, service and fraternal organizations was held by the older, more seasoned residents. As a consequence of these factors a move was launched in the late 1940s to establish a new community at the southeastern end of the basin. Homesteaders in the Panhandle and Coppock Bay area, who felt that the former War Relocation Authority Japanese internment camp at Newell would be an ideal townsite, spearheaded the effort. It had an abundance of surplus buildings; it was situated next to Highway 139 and the Southern Pacific Railroad line; and roadways, water, sewer and electric lines were already in place.

At the time that townsite status was proposed for Newell, it was under the jurisdiction of the Bureau of Reclamation. Responsibility for the 1,100-acre internment camp had been transferred from the War Relocation Authority on May 4, 1946, two months after the last Japanese internees had left the compound. As described in Chapter Seventeen, the Bureau's first responsibility was to supervise the dismantling of the camp and the selling of surplus buildings and equipment. In a country hard hit by war-caused scarcity, the 1,700 buildings and thousands of pieces of equipment, ranging from power lines to plumbing fixtures, were in high demand. Many of the items were given to the 1940s homesteaders, but other parties made application for buildings and equipment including "non-profit organizations such as schools, churches, service clubs, Boy Scouts, the forest service, potato growers' associations, irrigation districts and hundreds of farmers."[1] In March of 1947, Ruth King, reporter for the Klamath Falls *Herald and News*, wrote that "more than 200 [electrical] transformers ... miles of high tension wire, barbed wire, underground water and sewer pipe and thousands of other miscellaneous items left over from the city of more than 20,000 persons" were put up for bid.[2] Under the Bureau of Reclamation' distribution program, barracks and equipment from Newell were soon spread over a vast area encompassing Northern California and Southern Oregon.

Between May of 1946 and February of 1948, the Bureau of Reclamation mulled over the fate of Newell. Meanwhile, it became a place of residence for a variety of people. A number of homesteaders stayed in the barracks at Newell until their own farm homes were ready for habitation. On May 27, 1946, the Tulelake Growers' Association utilized part of the site as a farm labor camp. The organization initially brought in thirty-six Mexican laborers.[3] Two months later the program had been expanded to include housing for American-born migrants and by September, 1946 nearly 1,000 farm laborers were being temporarily housed in nine blocks of barracks formerly occupied by internees and WRA employees. Even some of the army camp barracks were pressed into service.[4]

The 1947 agricultural season brought improvements to Newell's farm labor camp but still no word from the Bureau of Reclamation on townsite status for the general community. The Tulelake Growers' Association had refurbished enough barracks to handle 160 migrant families. The average family was charged $5.00 per week that included "electricity and use of heating and cooking stoves and (a) kitchen table."[5] The camp was under twenty-four-hour supervision and meals were served mess-hall style for a fee of $1.50 per day for an individual and $2.50 per day for families. The migrants housed at the camp were from a mixture of American racial backgrounds, and the housing and eating arrangements reflected the racial attitudes of the country at the time. There were separate barracks and mess halls for whites, Blacks and Filipinos.[6]

Newell's facilities were not just used to temporarily house migrants and new homesteaders. They also began to develop a small economic base. Several warehouses at the southern end of the community and others across the Southern Pacific tracks to the west were leased to the Tulelake Growers' Association for the purpose of grain storage. A recreation hall, formerly used by the WRA administration, was leased from the Bureau of Reclamation and converted into a general store. The Bureau itself set up temporary offices for supervising local building utilization and the removal and dismantling of barracks.

The greatest boost for Newell came in 1947 with the formation of the Newell Homestead Club. It had been organized for many of the same reasons as the Tule Lake Community Club twenty years before—out of a need to develop schools, improve roads, bring in telephone and electric service, establish new mail routes, and to protect the interests of farmers. The club's first president was Paul Rogers, a 1946 homesteader. With the skills learned as officers and enlisted men during World War II, Rogers and the Homestead Club mapped out a battle plan and then launched an assault on local, state, and federal agencies to make their wishes known.

In the first quarter of 1948 the Newell Homestead Club entered into one of its first political fracases. The Bureau of Reclamation had announced that it was transferring ownership of sections of The Peninsula to the National Park Service. The primary rationale was to protect Indian Petroglyphs along its rock base and on the sides of Prisoner's Rock to the southwest. The Tulelake-Butte Valley Sportsmen's Association protested this move, and in a resolution passed on January 15, 1948, the organization said:

> We believe that the best interests of our Community demand that this area remain under the control of the Bureau of Reclamation for the following reasons;
>
> First, Only local supply of gravel and sand and road building material for new homesteaders.
>
> Second, Only desirable Site for local cemetery.
>
> Third, Ideal feeding lots for homesteaders' livestock.
>
> Fourth, The best known water supply for city and rural use. Five deep wells.
>
> Fifth, Trap shooting, rifle range and hunting grounds. Sportsmen traps established June 1939. Improvements cost $5,113.69. Present replacement cost estimate $8,000.00.[7]

But the Newell Homestead Club did not entirely agree with the Sportsmen's Association. In March the club passed its own resolution that said:

> We feel that the best interests of the immediate community, of which our members are the major portion, will be served if this transfer is effected as recommended, with one reservation - - that is: That the Trap Shooting and Rifle Range facilities belonging to the Tulelake Butte Valley Sportsman's Association be left outside the transferred area ... We list the following reasons why we endorse the said transfer:
>
> First: We feel that since the Peninsula is the gateway to the present Lava Beds National Monument, it should be included as part of the monument.
>
> Second: The Peninsula has invaluable historic significance. Its Petroglyphs and the role it played in the Modoc War are an integral part of the story of the Lava Beds National Monument.
>
> Third: The prospective feed lot or sand and gravel needs are totally unaffected for either the present or future residents of the area.[8]

Having expressed their views on preserving the Peninsula, the Homestead Club then set about securing badly needed services. Jim Stearns was now the club's president. Frustrated by the snail's pace of the U.S. Post Office in setting up new mail routes in the southern basin, Stearns wrote Congressman Clair Engle seeking his help:

> Dear Mr. Engle:
>
> As you know, an application for a new mail route to serve the 1947 homestead area was sent in to the Postmaster General by Mrs. Wanda Stark, Post-mistress at Tulelake, for approval early last summer.
>
> There seems to have been considerable time elapse (sic) since that was done, and so far no action has been taken by the Postmaster General. The reason or reasons for the delay are not apparent to us here in

the area. There may be no reason other than depart-
mental procedure, but it seems to us that some sort of
answer should have been forthcoming before now.

This letter, then is to ask you, in (sic)n behalf of the
Newell Homesteaders ... to contact the Assistant Postmaster General and attempt to expedite the approval
of the route.[9]

Apparently, Engle was able to provide the assistance requested, because four months later Tulelake Postmaster Wanda Stark
sent a letter to Jim Stearns announcing "that the new mail route
will start July 16th."[10]

In the summer of 1948, the Homestead Club entered into a
new battle with the federal government. This time it involved
government restrictions that limited the amount of individually
owned acreage that could be irrigated by federal projects to 160
acres. The club felt that this unnecessarily prevented farmers
from expanding their operations. But when they petitioned Clair
Engle for a remedy, they found him not as sympathetic as they
had hoped. In a letter sent to Gerwin McCracken, Secretary of the
Newell Homestead Club, the congressman said:

I will want to be shown how removing the 160 acre
limitation will tend to maintain the family size farm
and what safeguards will then remain to prevent
speculative profits to large landowners and others
from the investment of public funds in reclamation in
California.[11]

Undaunted by this setback, the Newell homesteaders then
embarked on their largest and most important crusade, the
creation of a school district. At the time of the 1946 to 1949
homestead allotments, there were three small schools serving the
area. These included Carr School, situated about two and a half
miles north of Newell at the intersection of county roads 101 and
112. Eighteen miles to the south was Tionesta (pronounced "tea-
o-nesta") school, serving local ranchers and the remnants of the
Tionesta logging community. And in Newell itself was Grandview
Elementary School, which had originally been established during
World War II for the children of WRA employees working at the
internment camp. With the influx of over 200 homesteaders,
many of whom were newly married and just beginning families,

these three schools could not possibly handle the bumper crop of children that would soon be in need of an education. Paul Christy, a 1946 homesteader, assumed leadership in the drive for schools. In April of 1949, as Secretary of the Newell Homesteaders, Christy wrote a letter to the California State Board of Education, requesting assistance:

> Within the next three to five years it will be absolutely impossible to handle the sudden influx of primary students with our present facilities. We feel, at this time, that what we are in need of more than anything else is expert unbiased advice. We want to know that can be done to prepare for the future of our children's education. [12]

In May of 1949, Edgar Parsons, Field Representative for School Planning, was sent to Newell by the State Board of Education. Parsons explained to the homesteaders the process for establishing a school district and for obtaining state and county money for school operation. Parsons's advice was put into action, and in the fall of 1949 Grandville Elementary was in operation for the children of the homesteaders. In January of 1950, Paul Christy sent a letter of appreciation to Edgar Parsons for his help:

> We have been waiting to thank you for your assistance ... until we could let you know that it had actually been a visit of real worth ...
>
> The school at Newell ... has been transferred from temporary status to a permanent school. We now have a school bus operating and are adequately taking care of the present school needs, which is giving us a breathing space to plan for the near future when the big influx of young students will take place. [13]

Meanwhile, the Homesteader's Club also had been hard at work lobbying the Bureau of Reclamation to give Newell townsite status. Their efforts persuaded Klamath Project Director Raymond Best to champion their cause, and in a letter sent to the Bureau's offices in Sacramento and Washington, D.C., Best said:

> Due to the recent opening of land for homesteading on the Tule Lake Division and Modoc Unit of the Klamath

Project, and in view of the opening of additional land to settlement next year, there is a demand for a townsite at the old Japanese War Relocation Center ...

Utilities, such as water, sewer and electric service are already available for serving the area. The Central Pacific [today the Southern Pacific] Railroad crosses one edge of the area ... Further development of railroad sidings to proposed industrial and commercial sites is proposed by the railroad company. The California-Oregon Telephone Company has already made application for the lease of a lot on which to construct a telephone exchange building which will serve the surrounding community.

There are approximately 50 families of the Bureau of Reclamation employees living in the camp at the present time. There is a store and cafe in the area and the Klamath Falls-Alturas Bus makes regular stops. Located within the proposed townsite is the Grandview School which was constructed during the period of the operation of the Internee Center. The school, at the present time, is being operated by Modoc County.

It is requested that approval of the townsite be expedited to the greatest extent possible as there is an urgent demand for commercial sites along the railroad, and it is desired that we receive approval ... in order that a public sale may be held late this summer.[14]

On June 1, 1949, the Bureau supported Best's position. A notice was issued announcing "A public hearing in connection with the establishment of a townsite on the Area formerly occupied by the WRA camp, will be held in the Theatre Building, at Newell, California, at 1:00 p.m., Monday June 10, 1949."[15] In preparation for the hearing, the Newell Homestead Club drafted a position paper that expressed strong support for townsite status. The paper said in part: "We feel that since the members of our organization form the great majority of the people living near the proposed site that the opinion and desire of [the] group be given primary consideration."[16]

Initially the Tulelake Chamber of Commerce expressed concern over the establishment of a town which would compete against established basin merchants, but when the Bureau of Reclamation conducted its hearing on June 10th, the only issue raised by the Chamber was over "the expenditure of any public money for maintenance of utilities already established at the townsite."[17] The organization was assured by officials of the Bureau of Reclamation that no funds would be spent for such purposes. Those speaking in favor of the townsite pointed out that "a town closer to the homesteads than Tulelake would improve police protection, fire protection, school facilities and accessibility to loading points."[18]

At the conclusion of the hearings, the Bureau of Reclamation ruled in favor of townsite status, but the actual sale of lots to private parties was delayed for two years. In the interim, the Bureau surveyed the townsite for lots and established the community's perimeter. The survey party established the eastern boundary at the firebreak that once separated the War Relocation Authority and Military compounds from the Japanese section of the internment camp. The western boundary was Highway #139. Utilizing the existing streets and blocks set up by the WRA, the townsite encompassed the former military camp to the north; the WRA residential quarters, motor pool, and administration headquarters in the center; and the old camp warehouses to the south.

In the spring of 1951, the Bureau of Reclamation finally announced that lots at Newell would be auctioned off at 9:00 a.m. on June 21st. A total of 300 lots was to be offered with minimum bids ranging from $10 to $1,000, depending upon the size and location of the lot.[19] But on the appointed day, the results were disappointing. In an article titled "Newell Sale Slow" the *Tulelake Reporter* described the auction:

> Bidding was sporadic and for the most part slow this morning as a crowd that never reached the 100-mark followed the bureau of reclamation auction truck around the Newell townsite.

> Most of the lots were being bought up in groups of three and four or more by a half-dozen buyers, most of them businessmen or dabblers in real estate.

Only the business lots fronting the highway prompted spirited bidding. Bob Jones purchased the store building he has been leasing for $3,600 [the Homestead Market], a figure that surprised most onlookers, who had predicted the choice item would go for $5,000.[20]

Eventually 209 lots were auctioned off at an average price of $147 each. The Bureau of Reclamation earned a total of $30,710 from the sale.[21]

Though the excitement over the sale of lots at Newell had only been lukewarm, the community's efforts to build an expanded school system remained in high gear. Under Paul Christy's direction, school development took place in three phases. The first step was an effort to unify the Carr, Grandview (Newell), and Tionesta schools into a single district, so that resources at the elementary grade level could be pooled. This was accomplished with relatively few problems. However, the second step, which involved deciding whether or not to pursue a totally independent K to 12th grade school system, was more complicated. The patrons of Carr School had tied themselves in with the Siskiyou Joint Union High School District, and their children went to Tulelake High School. Now those who resided in the Grandview School District, "comprising basically the Coppock Bay, Panhandle and southern fringe areas of the greater Tule Lake basin" had to decide whether to also ally with Siskiyou County.[22] An editorial in the January 11, 1951 issue of the *Tulelake Reporter* discussed the issue:

It is a credit to the spirit and foresight of the basin's newest homesteaders that they want to develop their own community center; their progress in unifying themselves to date through common effort for common gain and mutual pleasure is another lesson in Americana.

But we seriously doubt that even the energy and the independence of even so large and progressive a group as the new homesteaders should be placed ahead of the less glamorous but more matter-of-fact second level education of their children, and all basin youngsters.

Carr district parents have already solved their high school problem. Now Grandview parents must make a similar decision: turn to distant Alturas for provision of such high school education as that bonded district can afford; endeavor to build their own senior institution ... at best a 150-student second-rate plant comparable to Tulelake High in its more trying years.

The third choice: annexation with Siskiyou Joint Union High School District ... Plans to build a new, more modern institution are being considered to replace the congested conglomeration of buildings now in use.

The dream of a single, independent high and elementary district serving just these four centers [Grandview, Tulelake, Winema and Carr districts] is not remote. Together, these four areas represent an assessed evaluation of more than eight million dollars, enough to satisfy state requirements for university recognition; divided, or even pairs, the basin centers can never hope for independent and locally controlled school administration: Tulelake will remain under Yreka's yoke, and Grandview will struggle along as best it can with a costly second-class alternative.[23]

Though there was some objection by southern basin residents to the Tulelake Reporter's editorial, voters approved the unification at an election held on August 15, 1951.

The final phase in the school development plan called for the construction of a new elementary school that would draw children from Tionesta, Grandview, and Carr schools. At first everything went smoothly. In January of 1952, a $152,000 bond election was held, and it passed by a 10 to 1 majority. The "balloting saw 232 voters go to the polls despite snow drifts and icy roads."[24] In March, eleven acres adjoining Grandview Elementary School were selected as the building site, and the prospect of having a new school completed by the Fall of 1952 seemed to be a reality. Then a major problem developed. The federal government announced that it planned to open a detention center for "subversive persons" at Newell.[25]

Rumors that the Department of Justice was planning to build a prison at the old WRA camp had begun to circulate more than six months before the Newell School bond election. Equally worrisome was that the detention center was to be for those identified as "subversive." It should be explained at this junction that this was during the McCarthy Era, when many Americans were afraid that communists were close to taking over the country. The fall of China to Marxists, the French Indo-Chinese War, and the conflict in Korea all contributed to the paranoia. Consequently, the Justice Department had quietly identified a number of locations, including several former internment camps, as detention sites if a national emergency were declared.

On behalf of the residents in the Newell and Tulelake areas, Clair Engle had asked James V. Bennett, director of the Bureau of Prisons, whether or not the WRA camp was under consideration. Engle told Bennett: "The people of the Tulelake area are very much concerned about this rumor, remembering the unhappy experience they had with the operation of the Japanese Relocation Center. I would appreciate you confirming or denying these rumors."[26]

Bennett's reply to Engle stated that the site at Newell would only be used during the event of a national emergency. This seemed to put the issue at rest. But then in January of 1952, several weeks after the Newell School bond election, the Federal Bureau of Prisons announced that "the fenced-in portion [of Newell] known as the 'military area' is to be vacated."[27] This announcement put a hardship on the Tulelake Growers Association, which had been housing migrant workers in the facility, but it didn't cause any undue alarm among southern basin homesteaders because, as the *Tulelake Reporter* stated: "the bureau of prisons is merely preparing the site for possible use as a detention camp, but has no immediate plans to reactivate the old World War II prisoner of war center."[28]

Then in February local feelings began to change. It was learned that "about April 1 a small group of prisoners, all minor offenders, [would] be brought in to the camp to rehabilitate the buildings, putting "the future development of Newell as a community of schools, homes and other peacetime development ... 'up in the air'."[29]

Concern escalated, particularly because the proposed prison was in the proximity of the Newell School building site. Paul and Gertrude Christy remembered that the controversy reached the point that, "about half the people in the community were determined they didn't want the school built because of the prison. They could just see some prisoners bail out over the wall and latch onto their kids [as hostages]."[30]

The American Legion Post 164, whose membership was comprised of basin veterans, attempted to aid the residents of Newell by drafting a resolution to be sent to federal officials. The resolution was divided into four parts and stated:

> The proposed prison would be in the center of a highly developed and thickly populated area; the prison would be within 100 yards of a school, and it is not feasible to move the school to a new site; the government recently established Newell as a townsite; [and] the government owns millions of useless acres that could be much more readily adapted to a prison site. [31]

But the Bureau of Prisons turned a deaf ear and in May it was announced that 100 inmates would be sent to Newell to work on refurbishing the buildings. The situation placed the Grandview (Newell) School Board in a quandary. Many of the homesteaders' children were now reaching school age, and the community was desperate for a new facility. The site that had been selected for the new school had been ideal "from the standpoint of existing water facilities, foundation and central location near the highway."[32]

The school board, comprised of Paul Christy as chairman, Perry M. Hawkins, as clerk, plus Earl W. Parsons, Paul Rogers and Richard Fuller, determined that, given the immediate need for a new school, construction at the original site must begin as quickly as possible. This caused a division among the parents and in December of 1952, a number of families presented a petition to the Modoc County Board of Supervisors which requested they be allowed to withdraw from the Newell School District and join Siskiyou County's Tulelake Elementary School District. The petition was denied, giving the parents little choice but to stay with Newell School. [33]

Then, just as mysteriously as the prison camp project had developed, it disappeared. On April 23, 1953 the federal government closed the camp. Meanwhile, construction had begun on Newell Elementary School and when it opened its doors in September it boasted "seven 30 by 32-foot classrooms, and a multi-purpose room which also serve[s] as a cafeteria, gymnasium, auditorium, PTA meeting room and general purpose room."[34] Finally, after five years of effort the dreams and efforts of Paul Christy and the school board paid off.

Amid the controversy over the formation of a school district and construction of a new school in the southern basin, there were moments of poignancy and humor. For example, not long after the formation of the unified school district in the southern basin, the newly formed elementary school board visited Tionesta. A highly admired teacher ran the school there, and the local patrons were convinced that the board planned to close their little school and bus the children to Newell. After pleasantries over coffee and cookies were dispensed with, the board was asked point blank when the Tionesta School would be closed down. To their surprise, the board responded by saying: "It is your school and your community. If you want to keep your school the way it is then you keep your district. We have no intention of forcing you to send your children to Newell."[35] For several years after the meeting, Tionesta School continued to function. The children were frequently taken to Newell for "play-days" and holiday programs, helping acquaint them with children from other parts of the basin. Finally, Tionesta closed down and the children attended Newell School on a regular basis.

One of the most humorous events occurred in 1951, amid all the turmoil of trying to get the school district going and a bond issue passed to build a new facility. Just a matter of weeks before opening school in the fall, when all of the staff had been hired, temporary facilities in old barracks had been arranged, and the budget allocated, a group of parents unexpectedly presented the school board with a petition requesting the formation of a kindergarten. It seemed that California law required that if a majority of the parents signed a petition for kindergartens then the board was required to provide the program. Paul Christy remembered that: "This process of trying to get a school going was a howling mess. I'm not sure we even had enough teachers, rooms, or anything else ... and here as school is about to begin a bunch of parents show up with a petition that required us to have a kindergarten!"[36]

Paul had explained the situation with earnest expression. Then he added with a twinkle in his eye:

> Guess who was the first name on the petition—Gertrude, my wife! I looked at that thing and laughed. I said, you can have your kindergarten, all you're going to have to do is figure out where you are going to find a building and a teacher and the money![37]

Then Gertrude added: "Anyway, what happened was that we set up a carpool and until Newell School was completed the kids were taken to Tulelake where the district kindly found space for us."[38]

With the issues over schools, the prison camp, and townsite status out of the way, the future for the little community of Newell seemed bright. In the early 1950s a number of contributing factors made the potential for growth enormous. The city of Tulelake was having a great deal of difficulty with its deep water well and some merchants and residents were contemplating the possibility that they might have to move to Newell to get reliable water. Two great tracts of land, stretching from the western side of The Peninsula to just a mile south of the city limits of Tulelake had not yet been opened for homesteading. Known as the League of Nations and Frog Pond, if this land was allotted to homesteaders it would nearly double the population of the southern basin, and a majority of the potential newcomers would reside in the proximity of Newell.

There was also the promise of industrial development in the town. A consortium of local farmers bought five of the large WRA warehouses at the southern end of Newell and founded the Newell Potato Cooperative. The United States Pumice Supply Company leased an old, red, wooden warehouse at southeastern end of Newell that once housed the WRA camp's electrical and plumbing shops. Here they planned to use an ore known as scoria, mined from Glass Mountain (near Medicine Lake, to the southwest of Newell), to manufacture pumice blocks. These were to be used in cleaning restaurant-cooking grills.[39]

Other promises of growth came with the completion of the Tulelake Airport, located just to the east of Newell's city limits. On Sunday, June 24, 1951, just a matter of weeks after the auction of lots at Newell, an "air-fair" was put on which drew over 1,000 spectators. The *Tulelake Reporter* enthusiastically stated that it was "rated by 117 flying folk ... as one of the finest shows of its kind ever staged in a small community of the Pacific Northwest."[40] The paper then added: "The show was a wonderful tribute to the years of effort to obtain a landing strip to service this community. The airport was jointly sponsored by Modoc and Siskiyou counties and the federal government."[41]

The airport was important in the growth of Newell. It came to be used by sportsmen who flew into the facility and often stayed at the Flying Goose Hunting Lodge, located at the north end of town, while they hunted game birds, deer, and other basin wildlife. By the 1960s, Anderson's Spray Service was established at the airport, later to be taken over by Paul Macy. The extensive crop-dusting operation provided work for local residents and contributed to the town's economy.

Growth in Newell and the southern basin was also aided by the efforts of Jim Stearns, who worked tirelessly to improve local roads. The community of Newell was fortunate to already have red cinder roads left from the internment camp, but many of the outlying homesteads were served by little more than bladed paths that turned to quagmires in the winter. Stearns hounded government agencies for help and in 1950 ran for the Modoc County Board of Supervisors to make sure that the interests of the basin would be served. As a Supervisor he not only guided his road improvement program to fruition, but also helped southern basin residents establish fire protection.[42]

Newell was a city of mobile buildings. Many of its structures were either moved into the residential area from other sections of the former internment camp or were brought in from the outside. For example, when Carr Elementary School was closed down, the building was cut into two parts. One half was moved to Macdoel and became a home. The other half was taken to the Tulelake Airport and converted into an aircraft maintenance shop and office. In addition, a number of buildings were moved into Newell from the old Civilian Conservation Corps camp north of Merrill and placed just east of Newell Elementary School. These were primarily used for housing migrant farm laborers.

By March of 1952, progress in Newell and the southern basin was going so well that the services of the Newell Homestead Club were no longer needed. Eulogizing its contributions, the *Tulelake Reporter* stated:

> To homesteaders it has meant a champion for pioneers' rights, and a voice through which to speak their demands;
>
> To politicians and governmental agencies it was a name to fear and respect, the voice of a large and determined group of eager people;
>
> To housewives and children in that vast "new homestead" area, the name has meant a melting pot for social activity in an embryo community, a place to get acquainted with your neighbor;
>
> And to an entire community the name Newell Homestead Club will long be remembered as the strong force that helped mold a sprawling young basin into one great family of farms, homes and industry.[43]

Why did the club disband? Everett Lynham, the last president of the organization, said that it was "a case of having run out of things to do."[44] In reviewing the club's purpose and its accomplishments, Paul Rogers explained:

> We had an awful lot of our own specific problems, problems that we had to work out for ourselves. But now there is the P-TA (sic), the Farm Center and the Legion, each handling a specific part of the home-steader's problems. It's a matter of the homesteader infiltrating into the whole community, or the com-munity infiltrating into the homesteaders.[45]

Rogers was correct in his assessment that the community spirit of the basin had transcended the local interests of the Newell Homestead Club. Perhaps the best example occurred just a matter of weeks after the club disbanded. Two local men, Marvin Christy, a 1949 homesteader in the Panhandle, and Glendon M. Smith, manager of the Tulelake Growers Association, were killed when their small private plane crashed just south of the Tulelake Airport. The entire basin immediately rallied to provide support for Marvin Christy's wife and two young children. On April 30th, a number of his fellow 1949 homesteaders began to prepare his 80-acre farm for planting. The next day, on May 1, "there were so many tractors and other machines on the homestead [that they] had to start turning them away—there wasn't enough room to turn around in."[46] Soon after, a memorial fundraising campaign was initiated that led to the purchase and installation of chimes at the Tulelake Community Presbyterian Church.[47] Both acts were befitting of the tradition of caring in the basin that had begun many years before.

Growth at Newell and the southern basin continued until the mid to late 1950s and then it stagnated. Modoc County and the State of California constructed highway maintenance stations at Newell, but few other facilities or businesses were added. There were several reasons for the end of Newell's growth. The primary factor was that the League of Nations and the Frog Pond were never opened for homesteading. Both tracts were permanently turned over to the Fish and Wildlife Service to be included in the Tule Lake National Wildlife Refuge. Under their supervision, the land was only made available for leased farming, and no permanent buildings or residential structures were to be constructed. Consequently, there were simply not enough people in the southern basin to support a larger town. In addition, the city of Tulelake straightened out its water problems, ending concern that some of its residents might have to move out, and with the improvement of roads, local residents were no longer dependent upon Newell for major supplies. The end product was that Newell never had enough people to qualify for incorporation. It was listed on maps, but it did not have its own governmental body and the townsite was under the jurisdiction of Modoc County.

Over the past thirty years, Newell's hope for growth has had a number of additional setbacks. The pumice plant went out of business, as did a potato-packing warehouse. In 1982, Newell School was closed, the victim of declining student enrollment. (The school would remain closed until the 1990s.)

A combination of factors has kept Newell a viable community. Since the Tulelake Growers Association first used the former WRA military compound as a migrant camp, Newell has been a center of housing for farm workers. In the mid-1970s, members of the Tulelake Growers' Association, including John Cross, Tom Frey, and George Smith, spearheaded a cooperative effort with Modoc County and the State of California to build a permanent migrant labor camp toward the northeast end of Newell. Then in the late

1970s a federally sponsored housing program, known as the Great Northern Project, began to help low-income families build new homes. Clifford and Cindy Bell, who built a home in Newell under this program, are convinced that the project helped save the town. It was the first new residential housing to be constructed in years. It provided a means by which low income families could afford to own a home.

In the mid-1980s, there was hope for Newell's future. In 1984 a group of California businessmen purchased property at the south end of town with plans to build a potato flaking plant. Unfortunately, funding fell through and construction on the plant was never started. In spite of such setbacks, Newell has had a unique role in the history of the Tule Lake Basin. Born out of the tragedy of Japanese internment, the quiet, almost lethargic little town remains a hodgepodge of human life. Most basin residents feel that it will never grow dramatically, but that it will survive as a community for farm laborers, retirees, small volume business people, and for those seeking rural life but with some amenities of a town.

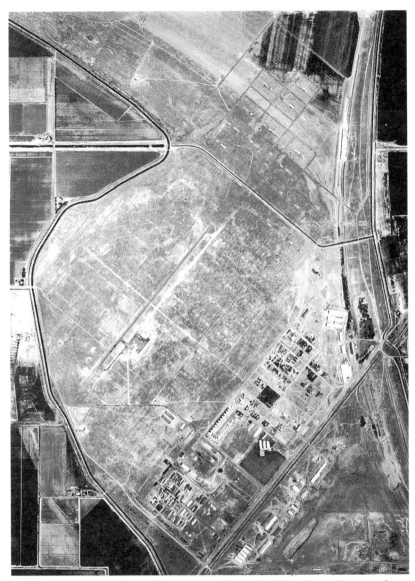

An aerial view of Newell taken in the 1980s when the roadways outlining the internment camp barrack blocks were still visible. Much of the open area on the left half of this photograph is now under cultivation. *(Photo courtesy Bureau of Reclamation)*

The Homestead Market. It was built as the recreation hall for civilian workers at the Japanese Internment Camp. *(Photo by author)*

Many of the newer homes in Newell were built on the site where the civilians were housed when the internment camp was in operation. *(Photo by author)*

CHAPTER 19

HOMESTEADING AND WILDLIFE PRESERVATION: A DIVISION OF INTERESTS

Even before the creation of the Klamath Project in 1905, it was apparent to western conservationists that reclamation was going to have a detrimental impact on millions of migratory birds in the Klamath Basin. Studies by the U.S. Bureau of Biological Survey (the forerunner of the Fish and Wildlife Service), and the National Audubon Society had shown that the complex of lakes and rivers that encompassed the planned reclamation project, including Upper and Lower Klamath lakes, Tule and Clear lakes, and the Klamath and Lost River systems were host to more than 80% of the birds using the Pacific Flyway - perhaps greater than six million a year.[1] With the planned draining of both Tule Lake and Lower Klamath Lake, thousands of acres of bird habitat would be destroyed.

Though President Theodore Roosevelt had signed the Newlands Reclamation Act into law in 1902, initiating the federal reclamation program, he also had a strong record in support of wildlife and wilderness preservation. He had been the first President to create a federal bird refuge when he issued an executive order on March 14, 1903 setting aside a 2 ½-acre plot on the east coast of Florida, known as Pelican Island. This became a sanctuary for the threatened Brown Pelican, and Roosevelt's actions set a precedent for the creation of other refuges throughout the United States.[2]

By 1908, the Audubon Society had gathered enough information to convince the President that federal action had to be taken to protect migratory birds on the Pacific Flyway. In addition to concerns voiced over the impact of the Klamath Project, it was found that hunters were killing huge numbers of birds on Lower Klamath Lake to supply the millinery market. "Cases were found where ... hunters in season were making from $400 to $500 a day selling bird crests, plumes, breasts, wings, etc. to milliners" who turned these into feathered hats for women.[3] As a consequence, in August of 1908, President Roosevelt issued Executive Order #924, which stated:

> It is hereby ordered that all islands in Lower Klamath
> Lake, and marsh and swamp lands unsuitable for
> agricultural purposes ... are hereby reserved and set
> aside for the use of the Department of Agriculture as a
> preserve and breeding ground for native birds.[4]

Though conservationists applauded Roosevelt's action, it was
greeted with mixed feelings in the Klamath Basin. Said the
Klamath Republican:

> By order of President Roosevelt, the sportsmen of this
> section will lose the finest duck and wild fowl hunting
> grounds in the country. The Lower Klamath lake has
> been made into a National bird preserve, and no more
> can the pot hunters of California or the sportsmen of
> Klamath flock to this famous shooting ground to
> slaughter the millions of duck and geese that breed in
> the swamps and tules in that vicinity.
>
> This order comes after one of the longest and hardest
> fights the Audubon Society has made and may be
> taken as the first step in what may result in a reserve
> policy as extensive as the forest reserves.
>
> These preserves mean that Klamath county will always
> remain one of the greatest game sections in the United
> States for the reason there will remain a sufficient
> number of places for the sportsman to hunt, while the
> Lower lake will act as a supply station for the game.[5]

In 1911, President William Howard Taft expanded the refuge
program within the Klamath Basin region by setting aside
protected land along Clear Lake Reservoir. In addition, funds
were allocated through the Bureau of Biological Survey to beef up
patrols around Lower Klamath Lake. A special launch was purchased and a system of record-keeping was initiated to keep
track of people visiting the lake and Bird Island, which was in the
central portion of the sanctuary. In explaining the Bureau's
action, Federal Game Warden J.J. Furber said:

> Parties desiring to visit Bird Island or wishing to take
> parties down must apply for permission from the
> warden. It is not the policy of the department to keep
> people away from the islands, but it is desired to know

who and how many visit them, and to prevent the undue exciting of the young birds.

No firearms are allowed on the reserve, and all species of birds, both water fowl and other kinds, are protected at all times of the year.[6]

In May of 1913, the Biological Survey and the State of Oregon expanded the area where no hunting was allowed to include the Klamath Straits, the Klamath River marshes, and Lake Ewauna.[7] In August of the same year, a temporary ban was placed on trapping along Lower Klamath Lake in order to preserve the rapidly decreasing number of fur-bearing animals.[8] The expanding wildlife preservation program precipitated rather hostile reactions on the part of some residents of Northern California and Southern Oregon. Said one attorney and sportsman from Yreka:

The most useless, uncalled for and aggravating situation ... is caused by this "Bird Preserve" ... I have read a report from the Hon. Secretary of the Interior, Mr. (F.K.) Lane, wherein he refers to the immense number of native birds who nest and breed on the shores of Lower Klamath Lake ... And he therein speaks of the great necessity of protecting these birds for the benefit of the San Francisco Market ... We stand ready to make proofs that the only birds that nest and breed in that vicinity are mallard ducks and pelicans—absolutely no others. The pelicans are a nuisance, of no use to man and a destroyer of the fish that abound in the lake. They ought to [be] extermated (sic). They nest, not on this land, but on floating islands in the lake. The ducks nest not on this land [but] on the hills overlooking this lake, among the sage brush. It is manifestly impossible for either of these birds or any others to nest or breed on this land, for the very good reason that during the breeding season the land is wholly underwater.

This "Bird Preserve" is one of the most absurd creations of our great government. Speaking of Mr. Lane's desire to supply the San Francisco Market, permit me to say: This 15,000 acres of land, if reclaimed will cut at a very conservative estimate two and one half tons of hay per acre per year, or 37,000 tons in all. This hay, so experienced men say, will winter through 37,500 head of stock cattle. Reckoning these cattle to average 560 pounds of dressed beef each, and a mallard duck to dress about four pounds, it would require 5,250,000 ducks to equal in weight the 37,500 head of cattle, with the admitted shortage of meat, and its high price ... is it not better policy for the Government to aid and encourage this additional supply of beef rather than to reserve this great field ... to preserve a few ducks, not 5,000,000 by any means, for the consumption of a few rich bon-vivants of San Francisco?[9]

The author of this position paper was not the only person concerned about the restrictions imposed by the Biological Survey. Officials from the Bureau of Reclamation also voiced objection, particularly to efforts by the Biological Survey to block the draining and reclaiming of Lower Klamath basin land.

In 1915, opposing interests approached President Woodrow Wilson with requests concerning Lower Klamath Lake. On one side were representatives from the Audubon Society and the Biological Survey, who favored halting reclamation and who wanted continued rigid enforcement of game preservation laws. On the other side were officials from the Reclamation Service who wanted to complete the Klamath Project's master plan that included draining Lower Klamath Lake and opening the land to homesteading. Weighing the merits of wildlife protection on one side with land reclamation on the other, Wilson came down on the side of the Klamath Project. Consequently, on May 14, 1915, the President issued Executive Order #2200, which reduced the size of the protected land at Lower Klamath Lake and allowed the reclamation program to continue on course. When the Southern Pacific Railroad dike was completed across the Klamath Straits, and the gates at Ady closed, the size of Lower Klamath Lake was quickly reduced to a fetid swamp, filled with water-borne botulism that killed thousands of birds.

By the mid-1920s, reclamation in the Klamath Basin had worked miracles for local farmers and homesteaders, but it wreaked havoc among the migratory birds, decimating great numbers who were unable to find suitable nesting areas. The situation became so severe that it caught the attention of several prestigious leaders of the American conservation movement, including T. Gilbert Pearson. Pearson began his career as a college teacher in North Carolina and he was an ardent supporter of the National Audubon Society. His deep involvement in the organization saw him rise quickly through the ranks and he soon became the Society's president. In the 1920s, the Biological Survey hired Pearson. In 1927, concerned with what was happening to birds on the Pacific Flyway, he made an inspection tour of what was left of Lower Klamath Lake. He was appalled at what he observed.

> I did not see a ranch, although I was told that there were a few somewhere. I only saw weeds—miles and miles of thickly growing weeds—and the only living creature we found was a scrawny, venomous snake that crossed the road and paused by the wheel track to shake his rattles at the two perspiring men in the car. Further on we came to open flats over which whirlwinds chased each other like ghosts of the wildlife that had departed. In despair, almost in bitterness, I fled.[10]

Pearson collected data on what had happened. Then, with the support of other deeply concerned conservationists, he returned to Washington, D.C. to lobby for an expansion of wildlife refuge land within the Klamath Project. His efforts paid off. On October 4, 1928, President Calvin Coolidge issued Executive Order #4975, which established the Tule Lake Bird Refuge. The 10,300 acre preserve was to be located on the west side of the Tule Lake Basin, and the executive order made it illegal to "hunt, trap, capture, willfully disturb, or kill any wild animal or bird of any kind whatever, or take or destroy the eggs of any wild bird, except under the rules and regulations as may be prescribed by the Secretary of Agriculture."[11] In the same year, Coolidge also set aside portions of Upper Klamath Lake for the same purposes.

In 1929, birds and wildlife along the Pacific Flyway were given additional help with the passage of the Migratory Bird Conservation Act. This law gave the federal government the authority to buy land needed for migratory bird refuges. Unfortunately, the impact of the act was blunted several years later when the Depression caused its funding to be curtailed.

The 1930s saw the Tule Lake Bird Refuge increase in size, but its role as a protector of birds and other wildlife was tenuous. The Bureau of Reclamation controlled the supply of water to the Bird Refuge, and it also controlled farm activities on federal lease lands in the surrounding area. Consequently, the two federal agencies often found themselves at cross-purposes. The Biological Survey saw as its paramount goal the protection of migratory birds coming into the Klamath and Tule Lake Basins. On the other hand, the Bureau of Reclamation felt obligated to provide as much acreage as possible for farming and home-steading. Both groups had sympathetic support in Congress and within the Executive branch.

In 1932, the Biological Survey won a minor skirmish with the Bureau of Reclamation when it was able to convince President Herbert Hoover to increase its acreage at Tule Lake by 700 acres. But most officials in the Biological Survey felt that the size of the refuge was still much too small to have an impact on saving nesting and feeding areas.

The dwindling number of migratory birds throughout the United States caught the attention of Franklin D. Roosevelt during his second year in office. In 1934, he formed the Presidential Committee on Wildlife Restoration. After a series of investigative hearings, the committee recommended that a program be established to sell bird hunting stamps. It was designed to regulate bird hunters and generate revenue that could be used to maintain and purchase additional bird refuge land. In March of 1934, the Migratory Bird Hunting Stamp Act was passed, but the battle to protect migratory birds in the Klamath Basin was far from over.

Noting President Franklin Roosevelt's support for wildlife conservation, officials representing the wildlife refuge system in the Klamath Basin approached the President with their concerns about migratory bird preservation. Of particular interest was the expansion of refuge land at Tule Lake. Roosevelt was in agreement and on April 10, 1936, he more than tripled the size of the Tule Lake Bird Refuge, from 11,000 to over 37,300 acres.[12]

Roosevelt's action was a positive step for wildlife preservation, but it did not resolve all of the problems in the Tule Lake and Lower Klamath Basins. Both Tule Lake and Lower Klamath Lake, which had been reduced to stagnant ponds, continued to be plagued by botulism, which killed a great many waterfowl. In addition, hungry birds ravaged grain crops grown on adjacent lease land, generating wrath among local farmers.

In 1937, an effort was launched to ameliorate the differences between the Bureau of Reclamation and the Biological Survey over the use of Tule Lake and Klamath Basin land. The two agencies commissioned a study to be done by Engineer J.R. Iakisch. The result was the famed Iakisch Report, which was described in some detail in Chapter Ten.

In brief review, Iakisch melded the needs of both the Refuge and the Klamath Project into a neat, well-defined package. He recommended that the size of the reclaimed area at Tule Lake be increased by reducing the amount of "sump land" set aside for collecting surplus water. In order to control the water level, since Tule Lake had no natural outlet, he proposed that a pumping station be constructed at the northwest end of Tule Lake and a tunnel be dug through Sheepy Ridge to the Lower Klamath Basin. Water pumped though the tunnel would be channeled to farmland and into Lower Klamath Lake. The flow of water through the entire system would reduce the incidence of botulism in both basins, and be of great benefit to bird life. The pumping station would reduce the risk of flooding around the Tule Lake sump.[13] By 1941, Iakisch's proposal was in full operation with the completion of the pump and tunnel system.

In the decade of the 1940s, the refuge system within the Klamath Project still remained in a tenuous position, particularly the Tule Lake segment. However, the war years provided an interlude for officials of the Klamath Project and the National Refuge system. Only a few minor changes occurred in the relationship between the two agencies. In 1942, jurisdiction and responsibilities were clarified. The Bureau of Reclamation was to continue coordinating and supervising the construction, operation and maintenance of irrigation dikes along and within the boundaries of the Refuge. It was also responsible for maintaining, under normal conditions, the water within the Tule Lake sump area at a level that was satisfactory to the Wildlife Refuge. In return, the Refuge, now known as the Tule Lake National Wildlife Refuge, was to assume responsibility for the construction, operation, and maintenance of structures within the sump area itself. In 1946, additional provisions were made for the Bureau of Reclamation to operate the pumping facilities that carried excess water by tunnel though Sheepy Ridge and into the Lower Klamath Basin. In return, the Refuge agreed to reimburse the Bureau of Reclamation for the first 50,000 feet of water that passed though the tunnel each year.

In 1948, the truce between the two agencies was shattered when 2,300 acres of land at the southern end of the Refuge was removed from the jurisdiction of the Fish and Wildlife Service and opened for homesteading. This action drew the attention of both sportsmen and conservationists, who feared that birds and other wildlife in the basin were threatened. In October, Henry Clineschmidt, president of the Associated Sportsmen of California, protested the action and the conditions at Tule Lake:

> This lake has been squeezed down from 25,000 acres 20 years ago to only 16,500 acres [and] ... they are continuing to drain the lake as fast as they can, pumping it into the Lower Klamath basin whenever rain swells the lake threatening the Holland-like dykes. However, when fresh water is urgently needed to halt an epidemic of botulism killing thousands of ducks in the lower lake area, no water is being pumped. The California Division of Fish and Game has tried everything it could to get [Bureau of Reclamation Regional Director] Richard L.Boke to release some water for the ducks dying on the lake shores today but without avail. It is such systematic waste as this which will, in the not too distant future, toll the death knell to the West's greatest duck refuge.[14]

On the other side, farmers in the area around Tule Lake were not without their own complaints. Their barley and wheat fields were attractive feeding grounds for thousands of ducks and geese and the results were often devastating. In a desperate attempt to protect their fields, farmers tried a variety of techniques to scare the hungry birds away. They fired shotguns loaded with blanks. Pilots were hired to buzz the grain fields and drop firecracker-like noisemakers. A searchlight, once mounted on one of the guard towers at the internment camp, was installed on the back of a truck and operated at night in the fields to roust the feeding birds.[15] Unfortunately, their efforts were not successful and they suffered significant crop losses.

Tule Lake farmers also had to face the yearly onslaught of hunters who thoughtlessly tramped across planted acreage in search of birds and game.[16] When confronted, the hunters were often belligerent. In analyzing these problems, the farmers placed blame at the doorstep of the Wildlife Refuge. The common argument was that the Refuge's policy on bird protection and a tandem program allowing seasonal hunting on the Refuge were to blame.

The conflict between farming interests in the basin and the Wildlife Refuge intensified at the conclusion of the 1948-1949 homestead allotment. More than 13,000 acres of land under Bureau of Reclamation control had not been released for homesteading. Instead, this acreage was being leased to basin farmers. Pressure was exerted on the Bureau to open this land, and the battle raged on for nearly four years.

In 1951, the Fish and Wildlife Service announced that it intended to exclusively manage 15,253 acres of land, including the League of Nations and Frog Pond, that had been under consideration for homesteading.[17] Farmers and businessmen in the basin protested this move, and in April drafted a four page brief which in part stated:

> While fractional when compared with the entire area already under Fish and Wildlife control, this land is, however, a substantial part of the crop economy of Tulelake and is reclaimed at our expense through construction charges levied on all homesteads.[18]

In June of 1951, the Bureau of Reclamation vaguely intimated that additional Tule Lake land would be opened for homesteading despite the Wildlife Refuge's plans to the contrary. However, the Bureau's position may have been more akin to political posturings. When Congressman Clair Engle asked the Bureau about its plans for Tule Lake, G.W. Lineweaver, acting Bureau of Reclamation Commissioner, replied that all plans were contingent on land classification and economic studies currently underway. He went on to say:

> Practically all the acreage now under consideration [for homesteading] has been farmed for a number of years on a rental basis. At the present time there is no intention on the part of the bureau to discontinue agricultural use of presently leased lands, nor does the bureau plan to unwater (sic) any additional areas now used for wildlife refuge purposes.[19]

In December of 1951, the *San Francisco Chronicle* published an article by Jim Thomas, an AP outdoor writer, which castigated the efforts of Tule Lake farmers, stating that further homesteading was a "major threat to waterfowl conservation in the

Pacific Flyway."[20] The *Chronicle* article, which had been reprinted in the *Tulelake Reporter* went on to say:

> In a nutshell, the reclamation bureau policy proposes to wreck the great Tule Lake waterfowl refuge in Northern California, nullifying millions of dollars which have been spent to preserve the duck population in its wintering grounds and to prevent crop depredations in California.

> [The] policy [of further homesteading] would mean the removal of approximately one-third of the 30,000-acre Tule Lake refuge, the elimination of the Tule Lake public hunting area and the wiping out of the entire area on which hundreds of thousands of geese use the refuge to feed and rest.[21]

Reacting with moral indignation, John B. Edmands, editor of *The Tulelake Reporter* responded to the Thomas's article with stinging rebuke:

> The 4,000 souls in this basin are ever aware of the tremendous responsibility placed upon us in the annual feeding and protection of the ducks and geese (you used the figure 12 million) that annually use the Tule Lake and Klamath basins while en route south.

> Mr. Thomas, I will bet you a new typewriter that there are more real sportsmen among the 4,000 souls in this Tulelake area than you have in the entire city of San Francisco ... and as sportsmen and Americans we are sickened at the viciousness and carelessness of so many of your Bay area and Los Angeles hunters who annually invade this haven for bird and beast.

> And we pay too, Mr. Thomas for this blessing we know we have. Not only in the licenses and tags, the guns and shells as do all hunters. But our ranchers pay and pay again with thousands of bushels of grain consumed each year off private farm land by these "12 million ducks and geese threatened with starvation by the greedy Tulelake farmers." Not a 30,000 acre refuge, Mr. Thomas; no, rather a 93,000-acre paradise

of water and grain and clover on which these birds feed each spring and fall at our expense.[22]

A week after Edmands's letter to Jim Thomas, the Bureau of Reclamation sought to cool down the issue by announcing that there were to be no more homestead allotments in the near future. Bureau of Reclamation regional director Richard Boke stated:

> To prevent any false hopes on the part of veterans who are seeking homesteads, we are making it clear that plans are still in the investigation stages. There are many factors to be considered, including flood danger, and the effect on waterfowl.[23]

In September of 1952, the Bureau of Reclamation's Klamath Project conducted a hearing on the lease-land and homesteading controversy in the Tule Lake Basin. During three hours of debate, the primary theme was that land at the League of Nations, Frog Pond, and land leased by Tulana Farms should be opened in 1953 to homesteading.[24]

A month later, it appeared as if the basin farmers had won a victory. On October 9, 1952, the *Tulelake Reporter* ran a banner headline that stated "Government Will Open 150 Basin Homesteads in '53." The article boldly proclaimed that:

> The Bureau of Reclamation today announced plans to open an additional 150 homesteads in the Tule Lake Basin and Klamath Straits. The openings will be drawn for sometime in the summer of 1953.
>
> In telephone conservation with The Reporter today, James G. Lindley, region director of the [Reclamation] O & M, said there is no question about the directive from Washington calling for prompt action on the homestead program.[25]

However, the *Tulelake Reporter* story was a bit hasty. "Regional Director Richard Boke denied that any homestead action was impending."[26] He indicated instead "the entire matter was still in the lap of Secretary of the Interior Oscar Chapman."[27] Two months later, Chapman was still trying to sort out the issues. In a December meeting with Reclamation Commissioner Michael

Straus, the Secretary of the Interior attempted to determine if "homesteading of the basin's land ... [was] mandatory under the deed by which the states transferred them to the federal government for reclamation."[28]

In January of 1953, Chapman evidently decided that all considerations pointed to opening the Tule Lake lands to homesteading. According to the January 8th issue of the *Tulelake Reporter:*

> On the desk of Secretary of Interior Oscar Chapman today is a memorandum prepared at his request—and awaiting only his signature before becoming effective—which provides that:
>
> 1. All lease land here will be re-leased through the Bureau of Reclamation this year.
>
> 2. Sometime this year a drawing will be set up through which 6,700 acres in the League of Nations and Klamath Straits areas will be homesteaded with 1954 slated to be the first crop years.
>
> 3. Upon release of this acreage to homesteading, Fish and Wildlife will take jurisdiction over all other public land in the Tulelake area proper, except that which is necessary to service the Bureau of Reclamation Project here. [29]

In a special box in the same issue of the *Tulelake Reporter,* a "bulletin" stated:

> Just before *The Reporter* went to press today the following telegram was received:
>
> RE YOUR CALL. SECRETARY CHAPMAN HAS NOT OFFICIALLY SIGNED MEMORANDUM BUT IS EXPECTED TO ON FRIDAY.
>
> CONGRESSMAN CLAIR ENGLE.[30]

Chapman finally issued his directive, which ordered the Bureau of Reclamation to:

Take appropriate steps to homestead as soon as practicable the following areas:

a. All of the lands in the Klamath Straits Unit except approximately 1,770 acres in the half-sections bordering the Oregon-California State line, and

b. Approximately 2,500 acres in the League of Nations Tract.[31]

Chapman went on to say in his directive: "These orders should be drafted so that the continued use of the refuges for wildlife purposes shall not be subordinated to use for reclamation homestead purposes."[32]

Chapman's directive angered basin residents because the amount of land to be homesteaded was substantially reduced— and because he apparently left a loophole with his final statement related to wildlife purposes not being "subordinated to ... homestead purposes." But not all hope was lost. Chapman was a lame duck, soon to leave office along with the rest of the Truman Administration. The new Secretary of the Interior, under the Eisenhower Administration, was former Oregon governor Douglas McKay.

When McKay took office, he declared that the general policy of his office would be "to preserve and protect wildlife as far as possible," and he said nothing about homesteading.[33] In an attempt to persuade Secretary McKay that more land should be opened for homesteading at Tule Lake, a basin committee drafted a brief, which stated in part: "We do not believe that it is to the best interests of our country and its great system of free enterprise to turn over large tracts of land to federal agencies for permanent ownership and management."[34]

At the same time, Wallace Myers, writing in the Klamath Falls *Herald and News* raised the issue: "Should thousands of acres of rich crop land be homesteaded and thus put on the tax roles as private land or should it be turned over to the Fish and Wildlife Service for leasing and remain federal land?"[35]

Outside forces began to mount a campaign against opening any new homestead land. In April of 1953, the *Tulelake Reporter* noted that:

> Three powerful organizations this week were in league against the Basin on the matter of homesteading vs. wildlife seeking not only to prohibit any further farm-productive use of the land here but also to set aside the Chapman "lame-duck directive" and give back the 6,700 acres scheduled to be homesteaded this year to fish and wildlife.
>
> The three groups are the California Farm Bureau, the State Chamber of Commerce, and the State Fish & Game Commission.[36]

In a last-gasp attempt to persuade the government to support the homesteaders' position, an intensive lobbying campaign was initiated. Frank King, a 1948 Coppock Bay homesteader, vividly remembers his efforts on behalf of the Tule Lake homesteaders as he lobbied his congressional district's congressman:

> We rented a commercial airplane and wined and dined him. We were simply lobbying to open up more land to private ownership. As far as we were concerned, the one thing that would make this area prosperous was to get it out of government control. The conflict in this area at the time was, "Who got there first, the Fish and Wildlife Service or private ownership?" We felt private ownership would generate more income and prosperity for our community.[37]

The efforts of the homesteaders were to no avail. The Bureau of Reclamation stonewalled the issue for the remainder of the 1950s. Although this gave the Tule Lake Wildlife Refuge a breathing spell, it still did not end the debate over ownership and management of the land at Frog Pond and League of Nations.

Finally, the issue was resolved in 1964. Heavy lobbying by conservation interests and officials from the Fish and Wildlife Service convinced California Senator Thomas Kuchel to introduce federal legislation to permanently protect refuge land within the proximity of the Klamath Project. Kuchel's efforts were successful and Public Law 88-567 placed control and supervision of all land in question under the direct control of the Secretary of the Interior. The Kuchel Act stated "all U.S. lands within the executive order boundaries of Tule Lake, Clear Lake, Lower Klamath and Upper Klamath Wildlife Refuges are dedicated to

Wildlife conservation."[38] At last, after thirty-six years of advocacy, the Tule Lake Wildlife Refuge had real control over the destiny of migratory birds in the Pacific Flyway.

By 1977, it was clear that the balance of power had shifted to the Wildlife Refuge. In February, an amendment to the National Wildlife Refuge System Administration Act of 1966, coupled with an agreement signed on August 2, 1977 between the Bureau of Reclamation and the Tule Lake Wildlife Refuge, established two key positions: first, the Fish and Wildlife Service was acknowledged to be in charge of administering the land and water within the boundaries of the refuge and all decisions made by the Fish and Wildlife Service affecting this area were binding. Second, the Bureau of Reclamation would prepare and conduct leasing programs on the land designated for agricultural use within the Refuge. These leasing programs, though conducted by the Bureau of Reclamation, would still be under the approval of the Fish and Wildlife Service.[39]

On February 11, 1980, the Refuge expanded its jurisdiction to include land encompassing The Peninsula. The ancient volcanic formation was placed under Refuge control because of its natural nesting sites for eagles, falcons, owls, and hawks. Acquisition of The Peninsula was the culmination of a study begun in 1974 to analyze the impact of off-road vehicles on the area. It was ascertained that vehicular use around the Peninsula was not only threatening basin wildlife, but was also causing deep scarring on the hillsides, particularly on the southeast slope.

When the Wildlife Refuge assumed control over The Peninsula and placed it off-limits to motorized vehicles, it rekindled the long simmering dispute over the government's role in the basin. Farmers and recreationists decried what they believed to be the heavy-handedness of Refuge officials. Conservationists, on the other hand, applauded the move as an additional step toward wildlife preservation.

Today, the Tule Lake National Wildlife refuge encompasses 38,118 acres of croplands, uplands, marshes and open water. Of that acreage, approximately 17,000 acres are leased out on a five-year basis to farmers who reside within a fifty-mile radius of the Refuge. Though local farmers and Refuge officials still keep a wary eye on each other, they have a working relationship that is mutually beneficial. The lease-land system provides local farmers with additional acreage for cultivation. Around the lease-land, the

Refuge maintains approximately 2,000 acres of barley that is designed to act as a buffer and attract feeding waterfowl. This has substantially reduced crop damage by birds. In addition, since many of the birds arrive in the Tule Lake area in the autumn, after the crops have been harvested, and return in the spring, before the crops are in danger of being eaten, there is even less risk for lease land farmers that they will have their fields damaged.[40]

Finally, by controlling the lease-lands and portions of the sump area, which are diked and fitted with connecting pipes, the Wildlife Refuge is able to provide a stable environment which matches the yearly needs of migratory birds and permanent wildlife in the basin.

Though conflicts will probably continue between the Wildlife Refuge and private interests in the Tule Lake Basin, the overall cooperation between farming and conservation interests has been remarkably successful. A permanent means of protection for migratory birds has been forged, and so has an opportunity for farmers at Tule Lake to expand their production. Reclamation, farming, and wildlife preservation are now banded together into a unique and important relationship.

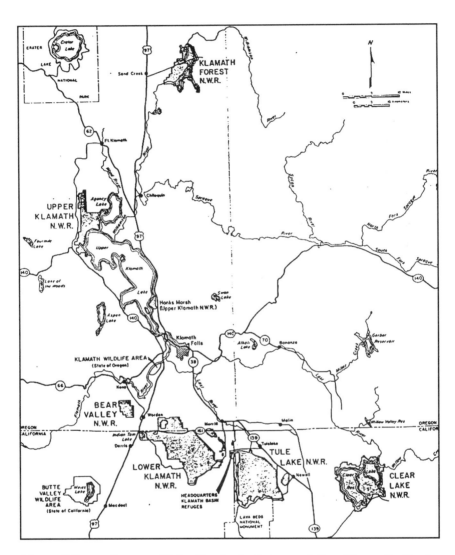

Map of the refuges within the jurisdiction of the Klamath Basin Wildlife System. *(Courtesy U.S. Fish and Wildlife Service)*

Klamath Basin National Wildlife Refuges Visitor's Center at the Tule Lake Wildlife Refuge. *(Photo by author)*

Pelicans at the Tule Lake Wildlife Refuge. *(Photo by Mary Hyde, courtesy Tulelake-Butte Valley Fair, Museum of Local History)*

CHAPTER 20

THE YEARS OF HARVEST

It has been more than eighty years since the inception of the Klamath Project. During that time, change has come rapidly to the Tule Lake Basin. John Muir, western naturalist and crusader for conservation, described the lake in 1874 as being, "fairly blooming in purple light, and is so responsive to the sky, both in calmness and color, that it seems itself sky. No mountain shores hide its loveliness. It lies wide open for many a mile, vailed (sic) in no other mystery than the mystery of light."[1]

Today the loveliness of the basin is manifest in symmetrical patchworks of green and gold. The nearly dizzy rate of growth through the 1940s and the decline of the fifties and sixties has been supplanted by stability. Aside from the frenzy of the planting and harvesting seasons, the basin has a sense of calm. It has been a time of harvest, of reaping the benefits of decades, even centuries of development.

In analyzing the direction of the Tule Lake Basin during the second half of the twentieth century, it is clear that two dominant factors have been at play: technological development and the unique character of its population. Together they have given shape and definition to the basin in its contemporary setting.

During the four decades since World War II, the greatest force behind basin change has been farm technology. It has had an impact on the region's population, farm size, crops, machinery, and finances. For example, by the 1960s, the average 80 acre homestead could no longer support a farm family. The reasons were tied to both technology and economics. With new machinery, a single farmer could manage many times the acreage that could be farmed twenty years before. The technology that spawned this capability also contributed to an enormous increase in expenditures for necessary equipment.

In the early 1930s, an adequate tractor cost less than $500. Fifty years later, in the 1980s the farmer must spend between $40,000 and $80,000, not including peripheral equipment needed for tilling, planting, crop maintenance, and harvesting. Combines used for harvesting wheat now run from $80,000 to over $100,000. The spiraling costs have forced basin farmers to make one of several choices: expand their operation, lease their land, or sell out. When asked about the economic burden and trend toward larger farms, homesteader and cattleman Frank King observed: "You just continue to need more and more land. You try and amortize a $40,000 or $50,000 tractor over 80 acres of grain, which is only producing maybe $30,000 gross a year, and you're only going to pull $5000 net off it. So what do you live off of?"[2]

The answer to the problem posed by King is the trend toward increasingly larger holdings. This move has not been without problems. Available land is extremely limited in the basin, and when homesteads are placed on the market they are quickly sold to local farmers anxious to increase their holdings. Inflation and the scarcity of land has caused the price per acre to steadily increase, contributing to an already substantial debt burden brought about by the purchase of expensive machinery. In addition, every time a local farmer increases the size of his farm he must contend with the government's 160-acre limitation on land irrigated by federal projects. To get around the law, farm units are often purchased in the name of individual family members—husbands, wives, children, and relatives.

On paper, the value of the farmer's land, buildings, and machinery is impressive, but the yearly investment in crop production has a leveling effect that leaves a precarious balance between profit and loss. In good times, net income can be generous, but when the market turns sour, or when disease and weather ruin crops, years of hard work can quickly be destroyed. Barbara Krizo, who with her husband Phillip homesteaded in 1946, summed it up best when she said: "No one has to be a better businessman or know more about business than a farmer."[3]

Though ever-increasing costs related to machinery and crop production have been a burden to farmers, technical improvements and scientific research have helped soften the impact. When potato production began in the basin in the 1920s, it was limited by many factors: the risks of attacks by pests and blight; by the backbreaking work needed to hand-plant and harvest; and by killing frosts that easily damaged the vulnerable vines of the plant. Over time, each obstacle was conquered.

Improvements in machinery helped increase the efficiency of potato production. Horse-drawn mechanical diggers, introduced in the late 1920s, brought the fully-grown potatoes to the surface. At the same time, the potato belt was developed. This simple device was worn around the waist and had hooks on its sides from which gunnysacks were suspended. Large groups of farm laborers wearing potato belts would descend on a field of harvested potatoes neatly placed in windrows by the mechanical diggers. They would quickly fill each sack, unhook them, and leave them standing in the field. The sacks would then be loaded onto horse-drawn wagons to be taken to storage or market.

In the 1930s, tractors came into use, leading to the development of larger potato diggers, and the introduction of conveyor systems to more easily move the sacked potatoes from the field to wagon or truck. However, the most rapid change took place after World War II, when machinery was developed that allowed only a handful of operators to plant, cultivate, and harvest entire fields. Today during harvest, giant mechanical diggers pile potatoes into three or four windrows at one time. A loader or bulker is then run along the rows, lifting the potatoes from the field to trucks running parallel to the machine. The crop is then taken to huge cellars where the potatoes are stored until they are shipped by truck or rail to market.

The amount of specialized equipment needed to grow potatoes, from mechanical planters to bulk loaders, has limited the number of farmers who do all their own work. It is not unusual to have some of the work "custom" done; that is, to hire another farmer who has the special equipment to come in and do the harvesting.

Potato production requires some of the most sophisticated equipment in the basin, but even wheat production involves expensive machinery. Generally the trend has been toward purchasing equipment that can handle ever-increasing amounts of land. Chisels, disks, harrows, and cultivators are larger and the tractors are more powerful. Some of the biggest tractors today are four-wheel drive and have huge dual wheels, front and rear. The tires are filled with calcium carbonate to increase their weight and improve traction. But there have been problems with the larger equipment. Though they are more efficient, their enormous weight can compact the soil, reducing the yield per acre. On the positive side, even the smaller tractors are vast improvements over the original Case, John Deere, International Harvester, and Ford tractors first used in the basin. Today they are equipped with such amenities as enclosed cabs, power steering, heaters, air conditioning, and radios. This has contributed to the exorbitant cost of new equipment, but has greatly improved working conditions for the operator. Nineteen forty-six homesteader Paul Christy reminisced about using his first John Deere tractor: "We sat there in the spring and fall, huddled up. The wind blew and the dust. It was cold ... but it was fun! I never regretted it. You just bowed your back and did it."[4] Even so, as his farm became profitable, Christy, like other basin farmers opted for newer equipment that provided protection against the elements.

At the same time new farm machinery has increased the amount of acreage an individual farmer can manage, crop yields have been substantially increased through scientific developments. The University of California Agricultural Extension Service has operated a branch office in the basin for over forty years. Located on the east side of Highway 139, next to the city of Tulelake, its research has helped basin farmers select the most appropriate and highest yield strains of seed. In addition, the service has provided crop-care analysis on a cost per acre basis— precious information when the profit margin is often razor thin.

Basin farmers have met scientific research that has promoted increased crop yields with enthusiasm. However, environmentalists have not always greeted it with equal support. For example, in the mid-1980s, a special bacterium was genetically engineered to help prevent frost damage to crops. Through research, it was discovered that frost forms around a special type of bacterium, and that by introducing a man-altered strain that causes frost to be formed at a lower temperature, crops such as potatoes could be more easily protected during the growing season. But environmental groups voiced concern. They were afraid that the long-term effects of the bacteria were unknown and that it might be drawn into the atmosphere, altering the temperature at which ice and snow are formed. Consequently, a court injunction was issued, preventing its experimental use in the United States. Then in 1987, all legal obstacles were removed and the bacterium was sprayed on plants at an experimental farm near San Francisco and on potato vines at the agricultural experiment station at Tulelake. The results of the experiments are yet to be determined.

One of the most important innovations in the basin has been the introduction of new methods of irrigation. Until the 1950s, the most common method was flood irrigation. It was an inexpensive method, needing only pumps to move the water from the irrigation canals into ditches and furrows between rows of crops. However, flood irrigation had its drawbacks. The fields had to be skillfully leveled and water was wasted as it sank below the root line in the porous soil. Repeated flooding leached traces of salt and alkali into the water, reducing crop output. Flooding also attracted greater numbers of insects. The introduction of sprinkler irrigation solved most of these problems. The amount of moisture delivered to each plant was easy to regulate. By watering at night, loss due to evaporation was substantially reduced. As an added bonus, sprinkler irrigation provided an effective means of combating frost.

There are generally two types of sprinkler systems used in the basin. The most common is the wheel-line, used principally in the production of wheat, barley, alfalfa, and clover. Wheel-lines come in twenty to thirty-foot sections, each with a large, spoked wheel and a "rain-bird" type sprinkler head. Linked together, the lines run from one quarter to one half mile in length, depending on the diameter of the pipe and the power of the supply pump. The line irrigates one linear section of a field at a time. It is then rolled to the next section by activating a gasoline motor located in the center of the line.

The second type of irrigation system, used primarily for potatoes, is the solid-set sprinkler. Though the system comes in sections, with one sprinkler head for each twenty to thirty-foot length of pipe, it becomes a semi-permanent part of a field during the growing season. Solid-sets are popular for potato production because they provide a means for watering an entire field at once. Not only does this alleviate the need to frequently move the system, but it also allows for an efficient means of frost control. A frost-monitoring device is set out in the field, and a transmitter activates a warning device in the farmer's home when the temperature approaches 32 degrees Fahrenheit. When the alarm goes off, the farmer turns on the solid-set system, which bathes the potato vines in water that is warmer than the air temperature. Unless there is a prolonged freeze, the crop is protected from damage.

Technical changes have been important in the Tule Lake Basin, but the key ingredient to its progress has been its people. There is great diversity in those who call the basin their home: original homesteaders, farm laborers, merchants, government employees, mechanics, and professional people. Many are newcomers, but a considerable number have lived in the basin since the first years of homesteading. Collectively, the basin's residents make up a tapestry that is rich and colorful.

Some pioneers of basin settlement, like 1922 homesteader Marie Gentry, modestly proclaim that every basin resident has had a role in its history. Marie defers suggestions that she and her late husband Karl were part of the leadership that secured schools, good roads, utilities, and the foundations for a new basin community. Brother and sister Ray Laird and Marguerite Dayton, who also came to the basin to settle in the 1920s, take pride in telling the Laird family history, which dates back to 1860 when their parents came to Siskiyou County by covered wagon. The family name is clearly marked on maps as "Lairds Landing," located at the southern end of the Lower Klamath Basin. Here, steamboats used to dock at the edge of the Laird ranch to take on passengers and freight destined for Klamath Falls.

Not all of the early settlers were homesteaders. Dorothy Ager, who moved from the basin in the 1970s, retains fond memories of her and her husband Earl's prime years spent helping build the community of Tulelake. Now in her eighties, Ager views homesteaders of the late 1940s, who themselves are now grandparents, as being mere youngsters in the history of the basin.

As a 1938 homesteader, Chet Main finds himself caught between two worlds. In terms of age, he is closer to those who homesteaded in the basin between 1922 and 1932. In fact, there was some debate at the time of the 1938 homestead that World War I veterans were too old and that younger applicants should be considered. Yet Main demonstrated that not only was his group capable of homesteading, but they also had the energy and resources to become involved in basin leadership. Chet was the first president of the Tulelake Growers Association and became a guiding force that led to the establishment of the Tulelake-Butte Valley Fair Grounds.

People such as Paul and Gertrude Christy and Otto Schaffner represent the "youngsters" among the original homesteaders, those who came between 1946 and 1949. Paul Christy, whose name was the eighth drawn in the 1946 homestead, not only led the fight for schools in the southern basin, but he is quick to pay tribute to the wives of the homesteaders. A considerable number were not from farms themselves, and, even if they were, had to put up with a great deal. Some worked in the fields side-by-side with their husbands. Others worked full-time in their homes - all faced taking care of children, preparing endless meals, continually washing dirty clothes, coping with dust storms, and putting up with long bleak winters. However, the Christys, like many basin families, exude a glow of pride. They survived the early years, and now approaching retirement, can enjoy the fruits of their years of labor.

Otto Schaffner was among the last three homesteaders in the basin. A former Navy radioman that had worked for Pan American Airlines in radio-navigation, Schaffner put his name in for both the 1948 and 1949 homestead allotments. When it was finally drawn in 1949, he was the fifteenth alternate. At first, the prospects of receiving a homestead seemed remote. However a number of plots at the northeastern end of the basin were high in alkali. Three remained unclaimed when the Bureau of Reclamation approached Schaffner. He accepted the challenge and spent eight years working amendments such as gypsum into the soil before the land would grow a profitable crop. In order to make a living, he had to lease a privately-owned farm unit nearby and also secure a government lease on the Refuge land to the southwest.

In 1954, Schaffner began to grow horseradish. In the late fifties he and his wife Margaret went into the horseradish processing business and with the help of a University of California food technologist developed a horseradish formula for a marketable sauce. They founded the Tulelake Horseradish Company and by the 1970s had accounts with large retail outlets that included Safeway and Albertson's. In the early 1980s, the Schaffners sold the company, but they have remained in Tulelake.

At eighty-four years old, Victoria Thaler is no youngster, yet her arrival in the city of Tulelake in 1942 makes her among the more recent of the "old timers." She had come to the basin with her husband to work at the Japanese internment camp, but it wasn't long before she was living in Tulelake. When the city clerk, Wanda Stark, became Tulelake's postmaster, Vicky was appointed to fill her position. She held the job for more than twenty years. Not content with just one government job, in the early 1950s she was elected as a city judge. Vicky Thaler's combination of fair but stern decisions, mixed with her sense of compassion, made the name "Judge Thaler" legendary.

Clifford Bell is a second-generation resident, born and raised in the Tule Lake Basin. Talk to the youthful Bell about his job working for the Newell Grain Growers' Hannchen Elevator, located about a mile southwest of The Peninsula, and he will describe with pride the intricate steps involved in processing wheat and barley, from grading and weighing to loading huge railroad hopper cars. During harvest, the busiest time of the year, his motions as he moves from one job to the next are fluid and business like. Yet it is clear that he enjoys his work.

As a truck arrives at the elevator, Clifford deftly moves to the checking platform where he quickly inserts a brass probe into the truck's load of barley. The captured grain is dumped into a container and then checked for moisture content and weight per bushel. It's an important test. If the barley is graded #1, it will be shipped to one of two major malting plants on the West Coast to be processed for use in the brewing of beer. The truck then moves to the weigh scale, where its fully-loaded tonnage is noted. The results of the test are then relayed to the driver. The barley is graded as #3, usable for animal feed, commanding a much lower price than a #1 grade. Clifford indicates to the driver to open the truck's unloading chute. As grain spills through open bars to a hopper and conveyor system below ground, he talks to the driver about the quality of the grain delivered. "They won't like to hear the results of the grade out where they are cutting," the driver responds.

Meanwhile, Bell turns on the platform hoist and the grain truck is angled into the air. As the front end begins to point skyward, the truck's load is quickly emptied. The ramp lowers and the truck is weighed again empty. A ticket is filled out indicating the grade and amount of grain delivered and the driver heads back to the fields to receive another load from the combine. By late August, when the harvest season intensifies, Clifford and his fellow workers will spend from morning to after dark filling the great cylindrical eighty-foot-high grain tanks that surround the Hannchen elevator.

Paulette Hinds considers her residency in Tulelake as relatively brief. She has lived in the basin for about eighteen years. Yet her roots in Tulelake's economy go deeper. She first came to the basin in the late 1950s with her brother and parents. They were migrant farm laborers who specialized in potatoes. Contrary to the notion that all migrant work is drudgery, both Paulette and her mother, Lavada Hance, talk with pride about their years picking potatoes in fields ranging from California to Washington State.

They worked the fields at a time before the widespread introduction of the mechanical potato-bulker and were experts at filling sacks hung around their waist from a potato belt. In her best years, Lavada could fill one sack a minute and the entire family could produce 1,000 sacks a day. They were paid $.06 per sack and $60.00 a day was considered good wages in the 1950s and early 1960s. But there was a price to pay for the work done by many migrants. A disturbing number ended up in poor health, victims of hard work, inclement weather and pesticides (it wasn't until the late 1960s that federal and state regulations restricted the use of pesticides when workers were in the fields).

There was another, less obvious, impact as well. Migrant workers, no matter where they were employed, were considered to be of low status, and consequently undesirable. They were often called "scabbies." For Paulette Hinds and her brother it meant that for years they were exceedingly reserved when meeting other people - insulating themselves from possible verbal derision.

Based on her experiences working in the fields of Tule Lake, Paulette swore she would never return to the basin. But after she married, she and her husband moved to Newell, where he operated a machine shop. Later they were divorced, but Paulette was determined to become a self-sufficient person and taught herself how to do bookkeeping. By the early 1980s, she was remarried and had been hired as the bookkeeper for the city of Tulelake. Though Paulette is still not prepared to express strong sentimental attachment for the basin, she does appreciate its rugged beauty and the friendliness of its people.

Andy Wilkins and his wife Ella are also recent arrivals. In 1971, Andy "retired" from his building contracting business in Southern California to purchase the Homestead Market in Newell. Then in the mid-1970s he sold the market and started doing electrical contracting work. His affable manner and his strong support for fellow basin residents has enabled him to become a well-integrated member of the community.

In 1967, John Moore was an out-of-work bartender in Redding, California. Checking for work at the local union hall, he became aware of an opening tending bar at the Sportsmen's Hotel in Tulelake. The next day he traveled to the basin on a Greyhound

Bus, and went to work at the Sportsmen that evening. Three months later, Moore's wife and children joined him and after little more than a year, he changed jobs and became produce manager at Jock's Market. On November 1, 1976 he purchased the Homestead Market from Andy Wilkins, and in the subsequent years developed the business into a profitable enterprise. Moore has endeavored to meet the needs of residents of the basin, particularly at Newell. Since many of the town's inhabitants are seasonal farm workers, he frequently keeps his store open late into the evening so that people coming home from work are able to purchase food. In many ways, his store is Newell's community center, where neighbors meet, the latest news is exchanged, and where emergencies, especially fires and accidents, are reported.

Cindy Wright and her husband Gary are one of the few young farm families in the basin to start farming without inheriting the land. In 1981, they purchased a tract originally homesteaded by Ralph Morrill in 1949. It has been a struggle for the Wrights. While attempting to make the farm profitable and keep up with the payments for the land and equipment, both Cindy and Gary have had to take outside jobs. Cindy works at the Tulelake-Butte Valley Fair Grounds as the assistant business manager, and Gary has been working for Ray Ackley at the Dry Lake Ranch, located south of the basin. To date, they have been limited to growing grain. This is because the expense involved with the equipment necessary for raising other crops has been beyond their means. In the future they hope to be able to work the land full-time.

Government agencies are well-represented in the basin, and include employees of the Lava Beds National Monument, the Tule Lake National Wildlife Refuge, the National Forest Service, and the Agricultural Extension Service. It is common for men like Jim Sleznick, director of the Lava Beds National Monument, to be involved in basin community service organizations such as Rotary. Sleznick's combination of businesslike management of the Lava Beds and friendly sense of humor add color to the basin. Once, in jest, he wrote an "official" memo to the National Park Service expounding the attributes of attaching cow magnets to the fuel lines of vehicles—claiming that it saved gas mileage. The letter, and Woody Gamble, the park employee who tried the experiment, made national news when the *San Francisco Chronicle* wrote an article about the experiment. Trouble was, if the magnets did work, they weren't consistent. One park employee claimed he actually got worse gas mileage when he attached them to his truck!

Perhaps one of the best indicators of the basin's diversity is David Porter Misso. His business card describes him as "philosopher at large" and his background working at many different jobs qualifies him as jack-of-all-trades. David was a product of the counter-culture revolution of the 1960s. He still describes himself as a "hippie" and a "commonist"—that is, a person supporting the causes of the common man. He is a veteran of the Vietnam War, but became an anti-war activist when he returned from his tour of duty. He and his former wife Sheila arrived in the Tule Lake Basin in 1973, refugees of smog and population-choked Los Angeles. Seeking to adopt a lifestyle free from dependence upon outside forces, David and Sheila's two-acre farm to the south of Newell contained no electricity, telephone, or running water. In 1981, the couple separated and then divorced.

Since David Misso first arrived in the Tule Lake Basin he has been fighting the "system," from standing up to Modoc County when it balked at his installation of a composting-toilet, to his prolific letter-writing campaign to congressmen, senators, California and Oregon politicians, the *Tulelake Reporter*, and the Klamath Falls *Herald and News*. His letters have stirred passions and pricked consciences. Yet his liberal, perhaps radical, views have come to be tolerated in the basin—the product of his hard work and his consistent willingness to live by his principles. David Misso has been a perennial candidate for political office, running countless times for the California State Assembly on the Peace and Freedom Party ticket. Knowing that his chances of winning were slim, his prime objective was to bring a message to people about the inequities that he believes exist in the United States. Then in the early 1980s, David ran for the Tulelake School District Board of Education and, perhaps surprising even himself, he won. His victory was not as unusual as it might have seemed. His willingness to speak out, even when people disagreed with him, had earned him support in his campaign to become the "conscience" of the school board.

These are but a few of the many people who call the Tule Lake Basin their home. The residents of Merrill, Malin, Tulelake, and Newell, and the hundreds of farm families living in the basin share a common bond that can be found throughout the extended community—a bonding of hard work and concern for one another. It is a tradition that began with the first pioneers— its origins are as old as the earliest humans to arrive in the basin 15,000 years ago. The tradition is still alive in the 1980s. Some of the accounts have already been told, such as when Buddy and Yvonne Booe's restaurant in Malin burned down, and members of the community pledged dollars and support to help them rebuild. Other examples have taken place since then, such as when Merrill farmer Randall Pope's potato crop was damaged during harvest. He shrugged off the loss and donated 43 tons to social service agencies in the State of Oregon to provide food for the needy. And in September 1982, basin farmers came to the aid of Bob Lillard. The 1947 homesteader had been hospitalized in August. He survived three operations in twenty-four hours, with complications that included blood clots, the amputation of his left leg, and a heart attack. During his ordeal, his main concern was for his crops! Rallying to his need, homesteaders Keith Vokach, John Bettendorff, and Phillip Krizo organized an armada of 11 combines. In several hours, Lillard's crop of barley was harvested. When asked why they came to his aid, the trio's response was unanimous: "It's the Tulelake way."[5]

"The Tulelake Way" is synonymous with people in the basin. They have about them an infectious sense of community. When people are in need, they are quick to help, and when their lifestyle is under fire, they are resolute. There is among Tulelake people a natural goodness, a strong sense of compassion, and an open and honest sharing of hospitality. The basin is a land of character, earned with the sweat, tears, and blood of a great range of inhabitants. It has a richness of history and tradition. The people who remain in the basin are proud; proud of their country and proud of their accomplishments. One homesteader who was interviewed said: "You put your roots deep around here."[6] It's easy to see why.

Newell Grain Growers Association's Hannchen Elevator, located west of Newell, California. The tanks are used to store various grades of wheat and barley. *(Photo by author)*

Clifford Bell runs a probe into a truckload of barley to check for uniformity and moisture content. Grain to be stored is recorded by Wendell Schey. *(Photos by author)*

Above and below: Tule Lake Basin farmland. *(Photos by author.)*

EPILOGUE: PART ONE

The Struggle for Water and Economic Survival

When this book was originally published in 1987, it appeared that eighty years of dreams and hard work by Tule Lake Basin homesteaders had created the "years of harvest." Little did anyone dream that, fourteen years later, the basin would be embroiled in a heated battle over water, pitting farmers and ranchers against environmentalists, Indian tribes, coastal fishing interests and government agencies.

It began in 1988, when two local fish, the short-nose and Lost River suckers, were listed as endangered under the Endangered Species Act. In the sixties, suckers had been so plentiful that members of the Klamath Tribes were able to pitchfork them into the backs of their pickups. By the 1980s, their numbers had severely declined and the U.S. Fish and Wildlife Service placed them on the endangered list.

From the outset, many people knew that placing the suckers under the umbrella protection of the Endangered Species Act would lead to problems in the Klamath and Tule Lake Basins. In the opinion of a number of biological studies conducted for the Fish and Wildlife Service, degradation of sucker habitat was directly attributable to the Klamath Project and irrigation. According to these studies, maintaining water levels in Upper Klamath Lake to protect sucker spawning and development was especially critical.

Sucker protection was not the only water issue in the basin. For years there had been conflicting water claims throughout the Upper Klamath drainage system. Among those involved were the Klamath Tribes, who lost their reservation in 1954, but had retained hunting and fishing rights granted to them in the treaty of 1864. Elwood H. Miller, director of the Department of Fish and Wildlife for the Klamath Tribes stated:

> Frequently the point is made that farmers have been working a piece of ground for four or five generations, and over this long time have developed an intimate relationship with the land. We, of all people, understand this way of thinking. The Klamath, Modoc

and Yahooskin people have been on this land for hundreds of generations, thousands of years before the ancestors of the pioneers had any idea that the North American continent even existed.

Our land was taken from us in stages from 1864 to 1954, until we were left with none.

If the agricultural community envisions the past decade as being like the Great Depression, just imagine how the tribal community must feel, having experienced great hardship and loss for a much longer time. When advertisements bemoan threats to "our water," imagine how the tribal people feel as they watch the rivers dry up.[1]

A myriad of farmers and small irrigation districts also had claims dating prior to 1909. In addition, the wildlife refuges of the Upper Klamath Basin needed water for wildlife and thousands of migratory birds within their protective boundaries.

By the mid-1990s, Senator Mark Hatfield (Oregon), attempted to resolve the multiple claims to water by forming the Upper Klamath Basin Study Group. The committee was made up of representatives from a broad base of interests. While Hatfield was in office, the committee had leadership that could prod them along, but in the late 1990s Hatfield retired from the Senate. Without strong leadership within the committee to forge equitable compromises, the work of the committee stalled.

In 1997, another fish within the Klamath drainage, the coho salmon, was added to the endangered species list. Like the suckers, the coho population had significantly declined. Commercial and sport fishing along the north coast of California and traditional fishing rights of several Indian tribes, including the Yurok and Karuk had been affected. Management of the coho was primarily the responsibility of the National Marine Fisheries Service. To protect the coho, NMFS adopted a biological study done by Thomas B. Hardy, director of the Institute for Natural Systems Engineering at Utah State University. According to the Hardy report, greater stream flows in the Klamath River below Iron Gate Dam were necessary to protect spawning salmon.

Environmental groups such as the Oregon Natural Resources Council believed that agricultural practices within the basin were detrimental to the general eco-system. They were most strongly opposed to farming on the Tule Lake and Lower Klamath Wildlife Refuge lease-lands, but a number of the groups were also of the opinion that farming should simply end within much of the basin as well. Their position was based on the premise that the land was originally semi-arid desert, artificially changed through the draining of Tule Lake and the Klamath Project irrigation system. They advocated the end of farming via federal buyouts and returning the land to its natural state.

Indian tribal interests also played an increasingly important role in the basin. For many years, other basin residents and the federal government ignored the tribes. Little was done to abide by or enforce treaty agreements. Once the suckers were listed as endangered, the tribes began to take a more aggressive stance and demanded the preservation of the suckers as a cultural resource. Several court rulings as well as written reports produced by the Fish and Wildlife service made reference to their treaty rights and culture.

In the fall of 2000, the Klamath Basin suffered one of the worst droughts in recorded history. By the following January, it became apparent there would not be enough water to adequately supply farmers, fish and wildlife. In light of the developing drought, the Fish and Wildlife Service and National Marine Fisheries took the position that Klamath Basin water must first go to the endangered suckers and coho salmon—even if it meant there would be no water for farming and ranching. The Bureau of Reclamation's Klamath Project was reluctant to take such a strong position, but they were faced with a no-win situation. Their historical mission had been to provide water for farming. Yet, the Endangered Species Act required them to place the highest priority on species protection. In preparation for a worst case scenario, the Project warned farmers that they might not be getting their summer water.

Further pressure was placed on the Klamath Project through several lawsuits filed in federal court. One was filed by the Pacific Coast Federation of Fishermen's Associations. The PCFFA claimed that the Bureau of Reclamation had not made a genuine effort to protect the coho salmon. Another was filed by EarthJustice Legal Defense Fund, which represented seven wildlife and environmental groups including the Oregon Natural Resources Council, Klamath Forest Alliance, Northcoast Environmental Center, Golden Gate Audubon Society, WaterWatch, the

Sierra Club and the Wilderness Society. The suit claimed the Bureau of Reclamation failed to consult the Fish and Wildlife Service on adequate protection for endangered suckers and bald eagles when they developed their 2001 operating plan.

Basin farmers responded with alarm to the Klamath Project's announcement that they might not be getting the water they needed for the 2001 growing season. They challenged the pending decision by claiming the federal government had long ago promised them they would always receive water. Water delivery was part of the Klamath Project's mission. Further, Tule Lake homesteaders had proof of their rights to water in the form of patents signed by various Presidents of the United States.

The farmers, through organizations such as the Klamath Water Users Association, also challenged the biological reports that claimed higher water levels in Upper Klamath Lake and greater flows in the Klamath River would protect the endangered fish. They cited the drought of 1992, claiming there were no large-scale fish kills in that year. They also produced their own biological study, which contradicted the studies adopted by the Fish and Wildlife Service and NMFS. The KWUA study said that higher water levels in Upper Klamath Lake were actually detrimental to spawning suckers. The study also claimed the additional water released into the Klamath River would be warm and therefore detrimental to salmon.

In an attempt to head-off the pending water cutoff decision and to address concerns for sucker and salmon protection, the KWUA proposed an alternate plan that would have provided water for both the endangered fish and the farming community. The proposal, which was rejected by the government agencies, contained the following components:

- Eliminate barriers to fish passage at Sprague River Dam near Chiloquin by dam removal or modification.
- Enhance natural lake and spring habitat for spawning suckers.
- Provide protected rearing habitat near the Williamson River and in Upper Klamath Lake for juveniles.
- Construct aeration or oxygen systems to improve water quality and reduce fish kills.

- Construct new, and enhance existing, wetlands fro nutrient and algae removal to improve water quality in Upper Klamath Lake.
- Conduct monitoring and compatible research for adaptive management.[2]

By April 2001, the die had been cast. A federal court in Sacramento, California agreed with the Pacific Coast Federation of Fishermen's Associations and ordered the Klamath Project to consult with the FWS and NMFS before issuing their 2001 operating plan. In effect, the court ruling by Saundra Brown Armstrong forced the Project to accept the reports supporting higher Upper Klamath Lake water levels and greater stream flows in the Klamath River.

Immediately after Judge Armstrong's decision, the Klamath Project issued its official operating plan for 2001, announcing there would be no water for basin farmers. The date was April 6th a date that became indelibly etched in the minds of basin farmers. Battle lines were quickly drawn. Responses from representatives of the various interest groups supporting and opposing the water cutoff were indicative of their positions. Marshall Staunton, Tule Lake Basin farmer said, "We knew it was coming. But we thought there would be some compromise. We didn't think it would be this drastic."[3]

Dave Solem of the Klamath Irrigation District said in frustration, "In a very short period of time, (suckers) went from being considered a nuisance to this endangered thing, which nobody could really understand."[4]

On the opposite side, expressing the opinion of many environmental groups, Felice Pace of the Klamath Forest Alliance said:

> For the first time, coho and other salmon in the Klamath River, as well as coastal and river communities that depend on salmon, will not be sacrificed in order to make full deliveries to Upper Klamath Basin irrigators. After years of struggle, we have finally achieved some balance.[5]

Glen Spain, Northwest Director for the Pacific Coast Federation of Fishermen's Associations, observed the ruling was "a step in the right direction and probably the best that can be done in a low water year."[6]

Once the cutoff was official, farming and ranching interests began a three-pronged effort to win back the lost water. In the legal arena they filed the first of several class action lawsuits, claiming the Klamath Project violated their contract rights to water under the Reclamation Act. The case was heard in Eugene, Oregon. Representing the farmers was the Klamath Water Users Association and two principal plaintiffs, Steve Kandra and John Cracka. The legal representation for the defendants represented a laundry list of groups that had strongly favored keeping all water in 2001 for the endangered fish. They included many environmental groups, Indian tribes and three federal agencies, Fish and Wildlife, the Bureau of Reclamation and the National Marine Fisheries Service. At the end of April, Federal District Judge Ann Aiken ruled against the plaintiffs, saying:

> The public interest weighs heavily on both sides of the dispute. Balancing these harms is a difficult task, and one that leads to no concrete determination. Given the high priority the law places on species threatened with extinction, I cannot find that the balance of hardship tips sharply in plaintiffs' favor.[7]

> I am bound by oath to uphold the law. The law requires the protection of suckers and salmon as endangered species and as tribal trust resources, even if the plaintiffs disagree with the manner in which the fish are protected or believe that they inequitably bear the burden of such protection.[8]

Judge Aiken concluded her ruling with advice to all parties involved in the lawsuit:

> The scarcity of water in the Klamath River Basin is a situation likely to reoccur. It is also a situation which demands effort and resolve on the part of all parties to create solutions that provide water for the necessary protection of fish, wildlife and tribal trust resources, as well as the agricultural needs of farmers and their communities. Continued litigation is not likely to assist in such a challenging endeavor. This court hopes and expects that the parties and other entities necessary to long-term solutions will continue to

pursue alternatives to meet the needs of the Klamath River Basin.[9]

In the political arena, basin farmers and their representative organizations began to heavily lobby local, state and federal elected officials. A series of impassioned meetings were held throughout the spring and summer. Some were heated, such as a Klamath County Fairgrounds gathering attended by Oregon Governor John Kitzhaber. Basin residents felt the governor had not taken an active role in advocating for their needs. The meeting at the fairgrounds was tense, the crowd less than receptive.

Other meetings were more positive. A contingent of community leaders from the Tule Lake Basin got up at 2:00 AM on May 22nd and traveled to Sacramento to testify before the State Assembly Committee on Water, Parks and Wildlife. It was an emotional meeting as speaker after speaker talked about the impact the water cutoff was having on their community. It wasn't long before the California legislature and the governor approved emergency funds to provide jobs and dig wells so basin residents could weather the crisis.

In the public venue, a series of small and large-scale demonstrations, followed by numerous acts of civil disobedience, gained nationwide media attention. The demonstration that was most meaningful to basin residents was a "Bucket Brigade" held on May 7th. A crowd of over 8,000 people gathered in Klamath Falls. After a round of speeches at Veterans Park deploring the water cutoff, the crowd formed a human chain stretching over a mile from Lake Ewauna on the west side of town to a footbridge over the "A" Canal on the east. Fifty buckets, each bearing the name of one of a state, were dipped into the lake. Eighty-five-year-old Tulelake homesteader John Prosser was the first to fill each bucket. He passed it to his son, also a farmer, who in turn passed it to his grandson. The buckets continued to flow along a line of thousands of individuals until they reached the "A" Canal, into which their contents were poured.

The Bucket Brigade of May 7th not only helped bring attention to the plight of basin farmers but elicited numerous editorials in northwest newspapers concerning the Klamath Basin water crisis. While basin residents would chafe at some of the contents, the editorials outlined many of the ongoing issues. Said the Portland *Oregonian*:

> This crisis is not just about the worst water year in recorded history in the Klamath, and not just about the federal government's decision to use the available water to protect endangered sucker fish and threatened coho salmon.
>
> It is about decades of failure to resolve conflicts over water rights that allow some upstream irrigators to take more water than they are entitled to, while others are left high and dry.
>
> It is about the facing the reality that the government long ago promised settlers and farmers more water than it could deliver without destroying some of the most significant marsh lands, wildlife refuges and wild salmon runs in the nation.
>
> The Klamath drought is a true crisis, and perhaps a catalyst for a serious re-examination of the Endangered Species Act. Put a picture of that little farm girl with the plaintive sign, "We need water," up against a shot of a slimy sucker fish, and for many people it's not even a close call.
>
> Yet it's not that simple, and nearly everyone close to the Klamath crisis understands that. It's also about people and communities downstream from the Klamath Basin, the commercial fishermen and their families who have lost their livelihoods, their way of life, because of the way water is diverted, sprinkled and polluted across the arid basin ... It's about the Klamath refuge system, among the nation's oldest ... They are last in line for water, behind suckers, salmon and farmers, and what little arrives through myriad dikes and ditches is polluted.
>
> There is a better way. It must begin with responsible elected officials, a strong local community open to change and a real commitment from the federal and state governments.

It should end with restored wetlands, a lake clean and sufficient enough for fish, a river with enough cool flow for salmon, and last but not least, a Klamath Basin with a sustainable level of irrigated family farms.[10]

The Eugene, Oregon *Register-Guard* added its perspective:

It's tempting—oh so tempting—to oversimplify and distort the Klamath Basin water crisis by declaring that it's all about protecting sucker fish and salmon at the expense of farmers.

It's ... (the) federal government—and not the suckers and salmon—that bears the ultimate responsibility for the Klamath crisis.

It's that same federal government that dug dams, drained marshes and built hundreds of miles of canals and ditches in the early 1900s, and then promised farmers that they would forever have irrigation water to feed crops—across the breadth of what once had been an arid basin.

It's that same federal government that for years has ignored its own scientists' warnings about the Klamath Project's devastating impact on the region's fish runs and waterfowl refuges.

It's that same federal government that has failed to craft a cohesive water policy that balances the needs of farmers against those of fish and wildlife—and the native American tribes, fishing industries and down-stream communities that depend on them.

Klamath Basin farmers can make it through this crisis intact, provided the federal government gives them the financial assistance they need and deserve, and moves quickly to develop a long-term strategy that balances the needs of the basin's people, its wildlife and the land itself.[11]

Throughout the summer, demonstrations continued, including acts of civil disobedience. Beginning at the end of June, there were a series of break-ins at the Upper Klamath Lake headgates, which allowed water to flow into the "A" Canal. On July 4th about 100 flag-waving protesters marched to the headgates in daylight and opened the valves. It was a symbolic act of defiance they dubbed "The Klamath Tea Party."

In order to prevent further break-ins, federal marshals were assigned to guard the headgates. By that time, a protesters' camp had been set up just outside and became known as "ground zero." Different tactics were then used to get water into the "A" Canal, including setting up pumps and running irrigation pipe around the headgates.

Protests also took other forms. Near the end of July, mounted horse-riders traveled from downtown Klamath Falls to the fence surrounding the headgates, expressing their support for basin farmers. The next day, protestors returned and placed several sheep and a donkey inside the fence. The Klamath Falls *Herald and News* explained the action. "Some (protesters) viewed them as farm animals in need of water. Others said the donkey represented Gov. John Kitzhaber and other Democrats, but a few said it was just a jackass that could be any number of government officials."[12]

The last large-scale demonstration occurred near the end of August, when "big rigs, riders on horseback, pickup trucks from several Western states and a horse-drawn wagon" arrived in Klamath Falls. Because of the size of the convoy, only a representative number vehicles were allowed into downtown Klamath Falls where they converged on Klamath County Government Center.[13] It was estimated that the parade and demonstration drew a crowd of at least 4,000 people. One of the features of the event was the delivery of a large steel bucket, made in Elko, Nevada, that commemorated the "Bucket Brigade" demonstration that had taken place three and a half months earlier.

There had been fears that the August 21st convoy would turn violent. Among those who announced they were going to attend were members of the far-right State Tyranny Response Team from the state of Washington and the Jarbidge Shovel Brigade from Nevada. Montana talk show host John Stokes, who had previously labeled environmental groups as "Fourth Reich" and "Green Nazis," also announced he planned to attend.[14] However the demonstration remained non-violent, even festive. It included lively speeches and a barbeque at the headgates.

Demonstrations at the headgates would continue until early September. The camp at the headgates closed shortly after the September 11th terrorist attack on the World Trade Center. Camp organizer Bill Ransom explained that in light of the attack, the protesters wanted to free up the federal marshals for other duties. He explained, "We are patriotic Americans, and this national emergency takes precedence."[15]

Assessing the months of demonstrations and acts of non-violent civil disobedience, Klamath Basin rancher Mike Connelly wrote in a guest editorial for the Eugene, Oregon *Register-Guard*:

> My goodness, this is a strange world we live in.
>
> On the right, we have conservative war veterans standing arm in arm, singing old spirituals, going against all odds in confronting what they see as oppressive oligarchies of political and financial power.
>
> On the left, we have Wendell Wood describing his employer, the Oregon Natural Resources Council, as "a law and order organization," and allegedly leftist commentators across the state are encouraging blind obedience to the coercive domestic policies of what they would otherwise consider the most heedless and rapacious government in the history of the industrial nation-state.
>
> The tragedy of the Klamath Basin stems not from the fact that the law has forced the economic devastation and cultural disillusionment of an entire community, but from the fact that our government has written multiple laws that contradict each other.
>
> Many of us here in the basin believe that, while we may be breaking some laws, we are defending others, such as the Reclamation Act of 1902, Oregon's state water rights laws, and that little piece of legal work called the U.S. Constitution.[16]

Months of demonstrations and appeals to politicians paid off in the form of two important decisions. On July 24th, Secretary of Interior Gale Norton announced that recent thundershowers, coupled with conservation by Upper Klamath Basin farmers would allow a limited release of water from Upper Klamath Lake. The next day, Klamath Projects Manager Jim Bryant and Merrill farmer Steve Kandra joined together to open the headgates to the "A" Canal. While basin residents praised Norton, groups supporting the use of the water exclusively for the fish accused her of bowing to political pressure. The water continued to flow into the canal for the next month.

The second major political event occurred during the first week of August. Secretary Norton said she planned to "ask the National Academy of Sciences to review the federal biologists' opinions that prompted the federal government to withhold irrigation water from farmers."[17] Her announcement pleased basin farmers. For months they had been not only questioning the science used that led to the water cutoff, but repeatedly asking that a review be conducted of the studies used as the rationale for the decision.

By the fall of 2001, the long series of demonstrations all but disappeared, while the battle within the legal and political arenas continued. At the end of August, Georgette Kirby, the daughter of a Tule Lake homesteader, filed a class-action lawsuit in Siskiyou County Superior Court in Yreka, California. The suit claimed that the Sierra Club, the Pacific Coast Federation of Fishermen's Associations, the Klamath Forest Alliance, the Golden Gate Audubon Society and the Institute of Fisheries Resources had conspired to fraudulently persuade the Bureau of Reclamation "that endangered suckers in Upper Klamath Lake and threatened coho salmon in the Klamath River need(ed) water that in past years (had) gone to farmers."[18] These organizations were targeted by the lawsuit because most of them had been involved in the federal case that had led Judge Saundra Brown Armstrong to rule that the Bureau of Reclamation had violated the Endangered Species Act. Another class action lawsuit was filed on the 11th of October by the Klamath and Tulelake Irrigation Districts. The suit claimed the government violated the Fifth Amendment of the Constitution by not paying for seized property (water intended for irrigation) and violated the Klamath Compact, which regulated irrigation water in the upper Klamath Basin. The lawsuit was patterned after a federal court ruling decided the previous April. In that case, the Fish and Wildlife Service and National Marine

Fisheries had ordered water cutoff from farmers in the Tulare Lake Basin Water Storage District to protect Chinook salmon and Delta smelt. Washington D.C. Federal Claims Judge John Paul Wiese ruled the federal government had taken property (water) away from farmers in Central California without compensating them.

In the political arena, Senators Gordon Smith and Ron Wyden, both from Oregon, had been attempting to get federal funding to promote long-term solutions for resolving the water crisis. The aid package they proposed would have provided $175 million to help ease future water conflicts by restoring fish and wildlife habitat, improving water quality, and reducing water demand. However, basin farmers did not enthusiastically embrace a number of the aid package's components—particularly funding to buy some of them out.

Efforts to pass federal aid continued through the spring of 2002. Final action was confounded by reductions in available federal dollars and by an amendment to the Smith-Wyden bill by Congressman Greg Walden. His plan was similar to one proposed by the Bureau of Reclamation in a draft report on its future long-term operation. The Walden amendment included removing most of the incentives for basin farmers giving up their land but added provisions that would create a "water bank." Under the plan, the government would buy water from farmers that would normally be used for irrigation. The resulting reduced demand for water would allow more water to be used to help the fish and wildlife refuges. Walden's plan would also provide funding to build a fish hatchery at Upper Klamath Lake to rear sucker fish. Finally, his plan would address concerns about wells on the California side of the border depleting the Tule Lake Basin aquifer. Several wells had already gone dry in the area around Malin and the hope was the water bank would reduce the dependency on California-side wells.

In October, the National Academy of Sciences announced it was moving forward with Secretary of Interior Norton's request for a review of the science used in making the decision to cutoff water to Klamath and Tule Lake Basin farmers. Twelve individuals were appointed to serve on the "Committee on Endangered and Threatened Fishes in the Klamath River Basin." Ten members were scientists from universities throughout the United States. One member was from the Institute of Ecosystem Studies in Millbrook, New York. The twelfth member was a consulting engineer from Victoria, British Columbia, Canada.

The committee was given a "fast track" timeline and asked to provide an "initial finding" by January 31, 2002 and a final report by April of 2003. Funding for the study was to come from Fish and Wildlife, the Bureau of Reclamation and the National Marine Fisheries Service. The three agencies charged the committee to:

- Review and evaluate the science underlying the biological opinions, as well as a 2001 biological assessment by Bureau of Reclamation.

- Review and evaluate what is needed environmentally for the suckers and salmon to survive as well as recover healthy populations.

- Identify newly available scientific information.

- Identify gaps in the science as well as the time and funding needed to develop strategies for saving the suckers and salmon from extinction.[19]

As the months of 2001 came to a close, there were tenuous but encouraging signs for basin water users. For one, it appeared the drought was finally over. By November and December, ample rain and snow were falling. Two, the lawsuit filed by the Klamath and Tulelake Irrigation Districts claiming Fifth Amendment violations had promise—if won, the suit would reaffirm the belief of homesteaders that they had contractual claims to Klamath Project water. Three, the long-sought review of the water cutoff decisions of the Fish and Wildlife Service, Bureau of Reclamation and the National Marine Fisheries Service had become a reality.

However, a 301-page study of the water crisis, done by Oregon State University, reminded all parties of the failures and painful experience of the year. Among the report's findings:

- There was a lack of "visionary" leadership to guide all parties through discussions, mediation and craft workable solutions;

- There was a high level of frustration over the uncertainty of future irrigation deliveries;

- There was an undercurrent of racism in the relations between the farmers and the Klamath Tribes.

- If the Klamath River flows had been allowed to drop below the levels identified in the FWS and NMFS biological opinions to protect salmon, as they had during the drought of 1992, there would have been no need to shut off irrigation to the Klamath Project.[20]

With the arrival of 2002, all parties with interest in the water of the Klamath Basin waited for the National Academy of Sciences report. In the meantime, some events began to play out in a fashion hauntingly similar to the previous year.

Near the end of January, the EarthJustice Legal Defense Fund warned the Bureau of Reclamation that they would once again file a lawsuit unless the agency prepared a plan for distributing limited water to farmers, endangered fish and wildlife refuges. Their attorney stated, "A year ago we were in a similar position. We don't want to go there again. The administration has 60 days to do what the law requires and we expect them to do that."[21]

Several days later the Bureau issued a draft biological assessment for the 2002 year. The document referred to past biological assessments, which required the Klamath Project to curtail water to basin farmers, and acknowledged that normal irrigation within the Project "could harm threatened and endangered fish most years."[22] The report suggested that more scientific studies needed to be conducted to learn exactly how much water was necessary to protect the endangered fish. It also proposed a water bank program (similar to the one Greg Walden wanted to add to the Smith-Walden federal relief plan). Finally, once the plan had been reviewed by FWS and NMFS, the Bureau wanted to begin developing a ten-year operating plan—doing so would give Reclamation the opportunity to study "how much water would be available for farms under a range of conditions, from drought to plenty, while meeting the government's obligations to Indian tribes and the Endangered Species Act." [23]

Almost immediately, environmental and commercial fishing groups criticized the new plan. Once again they threatened to file suit if water was not specifically allocated to endangered sucker fish and coho salmon. Glen Spain of the Pacific Coast Federation of Fishermen's Associations said, "This (plan) flies in the face of several legal opinions, ignores tribal obligations, ignores fisheries, and tries to assert a theory that is bankrupt, and this is that all water belongs to irrigators."[24] Steve Pedery of WaterWatch of Oregon also responded by noting, "This could have been the year they started negotiating a compromise. This is a recipe for more conflict over Klamath (water)."[25] Klamath Tribal Chairman Alan Foreman claimed the plan failed to recognize tribal water rights that had been guaranteed by treaty. Said Foreman, "In many ways, this proposal is more openly anti-tribal than previous Reclamation policies."[26]

On Wednesday, February 6, the long awaited interim report from the National Academy of Sciences' National Research Council was released. Titled "Scientific Evaluation of Biological Opinions on Endangered and Threatened Fishes in the Klamath River Basin," the report made the following conclusions:

> The NRC committee concludes that all components of the biological opinion issued by the USFWS (United States Fish and Wildlife Service) on the endangered suckers have substantial scientific support except for the recommendations concerning minimum water levels for Upper Klamath Lake ... The committee concludes that there is presently no sound scientific basis for recommending an operating regime for the Klamath Project that seeks to ensure lake levels higher on average than those occurring between 1990 and 2000.

> For the Klamath Basin coho, the NMFS (National Marine Fisheries Service) RPA involves coordination of operations as well as reduction of ramping rates for flows below main-stem dams and increased flows in the Klamath River main stem. Coordination and reduced ramping rates are well justified. The committee, however, did not find clear scientific or technical support for increased minimum flows in the Klamath River main stem. Although the proposed higher flows are intended to increase the amount of habitat in the main stem, the increase in habitat space that can occur through adjustments in water

management in dry years is mall (a few percent) and possibly insignificant.[27]

National Academy of Sciences panel member Peter Moyle explained the committee's criticism of the 2001 water cutoff decision. "It appeared to us that the status quo—what's happened in the last 10 years—is OK. That's enough to protect the fish in the short run." Moyle went on to say the ... "Incident of adult mortality (fish kills) ... have not been associated with years of low water level." In reference to the decision to increase water flows for coho salmon, Moyle stated, "The coho really likes cold water, and it doesn't matter how much water you release down the system if it's too warm."[28]

In balancing his statements, Moyle also rejected claims that the science used by FWS, the Bureau of Reclamation and NMFS was "junk." Referring to their efforts to come up with a fish protection plan, Moyle said "It's a biologically very complicated system. (The fisheries services) are really trying hard to err on the side of the fish, which is their job ... It's a real insult for people to call it junk science, because there has been a lot of good science done—it just hasn't provided a clear-cut result."[29]

Reaction to the National Academy of Science report from the groups that had supported the water cutoff varied. Officials from the Fish and Wildlife Service and National Marine Fisheries Service defended their original position. They reiterated that they were required to err on the side of the endangered fish.

The Klamath Tribes dismissed the report as inadequate, claiming "tight deadlines and 'crucial errors' led (the) National Academy of Sciences panel to incorrectly conclude there was no rationale for withholding water from Klamath Basin farmers to aid protect fish last summer."[30] Carl Ullman, attorney for the Klamath Tribes, said:

> The fundamental difficulty with the study is its narrow scope. The background chapter gives the reader almost no indication that native people have been in the basin for thousands of years and are affected by water management decisions. There's no reference anywhere in the document that tribal fisheries are so depressed—that the pain in the tribal communities is acute and has been for many years.[31]

When members of the Academy's committee conducted a hearing in Medford, Oregon on Monday, March 7, 2002 a series of speakers criticized their findings. Critics included biologists representing the various Indian tribes, government agencies and academic communities. Ronnie Pierce, fisheries biologist for the Karuk Tribe was reported to have "told the panel that it erred in concluding that the warm polluted waters running through the Klamath Project into the Klamath River may harm salmon."[32] Doug Markle, professor of fisheries at Oregon State University joined the critics when he was reported to have told the panel "that the connection between water levels in Upper Klamath Lake and the survival of short-nose suckers and Lost River suckers is much more complicated than their first report would indicate."[33]

While the National Academy of Science's report appeared to be a victory for basin farmers, it was nevertheless accepted with caution. First, it was an interim report with the final assessment not due until 2003. Second, many feared the issue would once again enter the arena of the courts, as threatened by the environmental interests. If another court order suddenly cut off water, it would be economically disastrous. Finally, it was uncertain when the Bureau of Reclamation's Klamath Project would issue their operating plan for 2002. Normally due on April 1, it appeared that it would once again be delayed—making it difficult for farmers to secure yearly startup loans from cautious banks.

Environmental groups continued their efforts to get the farmers off of the wildlife refuge lease-lands. One new tactic involved bidding on the lease-lands for the 2002 growing season. In early March, the Oregon Natural Resources Council was joined by the Klamath Forest Alliance and the Northcoast Environmental Center in making such an effort. Andy Kerr stated that if the bids were successful "We may grow waterfowl, which is in short supply, rather than crops that are in oversupply."[34] But their efforts may have been more symbolic than serious because their offer was $4,000 less than the winning bid made by two local farming brothers.

In mid-March, in an effort to help ameliorate the demand for Klamath Basin water and address the Klamath Tribes' interest in regaining lost reservation land, Secretary of Interior Norton announced that she would seriously consider turning over ownership of some National Forest land to the Klamath Tribes in exchange for their senior water rights within the Upper Klamath

Basin. In late-March, Secretary Norton traveled to Klamath Falls and joined other dignitaries on Friday, March 29 in opening the Upper Klamath Lake headgates for the 2002 irrigation system. Though the end-of-the-month act was encouraging to basin farmers, it was still viewed with caution. The Friday ceremony included protests from members of the Klamath and Yurok Tribes and from environmentalists. Collectively they claimed that Norton's action was politically motivated and would negatively impact both the fish and the environment. Threats of legal action were clearly implied.

As the weeks moved from early to late spring, the water war gradually diminished. A suit filed by the Pacific Coast Federation of Fishermen's Associations, demanding larger May water releases into the Klamath River for the benefit of salmon was rejected by Judge Sandra Brown Armstrong—the same judge that had ordered the previous year's curtailment of water deliveries to basin farmers and ranchers. Soon after this ruling, the National Marine Fisheries Service announced it would not challenge the Klamath Project's irrigation plan for 2002, but stated the Project's long-range plans would jeopardize the survival of coho salmon. Further, NMFS's biological opinion called for the Reclamation Service to set up a water bank to buy water from farmers willing to sell and in turn channel this water into the Klamath River for salmon.

With full deliveries of water, farming activity in the Klamath and Tule Lake Basins was at a fever pitch. Cover crops were greening up, cultivation for row crops was in full swing and farming appeared to be back to normal. Yet, there remained an undercurrent of concern. This was a one-year reprieve. The return of drought, future biological studies that favored withholding water for fish and wildlife, the continued decline of suckers and coho, and court rulings requiring the Bureau of Reclamation to once again shut off water to farmers and ranchers—any or all could return the basin to a crisis similar to 2001. Given the uncertainty of the future, the time was ripe for all concerned parties to establish a working relationship.

Upper Klamath Lake, focus of the controversy over appropriate water levels for irrigation and sucker fish protection.
(Photo by author).

A large crowd gathers for the May 7, 2001 Bucket Brigade in Klamath Falls, Oregon. *(Photo by Vi Montgomery)*

Above: Each bucket in the "Bucket Brigade" demonstration was filled by the Prosser family and passed along a line of people that stretched over a mile from Upper Klamath Lake to the "A" Canal. In the photo below, a Little League team from Tulelake joined many others in pouring buckets of water into the canal. *(Photos by Vi Montgomery)*

One of hundreds of signs that lined highways throughout the Klamath and Tule Lake Basins. *(Photo by author)*

EPILOGUE: PART TWO

The Years of Harvest Revisited

When the pulse of the Tule Lake Basin was taken in the mid-1980s, it was steady, reflecting a general sense of accomplishment among its residents. Homesteaders and their descendants spoke with pride about how vacant land had been turned into productive farms. Long-time residents and newcomers alike expressed their love for the basin. Binding them together were shared experiences, a strong feeling of community and a willingness to come to the aid of those in need—described as "the Tulelake way."

Fourteen years later, much of that character remained. Yet the forces of time and economic change had made a significant impact. The small towns of Merrill, Malin, Newell and Tulelake struggled to stay alive, faced with stiffened competition from the larger retail market of Klamath Falls. Farmers faced ever-increasing production costs and fluctuating crop prices. In the 1990s, passage of the North American Free Trade Agreement (NAFTA) caused more difficulties as farm produce from Canada and Mexico helped drive crop prices down. Then came the water crisis of 2001, sending the basin economy into a tailspin.

Clearly the water crisis was a defining moment in the history of the basin. It left many people feeling battered, vulnerable and wary. They experienced their extended community being torn apart by the decision to deny to them water, and they saw the painful results of that decision—people losing their jobs, auctioning off hard-earned equipment, some being forced to move, others losing the land they farmed, and many experiencing deep-seated anxiety about the uncertainty of the future. Yet the community did survive and, barring a repeat of the events of that spring and summer, it may have made them stronger.

While the four basin towns all struggled through the water crisis, the City of Tulelake was perhaps the most tested. Since the mid-1980s, it had continued to experience stagnation and decline. City Clerk Joe Cordonier had hoped the town of 1,000 would become a center for wildlife enthusiasts. He spearheaded several wildlife festivals, hoping they would become annual events and a springboard to building the town's reputation as a hub for visiting the wildlife refuges, Lava Beds and other local and regional attractions. But near the end of the 1980s, Cordonier left the City Clerk position and the festivals were no longer held.

In the decade of the 1990s, the city was still trying to find ways to stop the slow hemorrhaging of its economic base. One by one, the businesses and little shops that lined its wide downtown streets closed. By 2002, landmarks such as Tulelake Horseradish Company were gone. Its parent company, G.L. Mezzetta, Inc. kept the name and still purchased Tule Lake Basin-grown product but moved the bottling and packaging operation to Napa Valley. Also gone were the bowling alley, pharmacy, barbershops and beauty parlors. The hardware store became a seasonal irrigation supply firm.

Simultaneously, the 1990s saw very few business start-ups, and those that did often failed. There were several reasons for the high failure rate. The local market was just not large enough to keep them going. Overhead costs for starting and maintaining a business also played a heavy role. Old, established businesses had survived in Tulelake because when they started up, people still shopped locally. Hence, the owners were able to pay off the debts incurred for constructing their buildings, maintaining an adequate stock of merchandise and employing help. By the time business volume began to taper off, many of the original owners were able to get by even though sales had decreased. However, when they tried to sell their businesses, hoping to set aside money for retirement, they found few willing buyers. Those that did purchase firms were shouldered with new debt and many found their income insufficient to make the required payments.

Another obstacle to stemming the decline of local businesses was Tulelake's location in relation to Highway 139. Unlike Merrill, Oregon, where the highway went through the middle of town, Tulelake was purposely built to the west of the road. Doing so allowed it to be graced with wide and inviting streets, absent of the constant tangle with cross-through traffic. But in the long run, this layout was detrimental to the town's economy. When Highway 139 became a high-speed route and autos were able to travel longer distances between fuel stops, the town was bypassed by those hurrying north and south. By 2000, there were no gas stations left along the highway and the land paralleling the west side was uninviting—filled with dilapidated warehouses and infrequently used railroad tracks. Other than two signs at the northern and southern city limits announcing "Tulelake" and a speed zone in between, there was little left to indicate any reason for motorists to travel through the town.

In spite of these challenges, there have been efforts to revitalize Tulelake. Many of the town's leaders, business owners and citizens remain optimistic that once they have found a viable economic niche, the economy can be turned around. One of those advocates is Joe Cordonier, who returned to the City Clerk position after a ten-year absence. "Right now we are just a reduced speed zone," he says, explaining that one of his object- ives is finding ways to get people to turn west into downtown.[1] Capturing the business of even a small fraction of the thousands of travelers on Highway 139 would make a significant difference in the town's economy.

Cordonier believes that two major things will help the town. Economic diversification is one—finding businesses that aren't just reliant on local trade. These might include small manu- facturing firms and regional distribution centers. Another possi- bility is promoting Tulelake as a hub for regional tourism and wildlife enthusiasts. The city's central location is ideal for visiting the Tule Lake and Lower Klamath Wildlife Refuges, the Lava Bed National Monument, and the War Relocation Authority Intern- ment Camp at Newell.

One local business is already promoting the town as a central location for touring the area. Fe's Bed and Breakfast, started by Bob and Fe Galeoto in September of 2000, targets people who want to visit local and regional sites. In tandem with the bed and breakfast, Bob Galeoto operates LuCena West Tours, which offers guided tours including a bus for transporting groups. While the B & B is already popular, attracting not only tourists but relatives and friends of Tulelake residents, the tour company has not yet been utilized to its fullest extent. Galeoto knows that it will take more time and a lot of work to convince people that Tulelake is the ideal hub for visiting the region.

There are several other new and renovated businesses in Tulelake whose owners have been willing to swim against the tide of economic decline. Many of them are located along Main Street. Mike Collins bought and renovated the landmark "Jolly Cone" hamburger stand. A half block to the south, Carmen and Rogelio Villalpando opened a popular Mexican restaurant, "Villalpandos," in December of 2000. Further down Main, Mike Bunch expanded his automotive related businesses by joining his fiancee Christine Nelson in opening a specialty shop. "Ernest Gilbeys," named after Bunch's chocolate Lab "Ernie," sells gourmet foods, including Tulelake Horseradish, as well as candy, cigars and other unique items. Across the street, Barbara Hellman opened "Not Just One" in late 1999, a store offering consigned crafts and antiques. She expanded in 2001 and opened a cafe, the "Daily Goose," which is managed by her daughter, Vi Montgomery. The combined stores occupy the building that formerly housed Tulelake's pharmacy.

Rebuilding Tulelake's economic base is only one challenge faced by its citizens. Another is addressing the social needs of many of the basin's residents. Outside of school-based sports and clubs, the town has had very few youth and family centered activities and services—especially for the Hispanic community.

Concerned about the lack of community services and growth in local gang activity, business and school leaders began meeting several years ago to develop an action plan. Out of a lengthy series of meetings, they proposed to build a youth and community services center to be located on property adjacent to Tulelake High School. Their efforts paid off and they received several grants, including one from the California Youth Authority. The center, to be called the "Honker," will be completed in the summer of 2002 and will house a full-sized gymnasium, cafeteria, recreation rooms and offices. It will offer a wide variety of youth centered social and recreational activities, as well as support services for families within the Tule Lake Basin.

In the midst of the efforts to rebuild Tulelake's economic and social base, the drought and water cutoff of 2001 struck the basin. The impact on the town was significant. Many of the town's residents were directly connected to agriculture as field workers, farm managers, and small business owners. Collectively they faced losing their jobs and their businesses, and being forced to move. While at first the water crisis was debilitating for many, the event became a powerful unifying force that helped bring people together. Their energy became focused on the community's survival and gave additional meaning to "the Tulelake way." In the long run, this event may have been the catalyst for the revitalization of the town.

For several weeks after the April 5, 2001 announcement by the Klamath Project that water would not be coming to the Tule Lake

Basin, people in the community were paralyzed by disbelief. Why wasn't the long-range impact on people's lives taken into consideration when such drastic action was taken? How would they survive in absence of the economic base upon which they depended? By May, the community's despair had been transferred into action. In a pattern that matched efforts throughout the Klamath Basin, people became involved in a wide variety of efforts to keep the community together.

On the political front, perhaps the most important group effort occurred on May 22nd. A contingent of basin citizens, including Venancio Hernandez, Mike Byrne, his daughter Brianna, Tony Giacomelli, Sharron Molder and Nancy Huffman got up at 2 in the morning to travel by van to Sacramento. There they testified before the State Assembly Committee on Water, Parks and Wildlife at a hearing set up by Assemblyman Richard "Dick" Dickerson. Each presented information on the impact of the water cutoff and expressed their concern about the future of the community.

Everyone in the group spoke persuasively about the impact of the water cutoff. Tony Giacomelli, owner and manager of Jock's Supermarket in Tulelake, testified that "the economy (of the basic) is farming. That's it—if farming goes, everything goes."[2] Basin rancher Mike Byrne questioned the validity of the science used to make the water cutoff decision. His daughter, Brianna, a senior at Tulelake High School, expressed her concern about the impact the water crisis was having on students and the cloud it placed on their future as farmers. Sharron Molder, Principal of Tulelake High School, talked about the impact of the water crisis on her students. She expressed fear that many families would be forced to move away. Modoc County Supervisor Nancy Huffman testified on the impact the developing water crisis was having on the homesteaders and other residents in the basin.

Among the most powerful speakers was Venancio Hernandez who talked about his career in the Tule Lake Basin, beginning as a migrant worker in 1973, then as a farm manager and finally as an independent farmer. He and his wife Clementina, had raised five children—two still in the Tulelake schools, one married, one in the service and one in college. Though lower crop prices had made it difficult for him to make ends meet, he was surviving as a farmer until the water cutoff forced him out of business. He was unable to pay the rent on the land he farmed and had to auction off all of his equipment.

When the Tulelake contingent finished their testimony, they were unsure about its impact. Certainly members of the Assembly Committee had taken notice, but it was unclear whether any action would be taken. Tony Giacomelli remembers the discussion in the van on the way back home. "We talked about the impact of our testimony, how once again we told our story and felt our pain, but so what? Did they really hear us?"[3]

They were indeed heard. Within several weeks, residents of the basin were told that Governor Gray Davis and the California State Legislature were authorizing emergency funds for the basin. The funding came in several forms. Some of the money was used to finance the drilling of ten wells to provide the farmers with badly needed water. Other money went to the City of Tulelake to help with water improvement projects. Perhaps most important, funds were provided for job assistance and social service programs. The goal was to help farm workers and small business owners weather the crisis and provide families with a variety of social services. Coordination of these programs was through the Tulelake Community Partnership, housed in a building next to Tulelake Elementary School. Under the directorship of Joan Loustalet, the Partnership helped create jobs for many unemployed residents.

Among the beneficial spin-offs of the jobs program was pre-paid labor to help build a new central office and Museum of Local History at the Tulelake-Butte Valley Fairgrounds. The fair board had already set aside $101,000 for capital improvements, but this was far from enough to build the kind of facility that was needed. However, with funds for the labor coming from the emergency jobs program, and an outpouring of community support—including much of the lumber, cement and other building supplies provided at cost—the project became a reality. Construction began in early 2002, with a completion date of late spring to early summer. Fairgrounds Manager Cindy Wright coordinated the entire project and was the principal designer of the museum's layout. When done, it will trace the development of the Tule Lake Basin, from the first Native American inhabitants, through early white settlement, the Modoc War, reclamation of Tule Lake, homesteading and the WRA internment camp at Newell. The museum will also commemorate the contributions of basin veterans in the wars of the 20th century. Visitors to the museum will be given a cassette player and headphones to direct them through the labyrinth of displays. The dream of Wright and City Clerk Joe Cordonier is that the museum, which will be open year-round, will become one of the magnets to draw travelers off of Highway 139.

Though it has been more than a year since the start of the water crisis, there are still many reminders of the bitter fight. Only a fraction of the hundreds of signs that lined Highway 139 are left, but nevertheless the ones that remain are testimony to the strong sentiment in the basin.

OUR FUTURE DEPENDS ON WATER

WELCOME TO THE KLAMATH PROJECT, LARGEST WATER THEFT IN HISTORY

UNEMPLOYED FARMER WILL FARM FOR FOOD

WATER FOR FARMS, NOT FOR SUCKERS, AMEND THE ESA

KLAMATH   BUREAU   OF   RECLAMATION   SUCKER PROJECT

Perhaps the cleverest of the signs was one written by Malin area farmer Fred Simon. He put it up on Highway 139 near the California-Oregon border and it read "CALL 911, SOME SUCKER STOLE OUR WATER." The next morning, Walter Woodhouse, a Tulelake Elementary School student, was headed with his family to the May 6th Bucket Brigade demonstration in Klamath Falls. Needing to write something on a placard he was going to carry, he saw Simon's sign and jotted down the slogan. Walter was photographed at the demonstration and the picture of the sign was sent over the AP wires throughout the United States. Not long after, the slogan appeared on widely distributed bumper stickers. In the days that followed, Simon was surprised to learn that some members of the Klamath Tribes were offended by the slogan and by other signs that made negative comments about the sucker fish. Said Klamath Tribes member Adrian Witcraft "We're not telling anybody they have to eat a sucker. But you don't have to mock another culture. This fish meant something to my grandparents."[4]

At the north entrance to the Tule Lake Wildlife Refuge are two other signs that indicate the on-going tension between farmers and the federal government. The Staunton family, who owns land adjacent to the Refuge entrance, erected two signs patterned after the ones used by the nation's refuges and national parks. One of them says:

> PLEASE THANK THE
> U.S. FISH AND WILDLIFE SERVICE
> & MARINE FISHERY SERVICE
> FOR DESTROYING
> THE ECO-SYSTEM AND THE
> ECONOMY OF THE BASIN

The other sign references well water that local farmers sent to the Tule Lake Wildlife Refuge during the water crisis:

> PLEASE THANK
> TULELAKE IRRIGATION DIST.
> INDIVIDUAL GROWERS FOR
> SUPPLYING GROUND WATER
> TO AREA REFUGES
> COOPERATION AT WORK TO
> IMPROVE ECONOMY AND ECO SYSTEM

Phil Norton, Manager for the Klamath Basin Wildlife Refuges, has certainly felt the tension. He assumed the manager's position a year before the water crisis. Given the legal mandates of the Endangered Species Act, the strong environmental program of the Clinton Administration, and his own experience as a wildlife manager at other federal refuges, Norton advocated for an end to farming on the Tule Lake and Lower Klamath Lake lease-lands. It was a political landmine that he openly admits stepping into.

Norton initially believed that he had a solution for the lease-land controversy. He called it the "15 for 15 Program." The federal government would buy 15,000 acres of Tule Lake Basin land from farmers willing to sell. The land would then be turned over to the Tule Lake Irrigation District to lease out to farmers. In return, 15,000 acres of refuge lease-land would be taken out of production.

But most basin farmers soundly rejected the "willing sellers" or "15 for 15 Program." They believed it was part of a greater conspiracy to force them off their land entirely. Further, it was argued that removing 15,000 acres from production would harm the long-term economy of the basin. Besides, most basin farmers were of the opinion that farming on the refuges was good for wildlife, not detrimental.

Norton has since backed down from his "15 for 15" proposal and is now looking at various ways to promote farming and wildlife preservation as a unified effort. On the Tule Lake Refuge, as part of a pest management program, he's planning to rotate the location of the lease-lands and watered "sump" areas. He's also looking at model projects begun by farmers in other parts of California that promote the growth of crops and provide protective habitat for endangered species at the same time.[5]

When talking with basin residents, conversations invariably gravitate to their feelings about the 2001 water crisis. Phil Krizo, World War II veteran and 1940s homesteader, said he was shocked when the water was cut off.

> I don't think anyone thought something like this would happen in the United States. Maybe another country, but not the United States. One of the reasons ... is because the Klamath Project had a ... right to the water in Upper Klamath Lake and it states right on our title to our land, a title signed by the President of the United States, that we have title to that water and so do our descendants.[6]

Joe Victorine, another World War II veteran and 1940s homesteader said:

> In past years we got along just fine. We had drought years before and we shared. If people had just kept out of here ... (including those) "greenies" we'd be all right. These fish have absolutely nothing to do with it. The object was to stop agriculture in the Klamath Basin. Would you deprive four-hundred varieties of animals, fish and plants to save two? A (true) environmentalist would have never done that. They would have divided (the water) up and done the best they could. These greenies simply want the farmers out of here.[7]

Tulelake Elementary School Teacher Renee Kohler spoke of her experiences working with children in her classroom. "You know ... you teach them American democracy and how great this country is. Then you see the government take away their (families') livelihood. That was hard to explain to kids."[8]

Denny Kalina, owner of the Kalina Hardware store in Malin and a descendant of the founder of the little town, said his business volume was substantially reduced in 2001. He also commented on the overall decline of the basin's economic base— caused both by the water crisis and the competition created under NAFTA. "In 1980 there were twenty-nine potato sheds in the basin and now there are only three to five."[9]

In addition to being Fairgrounds Manager, Cindy Wright continues to farm and ranch with her husband Gary. During the water crisis they were able to stay in operation only because they were fortunate enough to sink a producing well. They were able to survive but witnessed many of their neighbors facing economic ruin. Wright says she felt guilty "because you looked at neighbors who didn't make it through."[10] Paul Christy, another World War II veteran and 1940s homesteader, agreed with Wright. He too felt guilty because he was fortunate to have been able to water his crops using a neighbor's well while all around him were dry fields.[11]

Sharron Molder, Principal of Tulelake High School, saw the impact of the crisis on her students. However, Molder proudly remembers how they became a strong force in support of the basin's farmers. They testified in front of committees and participated in many of the demonstrations. Molder also commented on the changes she had gone through since moving to the basin from the San Francisco Bay area. There she had been a member of the Audubon Society and supported preservation of bird habitat. She remains concerned about wildlife, but now questions the motivation of many environmental groups. She witnessed and experienced what she perceived to be strident behavior—an all or nothing attitude with no room for reasonable dialogue and compromise. Based on this experience, she concluded, "If they get their way, there will be no more us."[12]

Venancio Hernandez, who made such a strong impact on the California legislative committee, observed that the biggest losers in the fight over water have been the poor. "If it hadn't been for the California emergency assistance program, many families would have had to move away in order to survive."[13]

A relative newcomer to Tulelake is Jessie Larson. She and her recently deceased husband, moved to town in 1998 to be near a daughter living in Klamath Falls. Since that time she has become a tireless promoter of the basin—as a reporter for the *Lost River Star*, and as volunteer for many civil activities. She vividly remembers that people were indignant when the water was cutoff. They couldn't believe that it had happened. But, Jessie never saw anyone emotionally out of control. They were hurt and worried. They were mad, but never inappropriate.[14]

Luis Aceves has lived in Tulelake for thirty-three years and has watched the Hispanic community grow from a scattering of farm workers to become the town's majority population. He and his wife Alice raised three children of their own and a fourth child they took into their home. All of the children are college graduates. Aceves is deeply rooted in the community and cares deeply about its people. "The decision to stop water flowing to farm fields in the basin was devastating. I know personally of fifteen to twenty families that were forced to move away."[15]

Bill Ganger is the son of parents who homesteaded in 1928. Before moving to the basin in the early years of farming, his father had worked at the power plant at the Bull Run Dam, east of Portland, Oregon. As a long-time basin resident, Ganger compared the drought of 1992 with 2001. He didn't remember any reports of fish kills in 1992. Farmers were encouraged to conserve water, including not flood-irrigating their land. He believes that similar conservation efforts could have been made in the summer of 2001 and that cutting off all water was unnecessary. He is hopeful that in the future all of those with claims to Klamath Basin water will work out an acceptable compromise.[16]

John Crawford has been involved in water issues for over ten years. In that time he has immersed himself in the myriad details of the law and science related to fish habitat and survival. In advocating for farm interests in the basin, he's played the role of lawyer, biologist and politician. Crawford became a leading spokesman for farming interests and was often quoted in local and national media. He made at least fourteen trips to Washington, D.C. to speak with politicians and government officials about the developing crisis. What frustrates Crawford is that the agencies that made the decisions to cut off the water dismissed the scientific studies that took the opposite positions on sucker and salmon survival—specifically that higher water levels in Upper Klamath Lake were detrimental to suckers and greater flows in the Klamath River harmed the salmon. While Crawford is encouraged by the National Academy of Sciences report, which he believes supports the position that the decision to cutoff the water last summer was inappropriate, he remains worried that the issue if far from over. Like many other basin farmers, he is worried that the same federal judges will again order a water cutoff. However, he believes the federal court will rule more in their favor in the future, since the federal government has become more supportive of the farmers' position. What John Crawford wants more than anything else, for the sake of his family, is to be a farmer again. After all the years of battle, "all I want to do is be back on my tractor."[17]

Steve Kandra, past president of the Klamath Irrigation District, farms at several locations in the Tule Lake Basin. He has been on the Hatfield Upper Klamath Basin Working Group for much of the time it has been in operation. He's also been a spokesman for basin farms and a litigant in a class action suit filed in April, 2001 to get water released. When asked why something hadn't been worked out within the Hatfield Group before the water crisis, Kandra expressed frustration. He believed that the Working Group had come up with a number of proposals but "the agencies, (among them) Fish and Wildlife ... were more intent on regulation than they were in facilitating the projects." With a change in the leadership at the federal level, Kandra is now more optimistic that agreements can be worked out. "We have an administration that seems to be saying, 'What's it going to take to fix it? Let's do the projects and things we can do rather than saying, 'How can we regulate it?' "[18]

Kandra is also critical of some of the environmental groups that continue to push for a total water cutoff. He questions both their tactics and their motives.

> I call them "gadfly businesses." Crisis equals money and that's where those folks are at. I think some of (them) out there are not as concerned about the wildlife resources and ecosystem as they are about their personal agendas and their business, the politics and control they have. If they really cared, their budgets would be tied up in restoration rather than litigation.[19]

Kandra's comments were made while standing on land he owns just north of the Tule Lake Wildlife Refuge. During his conversation, he talked of the relationship between his land and the basin's wildlife.

> You know, all you need to do is stand here in this spot ... and in a few minutes there will be ten thousand snow geese flying around. Down in that ditch over there are coots and mallards swimming about. Later this evening you will see thousands of birds come into that field where there's grain. They're foraging on high protein material, and they'll come into that potato field and work on the dried starch. That's different from some natural systems, but I think that's good. With certain management practices, we are a natural fit. I love this place ... (that) is why I'm a little tenacious about it.[20]

What about the future? Will there be a resolution based on the lessons of the last year and a half or will the water crisis continue into the distant future? There have already been so many lost opportunities for finding mutually acceptable solutions.

It will be extremely difficult to develop long-range solutions that won't be challenged by one group or another. Yet, it is not an impossible task. Basin farmers continue to say they care deeply for the wildlife of the basin with which they share their land. They are open to proactive ways to maintain a healthy eco-system and have offered alternative plans to do so. What they are looking for is a balance, a plan that doesn't destroy their livelihood. They hope that reasonable environmental groups will emerge that are project oriented and not bent on forcing change through litigation. They want to deal with government agents that are oriented toward facilitation rather than regulation. Above all, they want programs that are balanced and fair.

Can mutually beneficial programs be developed? Yes, but it will take enormous effort, strong leadership, compromise, a sharing of the burden and assurances that people will not be forced off their land. The most extreme positions of all parties are going to have to be put aside. There will need to be recognition that some farming practices are harmful to wildlife, especially pesticides leaching back into the water delivery systems. There will need to be funding to assist farmers in developing wildlife habitat, experimenting with different crops and different growing techniques. There will also need to be acknowledgment on the part of environmentalists that farming is not inherently bad for wildlife, and that is not fair or realistic to expect people to abandon land that has been under cultivation for a great many years.

The Klamath and Tule Lake Basins are one of the last regions in this country not dominated by corporate farms. Contrary to the claims of some, the land is fertile and productive—for both crops and wildlife. Wouldn't it be unique and exciting to develop a model program in the basin that successfully incorporated farming and wildlife preservation? Instead of spending great sums of money and time in court, how about using all that energy and those dollars to develop experimental programs. It could become the "niche" Joe Cordonier has been looking for to put Tulelake on the map. "Come see the place where farmers work to feed America and preserve wildlife."

Idealistic? Maybe, but why not give it a try? Because if folks don't somehow manage to come together, this battle is going to go on for a long, long time.

A few signs still remain from the water war of 2001. By late spring of 2002, it was unclear whether the dispute would be resolved in the courts, through legislation or by compromise. *(Photos by author)*

Steve Kandra working land his family owns adjacent to the Tule Lake Wildlife Refuge. Millions of geese and other wildlife pass through here annually. *(Photo by author)*

At a Spring 2002 meeting at the Tulelake-Butte Valley Fairgrounds, homesteaders and basin residents talk about their experiences during the water crisis. <u>Above left</u>: Barbara and Phil Krizo, 1940s homesteaders. <u>Above right</u>: David Misso and Renee Kohler, both employees of the Tulelake Basin Joint Unified School District. <u>Below left</u>: Malin businessman Denny Kalina and Tulelake farmer Venancio Hernandez. <u>Below right</u>: 1940s homesteaders Ralph Morrill, David Hatfield, Joe Victorine and Roy Walldin. *(Photos by author)*

<u>Above left</u>: The new Tulelake-Butte Valley Fair offices and Museum of Local History under construction. Completion is scheduled for the summer of 2002. Displays will include an original barrack from the Tule Lake Internment Camp (shown on the <u>right</u>), later used as a homesteader home. <u>Below</u>: "Fe's Bed and Breakfast," one of several new businesses that have opened in Tulelake in the last two years. *(Photos by author)*

The Tulelake-Butte Valley Fair hosted the World Siphon-Tube Championship in the 1950s. *(Photo courtesy Tulelake-Butte Valley Fair, Museum of Local History)*

TULE LAKE BASIN HOMESTEADERS: 1922 to 1949

Tule Lake Basin Homesteaders Awarded Land

Alphabetical Listing Homesteader's Name	Homestead Number	Listing by Number Homesteader's Name	
Abel, Raymond D.	4323	4001	Buel, Ivan
Ablard, Louis Kenneth	5104	4002	Chenal, Edward M.
Ackley, Lawrence Lyle	5052	4003	Elzner, F.J.
Ackley, Orvin Ray II	5006	4004	Fayne, Michael
Adams, Evea	4039	4005	Gaines, Claude
Adams, J. Frank & Adams, Will W.	4038	4006	Hatfield, William H.
Adams, Robert S. & Adams, Evea	4101	4007	Lousenco, Felisberto
Adams, Will W.	4102	4008	McGuire, Thomas
Aikins, George R.	4212	4009	Michelbrook, Herbert S.
Aikins, Portia K.	4181	4010	Van Blaricom, Fred A.
Allen, Arthur Chapel	4432	4011	Viken, Sever O.
Anderson, Robert Franklin	4501	4012	Wall, Sam J.
Anderson, Samuel	4434	4013	Christensen, George Andrew
Anderson, Wesley Niles	4500	4014	McAuliffe, Eugene
Anderson, Wesley P.	4457	4015	Schultz, O.A.
Anderson, William H.	4243	4016	Hammond, Eugene W.
Anklin, William H.	4036	4017	Heiken, Ernest Harm
Arthur, Glen	5034	4018	Lewis, Paul D.
Askew, Thomas Read	4239	4019	Schultz, Alfred W.

Ayres, William Harvey	5099	4020	Ratliff, John Richard
Badker, Frank Albert	5033	4021	Street, Andrew Erwin
Bailey, Everett V.	4452	4022	Drazil, Vaclav
Baker, Raymond R.	4415	4023	Merevantz, John
Barcus, Maurice Claude	5046	4024	Johnson, William O.
Barks, Clyde Hobson	4316	4025	Micka, Jerry
Barks, William Pinkney	4559	4026	Victorin, Tony
Barleen, Virgil Henry	4577	4027	Johnson, Augusta Belle
Barr, J. Randolph	4279	4028	Coate, Andrew Joseph
Barrett, Harold Taylor	4497	4029	Pierce, Lester D.
Bartlett, Eugene Bickford	5054	4030	Campbell, Mary Ellen Eastwood
Beck, Albert	4322	4031	Durkee, Howard F.
Beck, Ardith L.	5038	4032	Pope, Dora O. (Owner)
Bell, Frank Eugene	4337	4033	Krejci, Joseph
Bell, James A.	4552	4034	Clogston, Lillian J.
Bentley, Ervan L.	4155	4035	Eldridge, William C.
Bergman, Peter C.	4281	4036	Anklin, William H.
Berry, Herbert F.	4306	4037	------------------------
Bertwistle, Clatus Earl	5005	4038	Adams, J. Frank & Adams, Will W.
Bettandorff, John N.	4529	4039	Adams, Evea
Bibby, Raymond Robert	4579	4098	California Oregon Power Co.
Bierly, Amos Walter	4498	4099	Great Northern Railway
Birtwistle, Lee	4458	4100	Central Pacific Railway
Bitter, Vernon E.	4409	4101	Adams, Robert S. & Adams, Evea
Bolesta, Eleanor Jane	4486	4102	Adams, Will W.
Bollenbaugh, Ralph	4380	4103	Brown, Andrew
Bone, John Burgess	4466	4104	Brown, Ross H.
Borrows, Robert Eugene	4560	4105	Brunton, J. Ernest
Bowen, Stone A.	4460	4106	Buell, Hathaway
Bradbury, Lloyd L.	4442	4107	Burriss, Lois E.
Bradbury, Stanley	4550	4108	Cacka, Frank
Bradley, Gale Jack	5101	4109	Cacka, John
Bradley, William E.	4574	4110	Cummings, Lawrence J.
Brainard, Lawson A.	4308	4111	Dobrovsky, James A.
Brown, Andrew	4103	4112	Donahoe, Robert
Brown, Andrew M.	4361	4113	Dunbar, F.G. (Floyd)
Brown, James M.	4401	4114	Dunnington, Clint Bryan
Brown, Jesse A.	4160	4115	Freund, Jethro Clarence

Name	No.	No.	Name
Brown, Lee E.	4171	4116	Garlick, Ray W.
Brown, Marion C.	4148	4117	Gentry, Karl D.
Brown, Patrick G.	4271	4118	Gray, Charles C.
Brown, Ross H.	4104	4119	Hammer, Oscar B
Brown, Roy L.	4350	4120	Hedlund, Lars J. (Johan)
Brownell, Austin B.	4391	4121	Higler, Joseph
Brunton, J. Ernest	4105	4122	Hogue, Ernest W.
Bryant, Oliver Earl	4538	4123	Howell, Frank
Buchanan, Walter Dean	4509	4124	Hoyman, Leonard I.
Buckingham, Bert G.	4532	4125	Lien, Ole N.
Buckingham, Keith Stanley	4488	4126	Lund, Bert
Buel, Ivan	4001	4127	McElroy, Harold M.
Buell, Cecil A.	4199	4128	Peterson, Benjamin F.
Buell, Hathaway	4106	4129	Reagan, Leroy B.
Burgess, William Polk	5049	4130	Reynolds, Walter S.
Burke, John F.	4262	4131	Simpson, Paul Quinton
Burman, John Rudolph	4170	4132	Spence, Preston J. M.
Burriss, Lois E.	4107	4133	Starns, Elmer
Bursik, Vaclav Jacob	5045	4134	Stewart, Merwin C.
Bush (or Busch), John	4400	4135	Treloar, Ernest
Byron, John Fredrick	4518	4136	Tucker, Everett L.
Cacka, Frank	4108	4137	Waldrip, Charles
Cacka, John	4109	4138	Wells, Leonal J.
Calhoun, Samuel T.	4241	4139	Williams, Charles J.
California Oregon Power Co.	4098	4140	Woldsen, Viggo
Callendine, Charles	4403	4141	Yordy, Ralph T.
Campbell, Mary Ellen Eastwood	4030	4142	Young, Armine O.
Campbell, Roy S.	4383	4143	Zlabek, Frank F.
Carman, David L.	5028	4144	Zumpfe, Joseph
Carter, Ralph L.	4459	4145	James, Christian
Casey, Patrick	4251	4146	McQuesten, Leavitt M.
Cashman, William James	5040	4147	Winter, Arthur L.
Central Pacific Railway	4100	4148	Brown, Marion C.
Chamberlain, Charles C.	4333	4149	Culver, Jesse Lea
Chambers, Woodrow J.	5059	4150	Halousek, William V.
Charles R. Dyer	4468	4151	Hatfield, William H.
Charley, Eldred Floyd	4478	4152	Lourenco, Felisberto
Chatburn, Thomas W.	4211	4153	Walsch, Richard
Chenal, Edward M.	4002	4154	Heim, Theodor
Cherry, Melvin W.	4359	4155	Bentley, Ervan L.

Christensen, George Andrew	4013
Christy, Marvin Miller	5093
Christy, Paul Edward	4542
Clink, Walter Livingston	4353
Clogston, Lillian J.	4034
Coakley, John Leonard	4168
Coate, Andrew Joseph	4028
Coley, Rufus	4289
Congdon, Shirley Albert	4535
Cooper, Edwin M.	4236
Corcoran, Gerald Eugene	4499
Corrie, John Quincy	4351
Costley, Eugene J.	4397
Coulson, John S.	4429
Cowling, Henry James	5064
Cox, Charles E.	4417
Craft, William U.	4451
Crawford, Daniel Martin	4412
Crawford, Lawrence Imber	4320
Crawford, William Marvin	4487
Cripps, A. Yarnell	4285
Cripps, Amos B.	4235
Criss, Marvin Delmer	5022
Crowther, George H.	4475
Cuddy, Clement William	4576
Culver, Jesse Lea	4149
Cummings, Lawrence J.	4110
Cushman, Melvin L.	4441
Dahle, Norman Grant	4334
Darrow, Glen Edward	4513
Davis, Charles S.	4220
Davis, Edwin A.	4221
Davis, Paul A.	4303
Davis, Wesley S.	4157
Day, George H.	4309
Dayton, Howard L.	4372
Dean, John Merlin	5063
Decker, Clifford J.	4476
Delaney, George A.	4276
Denton, Lee S.	4198

4156	Fugate, A. E. (Arden Edgar)
4157	Davis, Wesley S.
4158	Taylor, Jacob W.
4159	Turnbaugh, Lester
4160	Brown, Jesse A.
4161	Stearns, Carey Sumner
4162	Yanek, John
4163	Victorin, Frank
4164	Hannon, Richard K.
4165	Trippe, William Wells
4166	Mitchell, Harry Earl
4167	Storey, Walter
4168	Coakley, John Leonard
4169	Johnson, French E.
4170	Burman, John Rudolph
4171	Brown, Lee E.
4172	Maupin, Charles
4173	Kinsey, Roscoe R.
4174	Stewart, Earl Ulyssis
4175	Roberts, Harrison M.
4176	Minnas, Dean Hazlette
4177	Krupka, Henry
4178	Lidell, John A.
4179	Turnbaugh, David W.
4180	Hunt, John William
4181	Aikins, Portia K.
4182	Young, Roy O.
4183	Griffith, Levi J.
4184	Laird, Marion Raymond
4185	Sullivan, Tim T.
4186	Takacs, Stephen J.
4187	Sanders, James W.
4188	Taylor, Raymond
4189	Galarneau, Mike
4190	Klem, Joseph
4191	Taylor, Carl S.
4192	McCollum, Elmer
4193	Spolek, William M.
4194	Eastwood, Simeon W.
4195	Wolfe, Ival D.

Depuy, Ora Melvin	5107	4196	Kandra, John Jr.
DeShon, James Bernard	5096	4197	Ragnus, John Vaclav
Detwiler, Willard C.	4228	4198	Denton, Lee S.
Dobrovsky, James A.	4111	4199	Buell, Cecil A.
Donahoe, Robert	4112	4200	McMurphy, Fred E.
Douglass, George Alton Jr.	4494	4201	Markusen, Christian
Drazil, Vaclav	4022	4202	Smith, Richard M.
Duerksen, Irvin Earl	5024	4203	Trout, Frank M.
Duggan, Margaret O.S.	4284	4204	Snider, John T.
Dunbar, F.G. (Floyd)	4113	4205	Steyakal, Jacob
Duncan, Kenneth H.	4544	4206	Stevenson, James C.
Dunlap, Leeth S.	4341	4207	McDaniel, Edward
Dunnington, Clint Bryan	4114	4208	Schlichter, Mike H.
Durkee, Everett H.	4255	4209	Ziemenczuk, Henry
Durkee, Howard F.	4031	4210	Moore, Clyde E.
DuVall, Gaylord R.	5089	4211	Chatburn, Thomas W.
Easley, Roy B.	4463	4212	Aikins, George R.
Eastwood, Simeon W.	4194	4213	Riddle, Glenn N.
Edwards, Charles Welton	4480	4214	Rock, Elmer
Edwards, Wilbur S.	4340	4215	Keck, Asa Charles
Eisenbis, Walter	5007	4216	Newton, Thomas W.
Eldridge, William C.	4035	4217	Rockhill, Ferne D.
Elzner, F.J.	4003	4218	Golden, Walter C.
Elzner, Franklin W.	4545	4219	Frey, George H.
England, John W.	4264	4220	Davis, Charles S.
Ernst, Franklin H.	4443	4221	Davis, Edwin A.
Fabianek, John	4256	4222	Thacher, Boyd T.
Falconer, Richard Donaldson	5058	4223	Kirby, LeRoy C.
Fayne, Michael	4004	4224	Fugate, Roy B.
Fensler, Clarke W.	4305	4225	Peart, John
Ferrari, Frank	4298	4226	Heitz, Charles J.
Ferrel, larry	4492	4227	Tison, Albert S.
Finchum, Walter J.	4232	4228	Detwiler, Willard C.
Fish, Theodore J.	4420	4229	O'Keeffe, Patrick John
Fisher, Peter	4237	4230	Smith, Alfred D.
Fleming, Max William	4549	4231	Knight, Harvey A.
Flynn, Con	4250	4232	Finchum, Walter J.
Ford, Charles B.	4288	4233	Krizo, Frank
Frailey, Lum C.	4419	4234	Murphy, Jerry C.
Freund, Jethro Clarence	4115	4235	Cripps, Amos B.

Frey, George H.	4219	4236	Cooper, Edwin M.
Fugate, A. E. (Arden Edgar)	4156	4237	Fisher, Peter
Fugate, Roy B.	4224	4238	Motschenbacher, Lawrence W.
Fuller, Richard Lay	4484	4239	Askew, Thomas Read
Gaines, Claude	4005	4240	Newton, Almo H.
Galarneau, Mike	4189	4241	Calhoun, Samuel T.
Galloway, Harry R.	4422	4242	O'Keefe, Toby
Ganger, Ralph Andrew	4314	4243	Anderson, William H.
Garlick, Ray W.	4116	4244	Martin, Harry L.
Gentry, Karl D.	4117	4245	Havlina, Chester
George, Jeanne E.	4566	4246	Havlina, Vincent
Gilliland, Elmer A.	4414	4247	Havlina, Edward J.
Girvin, Russel Wayne	5041	4248	Rosenberg, John Wesley
Goldblatt, Arthur	4464	4249	Kelleher, Con
Golden, Walter C.	4218	4250	Flynn, Con
Goldlewski, Theophile	4526	4251	Casey, Patrick
Goodrich, Chandler P.	4265	4252	Kelleher, John
Goodrich, Fred G.	4278	4253	Lacey, Richard Owen
Gooing, Roy Elwyn	5095	4254	Stewart, Malcolm M.
Gorham, Thomas Albert	5002	4255	Durkee, Everett H.
Gray, Charles C.	4118	4256	Fabianek, John
Great Northern Railway	4099	4257	Kandra, William
Griffith, Frank C.	4310	4258	Kirby, Cecil J.
Griffith, Levi J.	4183	4259	Kirby, Emma
Grindrod, Orin E.	4299	4260	McDonald, Angus L.
Haas, Carl Fred	4408	4261	Peart, Arthur
Hackler, William Cyral	4318	4262	Burke, John F.
Hagerud, Oscar	4390	4263	Henagin, Clarence E.
Hall, Norman Dwight	5087	4264	England, John W.
Halousek, William V.	4150	4265	Goodrich, Chandler P.
Halstead, Herbert	4495	4266	Walldin, Jonas
Halvorson, Charles A.	4402	4267	Lee, Arthur J.
Hamilton, Ruben James	4395	4268	Walldin, Pete E.
Hamilton, William D.	4557	4269	Westlin, Jonas O.
Hammer, Oscar B	4119	4270	Lyons, Clement W.
Hammond, Eugene W.	4016	4271	Brown, Patrick G.
Hanna, Arthur Richard	5077	4272	Kozacik, John
Hannon, Francis P.	4321	4273	McAuliffe, Daniel
Hannon, Richard K.	4164	4274	Holbrook, David C.
Hardman, Alvah Webster	4376	4275	Landrie, Arthur J.

Hartley, Lawrence Wilbur	4517	4276	Delaney, George A.
Hartley, Leslie W.	4438	4277	McAuliffe, Michael D.
Hatfield, William H.	4006	4278	Goodrich, Fred G.
Hatfield, William H.	4151	4279	Barr, J. Randolph
Havlina, Chester	4245	4280	Scott, Emma M.
Havlina, Edward J.	4247	4281	Bergman, Peter C.
Havlina, Vincent	4246	4282	Slater, Herman C.
Heater, William Woodrow	5091	4283	Zerger, Rudolph
Heckman, Robert L.	4520	4284	Duggan, Margaret O.S.
Hedlund, Lars J. (Johan)	4120	4285	Cripps, A. Yarnell
Heiken, Ernest Harm	4017	4286	Seteyskal, William S.
Heim, Theodor	4154	4287	Slater, Thomas Clifton
Heiney, Robert Roy	4490	4288	Ford, Charles B.
Heiney, Roy C.	4407	4289	Coley, Rufus
Heitz, Charles J.	4226	4290	Stonecypher, Chester G.
Henagin, Clarence E.	4263	4291	Nelson, Hans
High, Rex E.	4431	4292	Prentice, Claud O.
Higler, Joseph	4121	4293	Staunton, Edward W.
Hirschback, Robert F.	4539	4294	Stevenson, George E.
Hodges, Roy A.	4485	4295	Trammel, Bird L.
Hofwegen, Arthur	4347	4296	Weitkamp, William H.
Hogue, Ernest W.	4122	4297	West, Homer L.
Holbrook, David C.	4274	4298	Ferrari, Frank
Holden, LaVant Horace	4565	4299	Grindrod, Orin E.
Holzhauser, Frank	4455	4300	Waldrip, Elmer M.
Hooper, William P.	4393	4301	Porterfield, Guy
Howard, Frank Lucian	4482	4302	Rose, Aaron Ivan
Howard, Frank Z.	4331	4303	Davis, Paul A.
Howell, Frank	4123	4304	Sodeman, Felix W.
Hoyman, Leonard I.	4124	4305	Fensler, Clarke W.
Huffman, Clyde Forrest	5102	4306	Berry, Herbert F.
Hughes, Edward W.	4307	4307	Hughes, Edward W.
Hull, John Oris	4578	4308	Brainard, Lawson A.
Hulse, Walter Max	4519	4309	Day, George H.
Hundley, Harry Howard	4536	4310	Griffith, Frank C.
Hunt, John William	4180	4311	Pence, Ora Cecil
Hurlburt, Don E.	4479	4312	Liddell, Wingham J. H.
Ihde, Earl	5065	4313	Pope, Lee C.
Irving, John A.	4527	4314	Ganger, Ralph Andrew
Isensee, Harry F.	4564	4315	Kadous, Tom B.

Isom, Robert Crocket	4567	4316	Barks, Clyde Hobson
Ivory, Frances Jeanne	5021	4317	Robinson, Fred B.
Jackson, Robert L.	5069	4318	Hackler, William Cyral
James, Christian	4145	4319	Mitchell, Edgar Malcolm
Jamison, Dwight L.	4381	4320	Crawford, Lawrence Imber
Jamison, Maurice Eston	5073	4321	Hannon, Francis P.
Jensen, Carl L.	4433	4322	Beck, Albert
Jensen, Leslie Raymond	4336	4323	Abel, Raymond D.
Johnson, Augusta Belle	4027	4324	Wright, Arthur Clyde
Johnson, Edward	5015	4325	Tingley, Washington I.
Johnson, Floyd	4348	4326	Tucker, Carl
Johnson, French E.	4169	4327	Jones, Frank Quantrell
Johnson, Gayle Myler	5003	4328	Meshke, Leonard Thomas
Johnson, Gerald Leslie	4493	4329	Taylor, Horace E.
Johnson, Walter Edward	4528	4330	Manero, Antonio
Johnson, William O.	4024	4331	Howard, Frank Z.
Jones, Charles J.	4345	4332	McGahey, Jackson B.
Jones, Charley	4362	4333	Chamberlain, Charles C.
Jones, Frank Quantrell	4327	4334	Dahle, Norman Grant
Jones, Lester N.	4428	4335	Yost, George G.
Jones, Vance Irwain	5068	4336	Jensen, Leslie Raymond
Jorgenson, Vincent Edward	5057	4337	Bell, Frank Eugene
Kadous, Tom B.	4315	4338	Tillotson, Lucius Edwin Jr.
Kandra, John Jr.	4196	4339	McClymonds, Arthur Erskine
Kandra, William	4257	4340	Edwards, Wilbur S.
Keck, Asa Charles	4215	4341	Dunlap, Leeth S.
Keeter, Eugene L.	5010	4342	Welsh, Thomas W.
Kelleher, Con	4249	4343	Stallings, William R.
Kelleher, John	4252	4344	Smith, Earle Clinton
Kennington, Forrest Weber	4561	4345	Jones, Charles J.
Kenyon, Lowell C.	4504	4346	Westfall, Fred J.
King, Edward Addison	4541	4347	Hofwegen, Arthur
King, Floyd F.	4378	4348	Johnson, Floyd
King, Frank LeRoy Jr.	5061	4349	Ott, James I.
Kinsey, Roscoe R.	4173	4350	Brown, Roy L.
Kirby, Cecil J.	4258	4351	Corrie, John Quincy
Kirby, Emma	4259	4352	Scott, Elmer Giggs
Kirby, Garvin Henry	4525	4353	Clink, Walter Livingston
Kirby, LeRoy C.	4223	4354	Lundy, Garner
Klassen, Jacob Jr.	5014	4355	McGinley, Morse

Klem, Joseph	4190	4356	Sutton, Martin L.
Kline, Henry	5086	4357	Lynch, Harry Michael
Knight, Harvey A.	4231	4358	Phillips, Samuel O.
Knoll, Alex A.	4405	4359	Cherry, Melvin W.
Knowlton, George Winslow	4571	4360	Owens, Jesse M.
Kongslie, Chester Eugene	5036	4361	Brown, Andrew M.
Kozacik, John	4272	4362	Jones, Charley
Krejci, Joseph	4033	4363	Laughlin, Cloyd F.
Krizo, Frank	4233	4364	Paulson, John C.
Krizo, Philip	4503	4365	Phillips, Vere Chesleigh
Krouse, Albert N.	4449	4366	Loudon, William T.
Krupka, Henry	4177	4367	Mahoney, John J.
Lacey, Richard Owen	4253	4368	Pritchett, Robert S.
Laird, Marion Raymond	4184	4369	Street, Herman T.
Landrie, Arthur J.	4275	4370	Palmer, Harry Hannond
Larson, Albert Paul	4439	4371	Wilkenson, Noble C.
Laughlin, Cloyd F.	4363	4372	Dayton, Howard L.
Law, Davis Brett	4505	4373	Mitchell, Arlie E.
Lee, Arthur J.	4267	4374	Lindsey, Gus
Lehman, Frederick Bryan	4524	4375	Sauer, Ludwig
Lemke, Cloyce Dudley	5044	4376	Hardman, Alvah Webster
Lesch, James Miller	5103	4377	Pritchett, Hubert A.
Lewis, Paul D.	4018	4378	King, Floyd F.
Lewis, Sheldon Wayne	4548	4379	Murray, Gladstone
Liddell, Wingham J. H.	4312	4380	Bollenbaugh, Ralph
Lidell, John A.	4178	4381	Jamison, Dwight L.
Lien, Ole N.	4125	4382	Weedon, Grover C.
Lillard, Robert Hughes	4507	4383	Campbell, Roy S.
Lindsay, Ernest Marvin	4543	4384	Redsull, James S.
Lindsey, Gus	4374	4385	McClymonds, William G.
Lloyd, Harry Earl	4471	4386	Mosebar, Frank Edward
Logan, John Mattison	5013	4387	Oland, Joseph E.
Loiselle, Roy S.	4413	4388	Minty, Chester A.
Loudon, William T.	4366	4389	Miller, Harry H.
Lourenco, Felisberto	4152	4390	Hagerud, Oscar
Lousenco, Felisberto	4007	4391	Brownell, Austin B.
Lund, Bert	4126	4392	Shelton, Ray H.
Lundberg, Charles Orvall	4569	4393	Hooper, William P.
Lundy, Garner	4354	4394	Olson, Harry A.
Lynch, Harry Michael	4357	4395	Hamilton, Ruben James

Name	Number	Number	Name
Lynham, Everett Lee	4537	4396	Templeton, Phillip H.
Lyons, Clement W.	4270	4397	Costley, Eugene J.
Mace, Jack Charles	4489	4398	McLaughlin, Edward Joseph
Macy, Paul R.	5008	4399	Norris, Alfred T.
Macy, William Elsworth	4522	4400	Bush (or Busch), John
Mahoney, John J.	4367	4401	Brown, James M.
Main, Chester J.	4446	4402	Halvorson, Charles A.
Manero, Antonio	4330	4403	Callendine, Charles
Markusen, Christian	4201	4404	Melgard, Sophus M.
Martin, Harry L.	4244	4405	Knoll, Alex A.
Masterson, John Leo	5020	4406	Spears, Charles C.
Mathis, Ernest Manuel	4581	4407	Heiney, Roy C.
Mauch, Barney	4474	4408	Haas, Carl Fred
Maupin, Charles	4172	4409	Bitter, Vernon E.
Maxwell, McKinley V.	4437	4410	Thomas, Marvin
McAtee, Paul William	5062	4411	Osborn, Ottis H.
McAuliffe, Daniel	4273	4412	Crawford, Daniel Martin
McAuliffe, Eugene	4014	4413	Loiselle, Roy S.
McAuliffe, Michael D.	4277	4414	Gilliland, Elmer A.
McClymonds, Arthur Erskine	4339	4415	Baker, Raymond R.
McClymonds, Robert Clendenin	4582	4416	Thrasher, George W.
McClymonds, William G.	4385	4417	Cox, Charles E.
McCollum, Elmer	4192	4418	Olsen, Leonard
McCoy, James Robert	5088	4419	Frailey, Lum C.
McCracken, Gewin	4554	4420	Fish, Theodore J.
McCullough, Patrick Claire	5042	4421	McFall, Earl J.
McDaniel, Edward	4207	4422	Galloway, Harry R.
McDonald, Angus L.	4260	4423	Rykman, Albert E.
McDonald, Lester Wills	5031	4424	Summerville, George V.
McElroy, Harold M.	4127	4425	Snyder, Donald A.
McFall, Earl J.	4421	4426	Wyatt, James C.
McGahey, Jackson B.	4332	4427	Puckett, Douglas J.
McGinley, Morse	4355	4428	Jones, Lester N.
McGuire, Thomas	4008	4429	Coulson, John S.
McKimens, Bayard T.	4447	4430	Slater, Lea Godley
McLaughlin, Edward Joseph	4398	4431	High, Rex E.
McMurphy, Fred E.	4200	4432	Allen, Arthur Chapel
McQuesten, Leavitt M.	4146	4433	Jensen, Carl L.
McVey, Vernon Elwood	4515	4434	Anderson, Samuel
Mehloff, Herbert Benjamin	5082	4435	Nuffer, Fred Jr.

Melgard, Sophus M.	4404	4436	Smith, George M.
Merevantz, John	4023	4437	Maxwell, McKinley V.
Meshke, Leonard Thomas	4328	4438	Hartley, Leslie W.
Meyer, Harlan Giffen	4530	4439	Larson, Albert Paul
Michelbrook, Herbert S.	4009	4440	Ruppert, David A.
Micka, Jerry	4025	4441	Cushman, Melvin L.
Miller, Gerald B.	4456	4442	Bradbury, Lloyd L.
Miller, Harry H.	4389	4443	Ernst, Franklin H.
Minnas, Dean Hazlette	4176	4444	Robison, Wade T. (may be Wate)
Minty, Chester A.	4388	4445	Stevens, Harry O.
Mitchell, Arlie E.	4373	4446	Main, Chester J.
Mitchell, Edgar Malcolm	4319	4447	McKimens, Bayard T.
Mitchell, Harry Earl	4166	4448	Schindler, Albert W.
Monroe, Nelson H.	4453	4449	Krouse, Albert N.
Moore, Clyde E.	4210	4450	Schweitzer, Edward C.
Morrill, Ralph B.	5094	4451	Craft, William U.
Morris, Clifford Dale	5027	4452	Bailey, Everett V.
Mosebar, Frank Edward	4386	4453	Monroe, Nelson H.
Motschenbacher, Lawrence W.	4238	4454	Scott, Albert M.
Mullins, Charles Leroy	5047	4455	Holzhauser, Frank
Murphy, Jerry C.	4234	4456	Miller, Gerald B.
Murray, Gladstone	4379	4457	Anderson, Wesley P.
Muther, Leland	5012	4458	Birtwistle, Lee
Naylor, Andrew J.	4551	4459	Carter, Ralph L.
Nelson, Hans	4291	4460	Bowen, Stone A.
Nelson, Willard Martin	5071	4461	Penhall, Leslie Walter
Neufeld, Cornelius N.	5080	4462	Terry, Stephen F.
Newkirk, Jack Leslie	5060	4463	Easley, Roy B.
Newton, Almo H.	4240	4464	Goldblatt, Arthur
Newton, Thomas W.	4216	4465	Vernon, Chester L.
Norris, Alfred T.	4399	4466	Bone, John Burgess
Nuffer, Fred Jr.	4435	4467	Schellenger, Nolan N.
O'Connor, Edmund Barry	5026	4468	Charles R. Dyer
O'Keefe, Toby	4242	4469	Powell, Ralph
O'Keeffe, Patrick John	4229	4470	Rudd, Olney Lee Jr.
O'Sullivan, John Patrick	4553	4471	Lloyd, Harry Earl
Oland, Joseph E.	4387	4472	Richey, Verne
Olsen, Leonard	4418	4473	Warring, Clayton F.
Olson, Elmer Earl	5066	4474	Mauch, Barney

Olson, Harry A.	4394	4475	Crowther, George H.
Oman, Donald LaVerne	4533	4476	Decker, Clifford J.
Oman, Laverne Frank	5092	4477	Reed, George Anthony
Osborn, Ottis H.	4411	4478	Charley, Eldred Floyd
Ott, James I.	4349	4479	Hurlburt, Don E.
Owens, Jesse M.	4360	4480	Edwards, Charles Welton
Palmer, Harry Hannond	4370	4481	Saylor, Ralph Eldon
Palmer, Marion Francis	5075	4482	Howard, Frank Lucian
Parsons, Earl Walter	5079	4483	Toler, Lester James
Paulson, John C.	4364	4484	Fuller, Richard Lay
Peart, Arthur	4261	4485	Hodges, Roy A.
Peart, John	4225	4486	Bolesta, Eleanor Jane
Pence, Ora Cecil	4311	4487	Crawford, William Marvin
Penhall, Leslie Walter	4461	4488	Buckingham, Keith Stanley
Perry, Oliver	5030	4489	Mace, Jack Charles
Peterson, Benjamin F.	4128	4490	Heiney, Robert Roy
Pettigrew, John William	5070	4491	Schwarz, Herbert James
Phillips, Ray Osman	5074	4492	Ferrel, larry
Phillips, Samuel O.	4358	4493	Johnson, Gerald Leslie
Phillips, Vere Chesleigh	4365	4494	Douglass, George Alton Jr.
Pickup, George Lloyd	5078	4495	Halstead, Herbert
Pierce, Lester D.	4029	4496	Stiles, Charles Webster
Pierce, Waverly Eugene	4584	4497	Barrett, Harold Taylor
Pope, Dora O. (Owner)	4032	4498	Bierly, Amos Walter
Pope, Lee C.	4313	4499	Corcoran, Gerald Eugene
Porterfield, Guy	4301	4500	Anderson, Wesley Niles
Portnoff, William Paul	5051	4501	Anderson, Robert Franklin
Powell, Ralph	4469	4502	Watson, Robert Eugene
Prentice, Claud O.	4292	4503	Krizo, Philip
Price, Roy William	5097	4504	Kenyon, Lowell C.
Pritchett, Hubert A.	4377	4505	Law, Davis Brett
Pritchett, Robert S.	4368	4506	Wallaert, Marceil F.
Prosser, Jess M.	4534	4507	Lillard, Robert Hughes
Pruitt, Raymon William	5083	4508	Solterbeck, Robert George
Puckett, Douglas J.	4427	4509	Buchanan, Walter Dean
Ragnus, John Vaclav	4197	4510	Sisemore, John E.
Ratliff, John Richard	4020	4511	Santana, William V.
Reagan, Leroy B.	4129	4512	Woodley, Merle Eugene
Redsull, James S.	4384	4513	Darrow, Glen Edward
Reed, George Anthony	4477	4514	Smith, George Arthur

Name	No.	No.	Name
Reimer, Bernhard	5004	4515	McVey, Vernon Elwood
Reimer, Lewis George	5053	4516	Wynn, John Sam
Reynolds, Walter S.	4130	4517	Hartley, Lawrence Wilbur
Richey, Verne	4472	4518	Byron, John Fredrick
Riddle, Glenn N.	4213	4519	Hulse, Walter Max
Roberts, Harrison M.	4175	4520	Heckman, Robert L.
Roberts, Robert Clell	5076	4521	Walter, Jesse Sims
Robinson, Fred B.	4317	4522	Macy, William Elsworth
Robison, Fred Allen	4523	4523	Robison, Fred Allen
Robison, Wade T. (may be Wate)	4444	4524	Lehman, Frederick Bryan
Rock, Elmer	4214	4525	Kirby, Garvin Henry
Rockhill, Ferne D.	4217	4526	Goldlewski, Theophile
Roderick, Augustine	5025	4527	Irving, John A.
Rogers, Paul Lewis	4562	4528	Johnson, Walter Edward
Rose, Aaron Ivan	4302	4529	Bettandorff, John N.
Rosenberg, John Wesley	4248	4530	Meyer, Harlan Giffen
Rossmiller, Robert J.	5105	4531	Stearns, James Gerry
Roth, Loren Lee	5043	4532	Buckingham, Bert G.
Rudd, Olney Lee Jr.	4470	4533	Oman, Donald LaVerne
Rund, Elmer Wayne	5100	4534	Prosser, Jess M.
Ruppert, David A.	4440	4535	Congdon, Shirley Albert
Rykman, Albert E.	4423	4536	Hundley, Harry Howard
Sanders, James W.	4187	4537	Lynham, Everett Lee
Santana, William V.	4511	4538	Bryant, Oliver Earl
Sauer, Ludwig	4375	4539	Hirschback, Robert F.
Saylor, Ralph Eldon	4481	4540	Sulivan, Frank James Jr.
Schaffner, Otto Henry	4583	4541	King, Edward Addison
Schellenger, Nolan N.	4467	4542	Christy, Paul Edward
Schey, Wendell A.	5032	4543	Lindsay, Ernest Marvin
Schindler, Albert W.	4448	4544	Duncan, Kenneth H.
Schlichter, Mike H.	4208	4545	Elzner, Franklin W.
Schultz, Alfred W.	4019	4546	Seus, Edward Alphons
Schultz, O.A.	4015	4547	Sprout, Dale Everett
Schwabenland, Peter	5056	4548	Lewis, Sheldon Wayne
Schwarz, Herbert James	4491	4549	Fleming, Max William
Schweitzer, Edward C.	4450	4550	Bradbury, Stanley
Scott, Albert M.	4454	4551	Naylor, Andrew J.
Scott, Elmer Giggs	4352	4552	Bell, James A.
Scott, Emma M.	4280	4553	O'Sullivan, John Patrick
Seteyskal, William S.	4286	4554	McCracken, Gewin

Seus, Edward Alphons	4546	4555	Walter, Ermine Leslie
Shaw, John J.	5035	4556	Smith, Robert L.
Sheckla, Leoard George	5009	4557	Hamilton, William D.
Shelton, Ray H.	4392	4558	Taylor, Jack Wallace
Silva, Manuel P. Jr.	5011	4559	Barks, William Pinkney
Simpson, Paul Quinton	4131	4560	Borrows, Robert Eugene
Singleton, John Jeremiah	5017	4561	Kennington, Forrest Weber
Sisemore, John E.	4510	4562	Rogers, Paul Lewis
Slater, Herman C.	4282	4563	Webb, Francis Melford
Slater, Lea Godley	4430	4564	Isensee, Harry F.
Slater, Thomas Clifton	4287	4565	Holden, LaVant Horace
Smith, Alfred D.	4230	4566	George, Jeanne E.
Smith, Delbert Wesley	5106	4567	Isom, Robert Crocket
Smith, Earle Clinton	4344	4568	Storey, Owen Robert
Smith, George Arthur	4514	4569	Lundberg, Charles Orvall
Smith, George M.	4436	4570	Workman, Robert
Smith, Richard M.	4202	4571	Knowlton, George Winslow
Smith, Robert L.	4556	4572	Will, Leonard I.
Snider, John T.	4204	4573	Yoder, Jack Dillon Kirmet
Snyder, Donald A.	4425	4574	Bradley, William E.
Sodeman, Felix W.	4304	4575	Victorine, Joseph J.
Solterbeck, Robert George	4508	4576	Cuddy, Clement William
Spears, Charles C.	4406	4577	Barleen, Virgil Henry
Spence, Preston J. M.	4132	4578	Hull, John Oris
Spolek, Edward James	5019	4579	Bibby, Raymond Robert
Spolek, William M.	4193	4580	Thomas, Derral Jackson
Sprout, Dale Everett	4547	4581	Mathis, Ernest Manuel
St. Peter, Wesley Joseph	5084	4582	McClymonds, Robert Clendenin
Stallings, William R.	4343	4583	Schaffner, Otto Henry
Starns, Elmer	4133	4584	Pierce, Waverly Eugene
Staunton, Edward W.	4293	4585	Thacker, Ernest Lee
Stearns, Carey Sumner	4161	5001	Worden, Wesley Allen
Stearns, James Gerry	4531	5002	Gorham, Thomas Albert
Stevens, Harry O.	4445	5003	Johnson, Gayle Myler
Stevenson, George E.	4294	5004	Reimer, Bernhard
Stevenson, James C.	4206	5005	Bertwistle, Clatus Earl
Stewart, Earl Ulyssis	4174	5006	Ackley, Orvin Ray II
Stewart, Malcolm M.	4254	5007	Eisenbis, Walter
Stewart, Merwin C.	4134	5008	Macy, Paul R.

Steyakal, Jacob	4205	5009	Sheckla, Leoard George
Stiles, Charles Webster	4496	5010	Keeter, Eugene L.
Stonecypher, Chester G.	4290	5011	Silva, Manuel P. Jr.
Storey, Owen Robert	4568	5012	Muther, Leland
Storey, Walter	4167	5013	Logan, John Mattison
Street, Andrew Erwin	4021	5014	Klassen, Jacob Jr.
Street, Herman T.	4369	5015	Johnson, Edward
Sulivan, Frank James Jr.	4540	5016	Swensen, Lynn Archie
Sullivan, Tim T.	4185	5017	Singleton, John Jeremiah
Summerville, George V.	4424	5018	Taylor, Leonard Andrew
Sutton, Martin L.	4356	5019	Spolek, Edward James
Swensen, Lynn Archie	5016	5020	Masterson, John Leo
Takacs, Stephen J.	4186	5021	Ivory, Frances Jeanne
Taylor, Carl S.	4191	5022	Criss, Marvin Delmer
Taylor, Horace E.	4329	5023	Westerhold, Harold John
Taylor, Jack Wallace	4558	5024	Duerksen, Irvin Earl
Taylor, Jacob W.	4158	5025	Roderick, Augustine
Taylor, Leonard Andrew	5018	5026	O'Connor, Edmund Barry
Taylor, Raymond	4188	5027	Morris, Clifford Dale
Templeton, Phillip H.	4396	5028	Carman, David L.
Terry, John Vivian	5085	5029	VanOsdel, Bob LaFay
Terry, Stephen F.	4462	5030	Perry, Oliver
Thacher, Boyd T.	4222	5031	McDonald, Lester Wills
Thacker, Ernest Lee	4585	5032	Schey, Wendell A.
Thomas, Derral Jackson	4580	5033	Badker, Frank Albert
Thomas, Marvin	4410	5034	Arthur, Glen
Thrasher, George W.	4416	5035	Shaw, John J.
Tillotson, Lucius Edwin Jr.	4338	5036	Kongslie, Chester Eugene
Tingley, Washington I.	4325	5037	Williams, Jack Wendel
Tison, Albert S.	4227	5038	Beck, Ardith L.
Todd, Clyde Elden	5072	5039	Withers, Thomas E.
Toler, Lester James	4483	5040	Cashman, William James
Trammel, Bird L.	4295	5041	Girvin, Russel Wayne
Treloar, Ernest	4135	5042	McCullough, Patrick Claire
Trippe, William Wells	4165	5043	Roth, Loren Lee
Trout, Frank M.	4203	5044	Lemke, Cloyce Dudley
Tucker, Carl	4326	5045	Bursik, Vaclav Jacob
Tucker, Everett L.	4136	5046	Barcus, Maurice Claude
Turnbaugh, David W.	4179	5047	Mullins, Charles Leroy
Turnbaugh, Lester	4159	5048	Voorhees, Carl Gordon

Van Blaricom, Fred A.	4010	5049	Burgess, William Polk
VanNortwick, Leon Bertrand	5050	5050	VanNortwick, Leon Bertrand
VanOsdel, Bob LaFay	5029	5051	Portnoff, William Paul
Vernon, Chester L.	4465	5052	Ackley, Lawrence Lyle
Victorin, Frank	4163	5053	Reimer, Lewis George
Victorin, Tony	4026	5054	Bartlett, Eugene Bickford
Victorine, Joseph J.	4575	5055	Wagler, Menno Jacob
Viken, Sever O.	4011	5056	Schwabenland, Peter
Voorhees, Carl Gordon	5048	5057	Jorgenson, Vincent Edward
Wagler, Menno Jacob	5055	5058	Falconer, Richard Donaldson
Waldrip, Charles	4137	5059	Chambers, Woodrow J.
Waldrip, Elmer M.	4300	5060	Newkirk, Jack Leslie
Wall, Sam J.	4012	5061	King, Frank LeRoy Jr.
Wallaert, Marceil F.	4506	5062	McAtee, Paul William
Walldin, Jonas	4266	5063	Dean, John Merlin
Walldin, Pete E.	4268	5064	Cowling, Henry James
Walsch, Richard	4153	5065	Ihde, Earl
Walter, Ermine Leslie	4555	5066	Olson, Elmer Earl
Walter, Jesse Sims	4521	5067	Warner, Irvin Jr.
Warner, Irvin Jr.	5067	5068	Jones, Vance Irwain
Warring, Clayton F.	4473	5069	Jackson, Robert L.
Watson, Robert Eugene	4502	5070	Pettigrew, John William
Webb, Francis Melford	4563	5071	Nelson, Willard Martin
Weedon, Grover C.	4382	5072	Todd, Clyde Elden
Weitkamp, William H.	4296	5073	Jamison, Maurice Eston
Wells, Leonal J.	4138	5074	Phillips, Ray Osman
Wells, Raymond Dean	5098	5075	Palmer, Marion Francis
Welsh, Thomas W.	4342	5076	Roberts, Robert Clell
West, Homer L.	4297	5077	Hanna, Arthur Richard
Westerhold, Harold John	5023	5078	Pickup, George Lloyd
Westfall, Fred J.	4346	5079	Parsons, Earl Walter
Westlin, Jonas O.	4269	5080	Neufeld, Cornelius N.
Whitaker, William	5090	5081	Younker, Donald Lee
Wilkenson, Noble C.	4371	5082	Mehloff, Herbert Benjamin
Will, Leonard I.	4572	5083	Pruitt, Raymon William
Williams, Charles J.	4139	5084	St. Peter, Wesley Joseph
Williams, Jack Wendel	5037	5085	Terry, John Vivian
Winter, Arthur L.	4147	5086	Kline, Henry
Withers, Thomas E.	5039	5087	Hall, Norman Dwight
Woldsen, Viggo	4140	5088	McCoy, James Robert

Wolfe, Ival D.	4195	5089	DuVall, Gaylord R.
Woodley, Merle Eugene	4512	5090	Whitaker, William
Worden, Wesley Allen	5001	5091	Heater, William Woodrow
Workman, Robert	4570	5092	Oman, Laverne Frank
Wright, Arthur Clyde	4324	5093	Christy, Marvin Miller
Wyatt, James C.	4426	5094	Morrill, Ralph B.
Wynn, John Sam	4516	5095	Gooing, Roy Elwyn
Yanek, John	4162	5096	DeShon, James Bernard
Yoder, Jack Dillon Kirmet	4573	5097	Price, Roy William
Yordy, Ralph T.	4141	5098	Wells, Raymond Dean
Yost, George G.	4335	5099	Ayres, William Harvey
Young, Armine O.	4142	5100	Rund, Elmer Wayne
Young, Roy O.	4182	5101	Bradley, Gale Jack
Younker, Donald Lee	5081	5102	Huffman, Clyde Forrest
Zerger, Rudolph	4283	5103	Lesch, James Miller
Ziemenczuk, Henry	4209	5104	Ablard, Louis Kenneth
Zlabek, Frank F.	4143	5105	Rossmiller, Robert J.
Zumpfe, Joseph	4144	5106	Smith, Delbert Wesley
-----------------------	4037	5107	Depuy, Ora Melvin

Total Tule Lake Basin Homestead Units, Acreage and Applications

Notice Number	Date	Units	Acreage	Applications Received
13	9/29/22	65	3,227	65
19	1/22/27	145	8,062	145
22	3/30/28	9	573	9
23	2/06/29	28	1,887	94
26	9/10/30	24	1,624	162
28	10/06/31	68	4,752	189
35	9/09/37	69	5,100	1,308
43	8/01/46	86	7,528	2,150
45	10/08/47	44	3,522	4,066
47	8/27/48	86	7,283	5,063
	Totals:	624	43,558	13,251

Sprinkler Irrigation in the Tule Lake Basin.
(Photo by author)

FOOTNOTES

CHAPTER 1: AN INTRODUCTION TO THE TULE LAKE BASIN

1. Carrol B. Howe, *Ancient Tribes of the Klamath Country*, p. 4.
2. John Cleghorn, *Historic Water Levels of Tulelake, California-Oregon and their Relation to the Petroglyphs, Klamath County Museum Research Papers*, No. 1, p. 5.
3. Rachel Applegate Good, *History of Klamath County, Oregon*, p. 5.
4. *Ibid.*, p. 5.
5. John Cleghorn, *A Geological and Archaeological Study of the Tule Lake Basin*, unpublished manuscript, p. 6.
6. *Ibid.*
7. *Ibid.*

CHAPTER 2: THE FIRST INHABITANTS

1. L. S. Cressman, *Prehistory of the Far West*, p. 69.
2. Emory Strong, *Stone Age in the Great Basin*, p. 42.
3. L.S. Cressman, *The Sandal and the Cave, The Indians of Oregon*, p. 22.
4. Strong, *op. cit.*, p. 38.
5. Stephen Beckham, *The Indians of Western Oregon*, p. 14.
6. Cressman, *op. cit.*, pp. 20-25.
7. Stephen Harris, *Fire and Ice, The Cascade Volcanoes*, p. 94.
8. Carrol B. Howe, *Ancient Modocs of California and Oregon*, pp. 41-42.
9. *Ibid.*, p. 39.
10. Keith Murray, *The Modocs and Their War*, p. 8.
11. Albert Samuel Gatschet, *The Klamath Indians of Southwestern Oregon*, p. xli.
12. L.S. Cressman, *Klamath Prehistory: Transactions of the American Philosophical Society, Volume 46, Part 4*, November, 1956, p. 397.
13. Gatschet, *op. cit.*, p. xxxiii.

14. Theodore Stern, *The Klamath Tribe, A People and Their Reservation,*
    p. 4.
15. Murray, *op. cit.,* p. 8.
16. Verne F. Ray, *Primitive Pragmatists, The Modoc Indians of Northern California,*
    p. xii.
17. *Ibid.,* pp. xiii-xiv.
18. *Ibid.,* pp. 202-203.
19. Murray, *op. cit.,* p. 9.
20. Ray, *op. cit.,* p. 82.
21. *Ibid.,* p. 4.
22. *Ibid.,* pp. 134-135.
23. *Ibid.,* pp. 18-19.
24. *Ibid.,* p. 26.
25. *Ibid.,* pp. 113-117.
26. *Ibid.,* p. 82.
27. Murray, *op. cit.,* p. 34.
28. Ray, *op. cit.,* p. 165.
29. *Ibid.,* p. 132.
30. Howe, *op. cit.,* p. 153.

CHAPTER 3: EXPLORERS AND TRAIL BLAZERS

1. Devere Helfrich, "The First Whites," *Klamath Echoes,* No. 8, p. 2.
2. K.G. Davies, ed., *Peter Skene Ogden's Snake Country Journal, 1826-27,* p. 36.
3. *Ibid.,* p. 42.
4. Helfrich, *loc. cit.*
5. Davies, *op. cit.,* p. 41.
6. *Ibid.,* p. 43.
7. *Ibid.,* p. 50
8. *Ibid.*
9. John Charles Fremont, *Narrations of Exploration and Adventure,*
    p. 488.
10. *Ibid.*
11. Keith Murray, *The Modocs and Their War,* p. 14.
12. *Ibid.,* pp. 14-15.
13. Fremont, *op. cit.,* pp. 492-500. (Note: Fremont in his description of the attack
    on his men is vague about the exact location. This has led to confusion,
    particularly in light of Lindsay Applegate's description of his party's
    discoveries at Lower Klamath Lake several months later.)
14. Rachael Applegate Good, *History of Klamath County,* Oregon, pp. 20-21.
15. W.H. Hutchinson, *California: Two Centuries of Man, Land and Growth in the
    Golden State,* pp. 102-103.
16. Lindsay Applegate, "The Old Emigrant Road," *The Malin Progress,* June 24 to
    July 15, 1926, pp. 1-2.
17. *Ibid.,* p 2.

18. Hubert Howe Bancroft, *History of Oregon, Volume 1*, pp. 543-544.

19. *Ibid.*, p. 544.

20. Applegate, *op. cit.*, p. 4.

21. *Ibid.*, p. 5.

22. *Ibid.*

23. *Ibid.*, p. 7.

24. Dr. Francis D. Haines, *The Applegate Trail: Southern Emigrant Route*, pp. 10-11.

25. Helfrich, "They Also Passed This Way," *Klamath Echoes, No. 8*, pp. 7-8.

26. Haines, *op. cit.*, p. 16.

27. *Ibid.*, pp. 16-17.

28. Applegate, *op. cit.*, p. 12.

29. Haines, *op. cit.*, pp. 20-21.

30. Samuel T. Frear, *Jesse Applegate, An Appraisal of An Uncommon Pioneer*, p. 23.

31. Haines, *op. cit.*, p. 25.

32. Applegate, *op. cit.*, p. 13.

33. Frear, *loc. cit.*

CHAPTER 4: EARLY RESISTANCE TO WHITE SETTLERS

1. Dr. Francis D. Haines, *The Applegate Trail: Southern Emigrant Route*, p. 27.

2. *Ibid.*

3. Keith A. Murray, *The Modocs and Their War*, p. 18.

4. Devere Helfrich, "They Also Passed This Way," *Klamath Echoes, No. 8*, p. 8.

5. *Ibid.*

6. Haines, *op. cit.*, p. 28.

7. Richard Dillon, *Burnt-Out Fires: California's Modoc Indian War*, p. 50.

8. Albert Samuel Gatschet, *The Klamath Indians of Southwestern Oregon*, p. viii.

9. F.A. Shaver, *An Illustrated History of Central Oregon*, p. 928.

10. Murray, *op. cit.*, p. 17.

11. *Ibid.*, p. 21.

12. *Ibid.*

13. *Ibid.*, p. 26.

14. *Ibid.*, p. 27.

15. *Ibid.*, p. 31.

CHAPTER 5: A PRELUDE TO CONFLICT

1. Keith Murray, *The Modocs and Their War*, p. 33.

2. *Ibid.*

3. Richard Dillon, *Burnt-Out Fires*, p. 55.

4. *Ibid.*

5. Dr. Frances Haines, *The Applegate Trail: Southern Emigrant Route*, p. 37.

6. Buena Cobb Stone, *Fort Klamath, Frontier Post in Oregon 1863-1890*, pp. 11-12.

7. *Ibid.*, p. 13.

8. Murray, *op. cit.*, p. 34.

9. Dillon, *op. cit.*, p. 57.

10. Jeff C. Riddle, *The Indian History of the Modoc War*, pp. 273-274.

11. Murray, *op. cit.*, p. 36.

12. Dillon, *op. cit.*, p. 59.

13. Columbus Delano, "The Quaker Policy", *New York Times*, April 16, 1873, p. 1.

14. Murray, *op. cit.*, p. 44.

15. Riddle, *op. cit.*, p. 32.

16. Murray, *op. cit.*, p. 59.

17. J.P. Dunn, *Massacres of the Mountains: A History of the Indian Wars of the Far West*, p. 465.

18. Walter H. Palmberg, *Copper Paladin, A Modoc Tragedy*, pp. 59-60.

19. Petition sent by the residents of Lost River and Klamath Basin to A.B. Meacham and General E.R.S Canby, January, 1872, Lava Beds National Monument Files.

20. Petition sent to Governor L.F. Grover, Oregon, January, 1872, Lava Beds National Monument Files.

21. Meacham. A.B., *Wigwam and War-Path, or the Royal Chief in Chains*, p. 358.

22. Palmberg, *op. cit.*, p. 38.

23. Memo from F.A. Walker, Indian Commissioner, Washington D.C., to T.B. Odeneal, Indian Superintendent of Oregon, April 12, 1872, Lava Beds National Monument files.

24. Letter from I.D. Applegate to T.B. Odeneal, May 8, 1872, Lava Bed National Monument files.

25. *Ibid.*

26. Letter from I.D. Applegate to T.B. Odeneal, May 16, 1872, Lava Beds National Monument files.

27. Letter from T.B. Odeneal to F.A. Walker, June 17, 1872, Lava Beds National Monument files.

28. Letter from T.B. Odeneal to Lieutenant Colonel Frank Wheaton, Commanding District of the Lakes, November 25, 1872, Lava Beds National Monument files.

29. Dillon, *op. cit.*, p. 122.

CHAPTER 6: THE MODOC WAR

1. Keith Murray, *The Modocs and Their War*, p. 91.

2. *Ibid.*, p. 92.

3. Murray, *op. cit.*, p. 93.

4. Stephen Powers, *Contributions to North American Ethnology, Volume III, Tribes of California*, p. 261.

5. Anonymous, "Uprising of Modocs in Southern Oregon," *Weekly Oregon Statesmen*, December 3, 1872, p. 2.

6. Anonymous, "The Indian Situation," *Weekly Oregon Statesmen*, December 10, 1872, p. 1.

7. Anonymous, "Latest From The Modoc Country," *Weekly Oregon Statesmen*, December 17, 1872, p. 2.

8. Memo from General Edward R.S. Canby Offices of the San Francisco Presidio, (undated), Lava Beds National Monument files.

9. Mary Case, "Creek-Spanning Blockhouse," *Klamath Echoes*, No. 1, p. 20.

10. Erwin N. Thompson, *Modoc War: Its Military History and Topography*, p. 46.

11. Anonymous, "Captain Jack's Fight From a Financial Point of View," *New York Herald*, January 22, 1873, p. 6.

12. Anonymous, "The Modoc War," *San Francisco Chronicle*, January 30, 1873, p. 2.

13. Thompson, *op. cit.*, p. 43.

14. Oliver Knight, *Following the Indian Wars, The Story of the Newspaper Correspondents Among the Indian Campaigners*, p. 106.

15. Thompson, *op. cit.*, p. 52.

16. Anonymous, "The Modoc War," *Weekly Oregon Statesmen*, April 8, 1873, p. 1.

17. Knight, *op. cit.*, p. 138.

18. *Ibid.*, p. 126.

19. Peter Palmquist, "Image Makers of the Modoc War: Louis Heller and Eadweard Muybridge," *The Journal of California Anthropology*, Volume 4, No. 2, Winter, 1977, pp. 209-214.

20. Thompson, *op. cit.*, p. 48.

21. Murray, *op. cit.*, p. 138.

22. Mark M. Boatner, *The Civil War Dictionary*, p. 118.

23. Dillon, *op. cit.*, p. 188.

24. Anonymous, "The Peace Commission," *Weekly Oregon Statesmen*, February 11, 1873, p. 2.

25. Thompson, *op. cit.*, p. 51.

26. Murray, *op. cit.*, p. 159.

27. Thompson, *op. cit.*, p. 54.

28. Walter H. Palmberg, *Copper Paladin: A Modoc Tragedy*, p. 127.

29. Personal letter from Second Lieutenant Harry DeWitt, 21st Infantry, South Shore, Tule Lake, April 29, 1873, Lava Beds National Monument files.

30. Thompson, *op. cit.*, p. 64.

31. Palmberg, *op. cit.*, p. 130.

32. Jeremiah Curtain, *Myths of the Modocs*, p. viii.

33. Thompson, *op. cit.*, p. 60.

34. Dillon, *op. cit.*, p. 228.

35. Anonymous, "The Modoc Massacre," *Chicago Tribune*, April 14, 1873, p. 4.

36. Anonymous, "Massacre, Bloody Treachery of the Modoc Indians," *The New York Herald*, April 13, 1973, p. 8.

37. Anonymous, "The Peace Policy," *Boston Globe*, April 14, 1873, pp. 4-5.

38. Anonymous, "The Modoc Tragedy - The Peace Policy," *Yreka Union*, April 19, 1873, p. 2.

39. Anonymous, "General Sherman's Views," *New York Tribune*, April 14, 1873, p. 1.

40. Anonymous, "The Modoc War," *New York Times*, April 15, 1873, p. 1.

41. Anonymous, "The Modoc War," *Boston Globe*, April 14, 1873, p. 5.

42. Dillon, *op. cit.*, p. 268.

43. Thompson, *op. cit.*, p. 91.

44. *Ibid.*, pp. 97-98.

45. Palmberg, *op. cit.*, p. 137.

46. Thompson, *op. cit.*, pp. 106-107.

47. Dillon, *op. cit.*, p. 293.

48. Thompson, *op. cit.*, p. 112.

49. Dillon, *op. cit.*, pp. 303-304.

50. Anonymous, "Massacre of Modoc Prisoners," *Oregon Statesmen*, June 10, 1873, p. 2.

51. Thompson, *op. cit.*, pp. 123-125.

52. Anonymous, "The Last of the Modoc Murderers, The Indian Question Again Before the World," *New York Herald*, Oct. 4, 1873, p. 6.

53. Dillon, *op. cit.*, p. 333.

54. *Ibid.*, p. 335.

55. Jeff Riddle, *The Indian History of the Modoc War*, p. 198.

56. Anonymous, Annual Report of the Commissioner of Indian Affairs to the Secretary of the Interior, 1873, Lava Beds National Monument files.

57. Anonymous, "Remnants of the Modocs," *Linkville Weekly Star*, May 10, 1884, p. 1.

58. Anonymous, "Modoc Indians To Come Here," *Klamath Republican*, December 8, 1910, p. 6.

59. Thompson, *op. cit.*, pp. 168-171.

60. Murray, *op. cit.*, p. 309.

CHAPTER 7: LINKVILLE, SETTLERS AND IRRIGATION

1. F.A. Shaver, *An Illustrated History of Central Oregon*, p. 939.

2. *Ibid.*, p. 976.

3. Rachel Applegate Good, *History of Klamath County*, pp. 212-213.

4. *Ibid.*, p. 146.

5. Shaver, *op. cit.*, p. 977.

6. *Ibid.*, p. 978.

7. *Ibid.*

8. *Ibid.*, p. 979.

9. *Ibid.*

10. Good, *op. cit.*, p. 97.

11. *Oregon Blue Book, 1931-1932*, p. 118.

12. "Weed Highway Finish Crown," *Klamath Herald*, 1936.

13. Elizabeth Byrne, "Brands of the Lava Beds and Devils Garden," *The Journal of the Modoc County Historical Society*, p. 49.
14. *Ibid.*
15. Devere Helfrich, ed., "First Settlers," *Klamath Echoes, No. 8*, p. 13.
16. Anonymous, *Tule Lake*, an unpublished manuscript, p. 5.
17. Helfrich, *loc. cit.*
18. Byrne, *loc. cit.*
19. *Ibid.*, pp. 50-51.
20. Evea Adams, "J. Frank Adams," *Klamath Echoes, No. 7*, pp. 16-17.
21. Helfrich, "Tule Lake Land Drawings," *Klamath Echoes*, No. 8, p. 28.
22. Good, *op. cit.*, p. 103.
23. *Ibid.*
24. *Ibid..*, pp. 103-104.
25. Devere Helfrich, "Dry Year Troubles," *Klamath Echoes, No. 7*, p. 7.
26. Helfrich, "The Adams Dredge," *Klamath Echoes, No. 7*, pp. 24-25.
27. *Ibid.*, p. 23.
28. Helfrich, "Lakeside Land Company," *Klamath Echoes, No. 8*, p. 20.

CHAPTER 8: MERRILL, ACTIVITY ON TULE LAKE AND WHITE LAKE CITY

1. Devere Helfrich, " 'Tulie" Lake-Gale-Merrill," *Klamath Echoes, No. 7*, p. 33.
2. N.S. Merrill, "The Father of Merrill," *Morning Express*, December, 1909, p. 6.
3. Helfrich, *op. cit.*, p. 37.
4. Merrill, *loc. cit.*
5. F.A. Shaver, *An Illustrated History of Central Oregon*, p. 981.
6. Interview with Marian Offield Hunnicutt and Frank Hunnicutt, July 16, 1984.
7. Anonymous, "Merrill School," *Klamath Republican*, December 1, 1904, p. 3.
8. Anonymous, "1000 Population By Next Fall," *Klamath Republican*, September 28, 1905, p. 1.
9. *Ibid.*
10. Anonymous, "Merrill," *Klamath Republican*, July 2, 1906, p. 2.
11. Anonymous, "Railroad to Merrill," *Klamath Republican*, February 14, 1907, p. 1.
12. Anonymous, "Merrill The Flour City," *Morning Express*, December, 1909, p. 5.
13. Anonymous, "$40,000 Fire at Merrill," *Klamath Falls Express*, April 6, 1911, p. 1.
14. Anonymous, "Town of Merrill Takes a Spurt," *Klamath Republican*, July 11, 1912, p. 8.
15. Anonymous, "Merrill Has Bad Blaze," *Klamath Record*, May 7, 1920, p. 1.
16. Anonymous, "Large Loss From Fire At Merrill," *Klamath Daily Record*, August 16, 1921, p. 1.

17. Anonymous, "Story of Merrill Volunteer Fire Department One of Slow Growth, Unselfish Aid," *The News and the Herald*, February 17, 1937, p. 4.

18. Anonymous, "Merrill Set For Renewal of Colorful Festival," *Tulelake Reporter*, September 7, 1951, p. 4.

19. Anonymous, "Parents Recall Fond Memories As Merrill School Destroyed," *Tulelake Reporter*, December 1, 1949, p. 1.

20. Anonymous, "Formal Dedication of New Merrill Elementary School Is Held Tonight," *Tulelake Reporter*, January 25, 1951.

21. Isabelle Barry, "Coppock Bay, Named for Klamath Homesteader, Soon Will See Land Rush," *Herald and News*, Wednesday, October 8, 1947, Section II, p. 1.

22. *Ibid.*

23. *Ibid.*

24. Anonymous, "Boats Were Important In Early Development of Klamath Basin," *Herald and News*, June 26, 1969, p. 6A.

25. *Ibid.*

26. Devere Helfrich, "Boating on Tule Lake," *Klamath Echoes*, No. 2, p. 74.

27. Barry, *loc. cit.*

28. *Ibid.*

29. Anonymous, "White Lake City," *Klamath Echoes*, No. 15, pp. 26-27.

30. Anonymous, "Will Start New Town," *Klamath Republican*, September 15, 1904, p. 2.

31. Anonymous, "From White Lake City," *Klamath Republican*, September 28, 1905, p. 1.

32. Anonymous, "White Lake City," *Klamath Echoes*, No. 15, pp. 28-29.

33. Anonymous, "Do You Remember White Lake City's Paper?" *The News and the Herald*, January 30, 1937, Supplementary Section.

34. Anonymous, "White Lake City," *Klamath Echoes*, No. 15, pp.27-28.

35. *Ibid.*, p. 33.

CHAPTER 9: MALIN - BOHEMIANS IN THE WEST

1. A.M. Collier, "Lakeside Land Co. Played Role in Malin's Founding," *Herald and News*, June 29, 1969, p. 6A.

2. *Articles of Incorporation of the Lakeside Company*, August 27, 1907 as amended between September and December, 1909, pp. 1-6, Malin Public Library files.

3. Emma Kalina Wilde, "Malin, 'Your Neighbor'," *Klamath Echoes*, No. 8, p. 55.

4. Evea Adams, "As Told by Frank Klabzuba," *Klamath Echoes*, No. 8, pp. 44-45.

5. Anonymous, "Bohemians Coming In," *The Evening Herald*, September 7, 1909, p. 1.

6. Anonymous, "Bohemian Settlers," *The Evening Herald*, September 27, 1909, p. 1.

7. *Ibid.*

8. Rachel Applegate Good, "Malin," *Klamath Echoes*, No. 8, p. 32.

9. Anonymous, "Bohemians Will Remain," *Klamath Republican*, September 30, 1909, p. 1.

10. Ruth King, "Malin Marks Fiftieth Anniversary," *Herald and News*, June 7, 1959, pp. 2-3.

11. *Ibid.*

12. Anonymous, "First Son Recalls Tales of Hardship," *Herald and News*, July 8, 1979, p. 34A.

13. Anonymous, "Life Was Hard," *Herald and News*, July 8, 1979, p. 42A.

14. Adams, *loc. cit.*

15. Anonymous, "Malin May Get Cheese Factory," *Klamath Republican*, July 20, 1911, p. 1.

16. Anonymous, "Bohemians Prepare For Fair," *Klamath Republican*, September 7, 1911, p. 5.

17. Devere Helfrich, "Malin Schools," *Klamath Echoes*, No. 8, p. 40.

18. Vaclav Kalina, Interview, July 24, 1984 and personal notes on Alois and Marie Kalina written in 1983.

19. *Ibid.*

20. Rachel Applegate Good, *History of Klamath County*, p. 137.

21. Good, *Ibid.*

22. Wilde, *op. cit.*, p. 61.

23. Anonymous, "Big Meeting At Malin," *Klamath Record*, April 11, 1919, p. 1.

24. Wilde, *loc. cit.*

25. Ruth King, "Growing Pains of Malin," *Klamath Echoes*, No. 8, p. 50.

26. Anonymous, "The Story of The Progress," from the *Herald and News*, January 10, 1937, *Klamath Echoes*, No. 8, p. 69.

27. Dr. Miroslav Tyrs, as published in the *Souvenir of the United American Sokols of the Pacific, Grand Pacific Festival, Malin, Oregon, July 3rd, 4th and 5th, 1928*, p. 3.

28. Ruth King, "A. Kalina Winds Up 25 Years As Mayor of Malin, City He Named, *Herald and News*, January 7, 1949.

29. Vaclav Kalina, *loc. cit.*

30. Anonymous, "Town of 600 Gives $60,000 to Restaurant," *Eugene Register-Guard*, February 16, 1982.

CHAPTER 10: RECLAMATION - A NEW LOOK FOR THE TULE LAKE AND KLAMATH BASINS

1. George Wharton James, *Reclaiming the Arid West*, p. 15.

2. Rachel Applegate Good, *A History of Klamath County*, pp. 212-213.

3. Anonymous, "Henley," *Klamath Echoes*, No. 15, pp. 38-39.

4. James, *op. cit.*, p. 293.

5. Frederick Haines Newell, *Third Annual Report Of The Reclamation Service, 1903-04*, p. 65.

6. Anonymous, "Farmers Meet," *Klamath Republican*, September 1, 1904, p. 2.

7. Anonymous, "Rousing Mass Meeting," *Klamath Republican*, December 1, 1904, p. 2.

8. Anonymous, *Annual History - Klamath Project, 1957*, p. 213.

9. Anonymous, "Klamath Canal Company To The Fore," *Klamath Republican*, December 22, 1904, p. 1.

10. Anonymous, "It Is Not The Government," *Klamath Republican*, December 29, 1904, p. 1.

11. Anonymous, "It Goes Well With K.C. Company," *Klamath Republican*, January 26, 1905, p. 1.

12. Editorial, *Klamath Republican*, February 9, 1905, p. 1.

13. Anonymous, "Force Out Canal Co.," *Klamath Republican*, April 27, 1905, p. 1.

14. Anonymous, "Klamath Canal Company Have (sic) Agreed To Sell," *Klamath Republican*, May 11, 1905, p. 1.

15. Anonymous, "Development of Irrigation," *Klamath Echoes, No. 8*, p. 16.

16. Anonymous, "Farce Enacted by the Federal Government," *Klamath Republican*, February 24, 1910, p. 1.

17. Anonymous, "Announcement From Ballinger," *Klamath Republican*, March 3, 1910, pp. 1 & 4.

18. Anonymous, "Irrigation Is Now Assured," *Klamath Republican*, May 12, 1910, p. 6.

19. Good, *op. cit.*, p. 106.

20. *Ibid.*, p. 108.

21. Herbert D. Newell, "Tule Lake Reclamation, Klamath Project," *Reclamation Record*, 1920, p. 260.

22. Good, *loc. cit.*

23. Anonymous, "Down Goes Tule Lake," *Klamath Republican*, December 5, 1907, p. 1.

24. Anonymous, "Tule Lake," *Klamath Republican*, December 5, 1907, p. 1.

25. Anonymous, "Great Lake Going Dry," *Klamath Republican*, November 28, 1907, p. 1.

26. Anonymous, "Offer To Drain Tule Lake For Homestead For Each," *Evening Herald*, as reprinted in the *Herald and News*, August, 1981.

27. Newell, *loc. cit.*

28. *Ibid.*

29. *Ibid.*

30. *Ibid.*

31. Anonymous, *Klamath Project: Mid-Pacific Region Water and Power Resources Service*, pp. 567-573.

32. Newell, *op. cit.*, p. 262.

33. Anonymous, *Chronology of Important Events, Klamath Project, 1903-1957*, p. 218.

34. *Ibid.*

35. J.R. Iakisch, *Report on Pumping From Tule Lake and Wildlife Refuge Development, 1938*, p. A.

36. *Ibid.*, pp. A to C.

37. Anonymous, *Chronology of Important Events, Klamath Project, 1903-1957,* pp. 220-221.

38. Anonymous, *Period Report of the Civilian Conservation Corps Camps Under The Bureau of Reclamation, 1936 to 1939.*

39. Anonymous, *Chronology of Important Events, Klamath Project, 1903-1957,* pp. 220-221.

CHAPTER 11: HOMESTEADING RECLAIMED LAND IN THE TULE LAKE BASIN - THE FIRST WAVE

1. Memo from A.P. Davis, Director and Chief Engineer, United States Reclamation Service, to the Project Manager of the Klamath Project, May 26, 1916.

2. Anonymous, "Tule Lake Land Opened Next Spring," *The Evening Herald,* Friday, January 5, 1917, p. 1.

3. Anonymous, "Final Rush Is Made For Tule Lake Opening," *The Evening Herald,* April 23, 1917, pp. 1 & 4.

4. Anonymous, "Winners of Tule Lake Land and Tracts Secure," *The Evening Herald,* April 28, 1917, p. 1.

5. Anonymous, "$10,000 Acres for Entry," *The Sunday Oregonian,* Sunday, September 24, 1922, p. 24.

6. Herbert D. Newell, Memorandum, United States Reclamation Service, Klamath Project, August 26, 1922.

7. Marie Gentry, "Experiences of an Early Homesteader," *Tule Lake Irrigation District, 1972 Annual Report,* p. 19.

8. Ten Broeck Williamson, *History of the 1946 Land Opening of the Tule Lake Division of the Klamath Project,* p. 3.

9. Anonymous, "Gives Reasons for Change on Tule L. Lands," *The Evening Herald,* Tuesday, October 10, 1922, p. 1.

10. Anonymous, "Tule Lake Is Too High Is Claim," *The Evening Herald,* March 11, 1927, p. 1.

11. Anonymous, "Tule Lake Lands Open To Entry," *New Reclamation Era, No. 3,* March, 1927, p. 40.

12. "Settlement of the Tule Lake Division, Klamath Project," *New Reclamation Era, No. 10,* October, 1927, p. 149.

13. Anonymous, "Opening of Tracts on Lake Planned," *The Evening Herald,* April 8, 1928, pp. 1 & 6.

14. Anonymous, "10,000 for Entry," *The Sunday Oregonian,* Sept. 24, 1922, p. 24.

15. Gentry, *op. cit.,* p. 21.

16. *Ibid.*

17. *Ibid.*

18. Ibid., p. 23.

19. Anonymous, "Dust Closes School," *Evening Herald,* October 26, 1922, p. 1.

20. Gentry, *op. cit.,* p. 21.

21. *Ibid.,* p. 31.

CHAPTER 12: CHANGES IN THE BASIN AND A
DEVELOPING SENSE OF COMMUNITY

1. Constitution and By-Laws of the Tule Lake Community Club, Article II, p. 1.
2. Anonymous, "Tule Lake Community Club, Klamath Project, Oregon," *New Reclamation Era, Vol. 19*, No. 7, July, 1928, p. 107.
3. Marie Gentry, "Experiences of an Early Homesteader," *Tulelake Irrigation District, 1970 Annual Report*, p. 27.
4. *Ibid.*
5. Letter from Joe Spence, Secretary of the Tule Lake Community Club to Herbert D. Newell, Project Director, Klamath Project, May 29, 1928.
6. Letter from Siskiyou County Superintendent of Schools L.S. Newton to H.A. Knight, President of the Tule Lake Community Club, June 14, 1928.
7. Regina Frey, Interview, August 7, 1981, Tule Lake Basin, California.
8. Newton, *loc. cit.*
9. Anonymous, *History of the Winema Welfare Club*, pp. 5-6.
10. Resolution of the Tule Lake Community Club, December 12, 1929, pp. 1-2.
11. Letter from Klamath Project Director B.E. Hayden to F.E. McMurphy, Secretary of the Tule Lake Community Club, March 6, 1930.
12. Letter from Bureau of Reclamation Commissioner Elwood Mead to the Hon. Harry L. Englebright, House of Representatives, May 13, 1930.
13. *Ibid.*
14. Letter from Bureau of Reclamation Commissioner Elwood Mead to the Hon. Harry L. Englebright, House of Representatives, June 30, 1930.
15. H.G. Mathewson, Secretary, Railroad Commission of the State of California to the Tule Lake Community Club, Malin, Oregon, June 3, 1930.
16. Letter from Klamath Project Director B.E. Hayden to Fred E. McMurphy, Secretary of the Tule Lake Community Club, January 16,1930.
17. Lorna Hansen, correspondence, Tule Lake Basin, California, September 16, 1981.
18. Gentry, *op. cit.*
19. Anonymous, "History of Tulelake All Written Since 1931," *The News and the Herald*, July 8, 1938.
20. Portia Aikins, Interview, Tule Lake Basin, California, August 7, 1981.
21. Anonymous, *Period Report of the Emergency Conservation Work Camps Under The Bureau of Reclamation, Seventh Enrollment Period*, November, 1936.
22. Anonymous, "Return From Lava Beds," *Klamath Republican*, May 25, 1911, p. 1.
23. Anonymous, "Big Party Sees Modoc Lava Beds," *Klamath Republican*, June 15, 1911, p. 7.
24. "CCC Speeds Up Development," undated news article, circa 1937, Lava Beds National Monument files.
25. Bill Brissenden, "History of Tule Lake Development," *Souvenir Program, 3'rd Postwar Tulelake Homestead Drawing, February 23, 1949*, p. 7.

26. Ten Broeck Williamson, *History of the 1946 Land Opening on the Tule Lake Division of the Klamath Project*, pp. 42-45.

CHAPTER 13:   THE CITY OF TULELAKE - A NEW TOWN ON THE LAKE BED

1. Letter from Herbert D. Newell to D.W. Turnbaugh, Secretary of the Tule Lake Community Club, February 21, 1929.
2. Letter from the Tule Lake Community Club to the Siskiyou County Board of Supervisors, August 9, 1929.
3. Letter from the Tule Lake Community Club to the Pacific Fruit and Produce Company, August 9, 1929.
4. Letter from the Tule Lake Community Club to the Railroad Commission of the State of California, August 12, 1929.
5. Dorothy Ager, Interview, August 17, 1984, Redding, California.
6. Anonymous, "History of Tulelake All Written   Since 1931," *News and Herald*, July 8, 1939.
7. Anonymous, "Sale of a Town to Draw Crowd," *The Evening Herald*, April 14, 1931, p. 1.
8. *Ibid.*
9. Anonymous, "Tule Lake Lot Goes For $530," *The Evening Herald*, April 15, 1931, p. 1.
10. Anonymous, "History of Tulelake All Written Since 1931," *News and Herald*, July 8, 1939.
11. Anonymous, "Nobody Would Pay Chet Havlina $125 for His Homestead," *Tulelake Reporter*, April 24, 1952, p. 13.
12. Letter from Mrs. Grace M. Hilgert to the Tule Lake Postmaster, July 29,1941.
13. Letter from Sara Welsh, Secretary of the Tulelake Chamber of Commerce, to Mrs. Grace M. Hilgert, August 1, 1941.
14. Malcolm Epley, "Today's Roundup," *Herald and News*, July 27, 1948.
15. Anne S. Horton, "The Youngest Sister," *Klamath Echoes*, No. 8, p. 75.
16. Dorothy Ager, *loc. cit.*
17. Anonymous, "Sodas, Service and Sociability: The Story of a 15th Anniversary," *Tulelake Reporter*, August 10, 1950, p. 1.
18. *Ibid.*
19. *Ibid.*
20. Dorothy Ager, Letter to Stan Turner, October 19, 1981.
21. Alan R. Beals and Thomas McCorkle, *Kroeber Anthropological Society Papers, No. 3*, "Lost Lake," p. 7.
22. Anonymous, "Story of Incorporation Reveals Names of Many Early Public Servants," *Tulelake Reporter*, April 24, 1952, p. 1.
23. Petition for Incorporation, City of Tulelake, October 3, 1936, Siskiyou County Court House files.
24. *Ibid.*

25. Anonymous, "Tulelake Swept by Flames," *The Evening Herald*, October 13, 1936, pp. 1 & 6.

26. *Ibid.*

27. Beals and McCorkle, *loc. cit.*

28. Anonymous, "Incorporation of Tulelake Talked," *The Evening Herald*, October 14, 1936, p. 6.

29. Anonymous, "Incorporation Move Voted by Huge Majority," *The Evening Herald*, February 27, 1937.

30. Anonymous, "Election Held for Tulelake Incorporation," *The News and the Herald*, February 27, 1937.

31. Anonymous, "Story of Incorporation Reveals Names of Many Early Public Servants," *Tulelake Reporter*, April 24, 1952, p. 1.

32. Endorsement of Incorporation, Frank C. Jordon, Secretary of State, State of California, March 1, 1937, 9:45 a.m., Siskiyou County Court House files.

33. Anonymous, "Tulelake Not On Map Until 1940," *Tulelake Reporter*, April 24, 1952, p. 7.

34. Hyman Wechsler & C.L. Fehle, *Tulelake Volunteer Fire Department Records*, pp. 1-4.

35. *Ibid.*, p. 1.

36. *Ibid.*, p. 5.

37. *Ibid.*, p. 6.

38. *Ibid.*, p. 7.

39. *Ibid.*, p. 1.

40. Victoria Thaler, Interview, City of Tulelake, California, August 8, 1984.

41. Anonymous, "Utilizing Methane Gas In Water As Tule's Gas Supply Probed," *Tulelake Reporter*, April 24, 1952, p. 16.

42. Anonymous, "Fire Loss May Reach 'Thousands'," *Tulelake Reporter*, May 25, 1950, p. 1.

43. Anonymous, "It's Softer, Smoother, Sweeter; But Most Folk Cautious Over New Water," *Tulelake Reporter*, September 27, 1951, p. 1.

44. Anonymous, "Miracle or Myth? Water Boosters Want New Well; Gold Fish Skeptical," *Tulelake Reporter*, October 4, 1951, p. 1.

45. *Ibid.*

46. *Ibid.*

47. Letter from J.W. Carlisle, Chairman of the Airport Committee, Tulelake Chamber of Commerce, to Mr. Arthur Ayres, Supervisor of Airports, Civil Aeronautic Administration, September 12, 1941.

48. Letter from E.R. Blank, District Manager, Tide Water Associated Oil Company to the Tulelake Chamber of Commerce, September 22, 1941.

49. Letter from R.W.F. Schmidt, Airport Engineer, Civil Aeronautics Administration to J.W. Carlisle, Airport Committee, Tulelake Chamber of Commerce, November 4, 1941.

50. Anonymous, "Big Opening for Airport," *Tulelake Reporter*, May 3, 1951, p. 1.

51. Letter from Sara Welsh to Paramount Pictures, November 8, 1941.

52. Chet Main, Interview, Tule Lake Basin, California, August 9, 1984.

53. John Staunton, Interview, Tulelake, California, March 27, 2002.

54. Russell Smith, Interview, Tule Lake Basin, California, May 7, 1982.

55. Chet Main, *loc. cit.*

56. *Ibid.*

57. Anonymous, "Over 3000 Attend Big Lite Night Fun," *Tulelake Reporter*, March 9, 1950, p. 1.

58. Anonymous, "Basin Schools Enroll Record-Breaking 737," *Tulelake Reporter*, September 11, 1952, p. 1.

59. Anonymous, "Tulelake Merchants Can Blame Selves for Losing Business, Chamber Told," *Tulelake Reporter*, March 19, 1953, p. 1.

60. Anonymous, "Tulelake Hotel Razed," *Herald and News*, December 13, 1984, p. 1.

61. Joe Cordinier, Interview, City of Tulelake, California, August 1, 1984.

62. *Ibid.*

CHAPTER 14: A PRELUDE TO THE INTERNMENT YEARS IN THE BASIN - WHY JAPANESE-AMERICANS?

1. John L. DeWitt, *Final Report: Japanese Evacuation From The West Coast, 1942*, pp. 26-27.

2. Bill Hosokawa, *Nisei: The Quiet Americans*, p. 151.

3. Richard H. Minear, ed., *Through Japanese Eyes, Volume II*, p. 117

4. *Ibid.*, p. 116.

5. Jacobus tenBroek, et. al., *Prejudice, War and the Constitution*, p. 39.

6. Anonymous, "Anti-Jap Bill Is Up In Congress," *Klamath Republican*, April 20, 1910, p. 2.

7. Anonymous, "Just Lower Element Fighting Japs," *Klamath Republican*, February 17, 1910, p. 1.

8. Anonymous, "Japs To Mine Manila Harbor," *Klamath Republican*, December 29, 1910, p. 1.

9. tenBroek, *op. cit.*, p. 29.

10. *Ibid.*, p. 30.

11. McWilliams, *Prejudice, Japanese Americans: Symbol of Racial Intolerance*, p. 147.

12. Minier, *op. cit.*, pp. 117-119.

13. tenBroek, *op. cit.*, p. pp. 43-57.

14. McWilliams, Carey, *Brothers Under the Skin*, pp. 148-149.

15. Hosokawa, *op. cit.*, p. 284.

16. *Ibid.*

17. Alan R. Bosworth, *America's Concentration Camps*, p. 73.

18. *Ibid.*

19. Henry McLemore, Editorial, *San Francisco Examiner*, January 29, 1942.

20. Hosokawa, *op. cit.*, p. 265.

21. Dillon Myer, *Uprooted Americans*, p. 22.

22. Michi Weglyn, *Years of Infamy*, pp. 59-61.

23. DeWitt, *op. cit.,* p. 10.
24. *Ibid.,* p. 18.
25. tenBroek, *op. cit.,* p. 351.

CHAPTER 15: THE WAR RELOCATION CAMP AT TULE LAKE

1. "Tulelake Chamber Draws Resolution in Opposition to Jap Evacuation Center," *Herald and News,* April 13, 1942.
2. *Ibid.*
3. Harry L. Englebright, Letter to Sara Welsh, April 28, 1942.
4. Henry L. Stimson, Letter to Harry L. Englebright, May 11, 1942.
5. *Ibid.*
6. John C. Page, Letter to Harry L. Englebright, May 17, 1942.
7. "Tule Lake Jap Camp Started: Lumber For First Unit Bought Here," *Evening Herald,* April 17, 1942, pp. 1-2.
8. "Jap Camp Moved to New Location: Crops Not To Be Disrupted This Year," *Evening Herald,* April 21, 1942.
9. "Jap Camp Causes Labor Shortage," *Evening Herald,* April 28, 1942, p. 9.
10. Richard H. Syring, "Portland To Be First Jap Free City," *Oregon Journal,* April 29, 1942, p. 1.
11. " 'Newell, Calif.' New Address for Jap Camp Center," *Evening Herald,* May 20, 1942.
12. "Tulelake Project Amazing for Speed of Construction," *Evening Herald,* May 23, 1942, p. 3.
13. Dorothy S. Thomas & Richard Nishimoto, *The Spoilage: Japanese-American Evacuation and Resettlement During World War II,* p. 38.
14. Shuji Kimura, "To A New World," *A Tule Lake Interlude,* p. 30.
15. Thomas and Nishimoto, *op. cit.,* p. 40.
16. *Ibid.,* pp. 40-41.
17. "Japanese Center 'Pointers'," *Evening Herald,* August 1, 1942.
18. Regina Frey, Interview, Tule Lake Basin, California, August 6, 1981.
19. Anonymous, "Gov. Sprague Asks Roosevelt to Force Japanese Internee Harvest Assistance," *Evening Herald,* October 16, 1942.
20. "Evacuees Having Differing Opinions of Treatment," *Evening Herald,* September 30, 1942.
21. *Ibid.*
22. "Japanese Name Found Painted on Petroglyphs," *Evening Herald,* September 30, 1942.
23. "California Game Chief Charges Violation of Federal Laws," *Evening Herald,* October 14, 1942.
24. "Radio Tokyo Lies," *Evening Herald,* October 15, 1942.
25. "Newell Jap Center Conditions Flayed: Japanese Charged With Duck Fishing," *Evening Herald,* October 14, 1942.

26. "Partial Report Made on Chamber Probe of Condition at WRA Tule Lake Center," *Evening Herald*, October 28, 1942.

27. "35 Years Ago: 1943, Looking Back," *Tulelake Reporter*, May 18, 1978.

28. Charles Palmerlee, Interview, Eugene, Oregon, September 20, 1973.

29. Anonymous, "Japanese Women At Camp Have Knitted 63 Shawls and Sent Them To Red Cross for Distribution to Servicemen," *Evening Herald*, December 3, 1942, p. 2.

30. Anonymous, "35 Years Ago: Looking Back," *Tulelake Reporter*, May 18, 1978.

31. Kenneth and Winifred Lambie, Interview, Klamath Falls, Oregon, May 9, 1982 and September 8, 1984.

32. *Ibid.*

33. Arthur Morimitsu, "Fleeting Impressions," *A Tule Lake Interlude*, p. 58.

34. Roger Daniels, *Concentration Camps, USA: Japanese Americans and World War II*, p. 110.

35. Morimitsu, *op. cit.*, p. 56.

36. Sada Murayama, "Loyalty," *A Tule Lake Interlude*, p. 31.

37. Anonymous, "A Nisei Diary," *A Tule Lake Interlude*, pp. 102-109.

CHAPTER 16: A NEW PHASE OF INTERNMENT - TULE LAKE BECOMES THE NATION'S SEGREGATION CENTER

1. Dillon S. Myer, *Uprooted Americans*, p. 132.

2. *Ibid.*, p. 133.

3. Roger Daniels, *Concentration Camps USA: Japanese Americans and World War II*, pp. 112-113.

4. *Ibid.*, p. 113.

5. Allan Bosworth, *America's Concentration Camps*, pp. 165-166.

6. *Ibid.*, p. 166.

7 Bill Hosokawa, Nisei, *The Quiet Americans*, p. 99.

8. Daniels, *op. cit.*, p. 113.

9. Dorothy Thomas & Richard Nishimoto, *The Spoilage: Japanese-American Evacuation and Resettlement During World War II*, p. 72.

10. Daniels, *op. cit.*, p. 114.

11. *Ibid.*

12. Thomas & Nishimoto, *op. cit.*, p. 73.

13. *Ibid.*, p. 74.

14. Haru Tanabe, Letter to Kenneth and Winifred Lambie, February 18, 1943.

15. Thomas & Nishimoto, *op. cit.*, pp. 79-80.

16. *Ibid.*, p. 63.

17. Audrie Girdner & Anne Loftis, *The Great Betrayal: The Evacuation of the Japanese-Americans DuringWorld War II*, p. 318.

18. Myer, *op. cit.*, pp. 79-80.

19. Michi Weglyn, *Years of Infamy: The Untold Story of America's Concentration Camps*, p. 163.

20. Senator Jack B. Tenny, et. al., *The Joint Fact Finding Committee On Un-American Activities in California (1943-45)*, p. 11.
21. Thomas & Nishimoto, *op. cit.*, p. 139.
22. *Ibid.*, p. 144.
23. *Ibid.*, p. 145.
24. *Ibid.*, p. 147.
25. Howard D. Hannaford, "The Situation at Tulelake," *The Christian Century*, December 15, 1943.
26. Thomas & Nishimoto, *op. cit.*, pp. 251-252.
27. *Ibid.*, p. 269.
28. *Ibid.*, pp. 271-272.
29. Anonymous, "Son of Tule Lake Jap Is Killed," *County Record*, Alturas, California, July 27, 1944, p. 1.
30. Jacobus tenBroek, et al., *Prejudice, War and the Constitution*, p. 175.
31. Thomas & Nishimoto, *op. cit.*, p. 353.
32. *Ibid.*, p. 349.
33. *Ibid.*
34. *Ibid.*, p. 351.
35. tenBroek, *op. cit.*, p. 179.
36. Weglyn, *op. cit.*, p. 259.
37. California Registered Historical Landmark No. 850-2, Tule Lake Basin, Newell, California.
38. JACL Hymn, 1945.

CHAPTER 17: THE LAST HOMESTEADERS

1. Ten Broeck Williamson, *History of the 1946 Land Opening on the Tule Lake Division of the Klamath Project*, p. 4.
2. *Ibid.*, p. 5.
3. *Ibid.*, p. 8.
4. *Ibid.*, p. 23.
5. *Ibid.*, pp. 19-20.
6. John A. Leveritt, "Future Homesteaders," *Reclamation ERA*, March, 1947, Vol. 33, No. 3, p. 66.
7. *Ibid.*
8. Williamson, *op. cit.*, p. 62.
9. *Ibid.*
10. *Ibid.*
11. *Ibid.*, p. 64.
12. Anonymous, "Board Reversed in Only 13 Vet Homestead Cases," *Herald and News*, November 14, 1946.
13. Lois Stewart, "Tension Grips Crowds At Homestead Drawing," *Herald and News*, December 19, 1946, p. 1.
14. Williamson, *op. cit.*, pp. 86.

15. Orin Cassmore, "Gold Mine in the Sky," *Reclamation ERA*, February, 1947, Vol. 33, No. 2, p. 29.

16. Lois Stewart, *loc. cit.*

17. Cassmore, *op. cit.*, p. 26.

18. *Ibid.*

19. *Ibid.*, p. 27.

20. Phillip Krizo, Interview, Tule Lake Basin, California, March 23, 1983.

21. Barbara Krizo, Interview, Tule Lake Basin, California, March 23, 1983.

22. Leveritt, *loc. cit.*

23. Williamson, *op. cit.*, pp. 87-88.

24. Malcolm Epley, "Today's Roundup," *Herald and News*, February 26, 1947.

25. Anonymous, "Farm Lottery: Veterans at Tulelake Win Land Developed in Wartime by the Japs," *Life Magazine*, January 20, 1947, p. 73.

26. Williamson, *op. cit.*, p. 90.

27. Stan Weber, "Banks Farm Winner Pleased With Luck," *Oregon Journal*, December 20, 1946.

28. Bill Brissenden, "History of Tulelake Development," *Souvenir Program, 3'd Postwar Tulelake Homestead Drawing*, February 23, 1949.

29. Anonymous, "Eight Veterans from Local Area Hit Jackpot in B of R Drawings Conducted at Klamath Armory," *Herald And News*, March 15, 1948 as reprinted in *The Tule Lake Reporter*, July 25, 1968, p. 6.

30. Ralph Morrill, Interview, City of Tulelake, California, March 24, 1983.

31. Anonymous, "Homestead Unit Taken," *Herald and News*, June 22, 1949.

32. Robert Anderson, Interview, Tule Lake Basin, California, August 6, 1981.

33. Bill Whitaker, Interview, City of Tule Lake, California, June 26, 1981.

34. Anderson, *loc. cit.*

35. Anonymous, "Life At Jap Center Draws near End as Hundreds of Buildings Moved Off Site," *Herald and News*, March 19, 1947.

36. File copy of barracks removal agreement, Bureau of Reclamation, Klamath Falls, Oregon.

37. Barbara Krizo, *loc. cit.*

38. *Ibid.*

39. A. D. Harvey and Orin Cassmore, "Golden Harvest at Klamath," *Reclamation Era, Vol. 34, No. 2*, February, 1948, p. 30.

40. Orin Cassmore , "Spotlight on the Pioneers," *Reclamation Era, Vol. 33, No. 11*, November, 1947, p. 238.

41. Anonymous, "Tulelake Lottery Winners Anxious to Start Building," *The San Francisco News*, January 2, 1947.

42. Frank King, Interview, Tule Lake Basin, California, August 5, 1981.

43. Phillip and Barbara Krizo, *loc. cit.*

44. Malcolm Epley, "Today's Roundup," *Herald and News*, December 16, 1946.

45. Cassmore, "Gold Mine in the Sky," *Reclamation Era, Vol. 33, No. 2*, February, 1947, p. 29.

CHAPTER 18: NEWELL - A COMMUNITY IN TRANSITION

1. Ruth King, "Life at Jap Center Draws Near End as Hundreds of Buildings Moved Off Site," *Herald and News*, March 19, 1947.
2. *Ibid.*
3. Anonymous, "Tulelake Expects Influx of Migrant Farm Hands," *Herald and News*, July 31, 1946.
4. Anonymous, "Migrants to Use Former Jap Colony," *Herald and News*, September 14, 1946.
5. Ruth King, *Herald and News*, May, 1947 (article title and date unknown).
6. *Ibid.*
7. John Coulson, President, E.L. Booth, Secretary-Treasurer, Resolution, Tulelake-Butte Valley Sportsmen's Association, January 15, 1948, Records of the Newell Homestead Club.
8. James Stearns, President, Resolution of the Newell Homestead Club sent to the Honorable Clair Engle, Members of Congress, California Second District, March 5, 1948, Records of the Newell Homestead Club.
9. James Stearns, letter to the Honorable Clair Engle, Member of Congress, California Second District, March 23, 1948, Records of the Newell Homestead Club.
10. Wanda L. Stark, letter to Jim Stearns, July 9, 1948, Records of the Newell Homestead Club.
11. The Honorable Clair Engle, Member of Congress, California Second District, letter to Gerwin McCracken, Secretary of the Newell Homestead Club, June 18, 1948, Records of the Newell Homestead Club.
12. Paul E. Christy, letter to State of California, Board of Education, April 18, 1949, Records of the Newell Homestead Club.
13. Paul E. Christy, letter to Edgar W. Parsons, Division of School Planning, State of California, January 10, 1950, Records of the Newell Homestead Club.
14. Raymond R. Best, Memo to Regional Director, February 16, 1948.
15. Notice of Public Hearing, United States Department of the Interior, Bureau of Reclamation, Klamath Project, Klamath Falls, Oregon, June 1, 1949, records of the Newell Homestead Club.
16. Wendell Schey, President Newell Homestead Club, letter to the Honorable Clair Engle, Member of Congress, California Second District, January 10, 1949. Records of the Newell Homestead Club.
17. Anonymous, "Townsite at Newell Gets Green Light," *Herald and News*, June 21, 1949.
18. *Ibid.*
19. Anonymous, "List Minimum Bids on 300 Newell Lots," *Tulelake Reporter*, Thursday, June 14, 1951, p. 1.
20. Anonymous, "Newell Sale Slow; First Buyers Listed," *Tulelake Reporter*, June 21, 1951, p. 1.
21. *Klamath Project Chronology, 1951*, Bureau of Reclamation, Klamath Falls, Oregon, p. vii.

22. Anonymous, "Grandview School Poser, Big Community Question," *Tulelake Reporter*, January 11, 1951, p. 2.

23. *Ibid.*, pp. 1-2.

24. Anonymous, "Newell Votes Tally Huge Majority for School," *Tulelake Reporter*, January 17, 1952, p. 1.

25. Anonymous, "No Plans For Using Relocation Center, Engle Indicates," *Tulelake Reporter*, May 3, 1951, p. 1.

26. *Ibid.*

27. Anonymous, "Clear Newell Labor Camp For Prison," *Tulelake Reporter*, January 10, 1952, p. 1.

28. *Ibid.*

29. Anonymous, "Washington Sheds Little Light As Basin Ponders Future of Newell Camp," *Tulelake Reporter*, February 21, 1952, p. 1.

30. Paul and Gertrude Christy, Interview, Tule Lake Basin, California, August 9, 1984.

31. Anonymous, "Seek Move Govt. From Newell," *Tulelake Reporter*, March 13, 1952, p. 1.

32. Anonymous, "Newell School Location Delays New Construction," *Tulelake Reporter*, June 26, 1952, p. 1.

33. Anonymous, "Board Denies Plea to Split Newell School Boundaries," *Tulelake Reporter*, December 4, 1952, p. 1.

34. "Homesteaders are Looking Forward to Third Reunion in July," *Tulelake Reporter*, June 21, 1979.

35. Paul Christy, Interview, Tule Lake Basin, California, August 9, 1984.

36. *Ibid.*

37. *Ibid.*

38. Gertrude Christy, Interview, Tule Lake Basin, California, August 9, 1984.

39. Anonymous, "Pumice Works Glass Mt. Location," *Tulelake Reporter*, July 26, 1951, p. 1.

40. Anonymous, "Over 1000 Visitors From Score of Towns Applaud Top Notch Tule Air Fair," *Tulelake Reporter*, June 28, 1951, p. 1.

41. *Ibid.*

42. Anonymous, "Fire Protection For New Homestead Areas Outlined," *Tulelake Reporter*, May 17, 1951, p. 1.

43. Anonymous, "Newell Homestead Club Ends Five Years of Wonderful Service To The Community," *Tulelake Reporter*, March 27, 1952, p. 1.

44. *Ibid.*

45. *Ibid.*

46. Anonymous, "Marvin Christy's Neighborliness Pays Off As Friends Seed 80-Acre Ranch," *Tulelake Reporter*, May 8, 1952, p. 1.

47. Anonymous, "Chimes Ring Out For First Time," *Tulelake Reporter*, Oct. 9, 1952, p. 1.

CHAPTER 19: HOMESTEADING AND WILDLIFE PRESERVATION – A DIVISION OF INTERESTS

1. Anonymous, *Klamath Basin National Wildlife Refuges, California-Oregon,* pamphlet, U.S. Department of the Interior.

2. Anonymous, *Celebrating 75 Years,* pamphlet, U.S. Department of the Interior, 1977.

3. Anonymous, "No Hunting on Lower Lake," *Klamath Republican,* August 27, 1908, p. 1.

4. Theodore Roosevelt, Executive Order #924, August, 1908.

5. Anonymous, "No Hunting On Lower Lake," *loc. cit.*

6. Anonymous, "Record To Be Kept Of Visitors To Bird Island - New Launch Purchased," *The Evening Herald,* June 19, 1912, p. 1.

7. Anonymous, "River, Lake Closed To Hunters," *Klamath Republican,* May 8, 1913, p. 4.

8. Anonymous, "Stop Trapping on Lower Klamath Lake," *Klamath Republican,* August 28, 1913, p. 1.

9. L.T. Coburn, *The Bird Preserve,* A Position Paper on file at the offices of the Klamath Project, Bureau of Reclamation, Klamath Falls, Oregon.

10. Frank Graham, Jr. *Man's Dominion: The Story of Conservation in America,* p. 222.

11. Calvin Coolidge, *Executive Order #4975,* October 4, 1928.

12. Franklin D. Roosevelt, *Executive Order #7341,* April 10, 1936.

13. J.R. Iakisch, *Report on Pumping from Tule Lake and Wildlife Refuge Development: 1938-1939.*

14. Anonymous, "Sports Official Predicts End of Tule Lake Refuge," *Sacramento Bee,* October 6, 1948.

15. Anonymous, "Revolving Light Used in Campaign to Scare Birds," *Herald and News,* September 9, 1946.

16. Malcolm Epley, "Today's Roundup," *Herald and News,* September 9, 1946.

17. Anonymous, "Wildlife Plan Scored Here," *Tulelake Reporter,* April 19, 1951, p. 1.

18. *Ibid.*

19. Anonymous, "Plan More Tule Basin Homesteads," *Tulelake Reporter,* June 28, 1951, p. 1.

20. Anonymous, "Homesteads Said Threat To Hunting," *Tulelake Reporter,* January 3, 1952, p. 1.

21. *Ibid.*

22. John B. Edmands, "Reporter Answers Charges Waterfowl Hurt By Homesteading In Tulelake Basin," *Tulelake Reporter,* January 10, 1952, p. 1.

23. Anonymous, "No More Tule Basin Homesteads In The Immediate Future," *Tulelake Reporter,* January 17, 1952, p. 1.

24. Anonymous, "Basin Speaks Out For Firm Govt. Policies On This Land," *Tulelake Reporter,* September 25, 1952, p. 1.

25. Anonymous, "Government Will Open 150 Homesteads In '53," *Tulelake Reporter*, October 9, 1952, p. 1.

26. Anonymous, "Bureau Does Homestead Flip," *Tulelake Reporter*, October 16, 1952, p. 1.

27. *Ibid.*

28. Anonymous, "Homesteads May Be Mandatory, Bureau Says," *Tulelake Reporter*, December 4, 1952, p. 1.

29. Anonymous, "Homesteads -- - 6,700 Acres, Wildlife --- All The Rest," *Tulelake Reporter*, January 8, 1953, p. 1.

30. *Ibid.*

31. Anonymous, "What Chapman Said," *Tulelake Reporter*, January 15, 1953, p. 1.

32. *Ibid.*

33. Anonymous, "McKay Pledges To Protect Ducks, Mum on Homesteads," *Tulelake Reporter*, January 22, 1953, p. 1.

34. Anonymous, "Voiding of Lame Duck Directive Asked," *Tulelake Reporter*, February 5, 1953, p. 1.

35. Wallace Myers, "Many Angles Apparent in Leaseland Problem," *Herald and News*, January 10, 1953.

36. Anonymous, "Groups Band Against Basin To Deny ANY Homesteads," *Tulelake Reporter*, April 2, 1953, p. 1.

37. Frank King, Interview, Tule Lake Basin, California, August 5, 1981.

38. Kuchel Act, Public Law 88-567, September 2, 1964.

39. National Wildlife Refuge System Administration Act of 1966 as Amended in 1976 and United States of America, Department of the Interior, Fish and Wildlife Service and Bureau of Reclamation, Cooperative Agreement, August 2, 1977.

40. Robert Fields, Project Leader of the Tule Lake National Wildlife Refuge, Interview, Tulelake Basin, August 3, 1981.

CHAPTER 20: THE YEARS OF HARVEST

1. John Muir, "Modoc Memories," *The Bulletin*, reprinted in anonymous manuscript on file at the Lava Beds National Monument, p. 2.

2. Frank King, Interview, Tulelake Basin, California, August 5, 1981.

3. Barbara Krizo, Interview, Tulelake Basin, California, March 22, 1983.

4. Paul and Gertrude Christy, Interview, Tulelake Basin, August 7, 1984.

5. Lee Juillerat, "Friends 'make hay' in Tulelake Way," *The Oregonian*, September 27, 1982.

6. Portia Aikins, Interview, Tulelake Basin, August 7, 1981.

EPILOGUE: PART ONE – THE STRUGGLE FOR WATER
AND ECONOMIC SURVIVAL

1. Elwood H. Miller, "Klamath Tribes' desire is return of robust land, water ecosystems," *Herald and News*, March 26, 2001.
2. Klamath Water Users Association, "Protecting the Beneficial Uses of Waters of Upper Klamath Lake: A Plan to Accelerate Recovery of the Last River and Shortnose Suckers", p. 1.
3. Michael Milstein, "Tensions flare over water rights," *Oregonian*, May 6, 2001.
4. Michael Milstein, "Endangered fish at center of swirling crisis," *Oregonian*, May 8, 2001.
5. Lee Juillerat, "Tribes, fishermen please with verdict," *Herald and News*, April 8, 2001.
6. *Ibid.*
7. Ann Aiken, United States District Judge, United States District Court, Steven Lewis Kandra, et al. vs. United States of America; Gale Norton, Secretary of the Interior, et al., p. 16.
8. *Ibid.*, p. 37.
9. *Ibid.*
10. Anonymous, Editorial, "The Klamath dust bowl," *Oregonian*, May 13, 2001.
11. Anonymous, Editorial, "Don't blame the fish", *Register Guard*, May 27, 2001.
12. Kehn Gibson & Anita Burke, "Evinger tells marshals it's time to go," *Herald and News*, July 22, 2001.
13. Lee Juillerat & Kehn Gibson, "Convoy brings strong support", *Herald and News*, August 21, 2001.
14. *Ibid.*
15. Kehn Gibson, "Officers freed to help in emergency," *Herald and News*, September 13, 2001.
16. Mike Connelly, "Farmers reacting to government lawlessness," *Register-Guard*, July 25, 2001.
17. Anonymous, Editorial, "A fortuitous review," *Register-Guard*, August 8, 2001.
18. Jeff Barnard, "Homesteader's daughter sues over Klamath water," *Register-Guard*, August 31, 2001.
19. Jeff Barnard, "Water review on fast track," *Herald and News*, October 24, 2001.
20. Jeff Barnard, "Klamath study mentions racial tension," *Register-Guard*, December 20, 2001.
21. Gillian Flaccus, "Activist groups threaten lawsuit over Klamath" *Register-Guard*, January 25, 2002.
22. Jeff Barnard, "New report rekindles Klamath water debate," *Register-Guard*, January 29, 2002.
23. *Ibid.*
24. *Ibid.*
25. *Ibid.*
26. *Ibid.*
27. National Research Council, "Scientific Evaluation of Biological Opinions on Endangered and Threatened Fishes in the Klamath River Basin," *National Academy of Sciences*, pp. 1-2, February, 2002.
28. Michael Milstein, "Scientists critical of Klamath water ban," *Oregonian*, February 4, 2002.
29. *Ibid.*

30. Michael Milstein, "Tribes fault Klamath report," *Oregonian*, February 22, 2002.
31. Anonymous, "Tribes take issue with Klamath water study," *Register-Guard*, January 26, 2002.
32. Anonymous, "Academy's Klamath report is criticized," *Register-Guard*, March 8, 2002.
33. *Ibid.*
34. Anonymous, "Environmentalists to bid on farmland," *Register-Guard*, March 12, 2002.

EPILOGUE: PART TWO – THE YEARS OF HARVEST REVISITED

1. Joe Cordonier, Interview, Tulelake, California, March 28, 2002.
2. Tony Giacomelli, Telephone Interview, April 9, 2002.
3. *Ibid.*
4. Michael Milstein, "Endangered fish at center of swirling crisis," *Oregonian*, May 8, 2001.
5. Phil Norton, Interview, Tulelake, California, March 27, 2002.
6. Phil Krizo, Interview, Tulelake, California, March 27, 2002.
7. Joe Victorine, Interview, Tulelake, California, March 27, 2002.
8. Renee Kohler, Interview, Tulelake, California, March 27, 2002.
9. Denny Kalina, Interview, Tulelake, California, March 27, 2002.
10. Cindy Wright, Interview, Tulelake, California, March 29, 2002.
11. Paul Christy, Interview, Tulelake, California, March 29, 2002.
12. Sharron Molder, Interview, Tulelake, California, March 28, 2002.
13. Venancio Hernandez, Interview, Tulelake, California, March 27, 2002.
14. Jessie Larson, Telephone Interview, April 24, 2002.
15. Luis Aceves, Telephone Interview, April 19, 2002.
16. Bill Ganger, Telephone Interview, April 25, 2002.
17. John Crawford, Telephone Interview, April 25, 2002.
18. Steve Kandra, Interview, Tulelake Basin, March 27, 2002.
19. *Ibid.*
20. *Ibid.*

Sacking potatoes in the 1950s.
(Photo courtesy Bureau of Reclamation)

BIBLIOGRAPHY: THE YEARS OF HARVEST

Books

Alt, David D. & Hyndman, Donald W., *Roadside Geology of Northern California*, Missoula, Mountain Press Publishing Company, 1975.

Alt, David D. & Hyndman, Donald, *Roadside Geology of Oregon*, Missoula, Mountain Press Publishing Company, 1978.

Bailey, Paul, *Concentration Camp U.S.A.*, New York, Tower Publications, 1972.

Baldwin, Edwart M., *Geography of Oregon*, Dubuque, Iowa, Kendall/Hunt Publishing Company, 1976.

Bancroft, Hubert Howe, *The Works of Hubert Howe Bancroft, Volume XXIX, History of Oregon, Volume 1, 1834-1848*, San Francisco, The History Company Publishers, 1886.

Beals, Alan R. & McCorkle, Thomas, Kroeber *Anthropological Society Papers, No. 3, Lost Lake*, Berkeley, University of California, 1950.

Beckham, Stephen Dow, *The Indians of Western Oregon: This Land Was Theirs*, Coos Bay, Oregon, Arago Books, 1977.

Binns, Archie, *Peter Skene Ogden: Fur Trader*, Portland, Oregon, Binford and Mort, 1967.

Boatner, Mark M., *The Civil War Dictionary*, New York, David McKay Company, Inc., 1959.

Bosworth, Allan R., *America's Concentration Camps*, New York, W.W. Norton and Company, 1967.

Brown, Dee, *Bury My Heart At Wounded Knee*, New York, Holt, Rinehart & Winston, 1970.

Clark, Keith & Donna (Eds.), *Daring Donald McKay or The Last War Trail of the Modocs*, Portland, Oregon Historical Society, 1971   (reproduction of 1884 edition).

Cleghorn, John C., *Historic Water Levels of Tule Lake, California-Oregon and their Relation to the Petroglyphs, Klamath County Museum Research Papers, No. 1*. Klamath Falls, Oregon, Guide Printing Co., 1959.

Conrat, Maisie & Richard, *Executive Order 9066*, Cambridge, Massachusetts, The MIT Press, 1972.

Curtain, Jeremiah, *Myths of the Modocs*, Boston, Little, Brown and Company, 1912.

Cranson, K.R., *Crater Lake, Gem of the Cascades*, Lansing, Michigan, KRC Press, 1982.

Cressman, L. S., *Prehistory of the Far West*, Salt Lake City, University of Utah Press, 1977.

Cressman, L. S., *The Sandal and the Cave, The Indians of Oregon*, Portland, Beaver Books, 1964.

Daniels, Roger, *Concentration Camps USA: Japanese Americans and World War II*, New York, Holt, Rinehart and Winston, Inc., 1971.

Davies, K.G. (Ed.), *Peter Skene Ogden's Snake Country Journal, 1826-27*, London, The Hudson's Bay Record Society, 1961.

DeWitt, John L., *Final Report: Japanese Evacuation From The West Coast*, Washington, Government Printing Office, 1943.

Dicken, Samuel N., *Oregon Geography: The People, The Place, and The Time*, Eugene, University of Oregon, 1973.

Dillon, Richard, *Burnt-Out Fires: California's Modoc Indian War*, New Jersey, Prentice-Hall, Inc. 1973.

Dott, Jr., Robert H. & Batten, Roger L., *Evolution of the Earth*, San Francisco, McGraw-Hill Book Company, 1981.

Dunn, J.P., *Massacres of the Mountains, A History of the Indian Wars of the Far West*, New York, Archer House, 1886.

Fey, Harold E. and McNickle, D'Arcy, *Indians & Other Americans: Two Ways of Life Meet*, New York, Perennial Library, Harper & Row, Publishers, 1970.

Fremont, John Charles, *Narratives of Exploration and Adventure*, New York, Longmans, Green and Co, Inc., 1956.

Gatschet, Albert Samuel, *The Klamath Indians of Southwestern Oregon*, Washington, United States Government Printing Office, 1890.

Girdner, Audrie and Loftis, Anne, *The Great Betrayal: The Evacuation of the Japjnese-Americans During World War II*, New York, The Macmillan Company, 1969.

Good, Rachel Applegate, *History of Klamath County*, Oregon, Klamath Falls, Oregon, 1941.

Graham, Frank, Jr., *Man's Dominion: The Story of Conservation in America*, New York, M. Evans and Company, 1971.

Guernsey, J. Lee & Doerr, Arthur, *Physical Geography*, Woodbury, New York, Barron's Educational Series, Inc., 1964.

Harris, Stephen L., *Fire and Ice, The Cascade Volcanoes*, Seattle, Pacific Search Press, 1980.

Howe, Carrol B., *Ancient Modocs of California and Oregon*, Portland, Oregon, Binfords and Mort, 1979.

Howe, Carrol B., *Ancient Tribes of the Klamath Country*, Portland, Binfords and Mort, 1968.

Hosokawa, Bill, *Nisei: The Quiet Americans*, New York, William Morrow and Company, 1969.

Hutchinson, W.H., *California: Two Centuries of Man, Land, and Growth in the Golden State*, Palo Alto, California, American West Publishing Company, 1969.

James, George Wharton, *Reclaiming the Arid West*, New York, Dodd, Mead and Company, 1917.

Johansen, Dorothy, *Empire of the Pacific*, New York, Harper and Row Publishers, 1967.

Josephy, Alvin M., Jr. (Ed.), *The American Heritage History of the Great West*, New York, American Heritage Publishing Company, Inc., 1965.

Knight, Oliver, *Following the Indian Wars. The Story of the Newspaper Correspondents Among the Indian Campaigners*, Norman, University of Oklahoma Press, 1993.

Leakey, Richard E., *The Making of Mankind*, London, England, Michael Joseph, Ltd., 1981.

McKee, Bates, *Cascadia, The Geologic Evolution of the Pacific Northwest*, San Francisco, McGraw-Hill, Inc., 1972.

McPhee, John, *Basin and Range*, New York, Farrar, Straus, Giroux, 1981.

McWilliams, Carey, *Brothers Under the Skin*, Boston, Little, Brown and Company, 1943.

McWilliams, Carey, *Prejudice: Japanese-Americans, Symbol of Racial Intolerance*, Boston, Little, Brown and Company, 1944.

Meacham, Hon. A.B., *Wigwam and War-path or the Royal Chief in Chains*, Boston, John P. Dale and Company, 1875.

Meacham, Hon. A.B., *WI-NE-MA and Her People*, Hartford, American Publishing Company, 1876.

Miller, Joaquin, *Unwritten History: Life Among the Modocs*, Eugene, Orion Press, 1972 (reprint of 1873 edition).

Minear, John, ed., *Through Japanese Eyes, Volume II*, New York, Prager Publishers, 1974.

Miyakawa, Edward, *Tule Lake*, Waldport, Oregon, House by the Sea Publishing Company, 1979.

Murray, Keith A., *The Modocs and Their War*, Norman, University of Oklahoma Press, 1959.

Myer, Dillon, *Uprooted Americans*, Tucson, University of Arizona Press, 1971.

Nakano, Takeo, *Within the Barbed Wire Fence: A Japanese Man's Account of his Internment in Canada*, Seattle, University of Washington Press, 1980.

Owen, Roger C., et. al., *The North American Indians: A Sourcebook*, New York, Macmillan Publishing Co., Inc., 1967.

Palmberg, Walter H., *Copper Paladin: A Modoc Tragedy*, Bryn Mawr, Pennsylvania, Dorrance & Company, Inc., 1982.

Powers, Stephen, *Contributions to North American Ethnology, Volume III, Tribes of California*. Washington, D.C., Department of the Interior, 1877.

Ray, Verne F., *Primitive Pragmatists: The Modoc Indians of Northern California*, Seattle, University of Washington Press, 1963.

Riddle, Jeff C., *The Indian History of the Modoc War*, Eugene, Oregon, Orion Press, reprint of 1914 edition.

Shaver, F.A., Rose, Arthur P., Steele, R. F., and Adams, A. E. *An Illustrated History of Central Oregon*, Spokane, Western Historical Publishing Company, 1905.

Stone, Buena Cobb, *Fort Klamath: Frontier Post in Oregon, 1863-1890*, Dallas, Royal Publishing Company, 1964.

Stern, Theodore, *The Klamath Tribe, A People and Their Reservation*, Seattle, University of Washington Press, 1965.

Strong, Emory, *Stone Age In The Great Basin*, Portland, Binfords & Mort, 1969.

tenBroek, Jacobus, Barnhart, Edward N., and Matson, Floyd W., *Prejudice, War and the Constitution*, Berkeley, University of California Press, 1970.

Thomas, Dorothy S. & Nishimoto, Richard, T*he Spoilage: Japanese-American Evacuation and Resettlement During World War II*, Berkeley, University of California Press, 1969.

Thompson, Erwin, *Modoc War: Its Military History and Topography*, Sacramento, Argus Books, 1971.

Unruh, John D., *The Plains Across: The Overland Emigrants and the Trans-Mississippi West, 1840-60*, Chicago, University of Illinois Press, 1979.

Washburn, Wilcomb E., *The Indian in America*, New York, Harper & Row, Publishers, 1975.

Wax, Murray L, *Indian Americans: Unity and Diversity*, Englewood Cliffs, New Jersey, Prentice-Hall, Inc., 1971.

Webber, Bert, *Retaliation: Japanese Attacks and Allied Countermeasures on the Pacific Coast in World War II*, Corvallis, Oregon State University Press, 1976.

Weglyn, Michi, *Years of Infamy: The Untold Story of America's Concentration Camps*, New York, William Morrow and Company, Inc., 1976.

Williamson, Ten Broeck, *History of the 1946 Land Opening on the Tule Lake Division of the Klamath Project*, Sacramento, U.S, Bureau of Reclamation, August, 1947.

Correspondence

Ager, Dorothy, former co-owner of Earl's Market, letter to Stan Turner, October 19, 1981.

Best, Raymond R., Memo to Regional Director, February 16, 1948, on file at offices of Klamath Project, Bureau of Reclamation, Klamath Falls, Oregon.

Correspondence from the files of the Tulelake Chamber of Commerce 1939-1942, as found in the document collection of the Tulelake-Butte Valley Fairgrounds Pioneer Museum, Tulelake, California.

Correspondence from the files of the Tule Lake Community Club, 1928 to 1931, as found in the document collection of the Tulelake-Butte Valley Fairgrounds Pioneer Museum, Tulelake, California.

Correspondence from the files of the Klamath Project, Bureau of Reclamation, Klamath Falls, Oregon, 1924 to 1942.

Correspondence and memorandums from Military and Government Personnel concerning the Modoc Indian War, 1872-1873, on file at the Lava Beds National Monument, Tulelake, California.

Davies, A.P., Director and Chief Engineer, United States Reclamation Service to the Project Manager of the Klamath Project, May 26, 1916, on file at the office of the Klamath Project, Klamath Falls, Oregon.

Englebright, Harry L. to Sarah Welsh, April 28, 1942, on file at the offices of the Klamath Project, Bureau of Reclamation, Klamath Falls, Oregon.

Hanson, Lorna, personal letter to Stan Turner, September 16, 1981, Tule Lake Basin, California.

Jones, Bob, former Tulelake Basin resident, personal letter to Stan Turner, October 25, 1982.

Newell, Herbert D., Memorandum for Public Notice on Tule Lake Lands, August 26, 1922, on file at the office of the Klamath Project, Klamath Falls, Oregon.

Page, John C., Letter to Harry L. Englebright, May 17, 1942, on file at the offices of the Klamath Project, Bureau of Reclamation, Klamath Falls, Oregon.

Stimson, Henry L., Letter to Harry L. Englebright, May 11, 1942, on file at the offices of the Klamath Project, Bureau of Reclamation, Klamath Falls, Oregon.

Tanabe, Haru, Letter to Kenneth and Winifred Lambie, February 18, 1943, Tule Lake WRA Camp, Newell, California.

Documents

Aiken, Ann, United States District Judge, *In the United States District Court for the District of Oregon: Steven Lewis Kandra; David Cacka; Klamath Irrigation District; Tulelake Irrigation District; and Klamath Water Users Association, Plaintiffs, and City of Klamath Falls, Klamath County, Modoc County, and Long Bailey, Plaintiffs-Intervenors; v. United States of America; Gale Norton, Secretary of the Interior; Don Evans, Secretary of Commerce, Defendants, and Klamath Tribes, Yurok Tribe; The Wilderness Society, et al., Defendants-Intervenors,* April 30, 2001.

Agreement By and Between the Bureau of Reclamation and the Fish and Wildlife Service, John C. Page, Bureau of Reclamation and W.C. Henderson, Fish and Wildlife Service, January 8, 1942, on file at the Tule Lake National Wildlife Refuge Headquarters.

Agreement By and Between the Bureau of Reclamation and the Fish and Wildlife Service, December 15, 1954, on file at the Tule Lake National Wildlife Refuge Headquarters.

Calvin Coolidge, *Executive Order #4975, October 4, 1928,* on file at the Tule Lake National Wildlife Refuge Headquarters.

Fish and Wildlife Service and Bureau of Reclamation Cooperative Agreement, August 2, 1977, on file at the Tule Lake National Wildlife Refuge Headquarters.

FWS-USBR Cooperative Agreement, Klamath Basin Refuges, Kuchel Act Lands, 1977, on file at the Tule Lake National Wildlife Refuge Headquarters.

Kuchel Bill: Public Law 88-567, 88th Congress, S. 743, September 2, 1964, on file at the Tule Lake National Wildlife Refuge Headquarters.

National Wildlife Refuge System Administration Act of 1966, on file at the Tule Lake National Wildlife Refuge Headquarters.

Franklin D. Roosevelt, *Executive Order #7341, 1936*, on file at the Tule Lake National Wildlife Refuge Headquarters.

Theodore Roosevelt, *Executive Order #924, August, 1908*, on file at the Tule Lake National Wildlife Refuge Headquarters.

William Howard Taft, *Executive Order, 1911*, on file at the Tule Lake National Wildlife Refuge Headquarters.

U.S. Department of the Interior, Bureau of Reclamation, *History of the Tule Lake Division, Including the Modoc Unit - Region II, Klamath Project, E.L. Stevens, Project Manager, February, 1952*, on file at the Bureau of Reclamation, Klamath Project, Klamath Falls, Oregon.

Interviews

Aceves, Luis, City of Tulelake resident, April 19, 2002.

Aikins, Portia, 1920s basin homesteader, Tule Lake Basin, August 7, 1981.

Anderson, Robert, 1940s basin homesteader, Tule Lake Basin, California, August 8, 1981.

Ager, Dorothy, former co-owner of Earl's Market, Redding, California, August 17, 1984.

Bell, Clifford, employee of Newell Grain Growers Cooperative, Tule Lake Basin, California, August 11, 1984.

Bell, Clifford & Cindy, residents of Newell, California, Newell, California, August 6, 1981, and August 11, 1984.

Bryant, James, Klamath Project Repayment Specialist, Klamath Project Office, Bureau of Reclamation, Klamath Falls, Oregon, August 4, 1981 and July 9, 1984.

Campbell, Mrs. Roy, former Postmaster at the Tule Lake War Relocation Authority Internment Camp, Tule Lake Basin, California, October 13, 1973.

Christy, Gertrude and Paul, 1940s basin homesteaders, Tule Lake Basin, California, August 9, 1984 and March 27, 2002.

Cordonier, Joe, Tulelake City Clerk, Tulelake, California, August 1, 1984 and March 28, 2002.

Crawford, Dan, basin homesteader, Tule Lake Basin, California, August 5, 1981.

Crawford, John, basin farmer, Tule Lake Basin, California, April 25. 2002.

Cross, Sr., John, Tule Lake Basin farmer, Newell, California, April 8 and May 7, 1982.

Dayton, Marguerite, 1930s basin homesteader, Tulelake, California, March 24, 1983.

Darling, Betty, former wife of the Reverend Marvis Keyser, minister of Tulelake Community Presbyterian Church, Stockton, California, August 20, 1984.

Fields, Robert, Project Leader of the Tule Lake National Wildlife Refuge, Refuge Headquarters, August 3, 1981.

Frey, Regina, 1920s basin homesteader, Tule Lake Basin, August 7, 1981.

Fults, Dan M., Project Manager, Klamath Project, Bureau of Reclamation, U.S. Department of the Interior, Klamath Falls, Oregon, August 18, 1982.

Ganger, Bill, son of 1928 Tule Lake Basin homesteader, April 25, 2002.

Gentry, Marie, August 2, 1981, 1920s basin homesteader, Tulelake, California, February 20, 1983 and March 24, 1983.

Giacomelli, Tony, owner and manager of Jock's Supermarket, Tulelake, California, April 9, 2002.

Hance, Lavada, retired migrant farm worker, Tulelake, California, August 13, 1984.

Hanson, Lorna, daughter of basin homesteader, Tule Lake Basin, California, June 23 and August 2, 1981.

Hatfield, David, farmer and employee of Standard Oil Company, Tule Lake Basin, California, August 7, 1981 and March 27, 2002.

Hernandez, Venancio, former farmer and Tulelake resident, March 27, 2002.

Hinds, Paulette, City Bookkeeper and former migrant farm worker, Tulelake, California, August 13, 1984.

Huffman, Clyde, homesteader, Tule Lake Basin, California, August 4, 1981.

Huffman, Nancy, Modoc County Supervisor, April 19, 2002.

Hunnicut, Marian Offield and Frank, Merrill, Oregon, July 16, 1984.

Kalina, Denny, owner of Kalina Hardware, Malin, Oregon, March 27, 2002.

Kalina, Vaclav, owner of the Broadway Theater and insurance broker, Malin, Oregon, July 24, 1984.

Kandra, Steve, Tule Lake Basin farmer, March 27, 2002.

Katagiri, George, head of the Department of Technical Instruction, Oregon State Department of Education and former Tule Lake WRA Camp internee, Eugene, Oregon, September 28, 1973.

King, Frank and Ginger, 1946 homesteaders, Coppock Bay, Tule Lake Basin, California, August 5, 1981.

Kohler, Renee, Teacher at Tulelake Elementary School, March 27, 2002.

Kolkow, Amy, City of Malin Librarian, Malin, Oregon, July 17, 1984.

Krizo, Barbara and Phillip, 1940s homesteaders, Tule Lake Basin, California, March 23, 1983 and March 27, 2002.

Laird, Ray, 1920s homesteader, Tulelake, California, August 8, 1981 and March 24, 1983.

Lambie, Kenneth & Winifred, retired accountant, Klamath Falls, Oregon, May 9, 1982 and telephone interview, September 8, 1984.

Larson, Jessie, City of Tulelake resident, April 19, 2002.

Main, Chester, 1938 homesteader, Tule Lake Basin, California, August 9, 1984.

Misso, David Porter, Employee of the Tulelake Basin Joint Unified School District and "philosopher at large," Tule Lake Basin, California, August 9, 1984 and March 27, 2002.

Miyakawa, Edward, architect and author, former Tule Lake WRA Internment Camp internee, Eugene, Oregon, May 15, 1981.

Molder, Sharron, Principal of Tulelake High School, March 28, 2002.
Moore, John, owner of the Homestead Market, Newell, California, August 7, 1981 and August 10, 1984.

Morrill, Ralph, Manager of the Tulelake-Butte Valley Fairgrounds and 1940s homesteader, Tulelake, California, March 24, 1983.

Myers, Bertha, resident, Malin, Oregon, July 17, 1984.

Norton, Phil, Manager of the Klamath Basin Wildlife Refuges, March 27, 2002.

Palmerlee, Charles, former WRA civilian employee at the Tule Lake WRA Internment Camp, Eugene, Oregon, September 22, 1973.

Porterfield, Donald and Frankie, basin farmers, Coppock Bay, Tule Lake Basin, California, August 3, 1981.

Rogers, Paul, 1946 homesteader and insurance salesman, Tulelake, California, August 7, 1984.

Schaffner, Otto, former owner of Tulelake Horseradish Company, Tulelake, California, August 8, 1984.

Scott, Ethel, wife of 1932 basin homesteader, Tulelake, California, August 12, 1984.

Smith, Russell, farmer, Tule Lake Basin, August 8, 1981.

Thaler, Victoria, former Tulelake City Clerk and Judge, Tulelake, California, August 8, 1984.

Whitaker, William, 1940s homesteader and former Tulelake City Clerk, Tulelake, California, June 24 and 25, 1981.

Wilkins, Andrew, owner Wilkins Electrical Contracting, Tulelake, California, August 8, 1984.

Wright, Cindy, Assistant Business Manager, Tulelake-Butte Valley Fair Grounds, Tulelake, California, March 24, 1983.

Manuscripts

Anonymous, *Tule Lake, Tulelake, California,* Tule Lake National Wildlife Refuge files, unknown date (unpublished).

Cleghorn, John C., *A Geological and Archaeological Study of the Tule Lake Basin,* unpublished, on file at Klamath Basin National Wildlife Headquarters, Tulelake, California, October, 1951.

Haines, Dr. Francis D., *The Applegate Trail: Southern Emigrant Route,* published under a grant from the American Revolution Bicentennial Commission of Oregon, on file at the University of Oregon Library, Oregon Collection, Eugene, Oregon.

Frear, Samuel T., *Jesse Applegate: An Appraisal of An Uncommon Pioneer,* A Thesis, Presented to the Department of History and the Graduate School of the University of Oregon in partial fulfillment of the requirements for the degree of Master of Arts, June, 1961.

Kalina, Vaclav, *Alois and Marie Kalina Family of Malin,* Oregon, 1983.

Kalina, Vaclav, *Vaclav and Hazel Kalina of Malin,* Oregon, 1983.

Minor, Rick; Beckham, Stephen Dow; and Toepel, Kathryn Anne, authors; and Aikens, C. Melvin, (Eds.), "Applegate Trail," *Cultural Resource Overview of the BLM Lakeview District, South-Central Oregon: Archaeology, Ethnography, History,* Eugene, University of Oregon Anthropological Papers No. 16, 1979.

Wechsler, Hyman & Fehle, C.L., *Tulelake Volunteer Fire Department Records,* Tulelake, California, date unknown (unpublished).

Miscellaneous

Constitution and By-Laws of the Tule Lake Community Club, 1928.

Newspaper clippings and notations from the files of the Lava Beds National Monument, 1925-1950.

Newspapers

Boston Globe, Boston, Massachusetts.

Chicago Tribune, Chicago, Illinois.

The County Record, Alturas, California

Daily Oregonian, Portland, Oregon.

Evening Herald, Klamath Falls, Oregon.

Herald and News, Klamath Falls, Oregon.

Klamath Falls Evening Herald, Klamath Falls, Oregon.

Klamath Falls Express, Klamath Falls, Oregon.

Klamath Record, Klamath Falls, Oregon.

Klamath Republican, Klamath Falls, Oregon.

Linkville Weekly Star, Linkville (Klamath Falls), Oregon.

The Malin Enterprise, Malin, Oregon.

The Malin Progress, Malin, Oregon.

Morning Express, Klamath Falls, Oregon.

New York Herald, New York City, New York.

New York Tribune, New York City, New York.

New York Times, New York City, New York.

The News and the Herald, Klamath Falls, Oregon.

The Portland Journal, Portland, Oregon.

Portland Oregonian, Portland, Oregon.

Register-Guard, Eugene, Oregon.

Sacramento Bee, Sacramento, California.

San Francisco Chronicle, San Francisco, California.

The San Francisco Examiner, San Francisco, California.

Tulelake Reporter, Tulelake, California.

Weekly Oregon Statesmen, Salem, Oregon.

Yreka Union, Yreka, California.

Pamphlets

Brissenden, Bill, *History of Tulelake Development, Souvenir Program*, 3'rd *Postwar Tulelake Homestead Drawing*, February 23, 1949.

Celebrating 75 Years: National Wildlife Refuge System, United States Department of the Interior, 1977.

Klamath Basin National Wildlife Refuges, Oregon-California, United States Department of the Interior, 1980.

Mertzman, Stanley A., *A Geology of the Lava Beds National Monument: A Summary*, Headquarters of the Lava Beds National Monument, California, date unknown.

Souvenir of the United American Sokols of the Pacific, Grand Pacific Sokol Festival, Malin, Oregon, July 3rd, 4th and 5th, 1928.

U.S. Fish and Wildlife Service, *Klamath Basin National Wildlife Refuges, Common Wildlife of Klamath Basin National Wildlife Refuges*, Oregon and California.

Periodicals

The Christian Century, December 15, 1943.

Cressman, L. S., *Klamath Prehistory, The Prehistory of the Culture of the Klamath Lake Area, Oregon*, Transactions of the American Philosophical Society, Philadelphia, The American Philosophical Society, November, 1956.

Gentry, Marie, "Experiences of an Early Homesteader," *Tulelake Irrigation District 1972 Annual Report*, Tulelake, California, 1972.

Geo Magazine, Vol. 4, February, 1982.

Klamath Echoes, No. 1, Klamath Falls, Oregon, Klamath County Museum, 1964.

Klamath Echoes, No. 8, Klamath Falls, Oregon, Klamath County Museum, 1970.

Klamath Echoes, No. 9, Klamath Falls, Oregon, Klamath County Museum, 1971.

Klamath Echoes, No. 15, Klamath Falls, Klamath County Historical Society, 1977.

The Journal of California Anthropology, Volume 4, No. 2, Winter, 1977.

The Journal of the Modoc County Historical Society, Alturas, Modoc County Historical Society, 1983.

Life Magazine, Vol. 16, No. 12, Time, Inc. Chicago, March 20, 1944.

Life Magazine, Vol. 22, No. 3, Time, Inc., Chicago, January 20, 1947.

Nakamura, George R., (Ed.), *A Tule Lake Interlude, First Anniversary Tule Lake WRA Project, May 27, 1942-1943*, Newell, The Tulean Dispatch, War Relocation Authority, 1943.

New Reclamation Era, Washington, D.C., Department of the Interior, 1924, 1927, 1928, 1929.

Oregon Blue Book, 1920 to 1984.

Palmquist, Peter, "Image Makers of the Modoc War," *The Journal of California Anthropology, Vol. 4, No. 2*, Winter, 1977.

Reclamation ERA, Washington, D.C, Department of the Interior, 1947, 1948, 1949.

Tulean Dispatch, Tule Lake WRA, Newell, California, February, 1943, on file at the offices of the Klamath Project, Bureau of Reclamation, Klamath Falls, Oregon.

Reports

Abney, Herbert M., Wildlife Biologist, *A Comparative Study of Past and Present Conditions of Tule Lake*, October 30, 1964, on file at the Tule Lake National Wildlife Refuge Headquarters.

Anonymous, *Annual History - Klamath Project*, Klamath Falls, Oregon, 1957.

Anonymous, *Annual Report of Civilian Conservation Camps Work*, Bureau of Reclamation, Klamath Project, fiscal year, 1939, on file at the Klamath Project, Bureau of Reclamation, Klamath Falls, Oregon, 1939.

Anonymous, *Annual Report of the Commissioner of Indian Affairs to the Secretary of the Interior, 1873*, Washington, Government Printing Office, 1874.

Anonymous, *Period Report of the Emergency Conservation Work Camps Under the Bureau of Reclamation*, Klamath Project, Seventh Enrollment Period, 1936, on file at the Klamath Project, Bureau of Reclamation, Klamath Falls, Oregon, 1936.

Anonymous, *Period Report of the Civilian Conservation Corps Camps Under Bureau of Reclamation*, Klamath Project, Ninth Enrollment Period, 1937 on file at the Klamath Project, Bureau of Reclamation, Klamath Falls, Oregon, 1937.

Anonymous, *Klamath Project: Mid-Pacific Region- Water and Power Resources Services*, Klamath Falls, Oregon, 1978.

Anonymous, *Chronology of Important Events, Klamath Project, 1903-1957*, Klamath Falls, Oregon, 1957.

Baghott, Kenneth G., *Potatoes In the Tulelake Area*, California Cooperative Extension Service, Tulelake, California, Tulelake Station, 1970.

Iakisch, J.R., *Report on Pumping from Tule Lake and Wildlife Refuge Development, 1938-1939*, on file at the Tule Lake National Wildlife Refuge Headquarters, Tule Lake, California, 1939.

Klamath Project files, *Klamath Project Reports, 1946, 1947, and 1948*, offices of the Klamath Project, Bureau of Reclamation, Klamath Falls, Oregon, 1948.

Klamath Project files, *Klamath Project Report: Chronology of Important Events, 1946, 1947, 1948, 1949, 1950, 1951, 1952, and 1953*, offices of the Klamath Project, Bureau of Reclamation, Klamath Falls, Oregon, 1953.

Klamath Water Users Association with assistance from David A. Vogel and Keith R. Marine, *Protecting the Beneficial Uses of Waters of Upper Klamath Lake: A Plan to Accelerate Recovery of the Lost River and Shortnose Suckers*, Klamath Water Users Association, Klamath Falls, Oregon, March 2001.

Minutes and Records of the Newell Homestead Club, 1948 to 1952. On file at the Tulelake-Butte Valley Fairgrounds Museum, Tulelake, California, 1952.

National Research Council, *Scientific Evaluation of Biological Opinions on Endangered and Threatened Fishes in the Klamath River Basin*, National Academy of Sciences, February, 2002.

Newell, Frederick Haines, *Second Annual Report of the Reclamation Service, 1902-03*, Washington, Government Printing Office, 1904.

Newell, Frederick Haines, *Third Annual Report of the Reclamation Service*, Government Printing Office, 1905.

Newell, Frederick Haines, *Fifth Annual Report of the Reclamation Service*, Government Printing Office, 1907.

Reed, A.D. and Baghott, K.G., "Costs to establish and Produce: Alfalfa, Potatoes," *Statistical Summary Sheets, California Cooperative Extension Service, Tulelake Station*, Tulelake, California, 1957 to 1978.

Stephens, Edward L., *History of the Tule Lake Division Including Modoc Unit*, Klamath Falls, Oregon, Bureau of Reclamation, 1952.

Tenny, Senator Jack B., et. al., *The Joint Fact Finding Committee on Un-American Activities in California (1943-45)*, Sacramento, April 16, 1945.

Voorhees, I.S., *History of the Klamath Project, Oregon-California, 1912*, Klamath Falls, Oregon, 1912.

The Peninsula looking northeast. *(Photo by Author)*